D1505502

ALSO BY CLIVE PONTING

The Right to Know:
The Inside Story of the Belgrano Affair

Whitehall: Tragedy and Farce

Breach of Promise: Labour in Power 1964–1970

Whitehall: Changing the Old Guard

Secrecy in Britain

1940: Myth and Reality

A Green History of the World

Churchill

ARMAGEDDON

ARMAGEDDON

THE REALITY BEHIND THE DISTORTIONS, MYTHS, LIES, AND ILLUSIONS OF WORLD WAR II

CLIVE PONTING

RANDOM HOUSE

NEW YORK

Copyright © 1995 by Clive Ponting

All rights reserved under International and Pan-American Copyright Conventions.
Published in the United States by Random House, Inc., New York.
Originally published in Great Britain by Sinclair-Stevenson,
an imprint of Reed Consumer Books Ltd., London.

Library of Congress Cataloging-in-Publication Data

Ponting, Clive.
Armageddon : the reality behind the distortions, myths, lies,
and illusions of World War II / Clive Ponting.
p. cm.
Includes bibliographical references and index.
ISBN 0-679-43602-2
1. World War, 1939–1945. I. Title.
D743.P59 1995
940.53—dc20   95-2995

Manufactured in the United States of America on acid-free paper
98765432
First U.S. Edition
Book design by Jo Anne Metsch

To Laura
with love and gratitude

The strong do what they have the power to do
and the weak accept what they have to accept.

Thucydides, *History of the Peloponnesian War*,
Book Five, 89

PREFACE

T HE CELEBRATIONS OF THE FIFTIETH ANNIVERSARY OF
V-J Day on August 15, 1995, recall the end of the most catastrophic
war in human history and the destruction of one of the most evil governments to have ruled a modern state. It was a war in which probably 85 million people died—the overwhelming majority of them
civilians. Why did all these people die? What was the purpose of the
war? In the immediate aftermath the answer was clear: it was, in the
title of one of the first books about the war, a "Crusade in Europe."
The war-crimes trials also led to what the historian A.J.P. Taylor has
called "the Nuremberg view of history." The responsibility for the
war was placed solely upon Germany and the Hitler government,
which in this view had been engaged in a conspiracy against peace
and had set out on a path of carefully planned aggression. The appalling atrocities committed during the war could all be blamed on the
Nazis and their associates. Unlike the 1914–18 war, the Second
World War was a clear contest between good and evil—perhaps the
closest approach ever to the medieval theologians' ideal of a "just
war."

There can be no doubt that the Nazi government was evil and that
if it had not been destroyed, the peoples of Europe would have lived
under a regime of terror and barbarity. However, this knowledge
does not in itself help us understand the complexities of the Second
World War. The aim of the following chapters is to try to discover

those complexities by abolishing a chronological framework and by taking common themes and seeing how the various belligerents (and neutrals) responded to common problems. The chapters attempt to see the war in a worldwide context and, as far as possible, avoid the British concentration on western Europe and the war in North Africa and the Mediterranean. There is little here on the detailed tactical handling of forces by military commanders, or maps and descriptions of particular battles. These have been exhaustively covered elsewhere and tell us little about the reality of the war. This book focuses on questions such as how the military equipment was produced in the first place, what strategy political leaders adopted, and what combat was like for the individual serviceman. In a war with so many civilian casualties, it is important to keep the focus on how societies, economies, and peoples were affected by the war, and not on how military commanders maneuvered on the battlefield.

CONTENTS

MAPS

CHRONOLOGY OF KEY EVENTS

1939

September
1   Germany invades Poland
3   Britain and France declare war on Germany
17   Soviet Union invades Poland
28   Estonia accepts Soviet ultimatum and agrees to Soviet military bases on its territory

October
5   Latvia forced to accept Soviet bases
10   Lithuania forced to accept Soviet bases

November
30   Soviet Union attacks Finland

1940

March
12   Finland accepts armistice and loss of territory to Soviet Union
30   Wang Ching-wei puppet government set up at Nanking

April
9   Germany invades Norway and occupies Denmark

May
6   Britain occupies Iceland
10   Germany invades Low Countries and France

15   Dutch surrender
May 27 to June 4   Evacuation from Dunkirk
28   Belgian surrender

June

10   Italy declares war on Britain and France
14   Fall of Paris
17   French request for armistice (signed June 22)
28   Rumania accepts Soviet demand for "return" of Bessarabia

July

1   Rumania denounces Anglo-French guarantee
3   British attack on French fleet at Mers el-Kébir
10   Britain closes Burma Road
mid-July to September 15   Battle of Britain
28   U.S. embargo on sale of aviation fuel and scrap iron and
steel to Japan

August

4   Italian invasion of British and French Somaliland
30   Vienna award by Hitler gives Hungary parts of Transylvania
and Bulgaria, and southern Dobruja, at expense of Rumania

September

3   Anglo-American destroyers-for-bases deal
14   Italy invades Egypt
23   Japan occupies northern Indochina
27   Tripartite Pact (Germany, Italy, Japan) signed

October

10   British reopen Burma Road
28   Italy invades Greece

November

5   Roosevelt reelected for third term
12   Molotov visits Berlin
20   Hungary, Rumania, Slovakia join Tripartite Pact

December

9   British attack in Egypt defeats Italians

1941

March

1   Bulgaria joins Tripartite Pact; German troops in Bulgaria
8   British troops arrive in Greece
11   Lend-Lease Act signed into law by U.S. Congress
27   Coup in Yugoslavia
31   First German offensive in North Africa

April

5   United States occupies Greenland
6   Germany invades Greece and Yugoslavia
13   Soviet-Japanese Non-Aggression Pact
17   Yugoslavia surrenders
27   British forces evacuated from Greece

May

2   British invade Iraq
20   German attack on Crete

June

8   Vichy forces in Syria and Lebanon surrender to British
22   German invasion of Soviet Union starts

July

7   United States occupies Iceland
23   Japan occupies southern Indochina
28   United States, Britain, and Netherlands impose oil and steel
embargo on Japan

August

9–12   Roosevelt and Churchill meet at Newfoundland; Atlantic
Charter signed
17   Fall of Kiev
25   Anglo-Soviet invasion of Iran

June

4   Battle of Midway; Japanese attack on Aleutian Islands

July

3   Germans capture Sevastopol

August

7   U.S. landings on Solomon Islands
9   Start of civil-disobedience campaign in India
12–15   Stalin-Churchill meeting in Moscow
19   Dieppe raid
31   Battle of Alam el-Halfa halts German invasion of Egypt

September

13   Battle of Stalingrad begins

October

23   Battle of Alamein

November

8   Anglo-American invasion of French North Africa
11   Germany occupies southern France and Tunisia; French fleet
scuttled

1943

January

11   United States and Britain give up extraterritorial rights in
China
14–24   Casablanca Conference

February

2   German surrender at Stalingrad
8   Soviet forces enter Kursk
14   Soviet forces enter Rostov

April

13   Germany announces discovery of Katyn massacre
19   Uprising in Warsaw Ghetto

May

11   U.S. invasion of Aleutian Islands
12   German-Italian surrender in Tunisia

July

5   Battle of Kursk salient
10   Invasion of Sicily
25   Dismissal of Mussolini

August

23   Soviet forces enter Kharkov

September

3   Invasion of Calabria; Italian surrender; German occupation of
north Italy
9   U.S. landings at Salerno
12   German forces rescue Mussolini
25   Soviet forces enter Smolensk

October

13   Italy declares war on Germany

November

5   Greater East Asia Conference in Tokyo
6   Soviet forces enter Kiev
22–26   Cairo Conference
28   Allied conference at Teheran begins

1944

January

12   Allied landings at Anzio
27   Relief of Leningrad

April

17   Major Japanese offensive in China

June

4   U.S. forces enter Rome
6   Invasion of Normandy

12   German V-1 attacks begin
15   U.S. invasion of Saipan

July
4   Japanese forces defeated at Imphal
20   Attempt to assassinate Hitler
23   Soviet forces occupy Lublin and establish Polish Committee of National Liberation

August
1   Start of Warsaw uprising
15   Allied landings in southern France
24   Allied forces enter Paris

September
3   Allied forces enter Brussels
5   Soviet Union declares war on Bulgaria
8   German V-2 rocket attacks begin
12   Rumania signs armistice
19   Finland signs armistice

October
15   British forces enter Athens
20   Soviet and partisan forces enter Belgrade; U.S. invasion of Philippines
25   Battle of Leyte Gulf (Philippines)

December
4   British forces attack partisans in Athens
16   German offensive in Ardennes begins

1945

January
9   U.S. landings on Luzon
12   Start of major Soviet offensive
17   Soviet forces enter Warsaw

February

4–12   Allied conference at Yalta

13   Soviet forces enter Budapest

13–14   Anglo-American bombing of Dresden

March

9   U.S. firebomb raid on Tokyo

April

1   U.S. invasion of Okinawa

5   Soviet denunciation of neutrality treaty with Japan

12   Death of Roosevelt

13   Soviet forces enter Vienna

28   Death of Mussolini

30   Hitler commits suicide

May

2   Soviet forces capture Berlin

3   British forces enter Rangoon

7   German surrender at Reims

9   Soviet forces enter Prague

July

16   United States tests first A-bomb

17   Allied conference at Potsdam opens

24   Allies call for Japan to surrender

August

6   A-bomb dropped on Hiroshima

8   Soviet Union declares war on Japan

9   A-bomb dropped on Nagasaki

14   Japan agrees to surrender

September

2   Formal Japanese surrender signed

I

ORIGINS

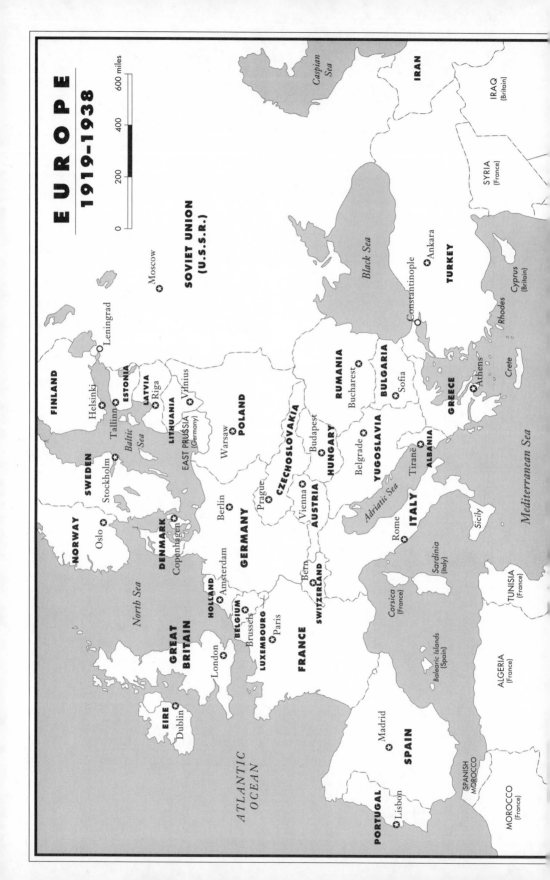

WHEN DID THE SECOND WORLD WAR BEGIN? FOR THE British and French the answer is easy: Sunday, September 3, 1939. For a German or a Pole the answer is September 1. A Lithuanian might suggest March 1939, when Germany seized the port of Memel. A Czech or a Slovak might argue for September 1938, the Munich settlement, or March 1939, the German occupation of Bohemia-Moravia and the declaration of Slovak independence. Did the war for the Soviet Union start with its attack on Poland in September 1939, its attack on Finland two months later, or, as Soviet historians assert, on June 22, 1941, when Germany invaded? For an American or Japanese citizen the answer is different again: December 7, 1941, the attack on Pearl Harbor. The Chinese would disagree. They would argue the war began on July 7, 1937, with the Marco Polo Bridge incident, which led to a full-scale Japanese invasion—or possibly in 1931, when Japan conquered Manchuria.

Although by December 1941 a number of different conflicts around the world had merged to become the Second World War, the origins of the war have to be sought in Europe. In 1940 the changes to the European balance of power drew the United States, once again, into a European quarrel, and without those changes it is difficult to imagine that Japan would have sought to alter the balance in East Asia and the Pacific and eventually launch an attack on the European colonial powers and the United States. The origins of "the last European war," from September 1939 until December 1941, can be found in the challenge to the existing European states and their empires posed by the emergence of a powerful Germany after 1871 and the peculiar weaknesses of the world and European power structures in the 1930s.

In European terms German unity came late (1870–71), and the destabilizing effect this had on the European power structure was heightened by rapid industrialization in the years before the First World War. In the 1880s Germany produced about 7 percent of the world's manufacturing output—less than a third of that of Britain. By 1914 its share had more than doubled and was greater than Britain's. In 1890 Germany produced only half the iron and steel output of Britain; by 1914 its output was twice as much. Germany's rapid growth to the position of foremost European economic power was not matched by a commensurate increase in political power. Britain and France had already acquired extensive colonial possessions, but by the time Germany was able to assert its claims it could establish control only over relatively unprestigious areas such as South-West Africa. By the end of the nineteenth century German colonial possessions were smaller than those of weaker European countries such as Belgium and Portugal, and there was little room for further expansion. Germany's imperial ambitions were no different from those of other European countries—it was just that the other powers had established control first and were unwilling to give up their gains to satisfy Germany.

Any attempt by Germany to increase its power within Europe and revise the status quo would destabilize the existing power structure. By the end of the nineteenth century the question of whether Germany was to have major economic power but not commensurate political power was still unresolved. Germany also faced a difficult situation within the larger geostrategic framework. Any bid for a significantly increased world-power role would inevitably challenge the position of Britain, a far smaller country that controlled almost a quarter of the globe. Either Germany accepted a situation of permanent subordination to Britain, or it attempted to transform the existing balance of power. It also had to take account of the rapidly

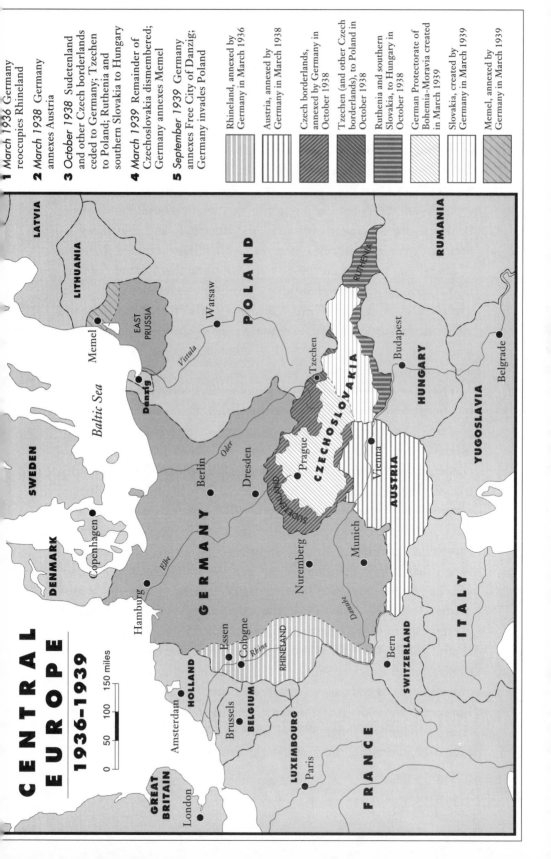

CENTRAL EUROPE 1936-1939

0   50   100   150 miles

1 *March 1936* Germany reoccupies Rhineland

2 *March 1938* Germany annexes Austria

3 *October 1938* Sudetenland and other Czech borderlands ceded to Germany; Tzechen to Poland; Ruthenia and southern Slovakia to Hungary

4 *March 1939* Remainder of Czechoslovakia dismembered; Germany annexes Memel

5 *September 1939* Germany annexes Free City of Danzig; Germany invades Poland

Rhineland, annexed by Germany in March 1936

Austria, annexed by Germany in March 1938

Czech borderlands, annexed by Germany in October 1938

Tzechen (and other Czech borderlands), to Poland in October 1938

Ruthenia and southern Slovakia, to Hungary in October 1938

German Protectorate of Bohemia-Moravia created in March 1939

Slovakia, created by Germany in March 1939

Memel, annexed by Germany in March 1939

GREAT BRITAIN
London

HOLLAND
Amsterdam

BELGIUM
Brussels

LUXEMBOURG

FRANCE
Paris

DENMARK
Copenhagen

SWEDEN

Baltic Sea

Hamburg

GERMANY
Essen
Cologne
RHINELAND
Rhine

SWITZERLAND
Bern

ITALY

Berlin
Dresden
Oder
Elbe

Nuremberg

Munich

SUDETENLAND

Danube

AUSTRIA
Vienna

Prague
CZECHOSLOVAKIA

Tzechen

LITHUANIA
Memel

EAST PRUSSIA
Danzig

Vistula

POLAND
Warsaw

LATVIA

RUTHENIA

Budapest

HUNGARY

YUGOSLAVIA
Belgrade

RUMANIA

growing strength of the continental powers, Russia and the United States. In making its bid for increased power, Germany faced three major problems. First, since expansion overseas was effectively blocked, attempts to increase German power were largely confined to Europe and directly affected the other European powers. Second, Germany was unable to find an acceptable ideological justification for its expansion. Other powers were able to do so: the first French republic and Napoléon adopted the rhetoric of liberal nationalism; Britain in the nineteenth century used free trade and European supremacy over lesser races. Later, the United States utilized the ideas of liberal capitalism, and the Soviet Union the ideology of communism. Germany could find nothing apart from the rather too open desire for greater power. Third, Germany found that there were too many other European and, eventually, extra-European powers who were in the last resort prepared to combine against an attempt by Germany to increase its power.

That Germany did attempt to increase its power was not surprising. In the first decade of the twentieth century it tried to expand its power by asserting its interests in colonial areas such as Morocco (under French tutelage) and by building a fleet that was seen as a challenge to British naval supremacy. This effort brought about a transformation in the European power balance. In particular, Britain, a state facing increasing threats around the globe, made deals with the powers it had long regarded as its most likely enemies, France and Russia, in order to protect its imperial position. This inevitably meant that Britain was increasingly ranged with France and Russia, who had been allies since 1894, against Germany and her main ally, Austria-Hungary. This shift in the balance of power only increased perceptions in Germany that it was encircled by hostile powers. By about 1912 the German government also knew that increasing industrialization in Russia, combined with faster mobilization times and a much improved railway system, meant that the German plans for a European war—defeating France rapidly before turning to face Russia—might no longer be possible in a war after about 1916. In July 1914, therefore, the German government was prepared to take advantage of the assassination of the heir to the Hapsburg throne at Sarajevo and risk a war. It encouraged Austro-Hungarian demands on Serbia, even though it was likely that Russia would support Serbia, thereby almost certainly bringing about a European war. Although other governments cannot be absolved of blame, Germany bears much of the responsibility for the outbreak of war in August 1914.

Despite initial successes, long-drawn-out battles of attrition, and the collapse of Russia, Germany was eventually defeated after growing American economic and military power enabled Britain and France to avoid defeat in the west and then, in the summer of 1918, gradually push the German armies back eastward. Before they had reached the frontiers of Germany the German leadership realized that the war was lost. In early November 1918, internal revolution overthrew the imperial state and ended the war. The Treaty of Versailles and other treaties with the defeated powers demonstrated the extensive nature of Allied, particularly British and French, war aims. Austria-Hungary was partitioned into new states and Poland resurrected. Although the Allies espoused the principle of self-determination, this was flouted in central Europe by the inclusion of the ethnically German areas of the Sudetenland in Czechoslovakia to give the new state defensible frontiers. Also, Poland was given a corridor to the sea at Danzig, which separated East Prussia from the rest of Germany. Germany was largely disarmed: no air force was allowed and its army was limited to a strength of 100,000. The Rhineland was to be demilitarized and Germany was to be occupied for fifteen years.

Although many of the provisions of the Versailles settlement were not in practice carried out—the high level of reparations proved to be unenforceable—the Allies had created major long-term problems. The Versailles Treaty was neither so draconian as to permanently cripple German power nor so lenient as to give Germany any incentive to accept the settlement. Germany was still the largest state in Europe, and once it had recovered from the postwar chaos it also regained its status as the strongest economy. The Allies' unwillingness to enforce Germany's permanent inferior military and political position ensured that the disparity between Germany's economic and political power would again become an issue.

A major element in the fragility of the postwar settlement was that the new states of central Europe that had been created out of the collapse of the German, Russian, and Austro-Hungarian empires were weak and riven by ethnic and territorial disputes, both internal and with other states. Part of the problem was that they all contained substantial minority populations. In Poland, a fifth of the population was not Polish—there was a substantial German minority in Upper Silesia—and the 1920 Treaty of Riga with the Soviet Union fixed the eastern border of the country far to the east of the Curzon Line that had been agreed at Versailles and incorporated large numbers of Ukrainians and Belorussians. Poland had territorial disputes with Lithuania over the city of Vilnius, which the Poles had seized in 1922, and with Czechoslovakia over the Tzechen area. Lithuania had taken over the German city of Memel in 1923 as its only port. Nearly a fifth of the population of Czechoslovakia was German, and if the Slovaks were counted as a separate group, then the Czechs were themselves a minority in the country they largely controlled. Rumania had a substantial minority of one and a half million Hungarians in Transylvania, an area Rumania had been promised by the Allies as a reward for entering the war. Yugoslavia was in many ways only prewar Serbia writ large, but the Serbs who dominated the state were less than a third of the population, and substantial minorities such as the Croats, Slovenes, and Muslims were largely excluded from power. All these states in central Europe were to face the challenge of a Germany whose power was reviving and of the Soviet Union as it emerged out of the chaos of revolution.

No major German politician was prepared to accept the permanent subordination that the Versailles Treaty implied, although some were willing to make tactical concessions during the 1920s. A large part of the German population and the political and military establishment did not accept the Weimar Republic, which had emerged in 1919, and defeat combined with revolution had spawned a series of right-wing parties that were dedicated to a revival of German power and the reestablishment of an authoritarian regime. Adolf Hitler and the Nazi party were one extreme example of this trend, and Hitler's ideas were far from being original. The Nazi party began as a small, extremist party in Bavaria; after the failure of the Munich Beer Hall Putsch in 1923, when Hitler tried to persuade other more senior figures such as General Erich Ludendorff into a coup d'état, he was imprisoned for a brief period, which he spent writing *Mein Kampf,* his political "philosophy."

In *Mein Kampf* and the later "Secret Book" written in 1928, Hitler displayed a crude anti-Semitism learned during his time in Vienna before the First World War. Anti-Semitism was nothing new in German politics, nor was Hitler's belief, shared with many of his contemporaries throughout western Europe, in white superiority—specifically that of the Aryan race—and in the proposition that ultimately all major political and international questions could be reduced to a racial basis. To this mixture Hitler added a virulent antibolshevism that was also common to most of the right across Europe. Hitler's ideas about foreign policy were equally unoriginal. They reflected the widely held views of the German nationalist right and the almost universal demand for a revision of the Versailles settlement. He argued that Germany needed *Lebensraum* ("living space") in the east for settlement and for resources. He objected to an alliance with the Soviet Union and argued that Germany could best achieve its aims by securing an agreement in the west with Britain and Italy so as to isolate France. In order to concentrate on eastward expansion Germany should drop its demand for the return of its colonies and for revision of the Versailles borders, so as not to alienate Britain. It is impossible to regard these writings on foreign policy as a blueprint for Hitler's actions in the 1930s—indeed, in many respects he carried out the opposite policies once in power. He had only vague and general aims of restoring German power and expanding in a way that was consistent with some of Germany's war aims in 1914–18.

Hitler and the Nazi party gained little support in Germany during the relatively prosperous years of the Weimar Republic in the mid-1920s. The onset of the worldwide depression after 1929, however, brought about a rapid rise in support for the Nazis. In 1930 the parliamentary system broke down, but it was not until January 1933 that the conservative and authoritarian parties of the right were prepared to allow Hitler to become chancellor. They believed that they could control him and that the Nazi party would provide popular support for their long-held aim of finally destroying the Weimar Republic. They were to be disappointed. It very quickly became clear that Hitler could control the authoritarians such as Vice Chancellor Franz von Papen and the politician and industrialist Alfred Hugenberg, and within a few months Hitler and the Nazis had, with the consent of the other parties of the right and center, seized power, ended the Weimar system, banned the Social Democrats and Communists, and set up an authoritarian regime.

When Hitler first took power, his foreign and defense policies were conventional and designed to appeal to the various conservative groupings in Germany—probably what any revisionist government would have done. Germany withdrew from the League of Nations and the Disarmament Conference in Geneva and signed a nonaggression pact with Poland, which removed any threat of an immediate attack while Germany rearmed in defiance of the Versailles Treaty. Secret German rearmament had been undertaken in the 1920s, and plans to build an air force and expand the army from the force of 100,000 men permitted under the Versailles provisions had been drawn up before Hitler took power. These plans were bound to take time to implement, however. In 1932, the German air force consisted of 250 aircraft, most of them converted civilian machines, and 550 pilots. The aircraft industry was very small—in 1932 it produced just 32 machines. After January 1933 the government began an expansion program; by 1934 nearly 2,000 aircraft had been produced, but about half of these were trainers to produce the pilots who had been drafted from the army. The new Luftwaffe was not even ready to begin operational maneuvers with the army until 1936. The army was expanded from seven divisions to twenty-one, but by 1936 it still numbered only about 500,000 men and was smaller and far less effective than that of France. Naval expansion was slower still. From 1933 to 1936 Germany spent about 5 percent of its national wealth on defense, no more than many of its rivals.

Nevertheless, German rearmament—openly avowed after 1935, when conscription was first introduced—posed major problems for France and Britain. This challenge to their position, the longer-term threat of increased German power, and perhaps demands for the revision of the Versailles provisions had to be met in particularly difficult circumstances. German power before 1914 had been contained by an alliance between France and Russia and the tacit British backing for these two powers. The threat of a two-front war had been a major constraint on German policy. Now the Soviet Union was largely shunned and distrusted by the capitalist powers of western Europe. Germany's eastern frontier was no longer shared with a substantial military power but with the weak states of central Europe, which posed no major threat and represented only a temptation for expansion. In 1917, with Britain on the edge of bankruptcy and the French demoralized by huge military losses, its armies on the edge of disintegrating, the two powers had been saved from a compromise peace only by the intervention of the United States. In 1919 the United States had withdrawn into political isolation; although it was prepared to cooperate on European economic and financial problems, particularly reparations, it was not a member of the League of Nations and would not provide any political support for Britain and France. The withdrawal of the Soviet Union and the United States left a power vacuum in Europe that weakened Britain's and France's ability to withstand German demands.

France's strategic position was poor. The German economy was the largest in Europe: by 1929 its steel production was already 60 percent higher than that of Britain and France combined. Also, the population from which its army could be drawn was three times that of France. In the First World War, France had lost a quarter of all men between the ages of eighteen and twenty-seven, a higher proportion than any other belligerent. After the war it had to provide for four million wounded, and even in the late 1930s war pensions took up over half of government expenditure. Much of France's overseas investments had been lost as a result of the revolution in Russia. The economic depression hit France relatively late and there was little economic recovery until 1937. Even in 1938, national wealth was 18 percent lower than it had been in 1929. These weaknesses were compounded by the lack of strong allies. Without support from the United States and the Soviet Union, and even without a formal guarantee of British support until late September 1938, it had little alternative but to turn to the new, weak states of central Europe and sign alliances with Poland, Czechoslovakia, Rumania, and Yugoslavia. The French wanted their support in case of a German attack but were far less keen to assist them if they were attacked by Germany. These countries, however, could never provide a military force capable of resisting a rearmed Germany.

If the strategic problems faced by France were bad, those facing Britain were far worse. A country with a population of just over 40 million, it was trying to control an empire comprising about a quarter of the globe. Although it had been the first country to industrialize, Britain had been in relative economic decline since the last quarter of the nineteenth century and now produced only 10 percent of the world's manufacturing output. Many of its old established industries such as shipbuilding, coal, iron and steel, and textiles were in decline, and its levels of industrial investment and productivity were low compared with those of its rivals. Its financial strength had been dissipated during the First World War, and by 1919 its national debt had risen elevenfold, so that interest on the debt took up about 40 percent of the budget of postwar governments. The maintenance of Britain's prestige and influence required a continuation of the status quo, but that was an increasingly difficult task as the balance of economic, financial, and military power in the world shifted. Britain lacked the resources to maintain a global empire in the face of increasing threats around the world.

By the late nineteenth century, the naval supremacy the British had achieved after 1815 was fast disappearing. In the Western Hemisphere, the strength of the United States was rapidly rising; war with the former colonies was ruled out out as impractical and therefore unthinkable. In the Far East, an alliance with the emerging power of

Japan was signed in 1902 to provide protection for imperial possessions such as Malaya, Singapore, Australia, and New Zealand. The
relative priorities of these two policies had to be decided at the
Washington conference on naval limitations in 1922. The British
government had already accepted in 1919–20 that they could not win
a naval race with the United States and had already conceded naval
supremacy to the stronger power. They were therefore keen to accept an American offer of naval equality and limitations. The price
the Americans demanded, though, was the end of the Anglo-Japanese
alliance. After an anguished debate the British government accepted
the proposals. The Japanese fleet was restricted to about 55 percent
of the British and American levels, but this was still sufficient to give
it local superiority in the Pacific. The British now had to plan on a
potentially hostile Japan threatening British possessions in the Far
East. They began construction of a major naval base at Singapore,
and although Australia and New Zealand were reassured that the
majority of the Royal Navy would be sent to the Far East if necessary, it was far from clear how this could be done if Britain faced
major threats elsewhere, especially in Europe.

During the 1920s this seemed no more than a distant, theoretical
problem. After the 1932 Japanese takeover of Manchuria, however,
the British government had to consider the possibility of war. In
1933, shortly after Hitler came to power, the British government felt
able, as the economy began to recover from the depression, to consider increasing defense expenditure. In 1933–34, rearmament plans
were drawn up that were based on an immediate threat from Japan
but a longer-term and more severe threat from Germany. The government decided to be prepared for a war at any time after April
1939. The British, facing threats in both Europe and the Far East,
were in a very difficult position. In 1934 the government considered
whether to reach a deal with Japan that, while not re-creating the old
alliance, might provide reassurance against an attack on British
possessions. The problem was that in order to achieve this, Britain
would probably have to accept a predominant position for Japan in
China, and the British government thought that this would not be acceptable to the United States. They could not afford to alienate the

Americans because they might need their financial and possibly even military help if a European war broke out. The British had therefore to continue to plan on possible conflicts in both Europe and the Far East.

This situation was made worse by the imperial ambitions of Mussolini. Until the early 1930s, Italy was a conservative state in foreign policy and remained close to its old allies, Britain and France. However, as Mussolini's internal revolution ran out of steam he turned increasingly toward foreign adventures as a form of compensation. His first aim was to take over Ethiopia, one of the last two independent African states, and avenge the humiliating Italian defeat at the end of the nineteenth century. As part of the "Stresa front," the Italians had joined Britain and France in seeking to maintain Austrian independence against Germany, and in June 1935 had concluded an important agreement with France for military assistance and mutual support against Germany. In its defense planning Britain had assumed that Italy, like France and the United States, would be a friendly power. The Italian attack on Abyssinia in the autumn of 1935 automatically involved the League of Nations, which had already failed to stop the Japanese takeover of Manchuria, and public opinion in Britain now demanded that the government take the lead in stopping aggression through collective security measures, including the use of sanctions. The government, however, ended up with the worst of both worlds. The attempt to reach a deal with Italy through the Anglo-French Hoare-Laval Pact, which would have allowed Italy to control a large part of Abyssinia, had to be abandoned under the pressure of public outrage. The international sanctions imposed were enough to alienate the Italians but not enough to stop the conquest of Abyssinia. By 1936 it was clear that Mussolini was moving away from Britain and France and toward Germany, and British strategic planning had to be based on likely Italian hostility in any war. Britain now faced a triple threat in different parts of the world: Germany in western Europe, Italy in the Mediterranean and Near East, Japan in the Far East. It simply did not have the financial, industrial, and military resources to meet all three threats.

In the spring of 1936 Hitler took advantage of the European pow-

ers' preoccupation with Abyssinia to reoccupy the demilitarized zone
of the Rhineland. This was a breach of the Versailles Treaty, but
short of starting an all-out war there was little that France and Britain
could do to remove German forces. From 1936, extensive rearmament commenced in most European countries. In Germany the
cautious economic policies adopted in 1933 were abandoned and
Hermann Göring was put in charge of a four-year plan, supposedly
modeled on the Soviet plan. In fact, German plans were chaotic, inconsistent, and hardly plans at all. The main policies were increasing
autarky (construction of synthetic oil and rubber production plants),
contracting barter deals to secure raw materials, and increasing arms
production. No clear date was set for when these preparations should
be complete, although the general understanding seems to have been
that Germany should be ready for war by the mid-1940s. By 1939 the
French were spending more on defense than in the last year of the
First World War. In Britain, defense spending was rising by about 40
percent a year. By 1939 the British were spending 18 percent of national wealth on defense (a higher proportion than Germany) and
seven times as much as in 1933. By 1939 British and French aircraft
production was a third higher than that of Germany. The most heavily armed state, however, and the one that was undertaking the greatest expansion in arms production, was the Soviet Union. In February
1931 Stalin said: "We are fifty or a hundred years behind the advanced countries. We must make good this distance in ten years. Either we do it, or they crush us." In 1932 the Soviet Union was already
producing 3,000 tanks and 2,500 aircraft a year. During the massive
and concentrated industrialization under the five-year plans in the
1930s, arms production took a very high priority. By 1940 aircraft
production had risen to 10,500 a year, and tank production rose six-
teenfold in the 1930s. Defense spending was taking up about a quarter of all industrial output.

   In the autumn of 1937, although the world situation was clearly
unstable (Japan had launched a major attack on China in July), it was
far from clear that war was inevitable. Hitler, though he had consolidated power in Germany and rearmed in defiance of Versailles,
had made no move to alter the borders imposed by the peace treaty.

In order to alleviate its desperate strategic situation Britain was considering reaching a deal with Germany or Italy. An agreement with the latter was made in early 1938, but it was limited and did not presage any change of sides by the Italians. An agreement with Germany proved to be impossible. At this time Hitler was discussing his future plans with his military advisers. At the Nuremberg war-crimes trial in 1945–46 much was made of the so-called Hossbach memorandum, a record made nearly a week later of Hitler's meeting at the Reich chancellery on November 5, 1937, with his military leaders. Its status is unclear. Both the original and the first copy are missing, and the copy used at Nuremberg came from private hands, not state archives. Whatever its provenance, it does not disclose a master plan for the launching of the Second World War—indeed, Hitler insists Germany will not be ready for war until well into the 1940s. Hitler does, however, make clear his willingness to use force, annex Austria, and deal with Czechoslovakia and the Sudeten problem. In March 1938 Hitler, through a combination of internal disruption caused by the Austrian Nazi movement and pressure on the government, was able to engineer a highly popular Anschluss, a union of Austria and Germany, in defiance of the Versailles Treaty. Italy, now virtually allied with Germany, accepted this change in the European balance, and Britain and France found that short of declaring war there was little that they could do.

The Anschluss with Austria ruined Czechoslovakia's defensive position. Hitler was now able to exploit the widely acknowledged grievances of Czechoslovakia's German minority. Under pressure from Britain and France, the Czech government began to consider some form of autonomy for the Sudeten region and in the early summer Britain sent a mediator to try to help bring about a settlement. By the beginning of September 1938 it was clear that autonomy would not be sufficient to satisfy either the Sudeten Germans or Hitler. Britain and France now considered the possibility of a cession of the ethnically German areas to Germany. The case for this, especially in terms of the Versailles principle of self-determination, was strong. The difficulty was the method by which the transfer might be accomplished—referendum or simple annexation by Germany—and how much pressure could or should be put on the Czech government. The British prime minister, Neville Chamberlain, flew to see Hitler twice, but in the end they could not reach agreement: neither Britain nor France would accept Hitler's demands for the straightforward annexation of the Sudetenland without a referendum. Hitler was, by the last week of September, ready to order German forces to attack Czechoslovakia. European war was avoided by Mussolini's intervention in persuading Hitler to accept a four-power conference at Munich, which agreed to the immediate transfer of some areas and a referendum in others. The Czechs were simply presented with a fait accompli and their country was dismembered.

Although the four powers agreed upon a guarantee of the remainder of Czechoslovakia, its independence lasted only four months; in March 1939 German troops entered Prague and set up a protectorate over the Czech lands (Bohemia and Moravia) and Slovakia became an independent state. It is often argued that at this point the British government finally saw the error of its ways—Germany had now moved beyond demands for a revision of the Versailles provisions and was thought to be bent on dominating Europe. This meant that "appeasement" was no longer possible. A revision of the position at Danzig and the Polish corridor to the sea seemed likely to be Hitler's next objective. Britain and France therefore gave guarantees to Poland, Rumania, Greece, and Turkey and prepared to fight Germany rather than make any further concessions.

In practice, the situation was much more complex and demonstrates many of the ambiguities that were to be so apparent during the Second World War. The guarantee the British gave Poland was of its independence, not its territorial integrity. The British and French hoped thereby to gain some control over Polish policy and bring about a negotiated settlement—the British were certainly prepared for a return of Danzig to Germany. The Poles were given no military assistance, only a credit of £8 million and no cash help until a week after war had broken out, and by then it was too late. Poland was seen by the British and French governments as a revisionist, expansionist, illiberal and anti-Semitic state and was particularly disliked after Munich, when it had taken advantage of the German pressure on the Czechs to successfully demand the handing over of the Tzechen area.

Three days after the British and French guarantee, Hitler ordered "Case White," the attack on Poland, to be ready for implementation by the end of August. The Poles had already decided to fight rather than negotiate. It is clear therefore that the primary responsibility for the situation that led to the outbreak of war lies with Hitler's decision to use force if necessary to achieve his ends. That, however, had also been the case during the Czech crisis a year earlier. The most interesting question, therefore, is why the British and French decided to fight over Poland when they did not do so over Czechoslovakia. In 1938 the British government had been advised by the Chiefs of Staff that they could do nothing to stop Germany from inflicting a decisive defeat on the Czechoslovak army. It would then be necessary, they argued, to continue the war to defeat Germany in order to restore Czechoslovakia, and this would involve the substantial risk that Italy and Japan would join the war with potentially catastrophic consequences. The situation over Poland was identical. The British and French recognized that there was nothing they could do to stop Germany from defeating Poland relatively quickly.

Why then were Britain and France prepared to accept a war in 1939 but not in 1938? To some extent it was a matter of prestige. As declining powers they felt that their status and world standing could not be sustained if Germany scored another major success. In such circumstances the influence of Britain and France in Europe, let alone outside the Continent, might suffer irreparable damage. It was also to some extent the last defiant throw by two declining powers. In particular the British government recognized that any war would probably lead to a massive reduction in British power and influence. Either Britain would be defeated by the combination of powers likely to be ranged against it, or, in the course of the war, the United States and the Soviet Union would be dragged into the conflict, thereby drastically reducing British influence and prestige. The vital questions for the British government were, therefore, when and for how long they could afford to fight a war with some chance of ultimate success.

Since 1934 the British had been planning on being ready for war after April 1939. Finding the resources to fund a major rearmament program became increasingly difficult as the size of the RAF was increased steadily through the various expansion schemes of the 1930s. In 1938 the Treasury was already cautioning the cabinet that rearmament on this scale probably could not be funded beyond 1940. In early 1939, Britain, already committed to massive air and naval rearmament, was faced by a French insistence that they provide a Continental army; without this "effort of blood," France threatened to reach a separate deal with Germany. The British felt they had little option but to agree; they decided to equip a thirty-two-division army for a Continental war and introduced conscription for the first time during peacetime.

Rearmament was placing major strains on the British economy. Arms production required large amounts of imports, and the diversion of industrial output from exports resulted in major balance-of-payments problems. By 1936 Britain had a small deficit, but this grew to £55 million by 1937 and £250 million by 1939. Far more worrying was Britain's lack of gold and dollar reserves. In the First World War, Britain had been on the verge of bankruptcy and had depended on American financial help after the spring of 1917. Now, under American legislation, it was prohibited from raising loans in the United States and would have to pay cash for all the raw materials, food, and arms it required. By June 1939 Britain's gold and dollar reserves had fallen to 60 percent of their level only a year earlier. The Treasury warned that Britain was in a far worse position than in 1914. Indeed, they thought that the reserves would last at best for three years and that survival would, once again, depend on large-scale American aid.

If by 1939 Britain had the financial resources to fight a war lasting at most three years, this was bound to have a profound influence on the time at which the British would be best placed to fight a war that the military advised would take at least three years to win. British military preparations had long been expected to reach a peak in early 1939. The rapidly expanding rearmament program, with its demands for raw materials and American arms, was beginning to use up Britain's limited financial reserves. The decision to build a Continental army as well as a major air force and navy would necessitate the creation of a war economy even in peacetime in order to allocate priorities correctly. To sustain the existing armed forces in the long term was probably beyond Britain's resources, especially since their equipment would have to be replaced when it became obsolete. The danger for the British was that if war was postponed beyond 1939 they would use up their limited gold and dollar reserves in peacetime rearmament so that they would not have enough left to fight for the three years it was estimated it would take to defeat Germany.

British and French preparations had been intended to reach a peak in 1939, and they felt they had just enough resources to survive for as long as it would take to defeat Germany without calling on American assistance, thereby preserving their status and prestige. This assessment was reinforced by a belief, which in practice turned out to be false, that Germany had been engaged in all-out rearmament for some years and that the economy was now at the breaking point and would not survive the pressures of war for very long. It was hardly a heroic stance by Britain and France, but it accurately reflected their weak position and declining power. They judged that 1939 was probably their last chance of having a reasonable prospect of defeating Germany with their own resources and therefore of maintaining their status in the world. They were therefore willing to see the test with Germany come over Poland: if Germany chose to fight, at least there was a chance of success; if not, so much the better.

After giving the guarantee to Poland at the end of March 1939 the British tried a number of parallel approaches to avoid war. They attempted to persuade the Poles to negotiate with Germany but were unsuccessful. In the middle of July, during four days of talks in London, Britain offered Germany a comprehensive agreement and a massive loan to help the transition to a peacetime economy. Hints were dropped that a nonaggression and nonintereference treaty linked to disarmament was acceptable and that in the event of a settlement Britain would drop the Poles. Hitler preferred a military solution. The British had taken this possibility into account since March, but it was difficult to see how any military help could be given to Poland without creating an alliance with the Soviet Union.

Even then the Poles would have to give permission for Soviet forces
to enter Poland, and this they consistently refused to do, believing
that the Soviet army would probably never withdraw. Under French
pressure desultory negotiations were opened with the Soviet Union
but by mid-August were deadlocked over the inability of the western
Allies to give the Soviets the assurance they needed about Polish attitudes to Soviet help.

In the summer of 1939 the Soviet Union held the key to the situation in Europe. Soviet leaders had always been obsessed by the idea
that at some stage the capitalist countries would combine against
them, as they had done in 1918–20 during the civil war. To some extent the Soviet advocacy of "collective security" in the mid-1930s
and protestations of help for Czechoslovakia during the Munich crisis were an attempt to embroil western Europe in a war from which
the Soviet Union might benefit. However, the increasing threat of
German expansion in the east and the latent threat that Britain and
France might do a deal with Hitler led the Soviets to reassess their
position. They had no expectations of making large territorial gains if
they fought Germany in alliance with Britain and France—indeed
the point of the war would be to re-create the Versailles settlement
from which the Soviets had suffered. For the Soviets, recovery of the
territories lost in the aftermath of the revolution, such as the Baltic
states and eastern Poland, had always been an objective, and if Britain
and France would not provide the framework within which this
could be done, then other alternatives had to be considered. In these
circumstances the weakness of the Versailles settlement became
clear. By removing the common frontier between Germany and
Russia that had existed until 1918 it removed a cause of hostility and
also provided an inducement to both powers to agree on how to divide up the area between them.

Hitler could not afford to ignore the Anglo-French negotiations
with the Soviets and risk a three-power coalition and a two-front
war—always the German fear since the late nineteenth century.
Before the end of July the German government was dropping diplomatic hints about a deal and the Soviets had instructed their representatives in Berlin to discuss the details. By August 19 the Soviet

government had decided to go ahead, and the German-Soviet Pact was signed in Moscow on August 23. It gave the Soviet Union what the British and French could not provide. In public it was a nonaggression pact, but in secret it divided eastern Europe into German and Soviet spheres of influence. The German-Soviet Pact marked the beginning of a new phase in European power politics. The effective alliance of the two dictatorships provided a major challenge to the existing European settlement. For the next fifteen months the two states were, independently but in tacit collaboration, to redraw the European map.

Hitler believed, rightly, that he had scored a diplomatic triumph. He had avoided the danger of a two-front war and thought that in the radically changed situation the Poles would have no choice but to negotiate. Even if this approach failed, he was convinced that Britain and France would not fight—thereby giving him the limited war with the Poles he had always wanted and expected. The British and French response was to sign a formal alliance with Poland in a last desperate attempt to deter Germany. Hitler still expected the British and French to give way, but although they tried to avoid war until the last possible moment they could not risk the blow to their status and prestige if they allowed their ally to be isolated. The German attack on Poland began on September 1, and two days later both countries declared war on Germany.

II

NEUTRALS

SOVIET EXPANSION
1939–1940

Part of Finland
Russian before 1917;
Finnish 1918–1940

Petrozavodsk

Gulf of Bothnia

FINLAND

Viborg

Helsinki

Gulf of Finland

Leningrad

SWEDEN

Tallinn (Reval)

Estonia
Russian before 1917;
Independent 1918–1940

Pskov

Gulf of Riga

Riga

Latvia
Russian before 1914;
Independent 1920–1940

Baltic Sea

0   50   100   150 miles

Memel

Lithuania
Russian before 1914;
Independent 1919–1940

Königsberg

EAST PRUSSIA

Vilnius

Grodno

Minsk

Eastern Poland
Russian before 1914;
Polish 1919–1939

SOVIET UNION (U.S.S.R.)

Warsaw

POLAND

Pinsk

Lublin

Kiev

GERMANY

Tarnov

Lvov

Przemysl

Eastern Galicia
Austrian before 1918;
Polish 1918–1939

Bukovina
Austrian before 1918;
Rumanian 1918–1940

Bessarabia
Russian before 1917;
Rumanian 1918–1940

SLOVAKIA

Uzhgorod

HUNGARY

RUMANIA

Kishinev

Odessa

Occupied by U.S.S.R., October 1939–December 1940

The German Reich by December 1940

Under German control or influence by December 1940

Black Sea

THE WAR THAT BEGAN IN SEPTEMBER 1939 WAS NOT A world war; it was not even a full-scale European war. The only parties involved were Germany, France, Britain and the Empire, and Poland. Unlike the First World War, when nearly all the combatants had joined the war within a week of its outbreak, this time the war took more than two years to reach its full extent. During this period, countries had to adjust to rapidly changing circumstances and try to preserve their independence. Between 1939 and 1941 there were major changes to the structure of international relations, and in particular there was a remaking of the European power system that had existed since 1918 (and in some respects, since 1871). This was brought about not just by Germany. The Soviet Union, though technically neutral in the war between Germany, Britain, and France, was equally aggressive in seeking the power changes it wanted. Italy made its own, smaller contribution. Many countries failed to find any way of adjusting to this new situation and were eventually dragged into the conflict. Few except the powerful neutrals such as the United States and the Soviet Union had much say over their own destiny. Nevertheless, even in Europe six states, excluding the Vatican, managed to preserve their neutrality until 1945. Neutrality, however, provided no certainty of avoiding the impact of the war. Countries such as Rumania were dismembered while still neutral, and all suffered in varying degrees from the effects of the war and had to make many of the same changes to their economies and societies as the belligerents. Many at times were hardly neutral: the United States gave massive economic, financial, and even limited military support to both Britain and the Soviet Union while still remaining "neutral"; Spain sent troops to the eastern front while remaining neutral toward Britain and the United States; Switzerland gave massive help to the German war economy; and Sweden was hardly neutral in providing transit rights and other facilities to Germany.

The existence of neutrals also posed problems for the states at war. Both sides needed raw materials and manufactured goods from neutral states but at the same time wanted to deny access to their opponents. The result was a careful balancing of interests by all involved, with the factors affecting that balance changing with the military situation. Few neutral countries wanted to alienate Germany during the period of its great successes between 1940 and 1942, whereas over the last three years of the war neutrals were more prepared to be accommodating to the growing power of the Allies. In general the British tried to use their naval supremacy to control neutral trade through war trade agreements. These agreements usually provided for import quotas based on prewar trade, control over exports, and limits on the neutrals' use of German materials. The Allies and Germany allowed Sweden a safe-conduct trade through Gothenburg because both needed Swedish goods. The Swiss were similarly allowed to bring in goods through Genoa and Marseilles and to transport them across Axis-controlled territory in special sealed trains. Both sides also tried to secure neutral raw materials through preemptive purchases, particularly in Turkey, Spain, and Portugal. This policy had to be used cautiously, however; otherwise it drove up prices and allowed the neutrals to make large profits.

Although the rights and duties of neutrals were carefully defined in international law, neither the Axis nor the Allies showed themselves willing to respect those rights when it was inconvenient. The Axis powers invaded eight neutral states after 1939 (Denmark, Norway, the Netherlands, Belgium, Luxembourg, Greece, Yugoslavia, and the Soviet Union). The Soviet Union attacked two (Poland and Finland), forcibly took over three (the Baltic states), helped dismember Rumania, and later invaded Bulgaria. The British, who were the first to violate the neutrality of Norway, contemplated doing the same to Sweden, invaded the territory of Denmark (Iceland and the Faroe Islands), and with the Soviet Union invaded Iran and took control of the country. The United States invaded the territory of Denmark (Greenland) and the colonies of a state with which it was not at war (Vichy-controlled North Africa). The Allies also violated the neutrality of Portugal by invading East Timor. Britain and the United States were less crude in their actions than the Soviet Union and the Axis powers; they tried to justify their actions as *raison d'état* and argued that they had a higher right on their side.

The first extension of conflict in Europe came when the Soviet Union attacked Poland just over a fortnight after the German invasion and annexed the eastern part of the country. This was followed by further aggressive Soviet action to secure territorial and strategic gains in agreement with Germany. They demanded military bases in the three Baltic states and attacked Finland. (All four countries had been placed in the Soviet sphere in the pact with Germany.) In October the Soviets demanded bases from Finland—in particular, Hanko on the Gulf of Finland, which would enable the Soviets to control sea access to Helsinki. They also demanded a nonaggression pact and revisions to the border established in 1917, which would mean Finland losing a strip of territory over forty miles wide near Leningrad. The German, British, French, and American governments all advised the Finns to accept the Soviet demands. They refused, and on November 30 the Soviet Union invaded Finland and set up a puppet government-in-exile in Moscow. Two weeks later, in its last action of any consequence, the League of Nations expelled the Soviet Union. For the next two months the Finns successfully resisted a startlingly inept campaign by the Red Army and created a situation that tempted Britain and France to intervene in Scandinavia.

For many in the British and French political and military elite this was an opportunity to fight what they saw as the real enemy—communism. The British foreign secretary, Lord Halifax, spoke of the danger created by the German-Soviet Pact of communism's spreading to western Europe and considered the possibility of declaring war on the Soviet Union. Churchill envisaged allying with Italy, Sweden, Norway, and Finland against the Soviets. As a consequence, Britain and France looked at various schemes to intervene and send forces to Finland. These would land in Norway and with or without the consent of the Norwegian and Swedish governments make their way (using force if necessary) to Finland. This would have, they believed, the additional advantage of allowing them to occupy the Swedish iron-ore fields, denying this vital raw material to Germany. Their economic intelligence was so weak they even thought that this might end the war within a few months through a collapse of the German war effort. None of these schemes got off the ground, because of poor political and military planning and outright opposition from Norway and Sweden to any violation of their neutrality. Eventually, greater Soviet military force proved effective, and in early March 1940 the Finns were forced to ask for peace terms. Although the Soviets stiffened their demands from those put forward the previous autumn— Finland lost more territory, including its second-largest city, Viipuri (Vyborg)—they dropped the puppet government and allowed Finland to keep its independence. Finland was not, however, reconciled to this substantial loss of territory and the establishment of Soviet bases dominating its main outlet to the Baltic. However, the German-Soviet Pact meant that it had no alternative but to accept.

Although Britain and France had to discard ideas of sending a major force through Scandinavia to help the Finns, they immediately reverted to an idea first raised in the autumn of 1939: sowing mines in Norwegian territorial waters to force ships carrying iron ore to Germany out into international waters, where they could be intercepted. This operation began on April 8, 1940, thus making Britain the first country to violate Norwegian neutrality. Allied interest in Scandinavia persuaded Hitler to change his mind about his strategic priorities. Originally he favored the maintenance of Scandinavian neutrality, since it would limit Germany's military commitments and allow the continued flow of vital raw materials. Four days after the Allied request on January 6 to Norway and Sweden to allow Allied troops passage to Finland, Hitler ordered his advisers to study possible counteraction. German planning for an invasion began on January 23. On February 17 British naval forces entered Norwegian territorial waters without permission to rescue British prisoners on the German merchant ship *Altmark*. A fortnight later Hitler issued a formal directive and settled the date for the invasion of Denmark and Norway—April 9.

Neither country had the capability to resist a German attack. Denmark capitulated within two hours. Although the Norwegians fought on in much more defensible terrain, Allied intervention, characterized by rapidly shifting objectives and very poor direction, proved of little help, and by the end of May German forces controlled the country. Until September 1943 Denmark remained a neutral state. Hitler had always been reluctant to invade Denmark and at first thought of asking for no more than the use of bases and transit facilities. The rapid Danish capitulation was based upon an assertion of neutrality that was accepted by Germany in return for the stationing of German forces in the country. German relations with Denmark continued to be conducted through the respective foreign ministries and ambassadors.

Denmark's anomalous status raised problems for the dependent territories of Iceland and Greenland. In 1937 the Icelandic parliament had decided to opt for full independence when its treaty of union came up for renewal in 1944. On April 9, 1940, the British asked the Icelandic government for defense facilities. The request was rejected and Iceland decided to remain neutral. On May 6 the British occupied the country. They then opposed any attempt by Iceland to declare itself independent. Early in 1941 the United States occupied Greenland with the permission of the Danish ambassador in Washington; he was promptly sacked by the Copenhagen government and the U.S. action was condemned. In July 1941 American forces took over from British troops in Iceland, and they allowed Iceland to become independent in 1944 without the consent of the Danish government.

After the successful occupation of Denmark and Norway, Hitler turned his attention back to the operation he had originally wanted to mount in the autumn of 1939: an attack westward. It finally began on May 10, and, as in 1914, German forces attacked the neutral states of

Belgium and Luxembourg. This time they also attacked the Nether-lands, which had remained neutral throughout the First World War. The Netherlands and Luxembourg were rapidly overrun and Bel-gium surrendered within three weeks. In a brilliantly conceived op-eration, German forces defeated the British and French, leading to the evacuation of most British forces from the Continent by early June and the French request for an armistice on June 17. This stag-gering success transformed the European power balance: Germany was now the dominant power to an extent not seen since 1812 and the Napoleonic conquests. The other European states had to adjust rapidly to the new situation. Britain, driven off the Continent, had little influence, although its continuing resistance at least suggested to some neutrals that they should take account of the fact that Ger-many might not ultimately win the war. In the new power balance two states caused problems for Germany. Italy had joined the war, but its ambitions were beyond its means, and its failed military opera-tions forced Germany to intervene in areas it wanted to keep neutral, in order to rescue its new ally. The Soviet Union took advantage of the new power balance to increase its control over eastern Europe and move toward challenging German interests in the Balkans, espe-cially Rumania and Bulgaria.

By the spring of 1939, after the occupation of Prague, Musso-lini seems to have believed that he should join the winning side—Germany. To impress Hitler he launched his own invasion of Al-bania. The necessary orders were given to the military only a few days before the attack, which, not surprisingly, turned out to be a shambles. Italy established control, and Hitler, who had wanted to keep the Balkans neutral, had little choice but to endorse the action. In May 1939 Mussolini at very short notice proposed, largely as a publicity gesture, a "Pact of Steel"—an alliance between Italy and Germany. The terms were drafted by Germany and were highly dis-advantageous to Italy, which had to provide unconditional support even in the event of an aggressive war launched by their ally. The Italians were told that Germany had no intention of attacking Po-land, and they agreed to launch a war in two or three years' time. At the end of July, Mussolini told Hitler that he fully supported him.

Hitler was shrewd enough not to believe his erstwhile ally. The Italians were not told about the attack on Poland until mid-August. Mussolini immediately developed cold feet about the forthcoming war. He refused to join Germany unless the Germans provided a vast amount of raw materials (6 million tons of coal, 2 million tons of steel, 7 million tons of oil—in total 17,000 trainloads), a list that Mussolini devised knowing that Germany could not provide it. September 1939, therefore, saw Italy repeating its actions of the First World War: deserting its ally and waiting to see which side was likely to win and offer the Italians the most. Mussolini thought that Germany was in a stronger position than in the First World War but was far from convinced that it was strong enough to guarantee victory. In the autumn of 1939 he was worried that the German-Soviet Pact would reduce the importance of Italy and was thinking of leading a neutral Balkan bloc. By December the Fascist Grand Council was even discussing the possibility of fighting alongside Britain and France. Because of the Italian need for hard currency at this time, Mussolini sold France tankers, railway trucks, six hundred aircraft engines and five hundred training aircraft. In practice, Mussolini's main concern during this period was to act as an international mediator—a role he had played well in the Munich crisis, had nearly brought to fruition in the last days of August 1939 during the Danzig crisis, and one that President Roosevelt twice thought he should play in the spring of 1940.

At the end of March 1940, Mussolini still thought a German attack in the west was improbable and argued that Italy should remain neutral for as long as possible. However, he was under increasing pressure from Britain and France. Italy lacked virtually any significant supplies of coal and during the 1930s had drifted from buying half its requirements from Britain into dependence on Germany. In March 1940 the British, in a very clumsy move, cut off the seaborne trade between themselves and Italy but offered British coal in return for Italian arms and a major shift in favor of the Allies. The rapid German military successes in May clarified Mussolini's mind. The British and French tried to buy him off as they faced defeat in the last week of May, but he thought their promises were worthless. Most of the influential groups around the Italian leader—the court, the military, parts of the Fascist party, and the Vatican—were against participation in the war, but Mussolini thought that this would be the last chance for Italy to jump on the bandwagon and secure long-term aims at little or no cost. In mid-June, Italy, tempted by the same "sacred egoism" as in the First World War, joined in the war.

The German successes in the summer of 1940 gave the Soviets the opportunity to extend their sphere of influence while Germany was preoccupied in the west. On June 15, following staged incidents, Lithuania was occupied, and the next day ultimatums were delivered to Estonia and Latvia. Within a week the three Baltic countries had formed popular-front governments. After rigged elections, the three parliaments voted on July 21 to become Soviet republics and apply for membership in the Soviet Union, which was magnanimously granted in early August. Germany was content to accept these changes because all three states had been allocated to the Soviet sphere of influence.

The next Soviet move, however, against Rumania, raised more difficult problems for Germany because it involved the Balkans, which had been excluded from the 1939 spheres-of-influence agreement and which Germany wanted to keep neutral so as to ensure the continued flow of vital raw materials. It was this Soviet move against Rumania that drew Germany into the complexities of Balkan rivalries and eventually dragged more states into the war.

Rumania was a key state in the Balkans. It had done well out of the First World War by joining the Allies, but this left it vulnerable to the powers that would benefit from any revision of the postwar settlement. These states, in particular Hungary and Bulgaria, tended to side with Germany and saw the changing European power balance in the summer of 1940 as an opportunity to secure gains they had long coveted. Hungary had been the biggest territorial loser in the 1919 settlement: it was reduced to a third of its historic territory and 40 percent of its prewar population, and a third of the Magyar people lived outside its boundaries. It had claims against all its neighbors, and the intensely conservative, landowning, semifeudal, anti-Semitic elite that controlled the country were prepared to pay a high price for territorial revision. After Munich, Hungary recovered part of south Slovakia and southwest Ruthenia from Czechoslovakia, and after the German occupation of Prague in March 1939 it annexed the rest of Ruthenia. Bulgaria also had a long-standing claim against Rumania to south Dobruja (an area that was ethnically 80 percent non-Rumanian), the justice of which was recognized by most powers, including Britain.

On June 23 the Soviets told the Germans they intended to demand the return of Bessarabia from Rumania. The ultimatum was issued three days later, and Hitler, who wanted to avoid any war in the Balkans, advised Rumania to accept and lose a substantial part of its territory. Britain, which had guaranteed Rumania at the same time as Poland in March 1939, could do no more than offer sympathy. In mid-July 1940, Germany intervened to counter Soviet pressure and offered to guarantee the borders of Rumania, but only after concessions had been made to both Hungary and Bulgaria. Negotiations between Hungary and Rumania collapsed in mid-August, and at the end of the month Hitler arbitrated the dispute and imposed a settlement. Hungary obtained about two thirds of its claims to Transylvania and a few days later Bulgaria took over southern Dobruja. In total, Rumania lost about a third of its territory and six million people, of whom about half were ethnically Rumanian. The result was that the authoritarian, semifascist, and corrupt dictatorship under King Carol II was overthrown and replaced by a regime under Carol's son Michael, run by General Antonescu and the Fascist-inspired Iron Guard. Rumania, despite its reduced status, had no alternative but to ally itself with Germany.

By the early autumn of 1940 Hitler could feel that he had successfully brought a new stability to the Balkans. The postwar settlement had been overthrown, the governments were sympathetic to Germany, and the raw materials and resources of the area were open to German exploitation. All of this had been done without a war and while maintaining the neutrality of the region. More important, Germany had managed to exclude the Soviet Union from any important influence in the area. However, this stability was to be shattered by

Italian actions, embroiling Germany further in the Balkans and raising again questions about Soviet intervention in the region. Eager for his own share in the glory of remaking Europe, Mussolini decided to attack Greece at the end of October 1940. Within days the invasion had been halted and the Greeks had begun driving the Italians back into Albania. Hitler initially stayed neutral in this conflict, but by the end of 1940 it was clear that the Italians were in desperate straits and that Germany would have to intervene in order to rescue them.

Any German attack on Greece would certainly have to involve Bulgaria and possibly Yugoslavia, too, for geographical reasons. Bulgaria was in a difficult position: the Soviet Union made clear to the Germans that they regarded it as part of their sphere of influence and offered Bulgaria a mutual-assistance pact in December 1940, under which Bulgaria was to make extensive territorial gains at the expense of Greece, Turkey, and Yugoslavia—a sign of Soviet intentions to redraw Balkan boundaries and extend their influence. Under continuing German pressure, however, the Bulgarians agreed in early January 1941 to start military talks and preparations for the deployment of German troops. Final agreement was not reached until Germany had accepted Bulgarian demands for territorial gains at the expense of Greece, and German troops entered Bulgaria on March 1, 1941.

Yugoslavia was to cause the Germans even more problems. The state, dominated by the Serbs, had survived as a democracy for only ten years after its creation and in 1929 had become a highly centralized, authoritarian royal dictatorship. Italy had long held expansionist aims in the area and for years had backed a series of Croat nationalists, including Ante Pavelic, leader of the extremist Ustasha movement. The internal divisions in the Yugoslav state between Serb, Croat, Slovene, Muslim, and other groups combined with territorial claims from Italy, Hungary, and Bulgaria gravely weakened its strategic position. The German military successes in the spring and early summer of 1940 and the entry of Italy into the war made a difficult situation even worse. The Yugoslavs turned to Moscow and opened diplomatic relations in June 1940, but surrounded as they were by states under German influence, they could expect little practical help from the Soviet Union.

In November 1940, Hitler tried to secure Yugoslav cooperation with a promise of Salonika, but the Yugoslavs, who had little expectation that the Italians would defeat the Greeks and reach Salonika or hand it over to them, remained noncommittal. Germany renewed its pressure in February 1941, once planning for its attack on Greece was under way. The German army wanted to use Yugoslav railways for nonmilitary supplies and the evacuation of the wounded. Yugoslavia was reluctant to join the Germany-Italy-Japan Tripartite Pact, signed in September 1940, as other Balkan states had done, but eventually agreed to do so when Germany agreed to respect the sovereignty and territorial integrity of Yugoslavia, recognize the Yugoslav interest in Salonika, not ask for the transit of German troops through the country, and not ask for Yugoslav military assistance. The Yugoslav government had scored a major diplomatic success: it had pledged itself to very little in return for major German concessions, which had not been given to any of the other neutrals who were part of the German sphere of influence in the Balkans.

During the spring of 1941 the British had also been trying to build a Balkan bloc to involve Yugoslavia and Turkey on the side of Greece. Their efforts were to no avail until Yugoslavia joined the Tripartite Pact on March 25, when British agents were able to encourage a coup d'état by Serb officers to remove the regent and install the underage King Peter on the throne. The British found, however, that the coup brought them few benefits—Yugoslavia remained a member of the Tripartite Pact and a British alliance was rejected. Hitler, though, chose to interpret the coup as an anti-German move by Yugoslavia and decided to implement contingency plans drawn up in the autumn of 1940 and attack Yugoslavia. The invasion began on April 6 (the same date as the attack on Greece), and the two million–strong Yugoslav army, especially the Croat forces, put up little effective resistance. Six days after the attack, an independent Croat state was proclaimed in Zagreb, and on April 17 Yugoslav forces surrendered.

The result was the disappearance of the Yugoslav state. Slovenia was partitioned between Germany and Italy, the latter getting Ljubljana and most of the Dalmatian and Adriatic coast. A Ustasha government was recognized in Croatia and given control of Bosnia-Herzegovina. Montenegro was given autonomy under Italian supervision, Italian-controlled Albania annexed western Macedonia and Kosovo, and a very weak collaborationist government was set up in Serbia. Hungary and Bulgaria made substantial gains. The former had joined the invasion and took control of the Vojvodina, the area it had lost at the end of the First World War. Thus, since 1938 Hungary had doubled in size, though it was still smaller than in 1918, and about half its population was now non-Magyar and subject to severe discrimination. Bulgaria, which had refused to take part in the invasion, nevertheless still received Macedonia. It had contributed the least of all the German satellite states and, while remaining neutral, had obtained the "Greater Bulgaria" borders it had coveted since the 1870s: it had taken control of the Dobruja and of parts of Thrace and Macedonia.

By May 1941, therefore, Germany occupied, or controlled through its Italian ally, both Greece and the former Yugoslavia. The remaining neutral states—Hungary, Rumania, and Bulgaria—were friendly. German domination of the Balkans was becoming increasingly important to Hitler as relations with the Soviet Union deteriorated. Stalin was seizing as much territory as possible in Poland, the Baltic states, and Rumania, although his aim was probably to keep out of the war as long as Soviet interests could be secured. Ideologically he saw no reason to intervene in a capitalist war unless the Soviet Union could expect to benefit. However, after September 1939 the Soviet Union for the first time had a common border with Germany and had to take account of growing German power, particularly after the fall of France and the expulsion of British forces from the Continent. Hitler too could not ignore growing Soviet power and influence. The main question for the two states throughout the period between September 1939 and the end of 1940 was whether the pact made in August 1939 could be sustained after the division of the territory between them had been accomplished and as their interests came increasingly into conflict.

At the end of September 1939 they were able to negotiate a revised partition of Poland, closer to the ethnic divisions, which gave Germany more territory, in return for which the Soviet Union was given Lithuania. Later, they concluded wide-ranging economic and military agreements. The opening up of German trade with the Soviet Union and the fact that the Soviets also allowed extensive German trade with China and Japan across their territory meant that the British blockade was largely ineffective. During 1940 and early 1941, Germany took nearly all Soviet exports of grain, timber, and petroleum, plus vital ores such as chrome and manganese used in armor production. German naval forces were also able to use Murmansk as a base. In return, the Soviets received metal and electrical products, together with military equipment, including five Me-109 fighters, two Ju-88 bombers, and the hull of the uncompleted battleship *Lutzow.*

In the winter of 1939–40 Germany had studiously stood aside from the Finno-Soviet war and refused to give any support, even diplomatic, to Finland. The further expansion of Soviet control in the summer of 1940, however, into the Baltic states and Bessarabia, raised more difficult problems for German strategy, which were not finally resolved until the end of the year. With Britain undefeated but relatively powerless Hitler was unsure how to proceed. One possible option, strongly advocated by Ribbentrop, the foreign minister, was an anti-British alliance between Germany, Italy, Japan, and the Soviet Union. However, this would depend on whether they could agree to a division of the world into respective spheres of influence. In June 1940 the Soviet Union hinted at a division of southeast Europe as part of an extension of the August 1939 pact. Italy was to be predominant in the Mediterranean and the Soviet Union in the Black Sea. The Soviets also asserted their claim to influence in Rumania and Bulgaria but by implication left the rest of the Balkans to be divided between Italy and Germany. Although Germany was prepared to allow the Soviets to take Bessarabia, it asserted its own claims to Balkan predominance in the carve-up of Rumania in August 1940.

The last attempt to reach a wide-ranging understanding came when Molotov, the Soviet foreign minister, visited Berlin on November 12, 1940. Ribbentrop proposed what was in effect a four-power agreement to dismember the British Empire. The Soviet Union would join the Tripartite Pact. Turkey and the Black Sea area would be in the Soviet sphere of influence, and Soviet expansion would be directed toward the Middle and Near East and ultimately the Indian Ocean. Molotov made no formal response during his visit but gave the Soviet reply a fortnight later in Moscow. In effect, the Soviet Union accepted the general thrust of the German proposals regarding the direction of its expansion but upped the price by asking for a greater sphere of influence in Europe—Finland and Bulgaria were to be allocated to the Soviets. Germany never made any formal response. In practice, Hitler decided that the price the Soviets were asking was too high and this removed any lingering doubts he had about launching an attack on the Soviet Union in the early summer of 1941. From December 1940 German policy was directed to that end.

Stalin's reactions to the European situation in the first six months of 1941 are very difficult to ascertain. To some extent he seems to have questioned whether Hitler would really embark on a two-front war and hoped that any war with Germany could be postponed, perhaps until 1942, when Soviet rearmament would be even more advanced. The Soviet Union therefore undertook no action that might alienate Germany. Large quantities of Soviet supplies continued to flow to Germany, and politically, too, Germany was appeased. In early May the Soviets withdrew recognition of the Belgian, Norwegian, Yugoslav, and Greek governments-in-exile and granted recognition to the pro-German regime in Iraq. Nor was any action taken against German reconnaissance flights over Soviet territory. There is, however, some fragmentary evidence that Stalin was taking a more cold and calculating view of Soviet interests. By the end of 1940 it was clear that the Soviet Union had probably expanded as far as it could in league with Germany. In an unpublished speech to the Soviet military academies on May 5 Stalin seems to have discussed this situation and hinted that the Soviets might have to take the initiative to secure their interests and attack Germany. Some commentators have even suggested that the forward deployment of Soviet troops along the frontier with Germany that took place in the spring of 1941 may have been the preliminaries for a Soviet attack on Germany.

During the summer of 1940, German consideration of a possible attack on the Soviet Union transformed the strategic situation of Finland. In June the Finns, under Soviet pressure, had made a series of concessions: Aland Island was demilitarized, Soviet troops were allowed to travel through Finland to their base at Hanko by train, and negotiations were opened with the British company that owned the strategically vital Petsamo nickel mines for their transfer to Soviet control. Throughout this period, in which the Finns feared either a Soviet attack or internal subversion, they received no support from Germany. In August Germany decided to give the Finns some support to bolster their independence while decisions were made about an attack on the Soviet Union. The Finns were allowed to buy arms from Germany and, owing to their concern about further Soviet expansion and driven by a desire to regain the territories lost earlier in the year, the Finns agreed to the German request for transit rights for their troops in north Norway. Some two thousand German troops were rapidly deployed to Finland, and the Finnish government took a highly cooperative line. There was no time limit on the deployment and no limit on numbers, unlike in the Finns' dealings with the Soviets over transit of their troops.

German plans for the attack on the Soviet Union assumed Finnish participation, and in April 1941 the Finns were told that Germany would support them if they were attacked by the Soviets. In May, Germany initiated preliminary political discussions. The Finnish government was convinced that Germany would defeat the Soviet Union and that they would regain their 1939 borders—which was to remain their requirement for entering the war. The Finns were then told of German intentions, and they made it clear that they wanted to appear to be drawn into the conflict rather than act as aggressor. This stance was difficult to sustain because Finnish troops were placed under German command before the attack was launched, mobilization had also begun, large numbers of German troops were deployed in Finland, and plans were laid to attack Soviet forces at Hanko. The Finns had become German allies in an aggressive war against the Soviet Union.

The German attack on the Soviet Union, which began on June 22,

1941, finally produced a full-scale European war. Western Europe, apart from Britain and five neutral states, was either occupied by or allied with Germany, and in the east, Finland, Hungary, and Rumania joined the German attack. The only other area of the world directly involved in the war at this stage was the Middle East. Egypt was technically a neutral state throughout the war, but the British effectively controlled all aspects of the Egyptian government, and a huge military base was developed as the center for British operations in the Middle East. Iraq was an independent state that had joined the League of Nations in 1932 on the cessation of the British mandate. However, the British maintained military bases in the country and effectively controlled Iraqi defense and foreign policy. In an unstable political system, the British opposed the nationalist groups led by Rashid Ali, which consequently turned increasingly to Germany for support. In April 1941, Rashid Ali seized power in an army coup but allowed British troops to transit through the country in accordance with the Anglo-Iraq treaty of 1930. The British sent troops to Basra but then refused to withdraw them. In retaliation, the Iraqis laid siege to the RAF base at al-Habbaniyyah. Four days later the British began full-scale warfare, bombing the Iraqi air force on the ground and moving in troops from Jordan. Rashid Ali tried to get support from Germany, but little was forthcoming. By June the British controlled Baghdad and installed a weak pro-British government, and the supporters of Rashid Ali were either executed, imprisoned, or confined in concentration camps. Although still a neutral state, Iraq was occupied by Allied military forces.

The entry of the Soviet Union into the war affected the position of Iran. In the 1930s the authoritarian, corrupt regime under Reza Shah was increasingly drawn toward Germany as a way of countering heavy British influence, exercised through the latter's ownership of the Anglo-Iranian Oil Company and the huge production facility at Abadan. In September 1939 Iran declared itself neutral. The British respected this position until June 1941, when the Trans-Iranian Railway became one of the few ways supplies could be sent to the Soviet Union. Iran refused a British request for the transport of weapons along the railway and for the expulsion of German personnel in the country. On August 16 a joint Anglo-Soviet ultimatum was delivered, requiring the Iranians to expel all Germans except diplomats. There was no threat of the use of force, although in fact the decision had already been taken to invade. On August 25, without any further warning, British and Soviet troops invaded Iran; they had already agreed to divide the country, with the British controlling the south, the Soviets the north, and the Iranians a central zone around Teheran. On August 30 the Iranians were told to withdraw their forces from the occupied zones, expel all Germans except embassy personnel, and allow the transit of supplies, weapons, and troops. When these demands were not accepted, British and Soviet troops moved to occupy Teheran to enforce the terms. They withdrew in October when the new Iranian government—the shah had abdicated in favor of his son—accepted the Allies' demands. Iranian neutrality had been destroyed, although a semipuppet government remained in nominal control of the country. It is difficult to see how British and Soviet actions in Iran differed from German actions in occupying and controlling Denmark. From the autumn of 1941 the Allies had established effective political control over the Middle East.

By 1941 the most powerful neutral state in the world, the United States, was playing an increasingly important role in the conflict and demonstrating just how "unneutral" it was possible to be without entering the war. The United States was, like the Soviet Union, forced to react to the major alterations in the European power balance and was at the same time expanding its power and influence. In September 1939 the United States was relatively unarmed; it was spending only about 1.5 percent of its national wealth on defense and had an army of 200,000, mainly equipped with First World War weapons, and an air force of 1,800 largely obsolescent planes, but a relatively modern navy. In Europe it relied on Britain and France to contain any threat from Germany, which remained remote, as far as the United States was concerned, as long as the European balance of power was maintained and war avoided. The Americans were, however, always prepared to take a more active, though still strictly limited, line in the Pacific. It was after the Japanese attack on China in 1937, which began to affect U.S. interests, that the Americans began to reenter the international arena. Although the United States held some limited discussions with British naval planners about the Far East situation in early 1938, it remained wedded to a policy of internationalism, free trade, and a possible major conference to resolve world disputes (an idea raised with the British in early 1938 but quickly dropped). President Roosevelt supported the Munich Agreement and as late as the spring of 1940 sent the deputy secretary of state, Sumner Welles, to Europe on a peace mission. Once war broke out, the Americans repealed part of the Neutrality Acts passed earlier, in the 1930s, so as to allow Britain and France to buy arms. This aided American economic recovery and was consistent with Roosevelt's policy of helping the Allies to contain and then defeat Germany. As long as they were able to do this there would be no need for American intervention.

The situation was transformed by the events of May and June 1940 and the rapid defeat of France. During the crisis Roosevelt offered the Allies little but moral support, and relations were distant. As part of the long-standing U.S. policy of trying to keep Britain and France fighting, the Americans supplied the British with 250,000 rifles, 130 million rounds of ammunition, and 80,000 machine guns in mid-June to replace equipment lost during the Dunkirk evacuation. However, the French surrender and the German domination of the Continent forced a rethinking of American policy. It was far from clear that Britain would survive, and given these doubts the safest American strategy seemed to be to concentrate on the defense of the United States and not to send any further arms to Britain, since they would probably fall into German hands. The main American worry was that in any armistice negotiations the British might hand over their fleet to the Germans in return for better terms. If they did so, U.S. control of the Atlantic would be jeopardized.

From mid-June, American policy shifted toward North American continental defense. U.S. war planning was based on the assumption that the United States would have to defend the Atlantic on its own. Talks with the Canadians were initiated on hemispheric defense. Massive rearmament plans were passed through Congress, and early in July Roosevelt endorsed an act that prohibited the sale of arms to other countries unless both the head of the army and the navy certified that such equipment was not essential for U.S. defense. Privately, Roosevelt thought that Britain would not stay in the war. Not until late July 1940, after he had been renominated for an unprecedented third term, and when British survival seemed a stronger possibility, was Roosevelt prepared to consider British appeals for help.

In mid-May, Churchill had asked for the loan of fifty First World War U.S. destroyers for convoy work; Roosevelt rejected the request. The British were desperate for any sign of U.S. assistance and raised the question again at the end of July, linking the request to the offer of bases in three British colonies in the Western Hemisphere. The U.S. government decided a deal would be advantageous but drove a hard bargain. When the deal was concluded at the end of August, in return for the fifty destroyers the United States gained leases on seven bases, together with a British declaration that they would sail the fleet to North America rather than turn it over to the Germans as a bargaining counter (an undertaking they had consistently refused to provide before). The agreement was clearly an "unneutral" act by the United States, but despite the limited help given to the British (the destroyers were of poor quality and took some time and work before they could be made operational), it was still consistent with previous American policy. The United States gained important bases for hemispheric defense and an assurance about the future of the British fleet without committing itself to keeping Britain in the war. The Americans were still hedging their bets—giving limited help to the British while gaining time for continued rearmament.

The United States had to make fundamental decisions about Britain at the end of 1940. By August the British cabinet knew that the limited gold and dollar reserves with which they had begun the war were rapidly running out, as huge orders were placed in the United States for arms and raw materials that could not be supplied from elsewhere. It seemed doubtful whether the reserves would last until the end of the year, by which time the uncertainty caused by the November presidential election would be resolved. The British had no alternative but to wait and hope that Roosevelt would be reelected and then be in a position to act quickly. In early December, Churchill sent a long letter to Roosevelt setting out Britain's weaknesses and asking for a vast range of American help. He admitted that Britain no longer had the resources to pay for U.S. goods and, since raising loans was not permitted, asked the Americans to provide everything free. Talks about Britain's financial position began in Washington at the same time.

The U.S. government decided that its best strategy was to continue with its policy of keeping Britain in the war so as to give itself time for rearmament. The only alternative was to face the consequences of the British making a compromise peace with Germany. At a press conference on December 17, using a vivid metaphor about a man lending his neighbor a hose to put out a fire and getting it back when the emergency was over, Roosevelt outlined the idea of "Lend-Lease." After Christmas, in a radio address to the nation, he put this help in the context of America's new role in the world, speaking of the United States as the "arsenal of democracy." The British were humiliated by having to show the U.S. administration in detail their financial affairs and the extent of their bankruptcy. They were not consulted over the terms of Lend-Lease and had to wait until March for Congress to pass the bill before any help was forthcoming. In the intervening period the British nearly defaulted on all their contracts in the United States. The Americans sent a warship to Cape Town to collect Britain's last £50 million of gold reserves, and only help from the U.S. administration over its contracts and loans of gold from some of the European governments-in-exile saved the situation for Britain.

The extension of massive financial, economic, and military aid to Britain did not mark a fundamental departure in U.S. policy: the Americans still wanted to keep Britain fighting while they continued to rearm. Lend-Lease was simply an extension of that policy brought about by British weakness. However, it inevitably changed the nature of Anglo-American relations. Although the United States remained neutral, it was increasingly tied to Britain's survival and as a consequence determined to exercise greater control over British strategy and diplomacy. It did not mean that the Americans were prepared to enter the war. Many in the British government had illusions about when the United States might enter the war: in early June 1940, to stop a French surrender; in the autumn, as British cities were bombed; in November, immediately after the presidential election. All of these hopes were disappointed. Indeed, the very existence of these hopes showed a profound misunderstanding of American policy. Roosevelt was well aware that American opinion polls consistently showed throughout 1941 that although about two thirds of the country wanted to help Britain, over 80 percent wanted to stay out of the war.

In these circumstances, and given the U.S. administration's assessment of U.S. security needs, Roosevelt proceeded very cautiously. In April, although the United States sent troops to Greenland and extended naval patrols eastward, they were not allowed to escort British convoys and could do no more than report the position of any U-boats to British forces. This limited development was still consistent with the American emphasis, apparent since the spring of 1940, on hemispheric defense. The same was true of Roosevelt's decision at the end of May to declare a state of "unlimited national emergency," and to take over the defense of Iceland from late June and extend naval patrols into the area. Although the British and Americans held staff talks about strategy and Roosevelt met Churchill at Newfoundland in August, neither brought U.S. entry into the war any nearer. In September, after the U.S.S. *Gear* was attacked by a U-boat off Iceland, Roosevelt introduced a new policy of escorting all convoys in the western part of the Atlantic. This lessened the escort burden on the British but was still only a limited step toward entering the war. Although Congress allowed the arming of U.S. merchant ships and agreed they could sail to belligerent ports, Roosevelt did not allow them to sail to Britain.

Until December 1941, therefore, the United States was in an extremely anomalous position in the Atlantic. Although technically neutral, it was giving massive aid to keep Britain in the war. (It did the same for the Soviet Union after June 1941.) It was also giving limited but nevertheless clear help to the British in fighting the U-boats, as well as extending its sphere of influence through the Caribbean and into the Atlantic with its bases in the Caribbean and on Newfoundland, Greenland, and Iceland. These were not the actions of a truly neutral power. However, the United States was by far the most powerful neutral. Hitler gave orders not to provoke the United States and tolerated the situation, partly because there was little he could do about it and partly because this limited American help was less damaging than U.S. entry into the war.

Although the United States was cautious in the Atlantic area, its policy in the Pacific was much more active and assertive. The dispute between Japan and the United States, both neutral in the European conflict, was to lead to the outbreak of war in the Pacific in December 1941 and the beginning of a worldwide conflict. Until the late 1920s Japan was a moderate pro-Western power. It had fought on the Allied side in the First World War and was an ally of Britain until 1922. It was industrializing rapidly (production rose over fivefold between 1913 and 1938) and was gradually establishing a dominant position in Asian markets. However, it felt slighted by the inferior position it was forced to accept under the Washington Treaty and by the racial immigration policies of countries such as the United States, Canada, and Australia. Until the Great Depression, Japan was trying to be integrated into the modern industrial world, but then, as part of a general reaction found in other parts of the world, it tended to retreat into an autarkic bloc and become more nationalistic in a growing reaction against Western values. The problem for the Japanese was that they were not economically self-sufficient—they depended on key imports, particularly oil, rubber, and tin—and this made them vulnerable to external pressure unless they could secure control of their own supplies.

After 1915 Japan played an increasingly influential political and economic role in China. As the latter disintegrated after the establishment of a republic, increasing factionalism and control by local warlords followed. Japan's role challenged the position of the United States, which had major economic interests in China and strong emotional ties through the Christian missions. The United States was opposed to any attempt to seal off China, and other parts of Asia, into a self-contained economic bloc dominated by Japan. Neither the United States nor Britain effectively opposed the first Japanese attempt to accomplish this when it took control of Manchuria in

1931–32 and set up its own puppet government in the new state of Manchukuo. Neither power had major interests in the area, and it proved impossible to agree, either bilaterally or through the League of Nations, on an effective response. In 1934 the United States rejected Japanese demands for naval equality in the Pacific, and Japan therefore abrogated the Washington Treaty. By then, increasing control over Japanese policy by the military, conservative business interests, and nationalistic groups meant that greater emphasis was placed on national expansion. How this could be done and whether it should be directed toward China, the Soviet Union in the north, or European colonial possessions to the south was, however, undecided. In November 1936 Japan signed the Anti-Comintern Pact with Germany. It was a weak diplomatic agreement, not an alliance, but it symbolized Japan's drift into the camp of the revisionist powers.

In July 1937, a localized outbreak of fighting between Japanese and Chinese troops near Peking rapidly developed into a full-scale undeclared war. Japanese aims were unclear, but by October 1938 all major Chinese cities were in Japanese hands and the Nationalist government had moved to the far west of the country, set up its capital at Chungking, and continued the war. The Japanese could not achieve a decisive victory and soon had over 700,000 troops in China in a conflict that was placing an increasing strain on the economy; rationing was introduced in 1938. By December 1941, Japanese forces had lost 180,000 dead in China. Although the European powers and the United States failed to agree to impose economic sanctions on Japan at the Brussels Conference in the autumn of 1937, they had broadly similar aims and policies. Both were content for the Japanese to be embroiled in China because it reduced the threat to their main interests elsewhere in the region. The United States continued to sell arms to Japan, together with scrap iron and steel vital to arms production. The change in American attitudes came in late 1938, when Japan openly advocated a "New Order" in Asia—an order that would reflect Japanese economic predominance and the exclusion of the United States and the colonial powers. Within a month the American administration was considering a change in policy. Loans were given to China to keep them fighting. Then, in July 1939, the

United States gave notice of its intention to abrogate the Treaty of Commerce and Navigation with Japan, signed in 1911, thus symbolizing American opposition to Japanese aims.

Within a month Japan's strategic position was radically altered. In the summer of 1939, when Germany signed the deal with the Soviets, Japan was embroiled in major fighting with the Soviet Union along the Mongolian border. At the outbreak of the European war the Japanese government stood aside and took time to reconsider its policy. It tried to negotiate a new trade treaty with the United States, but the Americans insisted on an end to Japan's special position and rights in China and so talks broke down. The drastic changes to the European power balance in the summer of 1940 had the greatest influence on Japanese policy. The defeat of France and the Netherlands and the need for the British to concentrate their very limited resources on home defense left their colonial empires extremely vulnerable, especially since the United States refused to give any guarantee of support. Nevertheless, Japan moved very cautiously. The Japanese government was unable to decide its long-term aims and therefore missed its best opportunity to take over the European colonial empires in the Far East at relatively little cost. Instead it sought only limited gains. Pressure was put on the British and French to close their supply routes to China; the British agreed, but only for a limited three-month period, and also withdrew their forces from the Japanese-occupied areas of China. When the Dutch refused the Japanese request for oil concessions in the Dutch East Indies, the Japanese took no action. Their only forward move was to send forces, with French permission, into northern Indochina as a base for operations against the Chinese. The U.S. response was to embargo aviation fuel and some types of scrap iron and steel.

Throughout the autumn of 1940 and the spring of 1941, the Japanese government remained undecided about future policy in the face of an extremely difficult strategic situation. That situation was made worse for Japan by the German decision to attack the Soviet Union, about which the Japanese were informed during a visit to Berlin by Foreign Minister Matsuoka in March 1941. On his return journey to Tokyo, Matsuoka stopped in Moscow and signed a neutrality pact, but this primarily benefited the Soviet Union. The Japanese also began a long series of talks in Washington aimed at trying to reach a settlement with the United States. The German attack on the Soviet Union forced the Japanese to reconsider their options. Should they join in the attack on the Soviet Union? The Japanese doubted the ability of Germany to secure victory, and the gains that the Japanese might make were not likely to be great. They could remain neutral in any world conflict, but the danger was that once Germany and Italy were defeated, the Americans would be able to put pressure on Japan so as to force a withdrawal from China. The other course was to try to take over the European colonial territories in the Far East before the United States intervened in the war. At a long series of meetings beginning in late June 1941 the Japanese government was unable to agree on a way forward except to make preparations for war with the Soviet Union (in case Germany succeeded) and to take over southern Indochina.

It was the latter operation that was to seriously foreclose Japanese options. On July 23 they forced the French colonial regime to accept Japanese forces in southern Indochina on the same basis as in the north; the French remained in formal control of their colony. The United States decided to take strong action: Japanese assets in the United States would be frozen and licenses would be required for the export to Japan of all important products. The Americans intended to sell just enough oil to satisfy Japanese peacetime needs and therefore reduce the risk of an attack on the Dutch East Indies. In fact, the Washington bureaucracy imposed a total embargo and the British and other Western powers followed suit. The United States was now prepared to take a much stronger line and assert its own interests because its rearmament program was beginning to bear fruit. Defense spending had risen from 1.3 percent of national wealth in 1939 to 11 percent in 1941. The number of service personnel had risen from 334,000 in June 1939 to 1.8 million in June 1941. New ships were nearing completion, advanced aircraft and army equipment were flowing from the production lines. The United States could afford to take the risk of Japanese counteraction—it could now fight a war with the almost certain assurance of success. It no longer needed to be cautious diplomatically, and although still technically a neutral in the European conflict, it could use its growing military strength to secure its objectives.

The Japanese had not expected such a strong reaction and were now faced with a situation in which their oil stocks would run out in about six months. Should they fight to secure supplies or should they come to an accommodation with the United States? What would be the American terms if they did try to negotiate? While the Japanese government decided what to do, the military drew up plans for an attack on Malaya, the Dutch East Indies, and Pearl Harbor. In early September the government decided to complete the preparations for war by the end of October, and in the meantime see what sort of settlement the Americans would offer. The talks that had been initiated earlier in the year in Washington continued. It was clear that the two sides were far apart. The Japanese offered not to undertake any further military expansion, to withdraw from Indochina, to guarantee the neutrality of the Philippines, and not to attack the Soviet Union as long as the latter stood by the neutrality pact. In return, the Western powers would have to stop military and economic aid to the nationalist Chinese, agree not to establish military bases in the Far East, and reopen trade talks. The key demand for the Japanese was a formalization of their position in China. The Americans were not prepared to concede. They argued that any deal would have to include the British, Dutch, and Chinese, knowing that the Chinese were bound to insist on a return to the pre–July 1937 position and possibly the restoration of Manchuria. In addition, the U.S. insistence on free trade and no discriminatory trading blocs would ensure that the Japanese would have to accept American economic predominance in Asia and the Pacific.

In mid-October the Japanese government was in crisis about the way ahead. The prime minister, Konoye, resigned and was replaced by General Tojo. However, the military-dominated government was still reluctant to attack the Western powers, despite the growing threat of economic strangulation through the trade and oil embargo. By the end of the month it finally agreed to negotiate until the end of November. With the talks deadlocked, the Japanese put forward a proposal to enable negotiations to continue. In return for a Japanese withdrawal from southern Indochina and a limit on their troops deployed in the north, oil supplies would be resumed. In effect it was a proposal to restore the pre–July 1941 situation. The United States was reading Japanese diplomatic traffic and knew that any rejection would mean the end of negotiations. The Japanese would then be faced with the choice of either fighting to obtain the oil they needed or giving in to the American terms. The United States rejected the Japanese proposals. On December 1 the Japanese government decided to fight rather than be humiliated. On December 7 they attacked Pearl Harbor, the Philippines, Hong Kong, and Malaya. The Pacific war, which in its origins was only remotely connected with the European conflict, had begun.

The last area of the world to be affected by the war was Latin America. With a population of 125 million, it was the largest raw material–producing area outside of great-power control. Germany provided about a fifth of the region's imports, but the United States and Britain accounted for about half. However, British trade was in steep decline, and the United States was determined to exclude British influence as much as possible. The United States, as the predominant political power, had dominated the Pan-American Conferences at Panama in 1939 and Havana in 1940, during which the main aim had been to ensure hemispheric security and the exclusion of European influence through a neutrality patrol zone in the western Atlantic. Once the United States had entered the war it called another Pan-American Conference, held at Rio de Janeiro in January 1942, and applied strong pressure to all states to break relations with Germany, Italy, and Japan. All except Argentina and Chile did so. Some went further and declared war. Given the level of American influence, some countries such as Panama had little alternative. For others this was purely an opportunistic way of gaining American aid: Somoza, the dictator of Nicaragua, obtained Lend-Lease materials, was allowed to export goods to the Panama Canal Zone, and obtained a commitment from the United States that it would build part of the Pan-American highway through the country. The American desire to secure the cooperation of its neighbor enabled the Mexican government to secure major concessions. U.S. companies had to settle for just 4 percent of their claims for compensation following earlier Mexican nationalization of the oil industry. In return, the Mexicans agreed to a joint defense commission with the United States, and after May 1942, when German U-boats sank Mexican ships, the country was effectively at war. Other countries simply took advantage of the situation: the Peruvian government appropriated all Japanese property and distributed it to members of the government and their friends.

Chile stood out against breaking relations with the Axis powers because the United States would not give any commitment to defend Chile against Japanese attack. It finally changed its mind in January 1943, when the chance of any attack had receded. Argentina, however, had taken the lead against American policy at the Rio conference, and the United States retaliated by labeling the government fascist and imposing an arms embargo, combined with a refusal to extend credit facilities and deliver key supplies. Britain, however, wanted a much more lenient policy, as it had major investments to protect and badly needed Argentine food exports, especially beef. Indeed, in 1940 it had considered offering to recognize Argentine sovereignty over the disputed Falkland Islands as a way of maintaining friendly relations. From 1942, therefore, Britain was quite content with a neutral Argentina. In June 1943 a military government seized power in Argentina and offered to break relations with the Axis if the United States lifted the arms embargo; the United States, determined to humiliate Argentina, refused. Not surprisingly, Argentina drifted closer to the Axis powers. However, when it tried to buy arms from Germany, the United States forced it to break off relations under the threat that its dealings would be exposed. The embargo continued and the Americans forced the British to cut back on Argentine food imports, despite the critical food supply situation. Once the Allies announced in late 1944 that no country that didn't declare war would be able to join the United Nations organization, the Latin American countries that had not already done so finally joined the war.

By early 1942 the world was at war. However, a number of important states in Europe remained neutral: Sweden, Switzerland, Spain,

Portugal, Turkey, Ireland, and the Vatican. They were, of course, heavily affected by the war and their neutrality was often far removed from the definition applied in international law. They had no guarantee that their neutrality would be respected by the belligerents and therefore had to trim their policies in an effort not to alienate their powerful neighbours.

Sweden had refused to intervene to help Finland in the winter of 1939–40, although it did sell supplies and allow volunteers to go to Finland. In the spring of 1940 Sweden put pressure on the Finns to make peace, knowing that the Soviets were prepared to allow Finnish independence and that there would continue to be a buffer state between Sweden and the Soviet Union. Sweden accepted German demands for strict neutrality during the invasion of Denmark and Norway, although it mobilized its army and refused to allow any German war matériel to transit through the country. The German conquest of Sweden's western neighbors and then the French armistice left Sweden in a weak situation—in particular, Germany dominated the Baltic and therefore Sweden's access to the North Sea. Given this control over Sweden's trade, Germany had little incentive to invade as long as the Swedes were cooperative. Sweden was dependent on Germany for imports of coal, steel, fertilizers, and machinery. In return, Sweden produced large quantities of high-quality iron ore and ball bearings, both of which were vital for German war production. After 1940, Swedish trade was reoriented toward Germany; by 1941 it was double 1938 levels, and ball-bearing exports had risen fivefold. Overall, Germany accounted for nearly half Sweden's trade.

In these circumstances the Swedes felt they had little option but to agree to most German political and military demands. In July 1940 Sweden accepted what it had earlier refused, the right for German troops to transit through the country on the way to Norway. The army was partially demobilized, the Norwegian government-in-exile was not recognized, and Germany was allowed a free hand in its dealings with Finland. In June 1941, at the start of the invasion of the Soviet Union, Germany made a series of far-reaching demands on Sweden. The Swedes were to allow the transit of a complete German division from Norway to Finland; single German aircraft were to fly over Sweden without restriction; aircrews and aircraft that landed were not to be interned; minefields were to be laid in the Baltic in concert with Germany; German sea traffic in Swedish territorial waters was to be under Swedish protection; and German vessels seeking shelter in Swedish ports were not to be impounded. Sweden refused only the request for additional rail transport—instead, German troop ships were escorted through Swedish waters by Swedish warships. These were not the actions of a truly neutral power; Sweden was virtually an accomplice of Germany in its attack on the Soviet Union. The minefield sowed south of Ölund completed the German Baltic minefield. Between July 1940 and October 1941, 670,000 German troops passed through Sweden. In the five months after the start of the attack on the Soviet Union, five thousand railway trucks of military supplies and seventy ships with 420,000 tons of supplies traveled through Sweden and its territorial waters. Sixty German courier aircraft a week were flying over Sweden on their way to Finland, and the Swedish forces had orders not to fire on either German or Finnish aircraft. A huge transit depot for food, fodder, and fuel was established at Luleä. Forty-five thousand tons of iron ore a day were exported to Germany, and military equipment and food supplies were sent to Finland. By the autumn of 1941 the Swedish government was cooperating with Germany in sequestering Norwegian ships chartered by the United Kingdom and stopping the export of ball bearings to Britain. The British, Soviets, and Americans regarded all of these actions as a major breach of neutrality but could do nothing.

Following American entry into the war, the Allies tried to put pressure on the Swedes to alter their policy. Little was achieved, although a small reduction in German transit traffic was agreed to in return for a guarantee of oil supplies. It was not until after the Battle of Stalingrad, when it became apparent that Germany might not win the war, that the Swedes were prepared to consider changing their policy. Even then, they did so only slowly and reluctantly, taking no action until after the fall of Mussolini in July 1943. During the summer, in a series of talks with the Allies, the Swedes agreed to end German transit facilities (though this was not carried out until May

1944) and reduce supplies to Germany—by 1944 exports were to be two thirds of 1942 levels. However, no action was taken over one of Sweden's key exports, ball bearings. Indeed, in 1943 exports to Germany were about 40 percent higher than in 1942. As Germany's power declined it took a very conciliatory line with Sweden in order to keep supplies moving. In the spring of 1944 Sweden rejected Allied requests for a major cut in iron-ore and ball-bearing exports to Germany, and in July 1944 refused to end all trade with Germany. It was not until September, when commercial insurance for voyages to Germany became virtually unobtainable, that Swedish trade with Germany declined sharply. In mid-October the sale of ball bearings stopped and Swedish harbors were closed to German ships, and in January 1945, with Allied armies inside Germany, Sweden finally stopped all trade.

Switzerland was in a much more difficult position geographically than Sweden: after June 1940 it was surrounded by German-controlled territory and the allies of Germany. Yet in some respects it was much tougher in resisting German demands—it never allowed the transit of German troops and even refused to allow war matériel to travel through the country. In other ways it was very cautious. In July 1940 the government issued instructions to newspaper editors that they should trim their pro-British views in order not to offend Germany. It also took a tough line on refugees. It was the Swiss government that in August 1938 asked the German government to put a "J" on German Jewish passports so that their bearers could be excluded—a piece of discrimination the German government had not so far adopted. Even after July 1942, when first reports about the scale of the killing of Jews were available, the Swiss turned back Jewish refugees at the border.

Both sides had an interest in maintaining Swiss neutrality. Germany would not have found it easy to conquer Switzerland. The country was fully mobilized in September 1939 and remained so throughout the war; it was the only country in the world to mobilize all adult males up to the age of sixty. Although Switzerland was dependent on Germany for raw materials, especially coal and food, it was a vital source of manufactured products. Overall, Swiss foreign trade declined sharply (by about a half by 1943), but exports to Germany rose sharply. By 1942 they were three times 1938 levels, and arms made up half the higher total. In addition, the Swiss produced specialist high-grade products Germany could not manufacture and also supplied large quantities of electricity. For the Allies, Switzerland acted as protecting power and it was also the home of the International Red Cross, which provided some protection for prisoners of war. Industrially, the Swiss provided three products the Allies could not find elsewhere: precision jewel bearings for instrument panels, specialist cloth used in grain and flour mills, and glass eyes. The Germans were prepared to allow the cloth to be exported by Switzerland, but the other two products had to be smuggled out of Europe.

The Swiss were therefore by 1942 a major supplier for German war production. In September 1942 they reached a "compensation agreement" with Germany that allowed the Swiss to import some key raw materials (rubber, copper, and chemicals) from the Allies in return for more exports of war equipment to Germany. Allied attempts to restrict trade with Germany were rejected. In April 1943, as a way of exerting pressure, the Allies stopped all supplies through the blockade and extended the "black list" of Swiss firms with whom they would not trade because of their contacts with Germany. By June the Swiss had agreed to restrict their exports to Germany to below 1942 levels, and in return, food supplies at half their previous level were allowed through the blockade. In 1944, export restrictions cut trade with Germany to half its 1942 level. In August 1944, trade was cut in half again, and all export of war materials was banned once Allied troops reached the Swiss frontier.

Spain did not face the geographical problems that so heavily influenced Swedish and Swiss policy, although German troops did reach the frontier after the French armistice. The Nationalists had received substantial help from Italy and Germany during the civil war, but Spanish policy was dictated far more by a poverty-stricken economy after the civil war, a desire for colonial gains, suspicion of Italy as a rival Mediterranean power, and pressure from the Allies, than by commitment to the fascist cause. Franco himself was not ideologically fascist (although the Falange clearly was), and he resented

German attempts to emphasize Spanish dependence and Germany's demands for repayment of loans advanced during the civil war.

In 1939 Spain made a War Trade Agreement with Britain that accepted the principle of British controls: the British were to make a series of six monthly agreements to allow key imports to Spain in return for important raw materials wanted by Britain. Franco was, however, keen to enter the war at the right moment and, like Mussolini, secure gains at minimal cost. He thought the moment seemed right in June 1940 as France collapsed. On June 12 Spain changed its status from a neutral to a nonbelligerent and two days later occupied the international zone at Tangier. Britain and France accepted the fait accompli. On June 19 he offered to join Germany and Italy, but only for a very high price: massive colonial gains, French Morocco, the Oran area in Algeria, expansion of Spanish Sahara and Guinea, plus huge amounts of German supplies (at least 400,000 tons of grain). Germany, as with Italy in 1939, refused to offer supplies on this scale and would do no more than "take note" of Spanish territorial claims. Hitler was playing a more subtle game in the Mediterranean. Allowing Spain to expand its influence in the area would only stir up the conflict he was trying to avoid. He privately told Mussolini that Spain would get no more than a slightly bigger Spanish Morocco, whereas the British were prepared to consider giving Spain the whole of French Morocco in return for continued neutrality.

The British, and later the Allies, had some leverage over Spain because of its dependence on both imported oil and large quantities of food. In 1940 the British allowed the import of 100,000 tons of grain a month in return for continued Spanish neutrality. British resistance also convinced Franco that the war might not be short and that the time to step into the Axis camp had not arrived. When he met Hitler at Hendaye in southwest France in October 1940, Franco repeated his earlier demands for supplies, together with the territorial demands, and added the Perpignan area in France for good measure. However, he would not commit himself to a date for Spanish entry into the war. Hitler was furious, demanding bases on the Canaries and domination of the Spanish economy through the German acquisition of all British and French firms. Franco refused, and Hitler more or less wrote off Spain as a useful ally. A faction of the German strategic planning staff favored a peripheral strategy against Britain, one stage of which would involve cutting off the Mediterranean supply route, and as part of this Spain could help in the capture of Gibraltar. Planning for an operation, including a number of German reconnaissance missions to Spain, continued through the winter of 1940–41, but Franco insisted on the German capture of the Suez Canal as a precondition for Spanish entry. In effect, he wanted a guarantee of German victory before stepping in to collect what he hoped would be a substantial prize. Germany decided Spain would be a liability as an ally.

The German invasion of the Soviet Union did provide Franco with an opportunity to demonstrate his anti-Communist credentials while remaining technically neutral. The Spanish government allowed the enlistment of the "Blue Division" and "Blue Squadron" of Spanish volunteers for the eastern front. They were under the command of Spanish officers but were directly integrated into the German army and swore allegiance to Hitler. By October 1941 they were in action around Leningrad but proved of little military value. About four thousand Spaniards were killed and over three hundred captured. U.S. entry into the war increased the amount of economic leverage that could be placed on Spain and finally convinced Franco that Germany would not win. After the Anglo-American landings in North Africa in November 1942, his room to maneuver was even more restricted. During 1943 the United States and Britain demanded that Spain stop refueling U-boats in its ports and withdraw its forces from the eastern front. Franco complied in October 1943, when Spain became officially neutral again. About 1,500 troops stayed on as genuine volunteers, but in April 1944 Franco announced that any soldiers doing so would have to renounce their Spanish citizenship.

The other Iberian neutral, Portugal, was more sympathetic to the Allies. Salazar, although a dictator, was an old-fashioned authoritarian Catholic conservative who regarded Hitler as a menace. He acted as a restraining influence on Franco and could afford to ignore German pressure because German troops were far from the Portuguese frontier and British naval influence remained strong. Portugal's main role was, with Spain, as a supplier of 95 percent of Europe's tungsten ore (wolfram), which was essential for the manufacture of high-speed cutting tools, armor plate, and armor-piercing shells. Portugal supplied ten times as much tungsten as Spain, and the state closely controlled the trade and made large profits as prices rose twentyfold in the year after August 1940, as Britain and Germany battled for supplies. Portugal allocated production from British-controlled mines to Britain, German-controlled mines to Germany, and originally 75 percent of the remaining production to Germany. After 1941, the Allies had enough tungsten supplies outside Europe but relied on preemptive purchases of Portuguese tungsten to deny as much as possible of it to Germany. In total, it cost the Allies $170 million to buy tungsten that would have cost $15 million at prewar prices, and even then the operation was only partially successful. Portuguese supplies to Germany were not drastically reduced until the summer of 1944, and by then deliveries were impossible because the Allies controlled western Europe. By this time the Portuguese had already surrendered to Allied pressure in other areas. Their neutrality had been violated in early 1942 when Australian and Dutch forces took over Portuguese East Timor; the Lisbon government could do no more than protest. In October 1943 they also had to allow Britain and the United States to set up air and naval bases on the Azores (the British had had plans since 1940 to capture the islands if necessary).

The other major neutral on the European continent, Turkey, had to maintain a difficult balancing act among at least four powers: Germany, the Soviet Union, Italy, and Britain. Britain and France had guaranteed Turkish independence in March 1939 and in October 1939 signed a mutual-assistance pact which was designed to reassure Turkey over Italian claims to Turkish territory, although it could also be seen as anti-Soviet. The Turkish position was transformed by the collapse of France, the entry of Italy into the war, the limited power Britain could deploy in the Mediterranean, and the extension of German influence through Rumania and into Bulgaria. Turkey was obviously worried by the German-Soviet Pact, and particularly by Molotov's visit to Berlin in November 1940, suspecting that this might presage a partition of Turkey or its allocation to a sphere of influence. In the spring of 1941 Turkey refused to join a British Balkan front that included Greece and Yugoslavia. It did not join the German attack on the Soviet Union (British power in the eastern Mediterranean still acted as a deterrent), and signed only a pact of friendship with Germany, which did no more than stop aid for the Soviets passing through Turkey. Nevertheless, Turkey remained interested in the consequences of any defeat of the Soviet Union, especially if German troops reached the Transcaucasian republics. At the end of August 1942, when this seemed likely, Sükrü Saracoglu, the Turkish prime minister, told the German ambassador that it would be best if at least half the Russians were killed, and if Germany ended Russian control of all the regions inhabited by the national minorities within the Soviet Union. Such action would obviously be in Turkey's interests—but these were hardly the sentiments of a neutral.

Turkey was also important as the main European producer of chrome ore, which was essential for the production of special steels. At the beginning of the war Britain and France had agreed to buy all Turkish production until January 1943 in return for arms supplies. In October 1941, as Germany seemed to be on the point of defeating the Soviet Union, the Turks signed a new agreement: in 1943 and 1944 all chrome production would go to Germany in return for arms. When the agreement came to be implemented, in January 1943, the military situation had altered, but the Turks refused to break the agreement, despite strong Allied pressure. Indeed, throughout 1943 the Turks resisted pressure to join the war on the Allied side. Churchill, who believed that huge strategic benefits would flow from such a decision, visited Turkey and insisted that they attend the Cairo Conference in November, but the Turks, who could see few benefits from such a decision, resisted the pressure and asked for huge quantities of arms. By 1944, chrome deliveries to Germany were in decline as the Germans failed to deliver the agreed quantity of arms. In April the Turks ended the agreement and two months later cut exports to Germany to half their 1943 level. In August they broke off diplomatic relations with Germany and finally declared war at the beginning of March 1945, mainly in order to secure a place at any peace conference and protect their position against the Soviet Union.

Most of the neutrals on the continent of Europe were subject to German pressure, especially in the period 1940–43, when German military ascendancy was at its height. Ireland (Eire), however, was subject to British pressure. Relations between the two states were heavily influenced by centuries of antagonism, and the bitterness over the battle for Irish independence after the First World War. Some in Britain still did not recognize the right of Ireland, which they viewed as technically still a dominion, to remain neutral in 1939. In addition, in 1938 Britain had handed back to Irish control the so-called "treaty ports," bases for the Royal Navy that could be important in protecting Atlantic convoys. The 1938 decision was probably inevitable, since the British could never have operated the ports in the face of active Irish hostility. However, they remained tempted to seize the ports.

In 1939 the British decided they had little choice but to allow the Irish to be neutral. Throughout the war they continued to recruit successfully: 60,000 Irishmen volunteered to join the British forces. (In Ulster, where conscription was not applied, less than one in five of the Loyalist male population volunteered, or 38,000 men.) Ireland was bound to be a strategic worry for the British; in early 1940 there were secret talks between the two countries about military assistance in the event of a German invasion. In practice, the Germans were content with Irish neutrality and knew that they lacked the capability to launch an invasion. There were a few contacts with the I.R.A., but far fewer than in the First World War. The situation was transformed by the collapse of France. The British were desperate for any help and wanted the treaty ports. In the last ten days of June a senior British minister went to Dublin three times in an effort to bring Ireland into the war. The British were at first prepared to offer no more than a joint defense council between Eire and Northern Ireland if the Irish joined the war. The Dublin government wanted Irish unity in return for continued neutrality. During the negotiations it was the British who gave way. By the end of the process they offered a guarantee of Irish unity (without consulting the government in Belfast) in return for an Irish declaration of war. After a long debate the Irish government rejected the offer because they did not trust the British to keep their word.

By the winter of 1940–41, when its strategic position had improved, Britain decided to adopt what many in the cabinet regarded as a much more congenial policy—putting pressure on the Irish. The Chiefs of Staff advised the government that Britain did not have the forces to effectively protect the treaty ports, even if the Irish cooperated, and that they would need ten divisions to hold down Ireland if the ports were seized forcibly. The British decided to use economic pressure instead. The Irish economy was dependent on Britain and in particular on the allocation of shipping space for supplies destined for Ireland. In early 1941 the British cut back supplies to Ireland by a quarter. The Irish had to introduce rationing for gasoline, coal, and tea. The British cut oil supplies in half in 1941 and then in half again by 1943, despite the fact that the Irish had allowed the British to charter the only seven tankers in the Irish merchant fleet. Electricity supplies collapsed, trains were difficult to run, and the Irish had to turn to burning turf as fuel. The Irish government continued to resist British pressure.

Until American entry into the war the British had to proceed with caution because of the influence of the Irish lobby in the United States. After December 1941 the British had more room to maneuver. Immediately after U.S. entry the Irish again rejected British demands for a declaration of war; the Dublin government still wanted some assurance on unity, but now the British felt under less pressure to discuss it. The American view was that strategically the Irish had nothing to offer the Allies and that the ports were not very important. U.S. forces were stationed in Northern Ireland, and the Americans gave a commitment that they would not be used against Eire; the British had always refused to give a similar pledge. In September 1943, however, Roosevelt was keen to ask the Irish to allow use of the ports and to break off relations with Germany as Ireland's contribution to the war effort. The British, however, were opposed to this approach. Many in the cabinet did not want to give the Irish the chance to come into the war and preferred, for political reasons, that they remain as neutrals so that they could be condemned. In the end, the Irish were asked to break off relations with Germany only in February 1944; they refused. Although there was some low-level intelligence cooperation from April 1944 and the Irish were prepared to allow some interned Allied aircrews to leave, the Irish government retained its neutrality until the end of the war.

The remaining European neutral, the Vatican, was not of course expected to join the war, but its moral position and authority were particularly important to both sides. Pope Pius XI in the early 1930s had been strongly anti-Nazi as well as anti-Communist. He condemned the Rome-Berlin Axis, and in his encyclical "Mit Brennender Sorge" of March 1937 he criticized Nazi racial theories as anti-Catholic, although he made no protests about German anti-Jewish policies. His successor, Pius XII, elected in March 1939, had been nuncio in Germany from 1917 until 1929 and as well as being deeply conservative and anti-Soviet was strongly pro-German. He consistently rejected any condemnation of Germany or criticism of Nazi policies. The Pope did not condemn either the takeover of Bohemia and Moravia or the attack on Poland. In his Christmas message for 1939 he made it clear that the real enemy was communism. Privately he told the German ambassador at the beginning of 1940 that he loved Germany and added that the widespread notion that he was opposed to totalitarian states was inaccurate. In 1940–41 he made no condemnation of the German attacks on Denmark, Norway, Yugoslavia, and Greece, he made a lukewarm one of the invasion of Belgium, and in early June 1940 he advised the French to seek an armistice. His proposals for peace in the summer of 1940 would have done no more than confirm the status quo of German domination. Pius XII recognized and endorsed the murderous policies of the Catholic Ustasha in Croatia.

The German attack on the Soviet Union was welcomed by the Vatican. In a radio address on June 29, 1941, the Pope spoke of the "high-minded gallantry in defense of the foundations of Christian culture and confident hopes for its triumph." He told papal representatives in Spain and France that he could not openly support Germany because of the continuing persecution of the Church, but he added that he had no more ardent wish for Hitler than to see him gain a victory over bolshevism. Two years later the Pope was increasingly concerned about the Anglo-American policy of allying with the Soviet Union, which, he thought, would do no more than allow the spread of bolshevism across Europe. He stated that he was very much annoyed at their policy and sternly condemned all plans aimed at weakening the Reich, arguing that a powerful German Reich was quite indispensable for the future of the Catholic church.

Similarly, the Pope refused to condemn Germany for its extermination of the Jews despite the clear evidence available to him that this was occurring. Indeed, to some extent the Vatican supported discrimination against the Jews. When the Vichy government introduced discriminatory legislation and planned to sequester Jewish property, the Vatican argued in August 1941 that there was nothing in the measures that they would wish to criticize, adding that the Church had never professed that the same rights should be accorded to all citizens. The Vatican restricted its criticisms to measures against Jews who had converted to Catholicism. In January 1943 the Pope rejected pressure from the United States to condemn Nazi policies, arguing that he could not condemn Germany without doing the same to the Soviet Union and suggesting that reports of the large-scale killing of the Jews had been exaggerated for the purposes of propaganda. As late as 1944, after Rome had been liberated, the Pope refused to condemn the last stage of the Holocaust, the sending of the Hungarian Jews to the death camps.

Despite pressure from both the Axis and the Allies a few states even in the heart of Europe managed to sustain their neutrality until the end of the war. Some, such as Turkey and the Latin American states, jumped on the Allied bandwagon at the last moment to take part in the peace conference and secure a seat at the United Nations. Some of those that did not, such as Spain and Ireland, were excluded from the United Nations; others, such as Switzerland, chose not to join. Most kept up their "neutrality" until the very end. Portugal declared two days of national mourning on the death of Hitler, and Eamon De Valera, the Irish leader, visited the German ambassador in Dublin to convey his condolences. Portugal, Sweden, and Switzerland did not break off diplomatic relations with Germany until a week after the death of Hitler, when the Dönitz government was on the point of unconditional surrender. Spain and Ireland did not do so until after the capitulation, when there was no longer a legal German government to recognize.

III

ALLIES

THE SECOND WORLD WAR WAS FOUGHT BETWEEN COA-litions. Both the Axis and the Allied powers, therefore, had to face difficult problems of coordination and cooperation, settle differences of interest, and try to ensure that the coalitions held together even in adverse circumstances. The nature of the coalitions and the relative power of different members had some similarities, although the Allied coalition was far larger than the Axis and its structure more complex. Both were dominated by a single power, Germany for the Axis and, after 1941, the United States for the Allies. Both had an important subordinate power, Italy for the Axis and Britain for the Allies. One power was also left to fight a largely separate war, Japan for the Axis and the Soviet Union for the Allies. Each side also had a cluster of minor allies—Finland, Rumania, and Hungary for the Axis, and the European governments-in-exile and the British dominions for the Allies—none of whom were given much say over the conduct of the war. Both sides were riven by disputes and the coalitions did not always survive the pressures of total war, particularly defeat, as was demonstrated by Britain and France in 1940. In such difficult circumstances agreements not to make a separate peace were ignored. On both sides, former allies finished up fighting each other: Germany with Italy, Rumania, and Finland, and Britain with France. Bulgaria even achieved the dubious distinction of being, for a short time, a member of both the Axis and the Allies and at war with both.

Both coalitions were a mixture of different types of states. The Axis, apart from Nazi Germany and the ideologically very different Fascist government in Italy, included authoritarian states such as Japan, Hungary, Slovakia, and Rumania as well as a democracy, Finland. The inclusion in the Allied coalition of the Soviet Union after June 1941 makes it impossible to sustain a claim that the Allies were democratic. The position of some of the other members was also ambiguous. The United States denied the vote to nearly all black Americans, practiced widespread and officially approved discrimination, and fought the war with segregated armed forces. South Africa was ruled by a white minority that denied the vote to the overwhelming majority of the country's inhabitants and practiced rigid discrimination, which was extended further during the war. The Chinese Nationalists were a corrupt dictatorship with a semifascist ideology. Neither did the Allies fight a war for democracy. Britain and France did not go to war in September 1939 to restore democracy to Germany—it was to preserve their own position as European and world powers. Until the end of 1941 it was official British policy to negotiate with a German military government if the army overthrew Hitler. Neither did the Allies restore democracy to Europe, only to western Europe: shortly after the end of the war eastern and central Europe were ruled by Communist dictatorships. In the Far East the Allies fought a war to reimpose colonial rule and, in the last stages, to extend Soviet territory.

The Axis states were held together because all of them, even Rumania, had something to gain from a change in the power balance. In some respects the Allied coalition was more divided: all the states had a direct interest in the defeat of Germany and Japan, but there was an underlying conflict between the United States and Britain on the one hand and between the United States and the Soviet Union on the other. The Allied coalition had also come together by accident—the Soviet Union joined only because it had been attacked by Germany. China had, to a large extent, been ignored between 1937 and December 1941; it was only the Japanese attack on the United States and European powers that made them interested in having China as an ally. In the last resort, though, both coalitions proved to be remark-

ably resilient. The Axis survived until military defeat drove Italy,
Finland, and Rumania to seek a separate peace; Germany then had to
use force to keep control of Hungary and some of the smaller satel-
lites. Despite very clear differences of interest, the Allied coalition
created in December 1941 did manage to hold together until victory
was achieved.

For the first nine months of the war Germany fought without allies. It then had little choice but to accept Italy as an ally; Mussolini
insisted on joining what he was convinced was the winning side. Hitler, despite some personal sympathy for the Italian dictator, was far
from happy with the arrangement, and in the event, Italy was to be
the source of more problems than support. Italy was highly dependent on Germany, which provided most of its coal, coke, and iron. By
1941 over 60 percent of Italian imports came from Germany, which
took about half of Italy's exports, most of which consisted of food.
Hitler also had to cope with unrealistic Italian demands. At the beginning of July 1940, when their contribution to the war effort had
been minimal, they asked for Nice, Corsica, Malta, Tunisia, Sudan,
Aden, and parts of central Africa in any peace treaty. Hitler suggested
that they might wait for some success on the battlefield before claim-
ing a final share-out of the spoils. Militarily they were advised to concentrate on North Africa and to stay out of the Balkans, which the
Germans had always regarded as their sphere of influence. Italy was
grudgingly allowed to send some aircraft to participate in the Battle
of Britain (their performance was so bad that they were quickly withdrawn), but Mussolini was told nothing about German political and
military plans.

By the late summer of 1940 it was clear that Italy had not achieved
its aims in entering the war. There was no peace treaty with France
and therefore there were no territorial gains. The British still had
forces in the Mediterranean and were able to maintain a precarious
naval supremacy. The Italians found that their status as allies of Germany was under threat as Hitler attempted to construct a wider coalition involving Vichy France and Spain. Hitler recognized that Italy
and his two potential allies had conflicting claims over French North
Africa and told his advisers that only by "grandiose deceit" could a

solution be found. At the beginning of October 1940 Hitler met Mussolini and told him that there would be no formal peace treaty with France without fulfillment of Italian claims. This was designed to reassure Mussolini, who was rightly suspicious that Hitler might abandon Italy in order to secure wider gains. However, Hitler's meetings with the French and Spanish later in the month were failures; neither would finally commit themselves to the Axis. Hitler was therefore left with Italy as an ally. He then went along with Mussolini's view that France should be kept out of the coalition and Spain should remain neutral, both of which positions were designed to enhance Italy's status.

Italy caused major problems for Germany, beginning with its attack on Greece, about which Mussolini casually informed Hitler during their meeting at the end of October. A month later and even before the British offensive in Egypt, Hitler felt that the dismal failure in Greece had had the useful effect of reducing Italian claims to something nearer their capabilities. By the end of 1940, as its military position crumbled, Italy had asked for German help in both Greece and North Africa. Hitler was worried that without aid Mussolini might negotiate a separate peace with Britain. In January 1941 the Italians were summoned to Germany and told that Germany was prepared to give political and military support but at the price of Italian subordination within the coalition. Any idea of an independent Italian strategy must be abandoned and Italian forces would be under German command. German troops were sent to Libya to stabilize the military situation; they eventually drove the British back into Egypt. Greece was to be attacked via Bulgaria. By May 1941, when Germany secured control of the Balkans, the Italians were allowed a sphere of influence and an occupation zone in Yugoslavia and Greece. They were told nothing about the German attack on the Soviet Union, but as loyal subordinates they were the first ally to declare war and sent about 40,000 men to fight on the eastern front. Hitler thought the troops would be more use fighting the British in North Africa but felt that he could not refuse the offer.

Between the summer of 1940 and the spring of 1941 Germany was able to bring together a coalition of states to support an attack on the

Soviet Union. In the late 1930s, and increasingly after the outbreak of the war, Germany secured economic domination of southeastern Europe. By 1940, Rumania, Bulgaria, and Hungary were sending about half their exports to Germany. Increasingly, their economies were becoming part of the German war economy, which limited their political room to maneuver. Rumania decided it might benefit from supporting Germany by regaining Bessarabia, lost to the Soviets in 1940. In the north, Finland joined Germany to seek revenge for its defeat in 1940. Rumania and Finland were given notice of the German attack; Hungary, a revisionist state long close to Germany, was kept out of the advance planning and joined only after German aircraft manned by Slovaks defecting to the Soviets bombed the town of Kassa. The bombing was blamed on the Soviets, and Hungary declared war a week after the German attack. (Britain did not declare war on these three states until December 1941, and then only after coming under strong Soviet pressure.) Bulgaria, though, had already achieved its territorial ambitions. In the summer of 1940 it had occupied the former Rumanian province of southern Dobruja and, by taking part in the attacks on Greece and Yugoslavia in April 1941, Thrace and Macedonia. Under the shrewd leadership of King Boris III, Bulgaria then claimed that its pan-Slav sympathies prevented it from attacking the Soviet Union, and it did no more than help in the occupation of the Balkans and provide transit facilities.

Rumania deployed fourteen divisions and was even given nominal command of the German Eleventh Army on the southern sector of the front. They recovered Bessarabia from the Soviets and fought reasonably successfully. Rumanian troops took part in some of the worst anti-Jewish atrocities and often had to be restrained by German forces. Their killing of nearly 60,000 Jews around the town of Odessa in October 1941 was the biggest single massacre during all the eastern-front operations. By 1942 Hungary had nearly 200,000 troops deployed, but they had to be kept well away from the Rumanians because of the strong animosity between the two nations. After bad defeats at Stalingrad and Voronezh most troops were withdrawn into Hungary in April 1943.

By the end of September 1941 the Finns had recovered the territory lost in 1940 and pressed on into Soviet Karelia and the area around Leningrad. The aim was to create a "Greater Finland," as envisaged in 1918–20, through the annexation of east Karelia and the Kola Peninsula (both of which had overwhelmingly non-Finnish populations). This would have cut off the Soviet Union from its only ice-free European port, Murmansk, and incorporated an area with huge natural resources. Achievement of these aims would have required the complete defeat of the Soviet Union and a close alliance with Germany in order to retain them. The Finns were slightly more cautious in the Leningrad area and agreed with the German policy of letting the city slowly starve itself into surrender. In November 1941 Finland became the only unoccupied and democratic country to join the German alliance system, the Anti-Comintern Pact, although it consistently refused to take any significant anti-Jewish measures.

Until 1943 and the German defeat at Stalingrad the German alliance system held together well. After this watershed, however, the alliances slowly began to disintegrate under the increasing likelihood of defeat. The first country to crack was Italy. By early 1943 the Italian military position was verging on the catastrophic. It had lost Abyssinia, Eritrea, and its North African colonies, its troops were in retreat on the eastern front, and both German and Italian troops were on the edge of defeat in Tunisia. The next target for Anglo-American forces seemed likely to be Italy itself. Internal pressure on the regime was also increasing: there were food shortages, growing strikes, and increasing political opposition and discontent within the armed forces, and the king, who had largely withdrawn from politics after 1922, was in touch with various politicians and was beginning to consider the removal of Mussolini. At the end of May, Hitler approved plans to take over Italy and occupy the Italian zones in the Balkans in the event of an Italian surrender.

On July 10, 1943, Allied forces landed on Sicily. The Italians asked for German help, but their ally refused to send extra troops or provide military supplies, fearing the latter might fall into Allied hands if the Italians surrendered. Within a week, elements in the Italian government were trying to open contacts with the Allies to establish conditions under which they might be able to surrender. Mussolini's meeting with Hitler on July 19 failed to resolve any of Italy's dilemmas, and opposition to the continuance of his rule was growing. Five days later, a meeting of the Fascist Grand Council effectively voted to end Mussolini's rule and the next day he was dismissed by the king. Marshal Badoglio took over the government in a coup by moderate Fascists and royalists, most of whom thought Italy would have to extract itself from the war somehow. Hitler did not believe Badoglio's protestations about continuing the war, but without any action from Mussolini's supporters he could not mount a countercoup. Instead, Germany prepared to occupy its ally; preliminary plans were being implemented by late July, and within a couple of weeks an extra seven German divisions had been deployed to Italy, despite German refusal to help Mussolini earlier.

The new Italian government agreed in early August to approach the Allies to try to negotiate peace terms. Badoglio met the Germans on August 6, but both sides were playing for time; the Germans knew of the Italian diplomatic moves and just wanted to continue with their military preparations. The formal Italian decision to surrender was made on September 1 and signed secretly two days later. Germany had already decided to invade and disarm the Italians. The formal German orders were issued on September 7, the day before the first Allied landings on the mainland at Salerno and the formal announcement of the Italian surrender. Within two days German forces had secured the Alpine passes, taken Rome (the king and Badoglio fled south), and disarmed Italian units across the Balkans. On September 11 Germany declared Italy a theater of war under German command. A military government was set up in the south, and Mussolini was eventually installed as leader of a collaborationist regime in the north. The German-Italian alliance had collapsed.

The Finns began to consider withdrawal from the war the day after the German surrender at Stalingrad. They hoped to hold on to conquered Soviet territory as a bargaining card but had to consider how to deal with the 200,000 German troops who were already in Finland. Finnish forces would not be capable of expelling the Germans, and therefore any attempt to surrender might mean extending the war onto Finnish soil. For over eighteen months they grappled with the problem. Finland was not at war with the United States, which in March 1943 offered to open channels for the Finns to negotiate with the Soviets. At this stage the Finns were unwilling to make any moves toward the Allies, apart from stopping recruitment to the Finnish S.S. battalion. In the autumn of 1943, contacts were opened with the Soviets in Stockholm but broke down over the frontier question, the Finns unrealistically expecting the Soviets to give up most of the gains they had made in 1940. The Finns kept the talks going through the spring of 1944 and even sent a mission to Moscow. At each round of talks the Soviets toughened their terms as their military position improved, yet the Finns continued to reject them. The Finnish government was caught between increasing Soviet pressure and their worries about how to remove German forces if they did try to surrender.

In early June 1944 the Soviets opened an offensive in Karelia, and before the end of the month the major Finnish city of Viipuri had fallen. As in 1940, this was the signal for the Finns to try seriously to make peace. Although the Finnish government had given the Germans a promise that they would not make a separate peace, they decided they now had little choice but to break with their ally. When they asked for Soviet peace terms at the end of August 1944 they found these had stiffened considerably. The Finns were required to break diplomatic relations with Germany and intern all German troops by mid-September and only then would peace talks open. This required a leap in the dark by the Finns, but they had little alternative: the Soviets were now threatening to occupy the country if there was no agreement. The Finnish government finally agreed on September 2, and a cease-fire came into effect three days later. The Soviet terms were, as so often in their dealings with Finland, tough but not harsh. The Finns had to accept the 1940 borders, together with the loss of the Petsamo area with its valuable nickel mines (which also gave the Soviets a border with Norway), and some territory near Helsinki. The Finns had to suppress all "fascist" and anti-Allied organizations, pay reparations, and release prisoners of war immediately; Finnish prisoners would be returned only when a peace treaty was signed.

Although Finland had extracted itself from the war with the Soviet Union, it now had to fight its ex-ally. German forces had prepared for a Finnish defection and were determined to keep control of the nickel mines around Petsamo. About 100,000 civilians were evacuated from Lapland as a vicious war raged in the winter of 1944–45. The Germans slowly retreated, destroying everything as they went— the nickel mines, the capital of Lapland, Rovaniemi, and all the farms. The Finns had only 75,000 troops and 75 aircraft, about a third of the German levels, with which to force the Germans out. The operation was not completed until April 1945, when Soviet troops moved into the areas they were to annex under the armistice.

Hungary, unlike Finland, was in a key strategic position for Germany and found that it could not change sides in the face of determined opposition from its ally. Although Hungary was formally at war with Britain and the United States, it took no action against them and in return it was not bombed until 1944. As early as 1943 it opened contacts with the western Allies to see whether, if it changed sides, it would be able to keep the substantial territorial gains it had made under German sponsorship in 1939–41. The response was not favorable. In March 1944 Germany decided to take greater control; eight divisions occupied Hungary, and the regent, Admiral Horthy, was forced to appoint a strongly pro-German government. About 450,000 provincial Jews were rounded up and sent to death camps, but those in Budapest were left in the ghetto. In August 1944, as the German position in the Balkans collapsed, Horthy, who still had some independence, sacked the government and tried to open talks with the Allies, but without success. On November 23, Soviet troops crossed the border and Horthy sent a delegation to Moscow to find out peace terms. The Soviets offered the same sort of deal as they had with Finland: Hungary was to change sides and fight Germany. When Horthy tried to announce this volte-face, the Germans mounted a coup, set up a full collaborationist government, and forced the Hungarians to fight on.

Compared with Finland, and particularly Hungary, Rumania and Bulgaria managed their change of sides relatively easily. In late August 1944, as Soviet troops neared the Rumanian border, the government declared war on Germany. The formal armistice with the Soviets was signed a fortnight later, and Rumania had to accept the Soviet territorial gains made in 1940. The Rumanians also declared war on their real enemies, the Hungarians, and fought on till the end of the war, losing 110,000 killed as their armies advanced into Hungary and Slovakia. The Rumanian volte-face posed real problems for the Bulgarians, even though they were not at war with the Soviet Union. They were the tacit allies of Germany in the hope of keeping their massive territorial gains. In early September 1944 the Soviet Union formally declared war and invaded. Bulgaria immediately declared war on its ally, and over 300,000 Bulgarian troops fought the Germans until May 1945, advancing with the Soviets as far as Vienna.

By autumn 1944, as its military position collapsed, Germany had lost all its significant allies apart from Japan. However, relations between these two countries had always been difficult and cooperation limited. Although the two powers had signed the Anti-Comintern Pact in November 1936 and shared a generally revisionist stance toward the existing world power structure, there was no formal alliance or any attempt to devise a common policy. Until 1938 Germany cooperated more with China than with Japan and the German-Soviet Pact of August 1939, which was fundamentally at odds with Japanese interests, led to a freezing of relations. Indeed, for the first six months of the war Japan cooperated with British blockade measures against Germany. The situation only changed with the German successes in the summer of 1940, which opened up new opportunities for Japan in the Far East.

Even in these new circumstances there was still no fundamental agreement about whether the two powers did have any common aims and objectives. Japan did not take advantage of the German successes to act against European possessions in the Far East. In September 1940 Germany and Japan signed the Tripartite Pact (with Italy), which appeared to commit Japan to a defensive military alliance against the United States. However, a secret clause limited the pact to a one-sided promise of German support. In practice, the pact was ineffective; the Japanese were not asked to coordinate a joint attack on the Soviet Union. When Germany did ask for help, the Japanese were beginning to think about moving south rather than against the Soviets. Germany did not favor a Japanese move against the United States but was not consulted about the talks going on between the two countries. By October 1941, when the Japanese were on the verge of deciding to attack the Western powers, they naturally wanted Germany to restrict its operations in the East and concentrate on the war against Britain and eventually the United States. By the time Japan launched its war in December 1941, however, there had been no military talks with Germany and no attempt to coordinate objectives and strategy. The two powers had arrived at a common war in a haphazard way. If they had coordinated their strategy and tactics, both would have been far more effective.

After December 1941 Germany and Japan created the rudiments of an alliance. Together with Italy, they agreed not to make a separate peace. In early 1942 they agreed that the already planned offensives by Germany toward Egypt and by Japan toward India constituted a "common strategy." However, there was no joint planning of operations or strategy—indeed, the distances involved made it difficult to see how they could be coordinated—and no idea of how they could bring the war to a successful conclusion. Not until the summer of 1943 did Japan and Germany agree that German submarines could operate in southeast Asia, and although they sank about one million tons of Allied shipping, earlier action would have made them far more effective. They did agree on military spheres of interest. Japan was allocated the Pacific and Indian oceans up to longitude 70 degrees E (approximately a thousand miles to the east of Madagascar), and Asia was divided along the Iran-Afghan border; the Soviet borders with Afghanistan, India, and China; and then the Yenisei River to the Arctic. This gave Germany the iron ore of the Urals and the coal of the Kuznetsk Basin and Japan the rest of Siberia. This agreement was relatively easy to reach because it was theoretical and any conflicts of interest were postponed. In 1943 Germany conceded Japanese primacy in China.

In practice, the alliance between Germany and Japan faced overwhelming difficulties. The two countries had very different traditions and there was no real meeting of minds. Neither of the ambassadors in Berlin and Tokyo was trusted by his government as a reliable source. Most fundamental of all were the facts of geography. Direct communication and trade had been cut off in June 1941 with the German attack on the Soviet Union, and after December 1941 the only option available was a long sea voyage in the face of Allied naval supremacy. The two allies agreed that the main requirement was to send essential raw materials to Germany and examples of German advanced technology to Japan. The trade was very limited: the Allies were deciphering German and Japanese codes and could intercept ships with some ease. Submarines were used, but their carrying capacity was limited and plans for cargo submarines were abandoned. Until 1944 Japanese blockade runners delivered about 44,000 tons of rubber and 50,000 tons of edible oils to Germany. In return, the Germans sent examples of a special steel-manufacturing process, artillery, optical equipment, a Würzburg radar set, a gun stabilizer, and a torpedo fire control system for ships. Blueprints of the Me-109 fighter and the new German jet aircraft were also sent. None of this, though, could compensate for Japan's limited industrial base and lack of raw materials. Even copying blueprints proved difficult—the Me-263 jet crashed on its maiden flight. Germany and Japan did not agree on a system similar to the Lend-Lease by which the Americans partly equipped the Allies. As late as January 1945, the two countries were still arguing over the terms under which Japan would be given access to the German synthetic-oil production process.

The problems of coalition warfare on the Allied side were equally complex. In 1939 Britain and France re-created the coalition arrangements that had applied in the First World War: a Supreme War Council to provide political and military direction by consensus between the two governments; joint purchasing arrangements in the United States but no formal integration of command. In early 1940 both countries agreed not to make a separate peace. These arrangements survived the "phony war" of the 1939–40 winter and the Scandinavian campaign but collapsed as different national interests came to the fore during the German attack in May and June 1940. In May 1940 the British contribution to the Allied forces was minuscule: the

British Expeditionary Force (B.E.F.) in northern France totaled nine divisions (smaller than the Dutch army), compared with the French army's eighty-eight divisions, raised from a population smaller than Britain's. The French suspected that Britain expected its ally to bear the brunt of the serious fighting on land. They believed that the battle in May 1940 was the crucial moment of the war and argued that all available resources should be used to try to stem the German advance. The crucial issues were the level of British support for the French; the conduct of British forces (particularly at Dunkirk); and, by mid-June, as the alliance disintegrated, the question of a separate peace for France and the future of the French fleet.

The first arguments were over the level of the British air effort, especially in view of the rapidly established German air superiority. At the beginning of the battle on May 10, the British, who had nearly forty fighter squadrons in Britain, decided to reduce the number of reinforcements moving to France. Only two squadrons were sent instead of the four originally planned. In the next five days they refused three times to increase this number and agreed to send four more only after the decisive German breakthrough at Sedan. As the situation worsened the British sent no further reinforcements and allowed aircraft to operate only from bases in Britain. By the end of May Britain had just three fighter squadrons operating in France (about 6 percent of their total force), and this level was actually less than at the start of the battle, despite the fact that overall the British had an extra six squadrons operational. Persistent French requests for help were rejected; the British wanted to keep their aircraft for home defense and believed that the battle for France was lost anyway.

The French were equally critical of British efforts on the ground. Although under nominal French command, once the B.E.F. encountered German troops in Belgium it began to retreat and rejected French orders to fight on the line of the river Senne and later to support the First French Army. The British did not fight their way back to the coast—they sustained only 500 casualties in the first eleven days of the campaign. They left the bulk of the fighting to the Belgians and the French and rejected five appeals to counterattack. The British were already concentrating on evacuating their troops from the Continent via the Channel ports, planning for which had begun on May 16—less than a week after the start of the German attack. By May 29, 73,000 troops had been evacuated, of which only 655 were French. Only on May 29 did the British tell their allies about the evacuation, and over the next two days another 83,000 British troops left the Continent, while only 23,000 French were evacuated. At the Supreme War Council meeting in Paris on May 31, Churchill, after strong French protests about the situation, offered them half the future evacuation places. Since at that stage there were only 50,000 British troops left compared with some 200,000 French, this was hardly a generous offer. Churchill also said that British troops would act as the rearguard, but no such orders were ever issued. The French felt that they had been let down, a feeling that was intensified when they discovered that the British had used the full strength of their fighter squadrons over Dunkirk, something they had refused to do to help their ally.

By the beginning of June the French had lost a quarter of their army; outnumbered two to one, they now faced a rapidly regrouping German army along the line of the Somme. The British had one division on the Continent (the French still had sixty-two left) and refused a French request for a unified air force command. It was clear to the British that the new German offensive that began on June 5 was no longer of any importance: the French were beaten and the only British interest was to keep them fighting as long as possible to enable British defensive preparations to be improved. The French evacuated Paris, and at the Supreme War Council meetings on June 11–12 at Briare and June 13 at Tours most of the important issues were not faced openly; furthermore, what was said gave rise to chronic misunderstandings later. By June 16 there was chaos within the two governments. The French prime minister, Paul Reynaud, wanted the British to refuse a separate armistice so as to strengthen his hand against those in the French government who wanted to ask the Germans for terms. The British then came up with the worst possible policy: the French could seek a separate armistice but only if their fleet was sailed to British ports. This undermined Reynaud's position, made it look as though the British were only interested in picking up the pieces from the French collapse, and removed the necessary protection of the fleet if the French government did decide to move to North Africa to continue the war. The British then confused the situation even further by offering a poorly-thought-out plan for an Anglo-French union. The result was that the French cabinet split, Reynaud resigned, and Marshal Philippe Pétain became prime minister and asked for an armistice.

Anglo-French acrimony now became even worse. The British were worried that the French fleet might fall under German control, thereby endangering their naval supremacy. They refused to believe French assurances that the fleet would not be surrendered. Hitler was shrewd enough not to ask for the fleet, and it sailed to ports in the French-controlled zone and to North Africa. The British still did not accept French assurances and after a long debate the British decided to take action. French ships in British ports and at Alexandria in Egypt could be taken over easily. The most difficult problem was posed by the ships at Mers el-Kébir, near Oran. On July 3 the British gave the local French commander a number of options, all of which would have violated the Franco-German armistice. When they were rejected the British opened fire. The attack was not a success—only one old battleship was sunk, and the two most modern were not even put out of action. Overall, nearly 1,300 French sailors were killed and 350 wounded. Within less than two months of the opening of the German attack the Anglo-French alliance had collapsed with bitter feelings of betrayal and open fighting.

The Allied coalition was created during the eighteen months after the French surrender. Britain was not alone in June 1940; it had the support of the dominions and the rest of the Empire as well as of the European governments-in-exile. In June 1941 the Soviet Union joined the Allies, but relations remained distant and cold. It was the entry of the United States into the war in December 1941 that transformed the alliance; the United States rapidly became the dominant partner. Also, as the war spread, especially in the Far East, new problems arose, particularly for the imperial powers, and also because China became an Allied power. The scope for conflicts of interest within this disparate grouping was enormous and often not resolved.

Nevertheless, the immediate identity of interest in the defeat of the Axis powers was just sufficient to hold the alliance together.

In 1939 the British found that the Empire had changed significantly since the First World War. Then, the dominions had been generally content to accept British leadership and strategic direction. During the interwar period, the white self-governing dominions had become more independent; in September 1939 a declaration of war by Britain did not automatically involve the dominions. Although Australia and New Zealand followed suit rapidly, Canada took over a week to do so. In South Africa the government was split, and it was only after the governor-general refused to allow the prime minister, Hertzog, who favored neutrality, to call an election that Jan Christian Smuts became prime minister and war was declared. Eire refused to join the war and remained neutral. Throughout the war the British were very reluctant to concede any effective say in decision-making to the dominions and treated their forces as British, to be deployed by the London government, not by the dominion governments. The Imperial War Cabinet of 1917–18 was not re-created. The dominion contribution to Allied forces was small overall, though significant as far as the British were concerned—although they tried to disguise this by referring to British forces when they meant imperial forces. In North Africa in November 1941, Indian, New Zealand, and South African troops made up nearly two thirds of the "British" total, and the actual British contribution was little more than that of South Africa. In January 1945 the British made up just 13 percent of the Allied forces in southeast Asia; they were nearly outnumbered by the African regiments and almost two thirds of the total consisted of Indian and Gurkha soldiers.

Canada was probably the least influential of all the dominions, despite its potential. In 1939 its forces were small: the navy had six destroyers and the air force thirty-seven modern planes, and the army was 4,000 strong. The Canadian government gave invaluable support in using its limited dollar reserves to support British purchases in the United States in 1940–41; it provided important bases for Atlantic convoys—the navy eventually had over 370 ships and there were sixteen coastal patrol air squadrons by 1943—and it acted as a center for training aircrew (over 130,000 in the course of the war). One division was sent to Britain for training in 1939 and another in 1940. Neither saw any action until the disastrous Dieppe raid in 1942. Although Canada had a Pacific coast it contributed little to the war in this area, apart from sending a few untrained troops to Hong Kong in 1941 and a small force to the Aleutian Islands. Canada did not seek an influential role in Allied strategic decision-making and proffered little advice. In fact, it was dominated by its strong neighbor to the south and was edging closer to the United States.

The South African contribution to the war was also limited, partly because of the severe split in the country about whether or not to participate. Many Afrikaners argued for neutrality, some had pro-German and pro-Nazi sympathies, and there was an active internal sabotage and subversion campaign. At the outbreak of the war, South Africa had no navy, six modern aircraft, and an army of 5,000. It was entirely dependent on Britain and the United States for its arms supplies and refused to take part in the Empire Air Training Scheme. Its main contribution was to create an army of almost 350,000, which, for political reasons, was restricted mainly to operations in Africa. South African units were first used in Kenya and Eritrea in late 1940, but once the North African campaign was completed in early 1943 the majority of troops returned home and the war effort was significantly cut back.

The defense of Australia and New Zealand was to cause major problems for the British. Before the war Australia and New Zealand had been reassured that in the event of any threat from Japan the bulk of the Royal Navy would be sent to Singapore. The course of the war was to show that these assurances were worthless. The German threat in the Atlantic and Italian entry into the war meant that the British did not have ships available to send to the Far East. The cabinet accepted the advice of the Chiefs of Staff that only one battle cruiser and an aircraft carrier could be sent east and they would operate in the Indian Ocean to protect the Cape of Good Hope route to the Middle East, not the Antipodes. The dominions were deliberately not told the details of the British assessment, merely that no reinforcements would be sent to help them, even if Japan declared war, until there was an actual invasion of either Australia or New Zealand on a large scale. During the period from the summer of 1940 to the autumn of 1941 the threat from Japan to Australia and New Zealand, though increasing, was still latent. Australia sent its army to the Middle East, its ships were placed under British control, and it participated in the Empire Air Training Scheme. The Australian government found it difficult to adopt an independent strategy; it relied on the British for intelligence information, it had no diplomatic service, and the heads of each of its armed services were seconded British officers.

The outbreak of the Pacific war and the rapid Japanese gains transformed the strategic situation for the Australians. There was now a direct threat to Australia itself. Churchill told the King that he expected parts of the country to fall to the Japanese. Nevertheless, the British still refused to help—only two capital ships were sent to Singapore and they were immediately sunk. The Australian government insisted on the return of some of its trained troops from the Middle East. The British agreed with bad grace, but then tried to divert these forces for the defense of Rangoon without Australian consent. The British refused to send any reinforcements to Australia and promised to send two divisions only if the Japanese invaded using at least eight divisions (two more than they had used in Malaya). The Australians therefore turned to the Americans. The arrival of American troops and General Douglas MacArthur to establish his South West Pacific Command in March 1942 stabilized the situation. The Australian government was not consulted over the creation of a joint command with the British, Americans, and Dutch in early 1942, they were excluded from the Cairo Conference in November 1943, even though strategy in the Far East was being discussed (even the Chinese were present), and they had no say in the drafting of the Potsdam Declaration in the summer of 1945 on the terms for Japan's surrender. The only leverage the Australians had was to withhold permission for their forces to be used, as they did in early 1942 and again in 1945 over the proposed invasion of Java. Although relatively close neighbors, the attitudes of the Australian and New Zealand governments were very different. They cooperated only once on an issue of any substance, protesting their exclusion from the Cairo Conference. New Zealand generally took a much more pro-British line than its fellow dominion. During the war a quarter of New Zealand's adult male population was in the armed forces, but unlike Australia, New Zealand contributed little to the Pacific war. Its main effort was in the Mediterranean and Europe, and it did not pull its division out of North Africa in early 1942.

The dominions were in an ambiguous situation. They were not fully independent states, yet neither were they as subordinate as other parts of the Empire, such as India. In 1939 the viceroy of India declared war without consulting any Indian politicians, and the Congress party promptly resigned from the provincial governments it controlled. The British were able to keep control of the country before 1942, partly by a promise to discuss the Indian constitution after the war. The outbreak of war in the Far East, in particular the advance of Japanese troops through Burma to the Indian frontier, radically transformed the situation. The British needed India as a source of manpower—the Indian army was increased from 189,000 in 1939 to 2.5 million by 1945—and as a base from which to reconquer its empire. The Congress party was in a major quandary in early 1942. It wanted the British to leave but had to recognize that it needed Britain to fight the Japanese. The British felt they had to make political concessions in order to retain control of India and they were also under American pressure to move decisively in the overall Allied interest. A senior member of the British cabinet, Stafford Cripps, was sent to India with an offer of a considerable degree of self-government in return for continued British control of defense policy. In July 1942, the Congress party agreed that British troops could stay in a self-governing India to resist Japan and give help to China. Britain would not concede immediate self-government, and by August 1942 the continuing "Quit India" campaign, initiated by the Indian National Congress, led to the imprisonment without trial of all the Congress party's leaders. Large-scale civil disturbances followed—over a thousand people were killed and sixty thousand arrested—and most British troops had to be used to maintain internal control. In 1943 the British government recognized that India was akin to an occupied and hostile country and could not be used as a major base from which to mount military operations.

The second constituent of the Allied coalition were the governments-in-exile. They all faced extremely difficult circumstances. Their countries were occupied and they had to continue to pursue what they saw as their national interests when they had very little, if any, power to wield. They had to assert their right to speak for their country but were often plagued by political disputes and factional fighting. They had virtually no say over the direction of Allied policy, but were usually allowed to maintain their own military units, subject to British and later Allied operational control. There were major disputes between the governments-in-exile and Britain, especially over the blockade. The British would not allow food through to the occupied countries, and the only concession they made was to allow the governments-in-exile to use their foreign exchange to buy food from neutrals such as Spain, Portugal, and Sweden within the blockade zone. The British resisted all pressure from the Americans to be more flexible: as late as March 1944 they rejected a U.S. scheme to provide limited relief for children and expectant and nursing mothers. In June 1941 sixteen governments joined in the Declaration of St. James's Palace, pledging mutual aid and assistance. It was symbolic of the changing balance of power that within a month of entering the war the United States was able to insist that the Declaration of the United Nations, involving twenty-six countries, be made in Washington on New Year's Day 1942.

The first government to go into exile was Poland's. By the end of September 1939 Poland had lost 200,000 killed and wounded, together with 400,000 prisoners in the war with Germany and nearly 300,000 in the war with the Soviet Union. It had also been subject to a fourth partition. Silesia and Pomerania were annexed by Germany, establishing a frontier far to the east of the old 1914 line; eastern Poland went to the Soviet Union; the area around Vilnius went to Lithuania; and a central area, called the General Government, was controlled by Germany. By October, General Sikorski was established as both prime minister and military leader of a Polish government-in-exile in Paris that was recognized by Britain, France, the

United States, and some neutrals. By June 1940 about 43,000 troops and civilians had been brought out of internment in Rumania and Hungary and another 44,000 troops recruited from the Polish community in France. Both the Polish navy and army fought in the Norwegian campaign. No sooner had the government begun to establish itself than the fall of France forced it to evacuate to Britain, together with about 20,000 military personnel. It took until well into 1941 to reestablish a small army, but two Polish fighter squadrons played a major role in the Battle of Britain and by the end of 1940 eight squadrons were operational.

The major change in the Polish exile government's situation was the Soviet entry into the war in June 1941. Under pressure from the British the Polish government-in-exile reached an agreement with the Soviet Union by the end of July. It recognized that the latter's August 1939 agreement with Germany was not valid as far as it applied to Poland, diplomatic relations were restored, and a Polish army was to be raised in the Soviet Union from among the prisoners and civilians whom it held. This agreement did not produce any degree of trust between the two old enemies, and it could not resolve the major problems facing the Polish government: how could they ensure their resumption of power in Warsaw together with a return to the 1939 borders after the war, and, in the interim, what would be the status of the territories annexed by the Soviets?

These questions would have to be answered if and when Polish territory was liberated. Meanwhile, the Polish government was determined to make a major military effort in order to increase its weight within the Alliance. The Polish army began forming in the Soviet Union in August 1941; it was headed by a Pole, General Anders, but under Soviet command. There were long arguments about the number of prisoners the Soviets were supposed to be holding and their refusal to allow Poles from the territories they had annexed in 1939 to join the army. In early 1942 both sides agreed that it was best to abandon the project. Starting in March, 70,000 soldiers and their families were evacuated from the Soviet Union via Iran and a new army was created in the Middle East. By 1944 the Polish II Corps was in action in Italy, thirteen squadrons were operational with the RAF, and an armored division took part in the Normandy landings. In total, the Poles provided over 130,000 servicemen for the Allied forces.

At the end of May 1940 the Norwegian government also went into exile in London. For much of 1940 relations with Britain were bad: many in the government felt the British had dragged them into the war and then given them no effective help. The appointment of Trygve Lie as foreign minister in November 1940 signaled a change of direction and a formal alliance was finally agreed in May 1941, although formal military collaboration had to wait until 1942. The Norwegian military effort was always small, four squadrons operating with the RAF and an army of 2,500 by 1943. Their contribution to the Allied effort came via the merchant marine, the fourth-largest in the world. Nearly one thousand ships were run from London and chartered to the Allies, providing the Norwegian government with a secure source of revenue and therefore independence. (The Norwegians rejected two British attempts to take over the fleet.) Until 1942 Norwegian tankers carried nearly half of Britain's petroleum supplies.

A Belgian government-in-exile was not formed until late 1940, when various politicians arrived in London from Vichy France. Their main contribution to the war effort was to lend Britain £60 million worth of gold in February 1941 in order to avoid bankruptcy while the British waited for the U.S. Congress to pass the Lend-Lease Act. The Dutch government arrived in Britain in May 1940 but spent much of the summer of 1940 considering whether to make a separate peace with Germany. They opened contacts with the Vichy government, and in mid-July the prime minister, Dirk Jan de Geer, proposed that they should approach Germany via Sweden to ascertain what peace terms might be granted. This idea was rejected, and in the late summer the Dutch decided to fight on. Their main concern was to protect the Dutch East Indies, and they twice considered moving the government from London to Batavia. The British refused until December 1941 to give the Dutch any guarantee that they would fight to protect their territory against Japan, and so, not surprisingly, the Dutch attempted to appease the Japanese by increasing oil and rubber supplies. The Dutch were treated rather like the Australians and were not consulted over many important decisions by Britain and the United States, such as the creation of the joint American, British, Dutch, and Australian command for the southwest Pacific in early 1942. The Dutch were allowed to sit on the largely powerless Pacific War Councils in Washington and London, but were excluded from the British-American Combined Chiefs of Staff, even when decisions affecting the Dutch East Indies were being made.

Both the Yugoslav and Greek governments went into exile in the spring of 1941, but they were riven by factional fighting stemming from prewar disputes and their legitimacy was in doubt. Both had only small armed forces, which played no effective part in the war. The position of the Czech government was anomalous for a considerable period. President Benes went into exile in October 1938, after the Munich Agreement. Czechoslovakia was occupied and divided in March 1939, but it was not until after the outbreak of the war that Britain and France thought it advantageous to recognize Benes. Even so, they recognized him as leading only a "national committee," not a government. In July 1940, desperate for allies, the British recognized Benes as heading a "provisional government." In the autumn, Benes lent the British £7.5 million worth of gold to fund purchases in the United States. A year later it was the Soviet determination to give full recognition to Benes that drove the British to do the same. Not until August 1942 did Britain disown the Munich Agreement and agree with Benes that all the boundary changes made in 1938–39 were invalid. Benes did not trust the British and French and believed that Czech friendship with the Soviets would be vital after the war. In December 1943 he went to Moscow and signed a treaty of alliance valid for twenty years. Sub-Carpathian Ruthenia, with its largely Ukrainian population, was ceded to the Soviets, and Benes accepted a major social-reform program and substantial Communist participation in the government. In return, the Soviets were prepared to install Benes as postwar leader when their troops liberated Czechoslovakia.

The greatest problems were caused by the French. After the armistice the French government under Pétain moved to Vichy and abolished the Third Republic but continued to control the southern, unoccupied, zone and the French empire. Although Britain had no formal diplomatic relations with Vichy, it was recognized as the legitimate government by countries within the Commonwealth such as Canada and South Africa and, most important, by the United States. The British kept open communications with Vichy through informal channels, and in the autumn of 1940 reached a modus vivendi. Vichy had much to offer the British, particularly control of the French fleet and the empire. As long as Vichy was not formally allied with Germany the British were prepared to work for limited cooperation and always hoped that at some stage Vichy might reenter the war on the Allied side.

Relations with Vichy severely complicated those with General Charles de Gaulle, who had left France just before the armistice. The British allowed him to broadcast to France at the time of the armistice, but until the end of June 1940 they hoped to find a more senior politician to lead a French movement of continued resistance. Eventually they recognized de Gaulle not as the leader of a government but simply as the head of a French Committee that directed the operations of Free French forces. The problem facing Britain and de Gaulle in the summer of 1940 was that he did not control any French territory. An attack by British and Free French forces on the key port of Dakar in Senegal was botched, and by the autumn de Gaulle was left in control of a few unimportant colonies in Africa. The British tried to replace him as leader with General Georges Catroux, the governor general of Indochina, who had defected to the Free French, but he preferred to serve under de Gaulle. However, when the latter declared himself leader of a French government, Britain did not accept his claims.

For the rest of the war relations between Britain and de Gaulle were characterized by vicious disputes as de Gaulle tried to assert French interests in very difficult circumstances. He resented being almost entirely financed by, as well as being militarily dependent on, the British. There were also severe personality clashes between Churchill and the Free French leader. The British tried in 1941 to bring de Gaulle under the control of a wider group of Free French leaders, but the plot failed and instead only succeeded in increasing de Gaulle's power. There were also major arguments about the British takeover of the Vichy-controlled colonies of Syria and Lebanon in the early summer. The British refused to hand them over to their Free French allies and instead started dismantling the French empire by declaring that the territories would become independent at the end of the war. The entry of the United States into the war only exacerbated the situation. They still recognized Vichy as the government of France, Roosevelt had no time for de Gaulle, and Churchill joined the Americans in trying to remove the Free French leader. The British and the Americans decided that during their invasion of French North Africa in November 1942 they would collaborate with Vichy to establish control and agreed that this would be the ideal opportunity to finally dispose of de Gaulle by recognizing a new French grouping partly based on the existing Vichy regime. Their plans fell apart and their candidate to lead the French, General Henri-Honoré Giraud, proved no match for de Gaulle, who was in a strong position, having backed the Allies since June 1940. Although a joint leadership was set up under Anglo-American pressure in early 1943, de Gaulle and his followers soon established control of the Committee of National Liberation (F.C.N.L.) set up in Algiers. The Committee controlled most of the French empire and directed the Free French forces. Britain and the United States, though, did not give it a status higher than that given the Free French in 1940—they were not prepared to recognize it as even the provisional government of France, something they had conceded to Benes and his Czech government. In June 1944, as the Allies prepared to invade France, there was still no agreement on how the country should be governed when it was liberated.

Three other states were minor Allies. In August 1942 Brazil became the first South American state to declare war on Germany and Italy. During 1942 the United States considered Brazil vital, as a factor in naval battles in the Atlantic and as a way of securing the route to West Africa. The United States provided Lend-Lease, major military supplies, and a number of troops and had operational control of the Brazilian navy. In January 1943, on his way back from the Casablanca

Conference, Roosevelt met President Getulio Vargas and agreed to
the deployment of Brazilian troops in Europe. Three divisions would
be trained in Brazil using American equipment and then be under
U.S. command in Italy. The British were strongly opposed but gave
in to American pressure. By early 1945, 25,000 Brazilian troops and
an air force contingent were fighting in Italy. The Brazilians hoped
that in return they would secure a permanent seat on the Security
Council of the United Nations after 1945, but they failed to do so.

The second minor ally, Mexico, sent a squadron of forty-eight aircraft to fight in the Pacific in 1945. The third state was Italy. After the
Badoglio government broke with Germany and signed a separate armistice with the Allies in September 1943 it declared war on its former ally in mid-October. However, the Allies refused to recognize
Italy as a full ally (they had still not signed a formal peace treaty) and
it was granted only cobelligerent status.

The most important Allied relationships were those between Britain,
the United States, and the Soviet Union. Britain had been dependent
on the United States for full-scale economic, financial, and military
help for a year before the latter joined the war. Inevitably this placed
the British in a subordinate position. However, the British were able
to build on the fact that during 1942 they would provide the bulk of
Anglo-American forces fighting the Germans and Italians. At a major
meeting in Washington in December 1941 and early January 1942
the structure of the Anglo-American alliance was decided and it became the most integrated of all the alliances during the Second
World War. A Combined Chiefs of Staff was set up to direct strategy
and Combined Boards were established to control shipping and raw
materials and to direct the industrial effort of the two powers. A series
of integrated military commands were established and collaboration
in areas such as intelligence and weapons development was extensive. However, there were also major political differences and numerous disputes, especially over policy in the Far East, where the
interests of the two states differed markedly and were at times directly opposed.

This situation of seeming equality also disguised major differences in effective power. The Combined Boards created to oversee the logistics of the war effort were dominated by the Americans because of their overwhelming economic power. The British had a significant say in Anglo-American strategy during 1942 and early 1943, but as U.S. military power was built up and deployed the Americans demanded and received a predominant role in strategic policy-making. The Combined Chiefs of Staff operated in Washington, and the British did not secure direction of the European war from London and the Pacific war from the American capital as they wanted. Instead, they had to settle for Anglo-American direction of the European war and a separate U.S. war in the Pacific, over which the Combined Chiefs of Staff had no effective say. When joint commanders were appointed they tended to be American. Eisenhower commanded the landings in French North Africa in November 1942 and was supreme commander in the Mediterranean and then in northwest Europe. The British were given the job in the Mediterranean only when it became a subsidiary theater. By 1944 the United States provided the overwhelming majority of forces in Europe and therefore dictated strategy.

The British had to recognize the overwhelming strength of U.S. military power at a time when they were even more dependent on the Americans economically and financially than militarily. Vast quantities of Lend-Lease equipment were required to keep British forces operational, and the Americans demanded a substantial quid pro quo. The British had to agree to open talks after the war aimed at liberalizing world trade and dismantling the protectionist barriers around the British Empire. As U.S. Air Force and Army units were deployed in Britain, British gold and dollar reserves, which had been exhausted by early 1941, began to grow. The Americans realized that this would only increase British postwar economic power and so they decided unilaterally to control Britain's foreign exchange reserves. They set a figure that they thought would be large enough to stop Britain's adopting an autarkic policy after the war but not so large as to make them independent of the Americans. The Americans were able to set the figure they wanted by making the British pay for goods that had previously been free under Lend-Lease. By the summer of

1944 the British realized that they could not continue the war against Japan after victory in Europe without substantial U.S. assistance, which would also be necessary to fund the transition to a peacetime economy. At the Quebec Conference in September 1944 the British had to ask for American help. They were forced to accept U.S. plans to dismantle the German economy (the Morgenthau plan) as part of the price of assistance. However, the United States went back on its commitments to provide help, and the British were left in a parlous economic and financial situation as peace approached.

The close nature of the relationship between Britain and the United States was unlike the relationship either of them had with the Soviet Union. Neither the British nor the Americans had chosen the Soviets as an ally; that decision was made for them by Germany—indeed, during the spring of 1940 the British and the French had been planning to sink Soviet ships in the Black Sea and bomb the oil wells at Baku as part of their plans to help Finland. Throughout the war, despite protestations about alliance unity from the British and the Americans on the one hand and the Soviets on the other, as well as a huge upsurge of popular support for the Soviet Union in the Western democracies, neither side trusted the other. The British and the Americans left the Soviets to fight their own war on the eastern front. They gave military and economic aid, but this, though important, was not vital to Soviet survival. Military missions went to Moscow but they were used mainly to spy on the Soviets. The supply convoys from Iceland to Murmansk and Archangel were essentially political gestures of support; they suffered high casualty rates in appalling conditions, but their military value was limited.

Britain and the United States knew that the Soviet Union was bearing the overwhelming weight of the war. Until the summer of 1944 it never faced less than 90 percent of the German army, and even after the Normandy landings the western Allies fought only about a third of the Wehrmacht. The British and Americans were content with a situation in which the very high casualties that would be necessary to defeat the Germans were borne by the Soviets. They saw no reason to increase their own casualties, and the British in particular could see advantages for themselves if the Soviet postwar position was weakened by their huge war effort. At no time were the British and the Americans prepared to adapt their own strategy to meet Soviet requirements. For their own reasons they rejected any attempt to create a second front in Europe in 1942, and the Mediterranean strategy adopted in 1943 did nothing to relieve the pressure on the Soviets. There was no attempt to create an Allied strategy; there was an Anglo-American strategy, and the Soviets devised their own.

Relations between the Soviets and Britain were distant. In the summer of 1941 the British and the Soviets signed an undertaking not to make a separate peace, but the only high-level political contact came in December 1941, when Anthony Eden, the British foreign secretary, visited Moscow after it was clear that the Soviet Union would continue the war into 1942. The talks were relatively unproductive. Molotov, the Soviet foreign minister, traveled to London and Washington in the spring of 1942 but failed to achieve recognition of the Soviet Union's political objectives, though he believed he had a promise about the opening of a second front in 1942. Churchill went to Moscow in August 1942 to tell Stalin that there would be no second front in 1942; their meeting was, not surprisingly, difficult and at times acrimonious. Churchill promised a second front for 1943 but by early June 1943 the Soviets knew that this promise, too, had been broken. It was not until late 1943 that there were effective alliance discussions—the meeting of foreign ministers in Moscow in October and the Teheran summit in November. These talks, and those that followed at the Yalta and Potsdam summits in 1945, were less about the conduct of the war than about the area in which the three powers felt that, in their own national interests, they had to reach some sort of agreement: the shape of the postwar settlement.

In fact, throughout the war the British and the Americans made a cold calculation that the Soviets had no choice but to continue fighting. At first they expected a rapid German victory; then, by the late autumn of 1941, they thought Soviet resistance might last well into 1942. During this period they guessed that a deal between Germany and the Soviets would not be possible because of German expectations of victory and the draconian terms they would be bound to impose if the Soviets sought peace. Once the tide of the war changed in the winter of 1942–43, Britain and the United States gambled that a repetition of the August 1939 pact and a separate peace by the Soviet Union was unlikely. Although Soviet archives are still closed on this sensitive point, there is some evidence that Stalin did not rule out a separate peace at this stage.

Stalin had not chosen to fight the war with Britain and the United States as allies, and in Soviet terms there was little to choose between these two powers and Germany: both were capitalist and imperialist and in the last resort antagonistic toward the Soviet Union. In December 1941 Stalin made clear to British Foreign Secretary Eden that the minimum Soviet objective in the war was the recognition of its 1941 borders, which were those achieved in collaboration with Germany. Throughout 1941 and 1942 the British and the Americans refused to give any commitments on this issue. By early 1943 the western Allies had already let down the Soviet Union over a second front in 1942, and Stalin was beginning to suspect that there would not be one in 1943, either. Even though the balance of the war was beginning to turn in favor of the Soviets, they still faced a long war with huge casualties before Germany could be defeated, and possibly with little help from their allies, either. It was not unreasonable for Stalin to see whether another deal with Germany was possible.

In the spring of 1943, after the German surrender at Stalingrad, there was a marked lack of activity on the eastern front. Stalin did not accept the Anglo-American formulation of "unconditional surrender" for the Axis powers agreed at the Casablanca Conference. He had already declared that the aim of the war was not to destroy all military forces in Germany. In late February, in his Red Army Day address, he did not mention the western Allies and spoke of the war as being purely German-Soviet. Unofficial contacts were opened in Stockholm but broke down over the Soviet demand for its 1941 frontiers; the Germans still thought they could retain a greater share of eastern Europe. The contacts appear to have been reopened in Stockholm in June 1943, after the Soviets were told that there would be no second front that year. The Soviet-German talks broke down again, even though the Soviets had hinted in public that Germany could keep some of its conquests, for example the Sudetenland. In early July the Germans opened their offensive around Kursk. After the Soviet military successes that summer initiatives toward a separate peace came from Germany in an attempt to split the coalition ranged against it. These approaches were rejected by the Soviets in September, and by the autumn the international situation had changed. The western Allies were convinced that the Soviets would beat Germany and that therefore they would have to be more accommodating toward their ally. At the Moscow Foreign Ministers Conference and the Teheran Conference, Stalin was convinced that the Soviet Union would achieve most of its territorial requirements by remaining in the alliance against Germany.

The position of the Soviet Union in the Pacific war was much more ambiguous. Although there had been border skirmishes between Soviet and Japanese troops in the late 1930s, the two countries signed a neutrality pact in April 1941, and this was reaffirmed after the outbreak of hostilities between Japan and the western Allies. In that war the Soviets remained neutral until 1945. The Americans asked for the use of Soviet bases for operations against Japan in early 1942 but were refused. Over three hundred American airmen who landed on Soviet territory after raids on Japan were interned, just as they would have been by any other neutral power. However, the Soviets realized that it would be in their interest to join the Far Eastern war once victory over Germany was achieved. Stalin told the Americans this in October 1943, and it was agreed in outline that the Soviets would attack Japan three months after the end of the war in Europe. In return they were to be rewarded with all the territory lost by Russia in the 1904–5 war with Japan, together with other gains. In April 1945 the Soviet Union denounced the neutrality pact. In August 1945 they rushed to join the war before the Japanese surrender and continued the war for nearly three weeks after the Japanese offer to surrender so as to secure the gains agreed on with the Allies.

The other ally in the Pacific war was China, which had formally declared war on Japan after Pearl Harbor. China's status was a matter of dispute between Britain and the United States. The Americans had many illusions about China, in particular that it was modern and democratic, and were determined to treat it as a great power and one that would be vital in the postwar world. Although undoubtedly right in the long term, this was a serious misreading of China under the Nationalists. The British, who were much more dubious about China, suspected that the Americans were only boosting the Chinese because they hoped China would support the United States in the postwar world, particularly in the United Nations; but they felt that they had little alternative but to go along with their stronger ally. In fact, the British position in China was slipping fast and was being replaced by American influence. In 1943, in an attempt to raise China's status, both the United States and Britain gave up their extraterritorial and other nineteenth-century treaty privileges.

In reality, China was not a modern nation-state at war; it was a political-military coalition of the Kuomintang (Nationalists), the Communists, and regional warlords. The pressure of war served only to increase the level of corruption and the failures of the system. The Chinese faced major problems of mobilization, food collection and distribution, stabilization of the currency and price controls, as well as military problems. These difficulties resulted in China's adding little to the Allies' war effort. The Nationalist regime was corrupt and inefficient and concerned more with containing the Communists in Yunan: by 1944, 500,000 of the best Nationalist troops were deployed against the Communists, not the Japanese. Within the territory nominally controlled by the Nationalist government in Chungking, it had only very limited influence. Most areas were run by local warlords who used their troops to control their region and exploit the local populations. The growth in the Chinese army from 200 divisions in 1937 to nearly 350 by 1945 had virtually nothing to do with fighting the Japanese; it owed more to local warlords trying to achieve supremacy over their rivals. Internally, China was on the point of collapse. It had lost so much territory to Japan that the grain harvest available to the government was half the 1937 level, but the army was twice as big. Seizures from the peasants increased, heavy forced labor was common, and inflation was rampant—by 1945 prices were 2,600 times higher than in 1937.

Despite these problems the United States continued to subscribe

to the myth that China was a major ally. This process peaked at the
Cairo Conference in November 1943, when Chiang Kai-shek and his
wife were feted by Roosevelt and Churchill and consulted about
strategy in the Far East. The United States attempted to re-form the
Chinese army and create about a hundred effective divisions from
the sprawling mass of the Nationalist "army." Because this cut across
the political requirements of the regime, however, nothing was
achieved. China had no modern munitions industry and so was dependent on foreign aid. This was limited. After the Japanese capture
of Burma in early 1942, the last road link to China was cut and supplies had to be taken by air over the Himalayas. Often as little as 100
tons a month could be transported, and even by 1943 total supplies
amounted to only 60,000 tons in a year, and most of that went to U.S.
Air Force units using Chinese bases. China received only 3 percent of
American Lend-Lease supplies, and the army deteriorated badly. By
late 1943 the army of 3 million men was equipped with just 1 million
rifles, 83,000 machine guns, and a miscellany of 1,300 artillery pieces.
As a consequence it was unable to withstand the Japanese army even
in the last year of the war. In August 1944 Japan launched a major
offensive, and the Chinese collapsed. They lost Hunan province and
other important rice-growing areas, together with over 300,000
troops. In late 1944 and early 1945 the Chinese lost more land and
people than in any other year since 1938.

By this time even the Americans had lost any expectation that the
Chinese would be of any use in the war against Japan. The U.S. military decided in early 1944 that the Chinese army would never be effective and that China was only useful to provide air bases for the
attack on Japan. However, once the Marianas, including Guam, had
been recaptured they provided better airfields than those in China.
Having built up the Chinese, and in particular Chiang Kai-shek, the
Americans found that they could not change course, despite their
growing interest in the Communists, whose army of 500,000 men, as
well as a 2 million–strong militia and partisan army, was proving far
more effective against the Japanese. China ended the war in chaos
and on the brink of civil war between the corrupt Kuomintang regime and the Communists. In effect it had contributed little to the

defeat of the Japanese, with whom it had been at war since 1937, apart from tying down part of the Japanese army.

Despite all the strains and tensions among its various members, the Allied coalition did hold together until Germany and Japan were defeated. The national self-interest of all the powers involved was sufficient to override other problems. Those problems surfaced almost immediately after the war was over, however, in particular the growing conflict between the United States and the Soviet Union.

IV

MOBILIZATION

F OR THE MAJOR BELLIGERENT STATES, ENTRY INTO THE war necessitated the mobilization of their economies and societies for total war. War was no longer simply a matter of deploying armies on the battlefield and moving fleets across the oceans. More important was the ability to produce armaments, finance the war, draft men and women into the forces, and provide a trained and efficient workforce. This meant that peacetime economies and societies had to be remodeled, often very rapidly, if the state was to survive the impact of war and find a route to victory. Decisions at this level were the most fundamental that states had to take—they determined the nature of the war a state could fight. Although many books about the Second World War concentrate on the way military commanders maneuvered on the battlefield, their options were in reality constrained by the nature of their societies and economies, together with decisions taken in government bureaucracies about the mobilization of resources.

The major belligerents began the war with very different social and economic systems, but the problems they faced and the solutions they found were very similar. The need to produce armaments was not a matter of production at all costs; instead, complex decisions had to be taken about priorities and about how those priorities were to be enforced. The size of the armed forces, for example, had to be related to how many people were required to produce the weapons that would keep the armed forces operational. Armaments production was clearly vital, but resources also had to be devoted to some civilian consumption to maintain the morale of the labor force, and investment in areas such as basic industry and the infrastructure had to continue or else arms production could not be maintained. Substitution was possible in a number of areas: capital investment could compensate for labor shortages, and production of synthetic materials could replace raw material supplies in some instances. Market mechanisms were largely abandoned by all the belligerents as being unable to result in the desired but difficult priority decisions that were required. Control of finance was less important than control over real resources, a situation symbolized by the fact that for long periods of the war the chancellor of the exchequer in Britain was not a member of the war cabinet. In the last resort the limits on production were often determined by the changes to society and the economy that governments thought desirable. After 1942 all the combatants were engaged in a war of production in which the advantage was bound to lie with the largest economies. Until 1944 all the major belligerents achieved massive increases in production, although these increases were, except in the United States, confined to military rather than civilian output.

At the core of the mobilization and direction of every economy was a system of priorities that became increasingly complex as the planners tried to resolve clashing alternatives as well as coordinate the allocation of raw materials and labor. In every case it was necessary for governments to devise systems that would provide much more information about the functioning of the economy. In no case were governments prepared to allow the military to decide priorities. In every state the military had highly optimistic views about the availability of labor and raw materials and the amounts of arms that could be produced; they naturally argued for large armed forces that in practice could not have been sustained because too much labor would have been diverted from production. Those behind the priority planning systems made little effort to discover the total level of inputs available to an economy and therefore the ultimate level of production that was theoretically possible. Instead, they worked in a more pragmatic way: cutting back military demands, imposing priorities, and changing those priorities as the military situation altered or as economic and social constraints intervened. All states found it difficult to impose priorities on the military and stop wasteful production. In 1943, for example, Germany was still producing 4.4 million pairs of scissors and 6.2 million ink stamps for the military.

Apart from the Soviet Union, none of the major belligerents entered the war with an effective planning system, and even the Soviets only undertook crude physical allocation. It therefore took time for these mechanisms to be developed. Germany had controlled raw materials throughout the 1930s, but not very effectively, and its strategy until 1942—fighting short, limited wars—was largely designed to avoid the problems involved in resolving conflicting priorities. Rival groups such as the military, the Ministry of Economics, the Ministry of Munitions, and the Four-Year Plan Office under Göring competed for Hitler's attention, and out of their struggles a policy of sorts emerged. The collapse of German strategy in early 1942 made it essential to plan the rational use of resources. Hitler was reluctant to have a strong, centralized planning system and would not give the function, and the power that went with it, to the armed forces, Göring, or the traditional bureaucrats of the Ministry of Economics. The least bad solution from his point of view was to use the Ministry of Munitions. By 1943 it had been transformed into the Ministry of War Production, run by Albert Speer, who through his close relationship with Hitler secured effective control over the allocation of raw materials, which enabled him to direct the war production effort.

In Japan there was no attempt at central direction of the economy until November 1942, and even then it was inadequate. In January 1943, Prime Minister Tojo suggested that he should have sole control, but this proved unacceptable to industrial interests, who insisted on maintaining their control over policy in each industry. It was not until November 1943 that a Ministry of Munitions was established, directed by the prime minister. By then it was too late to solve Japan's economic problems. In Britain, financial controls remained the predominant form of planning until May 1940. After this, effective controls based on the allocation of materials still took time to establish;

by January 1941 a basic system was in place. It relied not on a strong single ministry but on a cabinet committee to set priorities and allocate materials. The entry of the United States into the war and the establishment of an Anglo-American Combined Raw Materials Board and later a Combined Production and Resources Board forced the British to introduce a more effective planning system. Like Hitler, Churchill was reluctant to establish a single Ministry for Supply and Production because he felt this would create too great a concentration of political power. He therefore supported the minister of labor, Ernest Bevin, in rejecting such proposals and retaining a more diffuse system.

In the United States the first attempt at central planning, the War Production Board established in early 1942, was a failure, partly because it was controlled by businessmen. The result was chaos as the United States switched to a war economy. Truck factories were converted into aircraft factories, though it quickly turned out that trucks were a key requirement. Locomotive factories were converted to producing trucks, although shortages of locomotives were soon apparent. New factories were built with government money before it became clear that there would never be enough raw materials for them to begin production. The American economy was so large and the level of its underutilized resources so great that almost anything seemed possible in 1942. By 1943 it was clear that this was not the case, and the Controlled Materials Plan finally forced consumers of raw materials to plan coherently.

Every major belligerent apart from the Soviet Union recruited businessmen into the government bureaucracy, believing this was the way to achieve effective planning. The German authorities regarded this as no more than an unfortunate and temporary phenomenon and even then it was resisted by some parts of the Nazi state; ultimately, the S.S. built its own industrial empire. In Japan, the *zaibatsu* (industrial conglomerates) were very powerful and could effectively control industrial policy. In Britain, state control was exercised through the trade organization for each industry, thereby reinforcing the industrial status quo. Controls were applied only when shortages became apparent and the industry itself considered they were necessary. For example, rubber was not controlled until April 1941 and the allocation of rubber imports did not begin until January 1942. In the United States, huge incentives were given to industry. The cost of investment and expansion could be written off in five years and even excess-profits tax could be recovered after the war if a firm took a loss. As in Britain, most government contracts were undertaken on a costs-plus-fee-for-profit basis, thereby ensuring that losses did not occur. Most antitrust legislation was also suspended.

As war production crowded out civilian production and wages rose, all countries found that they had to reduce civilian spending power through increased taxation if they were to avoid spiraling inflation. Taxation was, therefore, increased everywhere: in Britain it financed 53 percent of war expenditure, in Germany 48 percent, and in Canada 55 percent. Only in the United States was taxation relatively low, 26 percent of war expenditure in 1943. The consequences of not raising taxes were apparent in Italy: prices rose 170 percent between 1938 and 1943. Only the Soviet Union, with its strong central controls, could avoid some of the problems, but even there taxation rose sharply.

For the minor belligerents, mobilization of the economy was not an option. Many countries such as the Balkan states had no arms industry of any importance and were therefore forced to rely on arms purchases to equip their armed forces. Armies could be mobilized but small populations meant that they could never be big enough to fight one of the major powers on their own. Some were nevertheless significantly affected by the war. Countries such as Canada and Australia found that their economies were transformed as orders created new industries and expanded others; industrial output rose 250 percent in both countries. In Canada the shipbuilding industry employed 4,000 people in 1939 and 126,000 in 1945. Aircraft production increased a hundredfold between 1939 and 1944. Other countries had to reorient their economies. Finland faced an acute shortage of oil and coal after 1940 and had to turn to its one indigenous resource, wood. It was used for fuel and to make wooden shoes and bedding, and buses were converted to run on gas produced by wood-burning stoves towed behind.

The economies of other states, even those not directly engaged in the war, were affected. Iceland, Egypt, and India became major international creditors by 1945 because of the foreign exchange earned by the stationing of large military forces on their territory. Trinidad moved from high unemployment to acute labor shortages as United States construction work expanded. So serious was the situation that sugar production, which provided the main export, slumped as workers went to earn higher wages elsewhere. On the South Pacific island of Tonga, copra production fell 80 percent because the population could make much more money renting out bicycles to U.S. troops for black-market dollars. Some primary producers were badly affected by the disruption to world trade. The exports of French West Africa fell to a third of prewar levels. By 1943 Honduran banana exports were at 10 percent of their 1930 level and national income had fallen by a third because the U.S. Navy requisitioned a large number of banana boats. Other countries benefited. The Cuban sugar crop rose in value during the war by 150 percent as world production collapsed. Chile and Bolivia went through an economic boom as demand for their main products—copper and tin, respectively—increased dramatically. Exports from the Belgian Congo doubled over prewar levels because of the Allied demand for raw materials.

Although all the world's economies were affected by the war, it was the decisions made by the major combatants—Germany, Italy, and Japan for the Axis; Britain, the Soviet Union, and the United States for the Allies—about how to mobilize their economies that determined the outcome of the Second World War. For all of them a basic starting point was deciding the proportion of the workforce to conscript into the armed forces so as to strike the right balance between fighting power and productive power. No country gave the military control over manpower policies, but all conscripted about one in five or six adult males into the armed forces. (The Soviet Union was the only country to mobilize all defense-industry and railway workers in their jobs and place them under military discipline.) Generally, conscription applied to men between the ages of eighteen (twenty in Japan) and either forty-five or fifty. This, together with the expansion of industry, meant that unemployment virtually disap-

peared; in Britain there were still 645,000 unemployed at the time of
Dunkirk, but none by 1941, or in the United States by 1943. The Soviet Union was the most heavily mobilized state; by 1943, 25 percent
of its workforce were in uniform and 33 percent were in war work.
Britain at its peak had 22 and 23 percent, respectively, Germany 23
and 14 percent, and the United States 16 and 19 percent.

Women served in the armed forces in very small numbers. Instead,
they were recruited into industry to replace the men drafted into the
military and to fill the new jobs created by the expansion of war production. In most Western countries the extra employment generated
by the war was about 15 percent. In Britain women made up 80 percent of the total addition to the labor force; in the United States it was
50 percent. Despite these increases, however, only about a third of
women worked in either of these countries. In Japan, although 14
million women were employed, there was little increase during the
war. The two exceptions to this general pattern, though in opposite
directions, were Germany and the Soviet Union. For ideological reasons the German government refused to recruit women into industry, and in 1944 there were still 1.3 million female domestic servants.
In the Soviet Union a high proportion of women had worked since
the 1920s, and by 1942 they made up over half the civilian labor
force, rising to over 60 percent by 1943; in some industries they made
up over 80 percent of the total.

In most countries workers were shifted away from agriculture into
industry. In Japan the male agricultural workforce fell by 1 million,
and in the Soviet Union, by a staggering 13.3 million (nearly 80 percent), as the rural population provided the majority of the Red Army.
In Britain, because of the need to restrict food imports as much as
possible, the farm workforce changed little.

The production of civilian goods was also cut back. In the Soviet
Union the number of people employed in this sector of the economy
fell by 60 percent between 1940 and 1942. A less drastic reduction
occurred in Britain. Poor-quality "utility" production was introduced
and the numbers employed in the distributive trades fell by a third.

Most countries also used foreign workers. In Britain there were
over 100,000 Irish workers in munitions factories alone, and Britain

also used over 224,000 prisoners of war, over half of them Italian. The Japanese employed about 1.5 million Koreans by 1945. It was Germany that used the greatest number of foreign workers, however. In 1939 there were about 300,000 foreign workers in the country. Until 1942 the program was largely voluntary, but afterward it relied on compulsion and labor drafts in the occupied countries. By 1944 there were over 7 million foreign workers in Germany, about a fifth of the labor force.

In every country labor was the ultimate resource limiting production, not just in terms of gross numbers but also in terms of the number of skilled workers that were available. Britain faced the most acute problems. A shortage of skilled labor was apparent even before the outbreak of war, and although over 300,000 workers were trained in government centers during the war and large-scale "dilution" of skilled workers took place, by 1942 there was an absolute shortage of labor. The manpower budget became the main tool for controlling the economy and by the end of 1942 munitions production estimates were based not on demand but on projected labor supply. The Soviet Union also recruited too many men into the armed forces and faced labor shortages by 1943, as did Japan in that year and the United States and Germany by 1944. In the United States, the allocation of defense contracts was normally decided according to which firms either had labor available or could recruit it locally.

One solution to this shortage was to work the labor force harder. In the United States the average work week rose from 38 to 45 hours, and in Germany and the Soviet Union it occasionally reached 70 hours, although that figure was rarely sustained for long. Japan set aside its 12-hour limit on the working day in late 1943, but productivity did not rise and few people worked longer hours as a consequence. In general, shift work was limited and unpopular. For those employed in arms production, earnings rose substantially: 80 percent in Britain, 70 percent in the United States, and by over 50 percent in the Soviet Union. Real wages, though, are difficult to calculate because of the effects of inflation, taxation, and the rationing of key goods. Only in the United States was there any major increase in living standards—by about 50 percent between 1939 and 1944. In Britain there was no real increase. Any improvement came simply from the longer hours worked. German workers experienced an increase in their living standards until 1941, but by 1944 they had fallen back to prewar levels. In Japan, workers suffered a major fall in their standard of living: by 1945 real wages were at best only 40 percent of the level a decade earlier.

The consequence of this experience was that the incidence of labor disputes and absenteeism increased in every belligerent during the war. In most countries, coal mining produced the greatest problems. In the Soviet Union, output per miner in August 1942 had fallen by between 25 and 40 percent compared with prewar levels. Absenteeism was up seventeenfold. In Britain in 1943, output per miner had fallen by nine tons a quarter from prewar levels. In Australia, a sixth of coal output was lost because of absentee workers in 1943 and the situation was so bad throughout industry that the government threatened to conscript absentee workers into the military. Other countries also experienced major labor disputes throughout the war. In both the United States and Britain there were more strikes each year than during the 1930s, despite the fact that in Britain strikes were effectively illegal during the war. In 1943 the United States lost 13.5 million man-days of work through strikes, three times the 1942 level. In 1944 Britain lost 1.6 million man-days in the coal industry alone—and 2 million tons of coal—almost as many as in the whole of industry in the previous year.

In Germany, Japan, and the Soviet Union, industrial disputes took the form of acute absenteeism because independent trade unions did not exist. In Germany the trade unions had been destroyed in the early years of the Nazi government. In Japan, although the labor movement had collapsed in the late 1930s and had been replaced by the government-sponsored Great Japan Patriotic Industrial Association, by 1943 strikes were at their highest level since 1937 and a year later absenteeism involved about one in six of all workers. In the Soviet Union, despite the tough regime and the supposed inspirational effects of the "great patriotic war," over one million people a year, or about 6 percent of the workforce, were taken to court and prosecuted for absenteeism, defined as being more than twenty minutes late for

work. They were usually given "corrective labor" in their job, reduced pay, and loss of seniority. After a third offense, individuals
were given a prison sentence of two to four months. About 200,000
people were convicted every year and many others simply went
missing and found jobs elsewhere. Conditions in the munitions industry were even tougher. Here, another 200,000 workers a year,
about 12 percent of the workforce, were convicted of unauthorized
"quitting." Altogether about 300,000 workers a year were sent to the
Gulag's forced-labor camps.

A fundamental consideration for all the belligerents, and many
neutrals, too, was to provide enough food to keep the population fit
for work. Governments also had to decide whether to take a role in
ensuring an equitable distribution of the available food. Decisions on
agricultural policy required complex judgments about the balance
between direct consumption of crops and feeding them to animals,
the amount of fertilizers required, the amount of shipping space
available, and the time required before investment in new agricultural land produced crops. The most vulnerable countries were those
with high levels of imports; Britain imported nearly three quarters of
the cash value of its food in 1938, and Japan about a fifth. However,
disruption of world trade patterns, brought about partly by the use of
shipping for other tasks, affected nearly every country. Britain had to
impose drastic meat rationing, even though vast surpluses were being
destroyed in Argentina, and Australia and the United States introduced sugar rationing, despite the fact that there were huge surpluses
in the West Indies and Cuba. The higher demand for food in wealth-
ier countries reduced their exports, and the poorer areas of the world
suffered a one-third reduction in food consumption.

The United States faced the least problems over food supplies because of its huge production potential. This was fortunate, as its agricultural policy was weak and ineffective. Food output rose 16 percent
between 1940 and 1944, but this was largely because of the removal
of the restrictions on output that had been imposed in the 1930s. The
increase was only half what the Department of Agriculture thought
was possible. In general, the planning system was inadequate. By

1945 the acreage devoted to the crops where supply needed to be increased had fallen in thirteen out of fifteen cases.

Germany faced few problems in feeding its population. Before the war it was almost self-sufficient and imported mainly vegetables, fruit, and eggs from southeast Europe, an area that remained the main source of supply, together with new supplies from western Europe after 1940. Overall imports were sufficient to avoid any problems until the German economy started to disintegrate, in late 1944, when Allied armies were on Germany's borders.

The countries that faced the most difficult problems were Britain, Japan, and the Soviet Union. British policy was successful, Japan's was not, and the Soviet Union's problems were probably unsolvable. Britain doubled the calorific value of the food it produced, by decreasing meat production by about a third and increasing the acreage devoted to wheat, potatoes, and fodder by two thirds. Output increased but variety decreased. Britain was able to make huge savings in the shipping space required to import food. In 1939, 22.5 million tons a year had been allocated. This was reduced to 14.5 million by 1941, and by early 1943 the annual rate was down to about 6 million tons a year, less than a third of the 1939 level. Although these restrictions meant a worse diet for some people compared with prewar levels, on the whole, food was more equitably distributed and the population was in better health than in the 1930s. Unlike Britain, Japan was heavily dependent on a single crop, rice. Before the war it had developed Korea and Formosa as colonial areas for food production, but the Allied attack on Japanese merchant shipping severely reduced capacity. By 1943, rice imports were at 10 percent of their 1940 level, and by 1944 they had ceased altogether. In the Soviet Union there was an acute food crisis. Two thirds of the country's prewar production came from areas controlled by the Germans in 1942 and food-industry output was therefore at about 40 percent of its 1940 levels. Because of the level of destruction in the Soviet Union, this had risen to only 50 percent by the end of the war. The result was that food consumption, which was poor even before the war, fell drastically; at times even the basic bread and potato rations could not be met.

All governments introduced rationing, not just of food but also other goods. The systems used and the products covered varied from country to country. In the United States, consumer output continued to rise throughout the war, and only those commodities in very short supply were rationed. Britain had a comprehensive system from 1940 onward that covered every basic item except bread and potatoes and was easy to enforce because of the high level of imports. A basic ration was provided, together with "points" that could be transferred between products and that the government could regulate according to its own priorities. In Japan, rationing began in 1938 and was extended in early 1941 to cover basic foods and clothing. Food was distributed through neighborhood organizations, but tickets were used for items such as salt, clothes, and soap. During the last two years of the war the system broke down under pressure, sugar and soap were rarely available after 1943, and fuel often consisted of the remains of burned-out buildings. Food supplies collapsed as more troops were stationed in Japan and imports fell; by 1945 average calorie intake was about two thirds that at the beginning of the war, most dogs had been eaten, pumpkins were the staple diet, and the government planned to make flour from acorns.

The food-production problems in the Soviet Union meant that rationing was extensive and severe. Food rationing, which had been applied in cities between 1929 and 1935 during the industrialization and collectivization drive, was reintroduced and extended in 1941. By November of that year virtually all goods for the urban population were rationed. Bread remained the basic source of food; provision of one loaf per person per day was the top priority and often it was the only ration provided. Food was not distributed equally; access depended on the work the person did. For most people rations were below the minimum levels to maintain health, especially for white-collar workers and children over the age of twelve. Because of the shortage of food, rations in the Soviet Union were not, as in other countries, a way of distributing food equitably—they were often mechanisms for deciding who should survive. Although food supplies for the urban population were poor, the situation in the countryside was far worse. Collective-farm workers were allocated no rations at all. Output fell as most male workers were conscripted and the government share of production was increased drastically. The remaining workers had to survive on what was left—usually not very much, and most of that, potatoes.

The level of mobilization differed greatly between countries. Britain was the least mobilized of all the major combatants; at its peak in 1943–44, the portion of its national resources Britain devoted to the war was about 47 percent. The United States mobilized late, but in the last three years of the war 53–54 percent of its resources were allocated to the war. Germany did not fully mobilize until 1942, when over half its resources went to the war; by 1943, the last year for which reliable figures are available, it had reached 60 percent. Even this effort was exceeded by the Soviet Union. In 1942–43 it was devoting three quarters of its national resources to the war effort—half as much again as Britain or the United States. The Soviet war effort is even more extraordinary when account is taken of what happened to the economies of the major combatants. Massive expenditure on arms brought about rapid economic growth for some states: U.S. national income was 50 percent higher in 1943 than it was in 1939, and Britain (31 percent) and Germany (16 percent) experienced a similar effect. The Soviet Union, however, lost huge areas of its raw-material resources and industrial output to Germany, and by 1942 its national income was only just over half its 1940 level. Some countries relied heavily on external support to see them through the war. Britain was the most dependent. After 1941 over a sixth of its national income was supplied free by the United States under Lend-Lease, and by 1944, 40 percent of its armaments came from abroad.

The significant differences between the major combatants' mobilization efforts reflected their different situations and objectives. German mobilization falls into two phases, 1939–42 (which was really an extension of prewar policies) and the last two and half years of the war. Germany faced a difficult strategic situation in the late 1930s. It controlled less materials and labor than in 1914; neither produced nor controlled any natural rubber or oil; and had to import copper, tin, and iron ore, and the metals vital for high-quality arms production: chrome, nickel, tungsten, molybdenum, and manganese. Although stockpiles of key materials were created after 1936 and synthetic oil and rubber production plants were built, Germany was not in a position to wage a long, all-out war.

Hitler's strategy, adopted against the advice of the military, was to plan on a series of short wars, designed to be achieved with only limited mobilization. To a large extent this was a highly rational strategy: Germany no longer faced a major power to the east, only a series of weak states that could easily be defeated in short campaigns. This strategy worked well between 1938 and 1941, and it was only when Hitler and his military advisers made the mistake of believing that the Soviet Union fell into the weak-state category that this strategy failed. Such a strategy also corresponded to the administrative shambles in the Third Reich, which could not have produced a coherent mobilization plan for total war. This option also fitted in well with Hitler's diplomatic strategy, his desire to avoid a repetition of the two-front war of 1914–18, and his reluctance to cut back civilian consumption because he thought it might endanger the stability of the regime. Between September 1939 and December 1941 the overall level of armaments production in Germany remained steady and lower than that in Britain. Consumer production rose in most major areas and remained higher than war expenditures until 1942— indeed, until 1944 the German standard of living was higher than the British. Hitler was able, because of the relatively low level of mobilization, to switch arms production from one area to another, depending on the campaign he intended to fight. Army ammunition production was doubled in the period leading up to the attack on France, and then was immediately cut back to concentrate on aircraft production for the Battle of Britain. Army production was increased again before the attack on the Soviet Union (though it was still below 1940 levels) and then cut back again in the autumn of 1941, when the Soviet Union appeared to have been defeated.

Germany was also able to exploit the economies of occupied Europe. Under the terms of the armistice the French had to pay Germany a sum equivalent to half its total public expenditure and about a third of its national wealth. In some areas German control was even greater, taking about 75 percent of French iron-ore production, 50 percent of its bauxite, and 15 percent of its coal. By early 1944, about 85 percent of train movements in France were for German purposes. In Belgium about half of the industrial output went to Germany, and in areas such as metalworking it was much higher. In general, despite some German theories of the time, it was the highly developed economies of western, not eastern, Europe that were the most productive for German exploitation. The levels of Soviet and German destruction meant that systematic exploitation in the east was impossible; under German occupation the output of Soviet coalfields was about 10–20 percent of their prewar level, although Germany did obtain about 90 percent of its manganese requirements from Soviet territory.

It was only after the failure of the initial onslaught on the Soviet Union in 1941 that Germany slowly moved toward the total mobilization that characterized the economies of the other major combatants. This was the sort of war that Germany could never win. However, as Albert Speer took an increasingly firm grip on the economy, an extraordinary productive effort was achieved. Between February 1942 and July 1944 German war output tripled overall. In some areas the increases were even greater: tank production rose sixfold in that period. German war output reached a peak in 1944. That year it produced the complete equipment for 250 infantry divisions and 40 armored divisions, far more than its front-line forces. German production collapsed only as the Allies overran its raw-material sources and then finally invaded Germany itself. Yet in many respects the German economy was never fully mobilized. Its consumer production remained far in excess of Britain's and the Soviet Union's. In 1943–44 it was still making 200,000 domestic radios, 150,000 electric bedwarmers, 3,600 refrigerators, 12,000 tons of wallpaper, and 4,800 tons of hair tonic.

Germany's first major ally, Italy, had the smallest share of world manufacturing output of any of the main combatants, less than 3 percent. It needed to import over 20 million tons of coal a year and its steel output was only 10 percent of Germany's. Over three quarters of its raw materials and foodstuff imports had to pass either Gibraltar or Suez and could therefore be interrupted. In essence, Italy was still only a semideveloped country: agriculture accounted for nearly half its working population and over a third of its national wealth. Autarky was not possible and there was no geographical area it could exploit economically; southeast Europe was dominated by Germany. All of these weaknesses were compounded by the lack of any clear strategic plan or mobilization of resources. Mussolini provided no guidance about when war might start, what sort of war it might be, what Italian objectives would be, and how the economy should be mobilized in support. The result was chaos.

Although Italy was spending about 10 percent of its national wealth on defense by the late 1930s, its military power was very limited. To some extent its rearmament had started too soon and so much of its equipment was obsolete. The navy was relatively strong, with modern battleships and over one hundred submarines but no aircraft carriers, because Mussolini did not believe in them. Italy had a regular army of 1.5 million but over 600 generals (one for every 33 officers), and a quarter of its divisions did not even have a full set of uniforms. The army's rifle was an 1891 design, and its best artillery remained that captured from the Austro-Hungarian army in the First World War. It had 1,500 tanks (all but 70 were light tanks equipped only with machine guns), and most had no radio and therefore had to be guided by the infantry walking in front of them. The air force was in a similar state. Few of its aircraft would have been regarded as first rate in any other major power: 40 percent of its fighters were still biplanes. By the late 1930s Italy's comparative strength, possibly even its actual strength, was in decline. This situation was made worse by the Italian decision to export large amounts of military equipment in a desperate attempt to earn foreign currency. In 1939 Italy was selling arms to over twenty-three countries, including France, China, and Japan, but the foreign-exchange reserves were still at 15 percent of their 1927 level.

After Italy entered the war in June 1940 there was no coherent plan to mobilize the economy. National wealth did not increase in the early years of the war and collapsed drastically after 1942; by

1945 it was over 40 percent lower than in 1938 and had fallen back to early-twentieth-century levels. Armaments production was not given a high priority and the level of mobilization was less than in the First World War. Aircraft production increased from 150 a month, but only to 300, and productivity in the industry was only a fifth of that in the United States and lower than that achieved in the First World War. In 1938 Italy made about 4 artillery pieces a month, a figure that rose to a wartime maximum of 200, but this was still only at a sixth of the level achieved in 1917–18. By 1942 tank production was only at 13 percent of the British level. The Italian planning system was almost nonexistent, which meant that the country's limited resources were not used effectively. Until 1942 it continued to build major fortifications along the border it shared with its ally Germany. In 1942 only 5 percent of its merchant fleet was being used to move supplies to its main military front in North Africa. The government's control of labor was equally incompetent. In 1941, shipyard workers were moved from Trieste and Genoa into the major naval base at Taranto, even though there were 5,000 unemployed shipyard workers in Taranto itself.

Like Italy, Japan was still only a semi-industrialized country; half its population was still employed in agriculture and it produced only 4 percent of the world's manufactured output and was heavily reliant on American investment. Like Britain, it relied heavily on imports of basic raw materials and food and was, therefore, extremely vulnerable to well-directed economic warfare. Prewar home production accounted for only 17 percent of iron-ore requirements, 60 percent of steel, 20 percent of oil, and none of the aluminum required to make modern aircraft. Unlike Italian weapons, however, Japanese weapons were, at least at the start of the war, of a generally high standard, and in particular its aircraft were equal to any produced elsewhere. Japan's strategic situation was similar to Germany's: it was surrounded by relatively weak states and therefore could expand fairly easily and without embarking upon full-scale mobilization. After 1937, though, the war with China placed an increasing strain upon the economy and society.

The Japanese convinced themselves that they might be able to fight a limited war against the Western powers, take over territory and key raw materials, and hope that their opponents would then accept the situation because they themselves were too embroiled in fighting Germany. It was clear by early 1942 that this was not the case and that they could not expect to withstand the economic might of the Western powers, despite the decision to fully mobilize the economy and fight for national survival. War expenditure was proportionately higher than in the United States, and national wealth grew by nearly a quarter during the war, but in key areas little extra output could be found, for example, steel and coal production barely rose in the four years after 1939. The government could, however, divert resources on a massive scale from the civilian economy, and consumer expenditure fell by a third during the war, which did allow major increases in armaments production. Between 1941 and 1944, when Japanese war production reached its peak, aircraft output rose over fourfold, army ammunition production doubled, and ammunition for the navy rose fivefold. However, this major effort could not produce enough weapons even to begin to match Allied output. In 1944 Japan produced just 4 percent of the number of mortars made in the United States, less than 5 percent of the tanks, and less than 1 percent of the bombs. Although economic warfare was not pressed home by the Allies in the same way as it was against Germany, the Achilles' heel of the Japanese economy was the level of imports. By 1945 Japanese imports had fallen drastically from 1941 levels: coal imports were at 8 percent of their 1941 level, iron ore at 5 percent, iron and steel at 18 percent, and rubber at 26 percent. Attacks on Japanese shipping meant that Japan was not able systematically to exploit the territory it occupied in southeast Asia. By 1945, tin production in Malaya was at 14 percent of its prewar level, and in the Dutch East Indies oil production had collapsed to 5 percent of prewar output. In these circumstances it is hardly surprising that the Japanese economy was on the point of collapse by the time the war ended.

The Achilles' heel of the British economy, as of the Japanese, was the level of imports. However, the British faced relatively weak naval powers that were unable to break the supply lines, and they had a large merchant fleet that, supplemented by Allied resources, was large enough to move the necessary raw materials, arms, and food. The problems were caused mainly by very long haulage lengths, a consequence of Britain's dependence on supplies from all over the world, and the capacity of its ports to cope with the level of imports under wartime conditions. Britain's problems stemmed less from the interdiction of supplies and more from its inability to finance the imports required, especially those from the United States. Britain's gold and dollar reserves were inadequate to sustain a major war, and by the autumn of 1940 they were nearly exhausted. Britain was rescued by the United States and from the end of 1940 was dependent on Lend-Lease to sustain its war effort. In total, Britain received $27 billion of aid during the war (equivalent to about $500 billion at current prices). Much of Britain's military capability was provided by the United States. By the end of 1943 the United States supplied 77 percent of Britain's escort vessels, 88 percent of its landing craft, 68 percent of its light bombers, nearly all of its transport aircraft and self-propelled artillery, 60 percent of its tanks, and all of its heavy tank transporters and ten-ton trucks.

British planning and mobilization of the economy was relatively effective, even though much of it came to depend on U.S.-supplied raw materials. Resources were redeployed into arms production and the value of consumer goods and services fell by over a fifth in the course of the war. There were major problems, however. It was difficult to increase steel production because iron ore took up so much shipping space. In addition, coal output fell by 20 percent during the war. Britain's resources were also heavily concentrated on the construction and operation of a heavy bomber force, which took up between a quarter and a third of the war effort. The aircraft industry expanded from 35,000 employees with an output worth £14 million in 1935 to 1,750,000 employees and a turnover of £800 million by the end of 1943. However, productivity in the industry remained low: at its peak it was only two thirds of the German level and 40 percent of that in the United States. Britain was the weakest of the three main Allied powers, producing only 12 percent of the Allied output of tanks, about the same level of artillery and truck construction, and 20 percent of the combat aircraft. Overall during the war, although Britain produced 40 percent more trucks than Germany, in every other area it produced less. Its combat aircraft output was 90 percent of Germany's, artillery was less than 80 percent, and for tanks the figure was below 60 percent.

To a large extent the United States was the arsenal of the Allies; furthermore, it was able to mobilize its economy knowing that it would not be directly attacked by its opponents. In the late 1930s the United States was still a sleeping giant in military terms, and to some extent in economic terms, too, owing to the continuing effects of the Depression. Recovery during the 1930s was patchy and there were still about 10 million people unemployed in 1939. However, the United States could rely almost entirely on domestic resources and had the biggest single economy in the world. In 1939 it was producing 30 percent more steel than Germany, even though two thirds of its steel plants were idle. Between 1939 and 1941 the U.S. economy was revitalized by rearmament—primarily the country's own (defense spending rose from just over 1 percent of national wealth to 11 percent in this period), but also from British and French orders and, after 1941, by full-scale war production. Between 1939 and 1944 America's national wealth increased by 52 percent, but the level of imports did not increase. War production rose from 2 percent of total output in 1939 to over 40 percent by 1943. In the same period, consumer purchases also rose by 12 percent. The United States was the only economy not to suffer from a diversion of resources away from consumers to war production, and there were only a few shortages of consumer durables. By 1944 nearly 19 million more people were employed than in 1939, and plant utilization had doubled. American productivity levels were also twice those in Germany and five times higher than in Japan.

The American productive effort was huge. Between 1940 and 1944 the United States increased its aluminum production fourfold. Even this effort was surpassed by the need to produce synthetic rubber to replace natural rubber, the only key raw material the United States lacked. In early 1942 the United States had a stockpile of natural rubber sufficient for twelve months' usage at peacetime rates. In 1941 it made just over 8,000 tons of synthetic rubber. By 1944 this had increased to over 750,000 tons. In 1939 the United States built 2,100 military aircraft; in 1944 the figure was 96,300. Between 1941 and 1945 the United States constructed 10 battleships, 18 fleet carriers, 119 smaller carriers, 45 cruisers, 358 destroyers, and 504 escorts. (In the same period Britain built just three major warships, a battleship, and two aircraft carriers, all ordered before the war began.) Overall, by 1944 the United States was producing 40 percent of the world's armaments and 60 percent of Allied output. The United States economy was the key element in the Allies' war effort. To a large extent it was only a matter of realizing the productive potential of the largest economy in the world in easy circumstances. The U.S. authorities could afford to make mistakes in their mobilization plans because of the room to maneuver with such a large economy. There were few problems in mobilizing society when well-paid jobs were being provided on an unprecedented scale, and the standard of living of the American worker rose 50 percent during the war.

The problems faced by the Soviet Union, however, were unprecedented and on a scale not encountered by any other belligerent. They required a major restructuring of the economy and a social effort of enormous scale. The main weaknesses of the Soviet economy were the low agricultural output, the relatively primitive communications systems, and the concentration of much of the industrial and raw-material production in the western part of the country, which was vulnerable to invasion. Soviet rearmament was a major constituent of the industrialization drive of the 1930s, especially in the last years of the decade. By 1940 defense spending was taking up 15 percent of national wealth and about a quarter of all industrial output and investment. By June 1941 the Soviet Union had 5 million people in the armed forces and 3 million employed in the arms industry.

The first six months of the war were catastrophic for the Soviet economy. By November 1941 the Soviet Union had lost territory that contained 40 percent of its population (78 million people). Also, Germany controlled—and continued to control throughout 1942 and most of 1943—a huge proportion of the U.S.S.R.'s industrial capacity: 74 percent of its coke output, 71 percent of its iron ore, 63 percent of its coal, 60 percent of its aluminum, 58 percent of its steel and 42 percent of its electricity output. In the agricultural sector Germany took over 60 percent of the Soviet stock of pigs, 38 percent of its cattle, 87 percent of its sugar output, and 38 percent of its grain production. Alone among all the major combatants the Soviet Union had to fight the war out of a diminishing, not increasing, national wealth and from a far smaller industrial base than it had before the war. By 1942 the Soviet Union's national wealth was only two thirds of the previous year's level, and agricultural output was under 40 percent of 1940 levels. By 1943 steel and coal production were less than half 1940 levels. At the same time the Soviet Union mobilized 12 million men and 1 million women for the armed forces in order to replace the huge losses during the summer and autumn of 1941, thus raising its overall strength from about 5 million to nearly 12 million. Only by an unparalleled national effort could it continue the war.

Part of that effort was to evacuate as many industrial plants as possible to the east. This could be undertaken only because the Soviet industrialization drive in the 1930s had begun to develop new industrial regions in the Urals and farther east. By 1941, however, this process was still in its early stages, and the Soviets had created only an infrastructure as the basis for wartime expansion. Only 7 percent of aircraft production and 18 percent of tank production was located in the east, and much of the latter depended on special steels still made in the west of the country. Between July and November 1941, however, 1,360 large industrial plants were moved eastward—about an eighth of the Soviet Union's industrial assets, taking up nearly 1 million railway truck loads. Stalin had first suggested moving the tank-armor rolling mills three days after the start of the German attack and a system of priorities was soon established: defense industries, then iron and steel production, then engineering and power supplies. In fact, it was soon clear that electricity supply was crucial and had to be moved to the east. If it was moved too early, however, production would be lost in the west. Over 7,400 miles of new railway lines had to be built. There were some successes: the first trainload of T-34 tanks left the Kharkov tractor plant, by then relocated in the Urals, on December 8, 1941. The Putilov arms factories were evacuated from Leningrad to the southern Urals and made over 18,000 tanks during the war. However, there was also much chaos and confusion. By the late autumn of 1941 the railway system was on the point of breaking down—the distance traveled by trains each day fell by half and railway truck turnaround times doubled. By mid-1942 only half of the evacuated metallurgical plants were operating. The major problem was the shortage of workers. Only about 30–40 percent of factory workforces moved east. During 1942 a second evacuation of industrial plants showed that little had been learned from the chaos of the previous year. Nevertheless, whatever the limitations of the evacuation effort, it was a major achievement.

In 1942 the Soviet economy was having to operate with the basic constituents of arms production—steel, coal, and machine-tool output—at about 40 percent of 1940 levels. Yet arms production overall rose by 86 percent; tank and artillery production was nearly nine times higher and aircraft output had risen by 150 percent. To some extent this could be financed by drastic cuts in already low civilian consumption, which was reduced by about a half. In 1945, shoe production was at a third of the 1940 level and real wages were at 40 percent of their 1940 level. However, Soviet planners discovered during 1942 that arms production had, not surprisingly, been expanded too quickly in the battle for survival during 1941–42. Other sectors of the economy were in chaos and it was increasingly apparent that the real constraints on output were the supply of metals, fuels, electricity, and transport. In 1942 the railways received just eight new locomotives and no new trucks. If this situation was allowed to continue the economic infrastructure would begin to disintegrate, arms production would inevitably decline, and the Soviet Union would be in a vicious circle. From 1942 more attention was paid to the infrastructure of the economy and arms output was generally stabilized in order to sustain the economy for the long war ahead.

Like the British, the Soviets received large quantities of aid. Overall the United States sent the Soviet Union under Lend-Lease 14,800 aircraft, 7,000 tanks, 376,000 trucks, 51,000 jeeps, 345,000 tons of explosives, and huge quantities of food; the last was the top priority in 1941–42. However, until 1943 deliveries of the P-39 Airacobra, U.S. aircraft were inferior to Soviet models and American tanks were not well adapted to conditions on the eastern front, where the Soviet T-34 performed superbly. The trucks and jeeps, though, were absolutely essential. British and Canadian supplies to the Soviet Union were concentrated in the period before the end of 1942 and included nearly 8,000 aircraft and 5,000 tanks, but they were relatively insignificant in value, about 10 percent of the U.S. supplies. Overall, Allied supplies were useful to the Soviets but not vital. At their peak in late 1941, they constituted about 10 percent of Soviet aircraft and tank production, but this figure dropped to 3 percent after late 1942.

The most important factor in deciding the outcome of the war was the massive surplus of Allied production over that of the three Axis countries. Regarding raw materials, the Allies produced over twice as much iron ore and steel as the Axis, just under twice as much coal and aluminum, but twenty times as much crude oil. Because of their control of world raw materials, their ability to transport essential supplies around the globe, and the strength of their economies, the Allies were able to turn these surpluses into a huge military superiority. In total the Allies produced 227,000 tanks (the Axis, 52,000), 915,000 artillery pieces (180,000), 658,000 mortars (73,000), 4,744,000 machine guns (674,000), 3,060,000 trucks (595,000), 417,000 combat aircraft (146,000), 103,000 training aircraft (28,500), and 43,000 transport aircraft (4,900). Once this superiority had been brought to bear the outcome of the war was inevitable. The strategic question for the Axis was whether they could win the war before the economic and financial superiority of the Allies was fully mobilized and the mass of military equipment it could produce was deployed on the battlefield. Strategic questions for the Allies were essentially concerned with how to use their superiority in the most effective way so as to achieve victory in the shortest possible time and at least cost.

V

STRATEGY

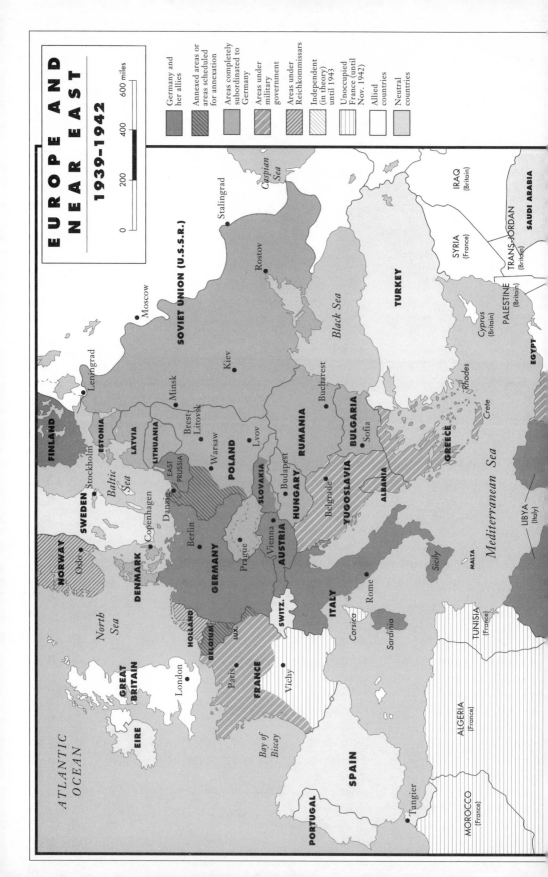

EUROPE AND NEAR EAST
1939–1942

	Germany and her allies
	Annexed areas or areas scheduled for annexation
	Areas completely subordinated to Germany
	Areas under military government
	Areas under Reichkommissars
	Independent (in theory) until 1943
	Unoccupied France (until Nov. 1942)
	Allied countries
	Neutral countries

0   200   400   600 miles

ATLANTIC OCEAN

EIRE

GREAT BRITAIN
London

North Sea

NORWAY
Oslo

SWEDEN
Stockholm

FINLAND

Leningrad

Moscow

SOVIET UNION (U.S.S.R.)

Baltic Sea

DENMARK
Copenhagen

ESTONIA

LATVIA

LITHUANIA

Minsk

Danzig

EAST PRUSSIA

Berlin

Brest Litovsk

Warsaw

POLAND

Lvov

Kiev

Rostov

Stalingrad

Caspian Sea

HOLLAND

BELGIUM

LUX.

GERMANY

Prague

Vienna

AUSTRIA

SLOVAKIA

Budapest

HUNGARY

RUMANIA

Bucharest

Black Sea

TURKEY

SWITZ.

Paris

FRANCE

Vichy

Bay of Biscay

PORTUGAL

SPAIN

Tangier

MOROCCO
(France)

ALGERIA
(France)

TUNISIA
(France)

Corsica

Sardinia

ITALY

Rome

Sicily

MALTA

Belgrade

YUGOSLAVIA

ALBANIA

BULGARIA
Sofia

GREECE

Mediterranean Sea

LIBYA
(Italy)

Crete

Rhodes

Cyprus
(Britain)

SYRIA
(France)

IRAQ
(Britain)

TRANS-JORDAN
(Britain)

PALESTINE
(Britain)

SAUDI ARABIA

EGYPT

North Sea

Uᴺᴛɪʟ ᴛʜᴇ ᴇɴᴅ ᴏꜰ 1942 ᴛʜᴇ Axɪs ᴘᴏᴡᴇʀs ʜᴇʟᴅ ᴛʜᴇ strategic initiative. In this period they tried to secure victory before the full economic potential of the Allied powers was brought to bear. Until the autumn of 1941 the dominant force in Axis strategy was Germany. Italy was a minor and largely ineffective power and Japan had not decided whether or not to become involved in the war. Throughout this period Hitler's overriding objective was to avoid the fatal mistakes of German strategy before and during the First World War.

Germany's strategic problems stemmed from its central position in Europe and the threat of a two-front war. Before 1914 German military planners relied on the unrealistic Schlieffen Plan (drawn up by Field Marshal Alfred von Schlieffen, and also known as the "swinging-door" plan) as an attempted solution to this problem in any European conflict. A rapid attack on France in the first weeks of the war would involve the overwhelming majority of the German army. Once France was defeated Germany would turn east and deal with the slowly mobilizing Russians. This strategy failed within a month of the outbreak of war in 1914 after the French won the Battle of the Marne in early September. Germany was then committed to a two-front war and made the situation even worse through its adoption of unrestricted submarine warfare in early 1917, which brought the Americans into the war in April. Even after Russia collapsed into revolution and signed a separate peace in early 1918, Germany still lost the war.

The strategy Hitler adopted from the mid-1930s into the early years of the war avoided many of these problems. He aimed to fight only limited wars as long as there was no possibility of having to fight a two-front war. Such a strategy was well suited to Germany's strategic circumstances: it did not require the full mobilization of the German economy, which Hitler wanted to avoid for political reasons, fearing the strain might lead to a collapse in morale as had happened in 1918; it was compatible with the inability of the competing agencies and ministries within the Nazi government to develop a coherent mobilization plan; and it reflected the fact the Germany in the east was faced not with the empires of Austria-Hungary and Russia but with the weak successor states established at Versailles. Having adopted this strategy, Germany did not require large armed forces capable of fighting a long, full-scale Continental war. An army of about fifty to sixty divisions, an air force of about two thousand aircraft, and a very small navy seemed adequate.

From 1936 to 1939 Hitler was able to make significant gains—the ending of the demilitarized zone in the Rhineland, the Anschluss with Austria, the incorporation of the Sudetenland, the final dismemberment of Czechoslovakia, and the regaining of Memel—at very little cost. Nevertheless he had to take account of the changing strategic situation, which in German eyes seemed to be remarkably similar to the 1912–14 period with its threat of encirclement. British and French rearmament was rapidly bearing fruit by the late 1930s, and the most heavily armed state in Europe, the Soviet Union, was potentially a threat, especially if Britain and France could bring it into alliance. The brilliant diplomatic coup of the German-Soviet Pact of August 1939 solved the central German strategic problem and avoided the threat of a two-front war. Although the British and French decided to fight after the invasion of Poland, Germany had still avoided the impossible situation of August 1914. In addition, the United States was unarmed and it was likely to be some years before it could offer anything more than diplomatic and possibly economic support to the Allies.

Hitler's decision to limit rearmament meant that the German armed forces in 1939 were still relatively small—Germany mobilized 1 million less men than in 1914—and poorly equipped. The idea that Germany launched a new type of warefare—the Blitzkrieg, involving masses of swiftly moving, heavily armored divisions—is a fallacy. ("Blitzkrieg" was not a German term; it was invented by a *Time* journalist after the attack on Poland.) In September 1939 the German army contained about 3,200 tanks, but 45 percent of them were a training model, armed only with two machine guns, which was obsolete when it was introduced in 1934. Another 40 percent were light tanks. In total, Germany had just 300 modern tanks adequately armored and gunned. In 1939 only about 50 tanks a month were being built, and in the entire year only 45 of the most modern Mk-IV models came off the assembly lines. The term armored, or Panzer, division was a misnomer. Although the so-called Panzer division had 2,000 vehicles to support the tanks, not one of them was tracked and only one type was armored.

The situation of the infantry divisions was worse. Only four were motorized, and eighty-six had less than a quarter of the transport required to make them fully mobile—nearly two thirds of them relied on requisitioned civilian vehicles. In reality German infantry divisions, like their First World War counterparts, relied on horsepower. In September 1939 the German army depended on 445,000 horses for basic transport and in the course of the war it used about 2.7 million horses, twice as many as in 1914–18. There were other major weaknesses. The standard rifle was based on an 1896 design, there were no heavy mortars, the main anti-tank gun was so ineffective it was known as the "door knocker," and the light and medium howitzers were based on a First World War design. Fifty divisions had no pistols, light or medium mortars, or 20mm anti-aircraft guns, and thirty-four divisions had no armored cars. The Luftwaffe was little better. Forty percent of its crews were not fully trained, and there was only one fighter pilot school, with the result that by 1941 half of the aircraft losses were caused by crashes and accidents.

Luckily for Germany, Poland faced an impossible situation. It could mobilize sixty divisions but had only 225 tanks, its aircraft were obsolete, and it had over three thousand miles of border to defend, with German troops on three sides and a flat terrain with few natural obstacles to hold up an advancing army. It also had to keep forces in the east to meet the expected Soviet attack, which came in mid-September. Poland was totally defeated by the end of September. The Germans lost only 10,500 killed and its total casualties were only 3 percent of the forces involved, although 10 percent of the tanks deployed were destroyed. With Germany's eastern frontier secure, Hitler could now concentrate on a single-front war in the west, once it was clear that the Allies would not make peace. At the end of September Hitler told his commanders of his intention to attack in the west in mid-November. The army was reluctant. It reported in early October that it had only enough ammunition for operations with a third of its divisions for fourteen days. Hitler was unimpressed by these arguments and only bad weather throughout the autumn and winter caused twenty-nine postponements to be made.

During this hiatus Hitler turned his attention to Scandinavia. It was not an area he had intended to attack until Allied intervention plans forced him to consider counteraction. When launched in early April 1940, the takeover of Denmark and the invasion of Norway were minor operations: only 5,300 killed, wounded, and missing. The postponement of the attack in the west proved to be highly fortuitous for Germany. Had it attacked in the autumn of 1939, as Hitler wanted, it is unlikely that a decisive victory would have been achieved. The intention was to carry out an unimaginative, scaled-down version of the Schlieffen Plan by means of an attack through the Netherlands and Belgium to push the Allies out of the Low Countries and northern France. It was exactly the attack the Allies were expecting, and one they would probably have countered very well. Hitler had begun to think about an attack through the hilly and wooded country of the Ardennes in order to penetrate the center of the French defenses at Sedan (a repeat of the Prussian strategy in 1870), but it was not until February 1940 that he adopted a plan drawn up by the army commanders responsible for this sector that placed the overwhelming weight of the German armored forces on this part of the front.

On May 10, 1940, when the German attack began, their forces were outnumbered. They had 135 divisions with 2.7 million men compared with an Allied (French, Belgian, Dutch, and British) force of 144 divisions and 3.7 million men. The French had 3,250 tanks and the Germans 2,500 (of which 1,500 were armed only with machine guns or light cannon and nearly 400 were captured Czech light tanks). The Allies had 14,000 artillery pieces, the German army 7,400. The British forces were completely mechanized whereas the German army was desperately short of trucks (only a quarter of German production was going to the army and that level was unable to replace normal peacetime wear and tear) and highly dependent on horsepower. The Luftwaffe had a small degree of superiority in the air. German strategy, however, compensated for this unpromising military position. The move through the Ardennes and the attack at Sedan were hugely successful. The French army disintegrated over a fifty-mile-wide front and within a fortnight German forces had reached the Channel and split the Allied armies before they could devise and carry out any counterattack. British forces were evacuated from the northern pocket around Dunkirk, the Belgians surrendered, and a renewed attack southward easily defeated the remainder of the French army. On June 17 the French asked for an armistice. Within six weeks Hitler had achieved, at very low cost, what the Imperial German armies had failed to do in four years. The campaign in the west cost Germany 27,000 dead and 130,000 wounded and missing, total casualties of just over 5 percent of the forces involved. It was a stunning victory that destroyed the European balance of power and left Germany dominant on the Continent.

The only country in Europe still fighting Germany was Britain. Hitler hoped that Britain would be prepared to accept the new power structure in return for retaining the Empire. He shrewdly realized that Germany would gain little from the destruction of the British Empire, believing that the main beneficiaries would be Japan and America. Hitler also realized that Germany had no capability to launch an invasion across the English Channel; it had neither the naval supremacy nor any of the specialized equipment necessary for an opposed assault. German planning and preparations for an invasion took place, but they were based on one fundamental premise: the British had to be on the point of defeat before the invasion was launched. Hitler was not willing to risk his prestige on a failed invasion, especially when Britain lacked the military capability to affect events on the Continent.

Hitler was, however, willing to allow Göring and the Luftwaffe the opportunity to defeat the British in the air and thereby establish the conditions for an "invasion" when Britain was already on the point of defeat. Before the war, theorists had speculated about the ability of air forces to secure victory on their own, but the war was to show that airpower was most effective when used in conjunction with ground forces. The Luftwaffe was equipped for this sort of operation, not for an independent air attack. In the summer of 1940 the German air force was embarking on an operation, an air assault aimed at defeating an opponent, that had never been tried before, and was doing it with the wrong type of aircraft. In addition to these handicaps, British fighter production was two and a half times greater than German production. By September the British had a larger force of front-line fighters than in July, whereas the Luftwaffe was at a third of its early summer level. Britain had also, in the late 1930s, developed a highly effective form of air defense based on radar detection and ground control of fighters. Furthermore, the Luftwaffe was unclear about its objectives. Was the main aim of the attack to destroy the radar stations, bomb the fighter airfields, draw the RAF into combat, or bomb cities such as London? Under Göring's erratic direction the Germans tried all these tactics at different times but never for long enough to achieve any significant results. By mid-September it was clear that the RAF had not been defeated, and in these circumstances Hitler had no intention of launching an invasion. On September 17 he postponed the plan indefinitely.

After June 1940 the German army was not involved in combat for the rest of the year. It was dragged into operations in early 1941 through Italian actions during the autumn of 1940—Italy's sole contribution to Axis strategy. Italian intervention in the war in June 1940 had little positive impact for the Axis. On mobilization only a third of the Italian army was ready for combat, and when it attempted to invade France after the French had already asked for an armistice, it was defeated by its heavily outnumbered opponents and its casualty rate was ten times as high. After this fiasco Mussolini developed no operational plans and was only concerned about giving the impression he was ready to fight. He vaguely considered an attack on Yugoslavia but this was vetoed by Germany. Italian forces successfully invaded British Somaliland, but it was of no strategic importance. In mid-September an offensive into Egypt stopped within three days after the British had fallen back fifty miles from the frontier. Mussolini intended to do little more until Britain was out of the war, and over 600,000 Italian troops were demobilized. His policy changed as a result of his exclusion from German policy-making on the Balkans. At the end of October Italy attacked Greece without informing Germany. Within days the invasion had been halted and Greek troops were driving the Italians back into Albania. Mussolini was now committed to a two-front war in Greece and North Africa and had inadequate forces to fight either. The British sent major reinforcements to Egypt—the one place they could actually fight the Axis. In December 1940 an attack by an Indian infantry division and an armored division (a total of 36,000 men) defeated two Italian corps and took 30,000 prisoners within three days at the expense of just over six hundred casualties. By early January 1941 British forces crossed the border into Libya, captured Tobruk and Benghazi, and destroyed eight Italian divisions. Italy had lost its war on both fronts and Hitler decided he would have to rescue his ally by sending troops to North Africa and attacking Greece. This marked the end of any independent Italian strategy in the war.

Like the Italians, the British faced the problem of a two-front war in the Mediterranean; like the Italians, they failed to get their strategic priorities right. In the autumn of 1940 the Greeks asked only for limited British assistance, mainly aircraft, as they believed the presence of British troops would only tempt the Germans to intervene. When they were on the brink of eliminating the Italians from North Africa the British, tempted by the prospects of a Balkan front, decided, in a series of ill-thought-out decisions, to divert the bulk of their forces to Greece. The result was disaster. Limited German forces in North Africa drove the British back to Egypt. On the Continent Hitler had originally offered to mediate between Greece and Italy in order to avoid a Balkan conflict. Even by the end of 1940, with the Italians on the brink of defeat, he was thinking only of securing the northeastern part of Greece and denying the British the use of air bases. It was the deployment of British troops at the beginning of March 1941 that changed German plans in favor of a complete occupation. The British-engineered coup in Yugoslavia convinced Hitler to invade that country too. German operations in the Balkans in the spring of 1941 were quick and effective. Of the twenty-nine divisions involved, only ten saw action for more than six days, and in the attack on Yugoslavia only a third of the units were involved in combat— and even this small force ended the campaign in half the time allocated. In total, German casualties were less than 5,000 and in Yugoslavia they lost only 150 killed.

The Balkan campaign remained a sideshow in terms of German grand strategy. After the conquest of western Europe, the main decision facing Hitler was whether or not to attack the Soviet Union, the state he had always seen as the ideological enemy. In July 1940, the military planners began a preliminary examination of the feasibility of an eastern campaign, at first without Hitler's specific authority. Hitler was involved in discussing outline ideas throughout the summer and autumn but would make no final decision while diplomatic discussions continued with the Soviet Union about whether the cooperation agreed to in August 1939 could be continued. It was not until the failure of the Molotov mission to Berlin in November 1940 and the final Soviet rejection of German terms for a further division of the world at the end of that month that Hitler finally decided to attack the Soviet Union in the early summer of 1941. A directive for Operation Barbarossa was finally issued to the armed forces in mid-December.

In retrospect it is clear that this decision eventually led to the defeat of Germany. Hitler has therefore been criticized for embarking on such an operation. In fact, his decision was highly logical and well adapted to the German strategic situation in 1940: it gave the best chance of an overall German victory. Hitler could not be sure that the Soviet Union would continue to abide by the terms of the 1939 pact. The Soviet Union's sphere of influence had widened considerably and German and Soviet interests were increasingly in conflict in eastern and southeastern Europe. Soviet forces on Germany's eastern frontier had doubled since September 1939, from 2 million to 4 million, and far outnumbered German forces. Overall German strategy in 1939–40 had been a slow-motion enactment of the Schlieffen Plan: Hitler had secured himself against a two-front war by the deal with the Soviet Union and had been able to defeat France and take control of most of western Europe. If war with the Soviet Union was inevitable it was best to strike now before Germany was involved in a two-front war again. If Britain sought peace, though this seemed unlikely by the autumn of 1940, then American intervention could almost certainly be discounted. If Britain stayed in the war, however, then U.S. intervention was a strong possibility at some stage, given their increasing support for Britain. Hitler calculated that if he did not attack American ships in the Atlantic, then U.S. intervention during 1941 on any significant scale was unlikely. Meanwhile, significant British military intervention could be discounted: between June 1940 and February 1941 the British did not fight the German army at all, and until the end of 1942 they never fought more than four weak divisions out of a total of over two hundred. If Germany could defeat the Soviet Union during 1941, then even if the United States came into the war it would face what the British and the Americans always regarded as an almost impossible task, launching an invasion against the full strength of the German army in western Europe.

Everything therefore turned on whether Germany could secure victory in 1941. Superficially, the Soviet Union seemed to be exactly the sort of weak state that Germany had defeated so easily in the previous eighteen months. After all, if France, which had resisted enormous German attacks in the First World War, could be defeated in six weeks, then surely Russia, which had collapsed in 1917, would go the same way? Such optimism was reinforced by the inept Soviet performance in the war with Finland and the extensive purges between 1937 and 1939, which had largely destroyed the officer corps. Hitler's views about the strength of the Soviet Union were widely shared.

LIMIT OF AXIS CONTROL IN EUROPE & AFRICA

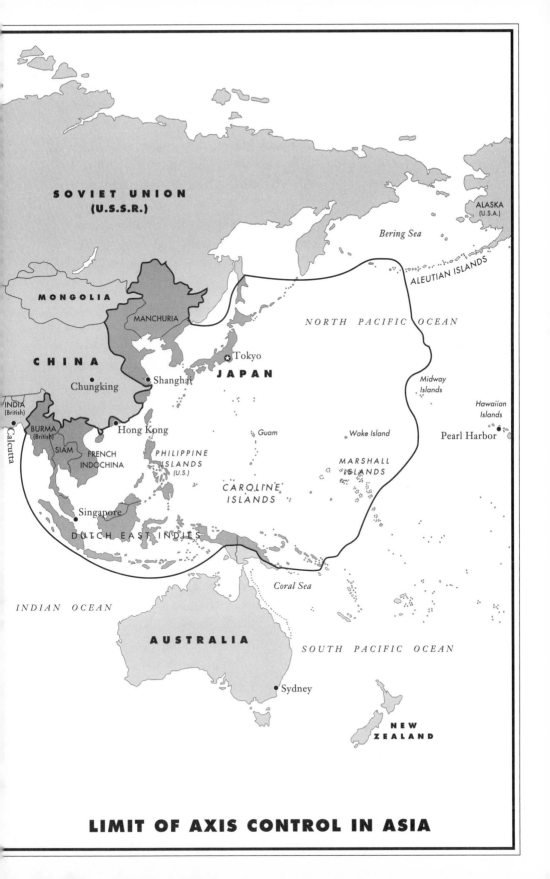

SOVIET UNION
(U.S.S.R.)

ALASKA
(U.S.A.)

Bering Sea

MONGOLIA

MANCHURIA

ALEUTIAN ISLANDS

NORTH   PACIFIC   OCEAN

CHINA

☆ Tokyo

JAPAN

Chungking

● Shanghai

Midway
Islands

Hawaiian
Islands

INDIA
(British)

Hong Kong

Pearl Harbor ●

Calcutta

BURMA
(British)

SIAM

FRENCH
INDOCHINA

PHILIPPINE
ISLANDS
(U.S.)

Guam

Wake Island

MARSHALL
ISLANDS

CAROLINE
ISLANDS

Singapore

DUTCH EAST INDIES

INDIAN   OCEAN

Coral Sea

AUSTRALIA

SOUTH   PACIFIC   OCEAN

● Sydney

NEW
ZEALAND

LIMIT OF AXIS CONTROL IN ASIA

The British believed that the attack would give them no more than a few weeks' breathing space. They thought that the Soviet Union would be defeated by August at the latest and British counterinvasion preparations were planned to peak in early September, ready for the expected German move back westward. The American administration shared these perceptions about the outcome of the campaign in the east.

The plans drawn up by the German High Command for the attack on the Soviet Union were woefully inadequate and demonstrated a failure to grasp the difficulties involved in such a campaign. The overall aim was not outright defeat of the Soviet Union. The Germans planned to stop east of Moscow, on a line joining the Volga and Archangel. They expected to keep some forty to fifty divisions as a shield against the Soviet government in Asia and an air force to continue bombing the industrial centers of the Urals, and to make a separate peace with puppet regimes in the west. They expected the campaign to continue through the winter and into 1942, even if the first assault was successful. Such an attack faced one major geographical problem: as German troops advanced eastward the front would have to become wider if it was to remain continuous. Before the invasion, during the summer of 1941, and in endless discussion since, arguments have been conducted about whether the weight of the German attack should have been in the north toward Leningrad, in the center aimed at Moscow, or in the south with Kiev, Kharkov, and Rostov as the objectives. These arguments were, and remain, largely theoretical because the Germans lacked the forces to carry out such huge operations. Operation Barbarossa envisaged a vast mobile campaign encircling huge numbers of Soviet troops. However, the German army was not equipped for this sort of warfare. It did not have enough tanks to create huge "pockets" or keep them closed while the slow-moving infantry caught up. German logistical arrangements were also inadequate. Reserves were based on a campaign similar to that in France and lasting five months. In practice consumption rates were about four times higher than in the French campaign, owing to the greater distances involved. The Germans also made few preparations to convert Soviet railways to the western European gauge, and so an effective supply system took a long time to establish.

The German forces that launched the attack on the Soviet Union in June 1941 were woefully ill equipped for the task. Arms production had been cut back in the autumn of 1940, and aircraft production fell 40 percent by early 1941. Of the 203 divisions in the German army, 80 percent were infantry and there were just 21 armored and 10 motorized infantry divisions. Although the number of Panzer divisions was doubled before Operation Barbarossa was launched, this was largely achieved by reducing the number of tanks in each division. In May 1940 a Panzer division theoretically had about 300 tanks, but by June 1941 the average was 160. Of the 3,300 tanks in the invasion force, 35 percent were obsolete Mk-I and Mk-IIs; five divisions were equipped with captured Czech models. Only 1,400 were modern tanks, and of these only 480 had the most modern guns. Four new motorized infantry divisions had been created, but they lacked any tracked transport. About half of the infantry divisions relied on captured foreign vehicles, but overall the army used 625,000 horses (far more than the total number of vehicles), and many divisions were supplied using captured one-horse Soviet carts. These ramshackle forces were spread thinly, and the tank density for the length of the front was four times lower than that for the campaign in France.

Despite these limitations the Germans scored some stunning initial successes against a Soviet army deployed too near to the frontier and reduced to chaos by the assault. Partial encirclements were achieved. Some 600,000 men and 5,000 tanks were captured around Bialystok, Minsk, and Smolensk in the early stages and another 600,000 men, 880 tanks, and 5,000 guns around Kiev in late September. Altogether, between June and December 1941 the Soviet Union lost as either killed or captured the equivalent of the entire Red Army strength in June plus its reserves. The Luftwaffe also destroyed most of the Soviet air force in the first weeks of the campaign. However, the Soviets were able to absorb these huge losses. By December the Red Army was larger than in June (3.2 million men were conscripted in the last six months of 1941), and its effective tank strength was at the same level. Most of the aircraft destroyed in the first weeks were obsolete, and by December Soviet front-line strength was higher than the Luftwaffe's. Because of the initial successes German arms production was cut further in the late summer of 1941 to 60 percent of its level earlier in the year. Only tank production was exempt from cutbacks, and although Germany built nearly 2,900 modern tanks in 1941 the Soviets produced over 4,000 modern T-34s.

By October the German assault was beginning to run into the mud of the Soviet autumn. In early October "Operation Typhoon," aimed at Moscow, had some initial success around Vyazma and Bryansk but was halted by Soviet reserves. A final assault on the Soviet capital in mid-November suffered a similar fate. In the south the Germans captured the Crimea but were turned back near Rostov. By late autumn the balance of forces was shifting in favor of the Soviets. Around Moscow they were able to deploy seventeen reserve divisions with 1,700 tanks. The German supply system was breaking down. By late August the army had suffered 440,000 casualties but only 217,000 replacements had been sent east. The Luftwaffe had only about 500 aircraft operational, whereas the Soviets had over 1,000 on the Moscow front alone. During the winter of 1941–42 the German army was effectively reduced to an infantry force with little transport. At the beginning of February 1942 it had 142 operational tanks on the whole of the eastern front; 30 percent of its trucks had been destroyed and another 40 percent were unusable.

The German army held the winter counterattack mainly because the Soviets undertook a broad-front assault instead of concentrating on a few key objectives. However, the strategic situation had changed profoundly for Germany with the entry into the war of the United States in December 1941. Although the United States did not declare war on Germany after Pearl Harbor, Hitler decided to formally join his ally Japan and declare war. He believed that such a declaration now made little difference. The United States was already giving immense help to both Britain and the Soviet Union, but its active intervention in the European war was likely to be very limited during 1942. If Germany could defeat the Soviet Union in the 1942 campaign, which both Britain and the United States still thought was probable, then the western Allies would still be left with the extremely difficult task of invading a German-dominated Europe when the overwhelming share of German strength could be deployed in the west.

Hitler's directive for 1942, issued in April, concentrated German forces on the south of the front and aimed at a big encirclement battle between the Donets River and Stalingrad, followed by the capture of the latter and a drive to Baku and the Caucasian oilfields. These objectives were far beyond German capabilities. Forces in the south could be built up only by taking troops and equipment from the divisions in the center and north. Even so, Panzer divisions were reduced to one tank battalion each and infantry divisions were at roughly half strength. The attack began at the end of June. This time the Soviets retreated and therefore denied the Germans any large encirclements. Hitler thought these tactics meant that the Soviets had no reserves left and so decided to attack Stalingrad and the Caucasus area simultaneously, even though Baku was 700 miles away. By the autumn the Germans were running out of supplies and reserves. By November the German forces around Stalingrad were reduced to an average of twenty-seven tanks in each Panzer division. As the German troops fought their way through the streets of Stalingrad, the Soviets prepared to counterattack. When they did so, on November 19, they deployed 500,000 troops, 900 high-quality tanks, 230 regiments of field artillery, and over 1,100 aircraft. Along a 250-mile front there were 7 German and 15 weak Rumanian divisions equipped with 300 tanks (most of them captured from the Czechs in 1939) and about 400 aircraft. Within four days the German front was, not surprisingly, smashed and the troops in Stalingrad surrounded. When the battle ended in early February at least 150,000 troops were dead and another 100,000 had been captured.

The last major German attack on the eastern front came in the summer of 1943, when they tried to eliminate the Soviet salient around Kursk, north of Kharkov and due south of Moscow. It was far from clear what they expected to gain even if they were successful, and the Soviets were content to let the Germans make the first move. The German army had recovered somewhat from its dire situation in early 1943, when it had just 495 operational tanks in the Soviet Union. By July it had concentrated 1,850 tanks and 530 assault guns around Kursk, half of the tanks in the entire army. The Soviets were well aware of German plans and concentrated 75 infantry divisions, 2,000 tanks, 20,000 guns, and 920 multiple rocket launchers in the area. In addition, there was defense in depth: on one front there were 3,000 miles of trenches and 400,000 mines, with four infantry armies and 1,500 tanks in reserve. The German attack began in early July and was called off within ten days. It was the largest tank battle in history, with over 1,000 vehicles engaged at one time. German casualties were huge and uncounted. The scale of the destruction can be gauged from the fact that the elite Grossdeutschland Division lost three quarters of its tanks in two days.

After Kursk the Germans never held the strategic initiative on the eastern front. Its other attempt to win the overall war, the U-boat battle against Allied convoys in the Atlantic, was collapsing at the same time. At the start of the war the Germans had very few submarines at sea, fourteen in the autumn of 1939, rising to twenty in the summer of 1940 and falling back to eleven by the end of the year. Yet despite these small numbers the Germans achieved the highest weekly total of sinkings for the whole war in this period, 1.5 million tons in the last six months of 1940. This was largely due to inadequate British countermeasures. The Royal Navy was short of escorts for convoy work, and its reliance on ASDIC* sonar for submarine detection was also misplaced because its range was so limited. British tactics were also poor, concentrating on the action of "hunter-killer" groups aimed at detecting U-boats on their transit routes rather than on fighting defensive battles around the convoys. There was also a severe shortage of aircraft to detect submarines, mainly because priority was given to RAF Bomber Command. In addition, British depth charges were largely ineffective. Germany was also reading about half of all Royal Navy signals. In 1941 Hitler increased the priority given to the Atlantic battle. U-boat construction was increased and in the second half of the year on average thirty-three boats were on patrol at any

*Anti-Submarine Detection Investigation Committee.

one time. Results were less than expected, though, because of British intelligence successes in breaking the U-boat codes and bringing improved radar into service.

In December 1941 Hitler rejected the option of adopting a holding strategy on the eastern front while concentrating resources on trying to break the supply lines between the United States and Britain, believing such a course would not work. In this belief he was right. Although the American failure to adopt the convoy system enabled the U-boats to have enormous success in early 1942 off the east coast of the United States, this was only temporary. Later in the year Germany had nearly 100 boats at sea at any one time operating in "wolf packs" and using multiple patrol lines to stop the Allies rerouting convoys, but without producing significant results. The massive convoy battles of spring 1943 were the last major effort in the Atlantic battle and by the end of May Admiral Karl Dönitz, the commander of the U-boat fleet, had accepted defeat. This was brought about by improved Allied equipment and tactics, including more escort vessels and aircraft carriers, better radar and direction-finding equipment, and the closing of the "air gap" through the use of very-long-range aircraft employing radar and lights. The crucial factor, though, as elsewhere, was the power of the Allied economies. Put simply, the Americans were able to build merchant ships far faster than the Germans could sink them. In 1940 the British lost 4 million tons of shipping and could build less than 800,000 tons (the losses were made up by taking over the merchant fleets of the governments-in-exile). By 1942, when the Germans sank 7.7 million tons, the Allies built 7.4 million tons of shipping, 5 million tons of it in the United States. In 1943 losses were reduced to 3.2 million tons and the United States built 13 million tons. The importance of the Battle of the Atlantic can also be overestimated. In practice, the British merchant fleet remained roughly constant throughout the war and the percentage of imports sunk was usually 5 percent or less.

The figures for merchant shipping production demonstrate that once the war had become one of production, Germany could not hope to win, especially when it was fighting a two-front war. After the German defeat at Stalingrad and failure in the Battle of the Atlantic, the strategic initiative passed to the Allies. German war production expanded greatly, but it could only delay the inevitable. From 1943 to 1945, Germany fought a very effective defensive strategy and hoped that the coalition facing it might collapse before victory came. It was the only strategy it had left.

The Japanese held the strategic initiative for a much shorter period than Germany but also faced the problem of a two-front war. Although the Japanese decided in the autumn of 1941 to attack the Americans and the European colonial powers, they were still deeply committed to the continuing war in China. In early 1942 the Japanese had twenty-two divisions in China, thirteen in Manchuria, but only eleven in the Pacific and southeast Asia. Few reinforcements were sent to the Pacific area, and in both 1943 and 1944 the Japanese mounted large and effective offensives against the Chinese. In early 1945 they still had one million soldiers in China and another 700,000 in Manchuria. The Japanese attacks in late 1941 and early 1942 were remarkably successful mainly because the Americans and Europeans had only weak forces in the area. The Japanese rapidly achieved all their strategic objectives. They captured Hong Kong, the Philippines, Malaya, Singapore (where 130,000 British and Commonwealth troops surrendered), the Dutch East Indies (where 98,000 Dutch troops capitulated), Guam, Wake, the Bismarck Archipelago, northeast New Guinea, the northern Solomon and Gilbert islands, and Burma. They already controlled Indochina and a puppet regime ruled in Siam. Japanese air attacks on northern Australia were also under way.

The Japanese appreciated that they could not win a long war of attrition with the United States. They hoped that the Americans, heavily committed in Europe, would accept the Japanese gains and leave them in control of the areas they needed for economic exploitation. It was a vain hope. By mid-1942 the Japanese had also lost the element of strategic surprise and U.S. forces were being deployed to the Pacific in increasing numbers. The Japanese advance was stopped on New Guinea and, after a vicious battle, on Guadalcanal in the Solomon Islands. The naval attack on Midway was turned into a disaster for Japan, both through the ability of the Americans to read Japanese naval signals and therefore deploy their limited resources in the right place—and luck: the U.S. air attack was launched just as the Japanese ships were at their most vulnerable because their fighters were re-fueling.

By the end of 1942 the Axis had lost the strategic initiative. For the last two and a half years of the war the Allies were able to dictate the shape of the war. The British, after their forces were expelled from the Continent, had to devise some sort of strategy by which they might win the war and, more important, convince the Americans of this. The cornerstone of this strategy stemmed from British weakness—they would never be able to build an army capable of mounting an opposed invasion of the Continent because the German army was four times the size of Britain's. In the spring of 1941 the British carried out a strategic review that concluded that the British army would reach its maximum size of 60 divisions in the autumn of 1942, compared with a German strength of 250 divisions. Even free American arms supplies could not compensate for this inferiority and the British military planners concluded that they could not hope to defeat the existing German army in the field and thereby secure victory.

The British therefore drew up a three-part strategy that they hoped might compensate for this military inferiority. The first element was continuation of the blockade of Germany. Throughout the summer and autumn of 1940 the British believed that the German economy might collapse by the end of the year. In fact, the German ability to exploit the resources of most of Europe meant that the British blockade could never be more than partially effective, and the limited level of mobilization meant that there was plenty of slack left in the German economy. The second strand of the strategy was to try to develop a widespread campaign of subversion across occupied Europe. This proved to be much more difficult to implement than the British expected, especially when most people on the Continent were unsure that Germany would ultimately be defeated. The final strand was the widespread bombing of Germany, in the hope of destroying the industrial base and the morale of the population. If all these elements worked, then it was hoped that a numerically inferior army might be able to reenter the Continent to deal the coup de grâce or possibly occupy an already defeated country. It was a strategy that the British were to cling to even after the German attack on the Soviet Union and U.S. entry into the war, when it no longer bore any relation to the respective strength of the two sides.

Throughout the second half of 1940 and the whole of 1941, British strategy was essentially negative. Once invasion by Germany was no longer a possibility, resources were devoted to keeping the sea-lanes open to maintain the flow of supplies, especially from the United States. The only active military campaign was in North Africa, against Italy. The attempt to intervene in the Balkans in the spring of 1941 was a fiasco and left Germany in control of the whole of the area. The British were able to defeat the even weaker Italians, but could not achieve success against the very limited forces Germany sent to Africa to prop up its ally. Hardly any resources could be spared for the poorly defended possessions in the Far East. The fleet in the area consisted of three modern and two old cruisers together with five old destroyers, while the army had three brigades available to defend Malaya and the RAF could muster eighty-eight front-line aircraft. The British realized that only the Americans could provide the resources to defend the Empire in the Far East, but the United States consistently refused to give any guarantee that they would do so.

The central element of British strategy, the mass bombing of Germany, faced major problems. Unfortunately, although the RAF had adopted the idea of a strategic bomber offensive since the early 1920s as the best way of preserving its independence from the army and navy, it was singularly ill equipped to carry out that role. At the outbreak of war the RAF discovered very quickly that casualty levels in daylight raids were prohibitive. This meant that when the RAF was launched into bombing German cities by night in May 1940, it was untrained and ill equipped to cope with the enormous difficulties of navigation and target finding such operations involved. The RAF had no adequate bombsight until 1942 and its primitive navigation systems were largely ineffective. In August 1939, during a carefully planned training exercise, 40 percent of the bombers involved could

not find a designated "target" in broad daylight in a friendly city with
no fighter defense. Given this level of competence, it was not surprising that night flying proved even more inaccurate. Until late 1942 the
RAF also lacked heavy four-engine bombers and they rarely dropped
more than 4,000 tons of bombs a month—less than the Germans
dropped on Britain during the Blitz, and the British were dropping
their bombs over a much bigger area.

In the summer of 1941 the British carried out a survey of the effectiveness of the bombing campaign. The conclusions were devastating. The RAF was losing more men than the number of German
civilians it was killing. Its navigation was so bad that although two
thirds of the crews thought they had found the target, only one in five
aircraft was bombing within five miles of the target (which meant
within an area of 78 square miles around the target) and two thirds of
the bombs dropped fell on open ground or on decoys. Over the key
industrial area of the Ruhr, accuracy was even worse: only one crew
in ten dropped its bombs within ten miles of the target. On moonless
nights accuracy was worse still: only one aircraft in every fifteen
dropped its bombs within five miles of the target. Despite these very
discouraging results the British felt they had little alternative but to
continue. They had no other way of attacking Germany. Also, by late
1941 the bomber offensive was taking up about a third of the British
war effort and it would be very difficult to change priorities and real-
locate resources.

By the summer of 1941 the British gave up what little pretense
they ever made that the bomber offensive was directed at military
and economic targets. The RAF was simply not capable of doing
anything other than hitting German cities. The chief of the air staff
argued that the weakest point in the German war machine was the
morale of the civilian population and in particular of the industrial
workers and that this could best be affected not just by killing large
numbers of them but also through the general dislocation of industrial and social life caused by damage to industrial plants, dwelling
houses, shops, and utility and transportation services and from the re-
sultant absenteeism. He suggested that the bombers should concentrate on the most densely populated towns. In a new directive to

Bomber Command in February 1942 the chief of the air staff stated that aiming points were to be built-up areas and not, for instance, dockyards or aircraft factories. In public the government lied about its policy. It told the House of Commons in March 1943 that the targets of Bomber Command were always military.

In the spring of 1942, even after the introduction of the first airborne navigation aid, RAF performance was still dire. Less than a third of the bombers were even attacking the target, let alone hitting it. Even after the introduction of specialist Pathfinder squadrons and the use of airborne radar in the summer of 1942 the average error in bombing accuracy at night was still three miles. It was not until mid-1944 that accuracy improved significantly, after the adoption of low-level marking and target-indicator bombs. By the end of 1944 half of the bombs dropped were within a mile of the aiming point and 95 percent fell within three miles. The weight of the bomber offensive was also increasing—the number of sorties rose from 8,000 in June 1943 to 35,000 in July 1944. (The Allies dropped a total of nearly 2 million tons of bombs during the war, twenty-seven times more than the Germans dropped on Britain.) In 1944–45 the British stuck to a policy of area bombing of German cities, even though they were capable of attacking specific industrial targets. Key targets were attacked occasionally, but never in such a way as to achieve long-term results. The synthetic-rubber plant at Hüls was put out of production in June 1943 and German stocks fell to a six weeks' supply. However, the plant was repaired and was never attacked again and production reached a peak in March 1944. The production of aviation fuel depended on just four factories capable of making the key additives tetraethyl lead and ethylene dibromide. None of these plants was attacked.

Overall the bomber offensive was a failure and was a poor use of scarce resources. It cost the British 8,000 aircraft and over 50,000 dead, yet it failed to damage German civilian morale (its primary objective) or reduce significantly industrial output. In fact, German war production reached a peak under the full weight of the bomber offensive in 1944. The official Allied survey after the war estimated that Germany lost just under 4 percent of its productive capacity to the bomber offensive, and even badly bombed cities such as Hamburg were back at around 80 percent of productive capacity within a few weeks. In 1945 German machine-tool capacity was actually higher than in 1939.

Anglo-American strategy after December 1941 was constrained and influenced by decisions made earlier by Britain, in particular by its decision to fight its primary land campaign in North Africa but also by the ideas developed in 1940–41 about how it might win the war. At the first military staff talks in Washington in early 1941 (when the United States was still "neutral") the Americans had expressed considerable skepticism about the value of the North African campaign as a way of defeating Germany. However, they did agree that if the United States were to enter the war, the strategic priority should be "Germany first." After Pearl Harbor the British and Americans had to decide on the best way of employing the vast military resources the United States would produce. This involved decisions about the relative priorities to be given to the production of various types of weapons, the movement of hundreds of thousands of men around the globe, the use of vast quantities of shipping, and the construction of huge bases and support facilities. Given the scale and complexity of these operations, it was not possible to change course rapidly. Once a strategy was decided it had to be followed decisively, otherwise Allied material superiority would be neutralized and the war would be prolonged unnecessarily. As it turned out, the British and Americans did exactly that and failed to follow through with the most effective strategy.

In early 1942 the Americans proposed a simple strategy. Enough forces were to be sent to the Pacific to contain the Japanese. The top priority, though, was to build up forces in Britain for a cross-Channel invasion in the spring of 1943. An invasion of northwest Europe would open the shortest route to Germany (in particular the Ruhr) and enable existing British bases to be used to obtain air supremacy. The Atlantic route from the United States to Britain was also the shortest and there were sufficient ports to cope with the huge influx of men and equipment. This route had to be kept open even if an invasion was planned elsewhere. During 1942 other operations were to be limited, although a five-division attack on Europe was a possibility either if Germany collapsed or if a diversion was needed because the Soviet Union was on the point of defeat. The British accepted this plan as embodying one of the classic principles of war: concentration of strength against the main enemy. It called for a buildup to 540,000 troops in Britain prior to invasion.

By the end of July this clear strategic plan for winning the war in 1943 had been abandoned. There were three main reasons for this change of strategy. First, the Soviet Union, facing the full weight of the German army, was pressing hard for a second front to be opened in Europe in 1942. Second, Churchill was going through a political crisis in which his direction of the war was under increasing criticism and he desperately needed a military success in North Africa, where British forces had been forced back into Egypt and seemed on the point of total defeat. Third, Roosevelt, facing midterm elections in November, wanted American troops in action in the European arena before then. Churchill therefore proposed and Roosevelt agreed that Anglo-American forces should invade French North Africa, thereby threatening the supply lines of German forces in Egypt and hopefully securing a cheap military success. American and British military advisers were clear that this was the wrong strategy and told Roosevelt and Churchill that such an invasion ought not to be undertaken. They also made it clear that any invasion of French North Africa would rule out a cross-Channel invasion in 1943: the diversion of forces would be so great that they could not be moved back to Europe in time. They argued that adopting such a course would be both indecisive and a heavy drain on resources. Nevertheless, Roosevelt and Churchill insisted on their new strategy, and Anglo-American forces invaded French North Africa in November 1942.

Without this change of strategy there is little doubt that a successful invasion of northwest Europe could have been mounted in 1943 rather than 1944. German war production was only beginning to increase and the Allies would have faced fewer German forces (49 divisions rather than 57 in 1944) and less coastal fortification, would have had a greater advantage in tank numbers, and would still have had air superiority. The decisions made in the summer of 1942 by Roosevelt and Churchill, against the clear warnings of all their military advisers, ensured that the Anglo-American war effort was not used to its best advantage. The consequence was a massive diversion of effort. The principle of "Germany first" was abandoned. In 1943 the Americans deployed nearly 1.9 million men in the Pacific, more than those in Europe; the U.S. Navy had 713 vessels there as opposed to 515 in the Atlantic; and there were 7,900 aircraft in the Pacific and 8,900 in Europe (fifteen groups of U.S. aircraft were diverted from Europe to the Pacific). After the invasion of French North Africa the level of forces in the region increased still further. In early 1943 the United States had 388,000 troops in the Mediterranean region and only 50,000 in Britain. Half of the American aircraft in Britain were sent to North Africa.

By early 1943, when the Americans and the British met at Casablanca to discuss the strategy to be adopted after the completion of operations in North Africa (which were taking far longer than expected because of stiff German resistance), there were serious disagreements between the two countries over how to proceed. The British retained the assumption they had developed in 1940, that an invasion should not be carried out until Germany was on the point of collapse. In addition, they favored continued operations in the Mediterranean, where they constituted the majority of Allied forces and were therefore able to have greater influence over decision-making. In fact, the British and the Americans had little alternative but to adopt a Mediterranean strategy in 1943: huge numbers of troops had been deployed in North Africa, and they could not be shipped back to Britain in time for a cross-Channel invasion, so they might as well be employed usefully while waiting for a 1944 invasion. The British wavered between invading Sicily or Sardinia but eventually plumped for the former. The Americans, badly prepared for the conference, reluctantly agreed, but there was no consensus over what to do after that. When the British and the Americans met at their next major conference in Washington in May 1943 the disagreements had become stronger. The British wanted an invasion of Italy after Sicily with the aim of forcing an Italian surrender, thereby allowing, they hoped, Allied troops to reach the Alps quickly. They assumed there would be no invasion of France until possibly 1945 or even 1946. The Americans were much better prepared for this conference and more determined to insist on their preferred strategy as they took on a greater share of the Anglo-American war effort. They wanted an invasion in May 1944 and the withdrawal of seven divisions from the Mediterranean in November 1943 (this was the maximum that Allied shipping could move).

The invasion of Sicily finally took place in July, and only after that did the Americans finally consent to invade the mainland. The British still opposed a cross-Channel invasion in 1944; they wanted to continue with the Italian operation, possibly invade Norway, and develop new operations in the eastern Mediterranean. The American secretary of war, Henry Stimson, visited London in July 1943 and reported to Roosevelt on British attitudes. On the invasion of northwest Europe he told the President that the British did not have their hearts behind such an operation and that they really believed that Germany could be beaten by battles of attrition in northern Italy and the eastern Mediterranean and in Greece, the Balkans, Rumania, and other satellite countries, and that the heavy fighting could be left to the Soviet Union. He told Roosevelt that the United States must insist on a cross-Channel attack and the U.S. Joint Chiefs of Staff agreed, arguing that the allocation of additional forces to the Mediterranean was uneconomical and assisted Germany to create a strategic stalemate in Europe. They concluded that British ideas imperiled ultimate victory. Roosevelt accepted his advisers' conclusions. The British were summoned to another conference at Quebec in August 1943. There, the Americans insisted on the adoption of their strategic priorities. The British, clearly the minor ally, had little choice but to agree. In fact, the Italian campaign, on which the British placed so much hope, turned out to be a major diversion of effort that achieved little. The Germans reacted quickly to the Allied invasion of the mainland and the Italian attempt to change sides by moving in reinforcements and securing control of the country. The topography of Italy gave immense advantages to the defender, and so inferior German forces were able to reduce the Allied advance up the peninsula to a crawl. It took them nearly a year to move from near Naples to Rome, and by the spring of 1945 they had still not reached the main cities of the north.

By late 1943 the British had little influence over Anglo-American strategy. The U.S. government insisted that since it was supplying the bulk of the forces in Europe, its priorities would have to be accepted. The invasion of France, perhaps the most complex operation of the war, finally went ahead successfully in June 1944. Although the battle in Normandy took longer than Allied planners expected, it led to the disintegration of German forces across northwest Europe. The British had rightly opposed the Americans over their determination to have an invasion of the south of France. Originally this had been scheduled for the same time as the landings in Normandy. However, it was postponed because the landing craft were needed in a vain attempt to speed up the stalled Italian campaign. By the time they were released the attack on the south of France had been delayed until mid-August. By then, however, it made no strategic sense: the Allies had already broken out of the Normandy bridgehead and France was on the point of being liberated. These arguments were the last Anglo-American disputes over strategy. Once the cross-Channel invasion had been agreed on, operations were in the hands of the military commanders. The supreme Allied commander was an American, and the Americans had fifty-five divisions deployed in northwest Europe to Britain's thirteen. Not surprisingly, in this situation they dominated decision-making.

In terms of the overall strategy of the war the Anglo-American disputes about how best to deploy their forces were relatively unimportant. The outcome of the Second World War in Europe was decided on the eastern front. The Soviet Union faced the overwhelming mass of the German army, and it was their efforts that broke its strength. Of the roughly 13.5 million German casualties and prisoners during the war, 10 million occurred on the eastern front. Nearly 5 million German soldiers were killed or wounded on the eastern front, and less than 600,000 in northwest Europe. Compared with the huge battles of the eastern front, those in other theaters of the war were small. In June 1941, at the start of the German attack, the Soviet Union faced over 98 percent of the combat strength of the German army,

134 divisions, while the British were fighting 2 understrength divisions in the North African desert. Even after American entry into the war this situation did not change fundamentally. Before June 1944 the western Allies never fought more than 10 percent of the German army, and usually it was nearer 2 or 3 percent. At times, such as June 1943, they were not engaged in any fighting at all. Even after the Normandy invasion, the overwhelming bulk of the German army remained on the eastern front; in the autumn of 1944 the Germans had three times as many tanks on the eastern front as they had facing the western Allies. The Soviet Union never at any stage of the war fought less than about 150 German divisions. The scale of the Soviet effort can be judged from the fact that Britain and the United States together on all fronts (including the Pacific) lost just under 600,000 men killed. The Soviet Union lost over 11 million killed on the eastern front.

The Soviets were left to fight this huge eastern-front war on their own; there was very little coordination of strategy between the western Allies and the Soviets. Soviet demands for a second front in 1941 were ignored, and even in 1942 the British and the Americans only invaded French North Africa. The Mediterranean strategy adopted in 1943 also failed to take the weight off the Soviet Union. In the four months after November 1942 the Germans moved seventeen divisions from western Europe to the eastern front. Once the invasion of Sicily demonstrated to the Germans that there would be no cross-Channel invasion in 1943 they moved more reinforcements to the east. The nearest approach to a unified strategy came at the time of the Normandy landings; the Americans and British had asked for a simultaneous Soviet attack and this was launched just over a fortnight after D-Day, once the Soviets were sure that the invasion was not a failure. Only in the last stages of the war was there any detailed coordination, and that was simply over where the two armies would meet in the center of Germany. Soviet grand strategy was at a much lower level than the Anglo-American debates. They did not have to decide where to invade. It was more a matter of shifting the balance of their forces from one part of the front to another in order to take maximum advantage of any German weaknesses. It was fitting, given their enormous military effort, that it was Soviet forces that captured Berlin in April and early May 1945.

Like the war on the eastern front, the Pacific war was also largely conducted as a separate theater. Here the Americans conducted their own war against the Japanese, and the other Allies were allowed little say in the way the campaign was conducted. U.S. strategy was largely determined by interservice rivalry. In 1942 General MacArthur was defeated in the Philippines and established his base in Australia. His strategy was based on a thrust from New Guinea, through islands such as the Solomons to the Philippines and thence on toward Japan. The U.S. Navy, however, refused to operate under an army commander and persuaded Roosevelt to establish two separate command areas for the army and navy: the navy was to control the central Pacific with an attack westward from Hawaii through the Marianas to Formosa. The Japanese garrisons in this area were not large, and the area was of little strategic importance. The result was that the United States engaged in two widely separated, uncoordinated axes of attack against Japan, which wasted resources and lives. No overall commander was appointed, even after the American recapture of the Philippines and a joint assault on Okinawa was undertaken. The Americans also failed to use their naval superiority to best effect against the Japanese economy. Not until 1944 were U.S. submarines ordered to give priority to attacks on oil tankers; if they had started a year earlier the Japanese would have faced an acute shortage by the end of 1943.

The British campaign in the Far East, concentrated first on the defense of India and then an attack into Burma, was always a sideshow, not only for the Allies but also for the Japanese. The British never faced more than 15 percent of the Japanese army and usually the figure was far lower. Their contribution to Pacific naval operations was also small. When they did finally manage to send a fleet to the Far East in February 1945 it consisted of 4 carriers (79 U.S. carriers in the naval operations), 2 battleships (23), 3 cruisers (45), and 10 destroyers (296). If Japan had been invaded in 1945–46 the United States intended to limit British and Commonwealth participation to three divisions, all of which were to be equipped with U.S. weapons and to operate only as reserves within the U.S. Army.

By the last two years of the war Allied strategy had become little more than the use of brute military power, for Allied economic superiority meant that they could outproduce Germany and Japan in every area. Sheer mass of numbers on the battlefield meant that success was guaranteed, and even German tactical superiority and flair could not compensate for gross numerical inferiority. The picture was the same in every area. In the Mediterranean theater the pattern had been clear since 1942. At the battle of El Alamein in October 1942 Germany could deploy 242 tanks with 22 in reserve. The British had 1,029, together with another 1,200 in reserve. By the end of the battle the Germans were operating with 12 tanks. When the fighting moved to Italy the German army had 229 tanks facing over 2,000 Allied vehicles. By April 1944 they were down to 60 operational tanks, an average German division had the same fighting strength as an Allied battalion, and Allied aircraft outnumbered the Germans about ten to one.

The Normandy invasion took place in conditions of overwhelming Allied military superiority. The Allies had 12,800 aircraft operating on D-Day, the Germans 319. On the ground most German divisions were at half strength and by August most Panzer divisions were down to between ten and fifteen tanks, and two had none at all. When Hitler concentrated his forces in the west for the Ardennes offensive in the winter of 1944–45 he had over 2,500 tanks available, as many as had been used in the attack on France in 1940. They were of little military significance; the Allies had over 7,000 medium tanks alone. By the time of the crossing of the Rhine two Panzer divisions had four tanks each with about 1,500 men and seventy-five guns. They had to face the British XII Corps, which had an armored division, two armored brigades, and three infantry divisions, using nearly 700 guns. The situation was the same in the air. The Luftwaffe was able to maintain a front-line strength of 5,000 aircraft from June 1943 until December 1944, a period during which British and American strength rose from 23,000 to 43,000. The major German problem was that they could no longer train pilots adequately. The Americans were training 105,000 pilots a month in early 1945, by which time the Germans were planning on taking members of the Hitler Youth, giving them a quick course of glider training, and then letting them fly the new jet fighters. A quarter of all aircraft being flown from the factories to the operational squadrons crashed because of inadequate pilots. By this time it hardly mattered anyway, because there was so little fuel to fly the aircraft. Horses and oxen were being used to tow aircraft to their takeoff points.

The situation was the same on the eastern front. By late 1943 the whole of the German Army Group North had 49 operational tanks facing over 1,000 Soviet models. In the south of the front, seventeen Panzer divisions could muster less than 500 tanks and assault guns. By the end of 1943 no Panzer division on the eastern front could deploy more than 20 tanks. Expanded German production could make little difference in the face of huge losses and the much higher rate of Soviet production. In September 1944 the Germans had 1,437 serviceable tanks, whereas the Soviet Union had just over 13,400. The Soviets also had 31,000 artillery pieces, the Germans 5,500; and over 4,800 planes, compared with Germany's 300. The size of the German army was also falling as it ran out of reserves. Between August and October 1944 the Germans had over 672,000 casualties on the eastern front but could find only 201,000 replacements. The real state of the German army was revealed in January 1945 as the Soviets deployed over 14,000 tanks. Hitler established a new "tank-destroyer" division. It consisted of overage recruits and Hitler Youth equipped with anti-tank grenades and operating on bicycles.

The picture was the same in the Far East. In October 1944 at the Battle of Leyte Gulf the U.S. Navy deployed 1,400 aircraft and the Japanese 400. By June 1945 the United States deployed 22,000 aircraft against a Japanese force of 4,000, of which about only 20 percent were operational. In the same month the remains of the Japanese fleet were sunk by American aircraft in Kure harbor, but it was no longer operational because there was no fuel left. In Burma the British and the Americans mounted 30,000 aircraft sorties in five months, the

Japanese less than 2,000. During the final attack on Rangoon in 1945 the Japanese could muster four divisions on paper, but they consisted of 20,000 emaciated and badly equipped men. The British Fourteenth Army had over 260,000 men. In addition, the Allies had 4,600 planes operational against a Japanese total of 50.

This situation in every theater of the war was the consequence of a greater Allied economic strength that could be mobilized and translated into greater military strength. Once this mobilization had been achieved the outcome of the war was assured.

VI

TECHNOLOGY

THE SECOND WORLD WAR IS OFTEN SEEN AS A CONFLICT in which scientific research and technological developments played a crucial part in deciding the outcome. Technology was certainly important, and states that lagged behind could find themselves at a severe disadvantage. In the last resort, however, technology could never compensate for greater numbers and the sheer brute power of the military force created by the largest mobilized economies. The Second World War did not witness a period of unprecedented technological advance and there is little evidence that the overall pace of change increased.

To some extent the most revolutionary changes in warfare took place during the 1930s. Most of the Second World War was fought by equipment either in service or designed during the 1930s. It was only in 1944–45 that major new developments such as jet engines, pilotless bombs, long-range rockets, and the atomic bomb were operational, and their impact was therefore limited. Some states, such as Italy and Japan, did not participate in this technological change because they lacked the industrial and scientific resources—their technology was essentially imitative. They therefore found themselves at an increasing disadvantage. For example, the Japanese began the war with excellent aircraft, such as the Zero, which outperformed most Allied aircraft, but by 1943–44 the Zero itself was outclassed. The most important advances were largely confined to the United States and Germany. Britain, for example, despite its important contribution to early theoretical work, decided that the development and production of the atomic bomb would divert too many resources from more immediately important war production. The United States funded five different ways of producing the materials required for the A-bomb, because they did not know which one might work, and at the same time also found the resources to become the world's strongest military power and supply huge quantities of aid to its allies. Some of the greatest technological advances were made in Germany—jet- and rocket-propelled aircraft, pilotless bombs, and rockets capable of traveling several hundred miles.

During the 1930s there were important changes in all three areas of warfare, but most fundamentally in air warfare. In the early 1930s fighters were lightly armed, fabric-covered biplanes capable of about 200 mph. By the late 1930s they were replaced by aluminum monoplanes with multiple machine guns or cannons, cockpit armor, self-sealing fuel tanks, and very powerful engines producing top speeds approaching 400 mph. Two-engine short-range medium bombers capable of carrying a small load over a few hundred miles were standard by the late 1930s, but already Britain and the United States (but not Germany and the Soviet Union) were working on heavy four-engine machines designed to carry a much heavier bomb load over a range of about 2,000 miles. By the end of the war the United States had the B-29 operational; conceived in the mid-1930s, it needed an 8,000-foot-long runway, cruised at 30,000 feet, and had a crew of eleven in two pressurized cabins, and virtually all its systems were electric rather than hydraulic.

At the beginning of the 1930s it was universally assumed that no effective defense could be mounted against bombers: without advance warning it was impossible to keep enough fighters airborne to locate and intercept incoming aircraft. This problem was solved in the mid-1930s by both Britain and Germany through the development of radar, the use of radio waves to locate attacking aircraft. Once radar stations were linked to ground control centers and these were linked by radio to fighter aircraft, it was possible to guide the fighters onto the bombers. Britain had an integrated air defense system operational by 1939, Germany by 1941. This significantly tilted the balance in favor of defense.

Important advances were made in other fields. More efficient engines meant that tanks could become heavier and carry more armor and larger guns. The light tanks armed with machine guns that characterized the early 1930s were being replaced by heavy tanks with 75mm guns. At sea there were few changes to battleship design, but aircraft carriers were increasingly becoming the prime capital ship, and the introduction of ASDIC (location by sound—sonar) provided at least a minimal capability to detect and attack submerged submarines.

In general, technological advance in the Second World War was characterized not by revolutionary new technologies but by improved production techniques, general improvement to basic types, improved firepower, greater mobility, and substitution of materials. One of the most effective ways of attaining greater military power was to improve industrial output through greater productivity, better design of equipment and, as a corollary, to find better ways of using the equipment. The development of management and engineering techniques was therefore important, particularly through greater investment in mechanized production. Before 1939 the world machine-tool industry was dominated by the United States and Germany. British manufacture of Merlin engines for the Spitfire and the production of various types of valves and fuses depended on U.S. machine tools, and some types of bomb and shell manufacture depended on machine tools from Germany. In 1940 over half of Britain's machine-tool requirements were filled from the United States, although the British were then able to copy designs and produce their own models. However, British productivity lagged behind that of their rivals: in 1943 Germany had two-thirds more machine tools, and in the United States machine-tool output rose sevenfold between 1939 and 1942. The result was that U.S. armaments productivity levels were far higher than those in Britain: the average American aircraft factory (which was about twice the size of the average British factory) produced sixty aircraft a week, an average British factory ten.

Another way to improve output was to simplify designs. In the Soviet Union an Ilyushin 4 bomber in 1941 took 20,000 man-hours to manufacture; by 1943 this had fallen to 12,500 hours. In the United States the time to make an Oerlikon antiaircraft gun was reduced from 132 hours to just 35. During the war the cost of making a U.S. bomber fell to a third of its 1940 level. One of the most remarkable changes was in merchant-ship construction. During the war the United States adopted standardized designs: the so-called Liberty ships. In particular, after 1940 welding was used instead of riveting. Average construction time fell from thirty-five weeks in 1939 to fifty days in 1943. Britain was slow to adopt such a new technique; it was not used until late 1943. To some extent, though, designs could not be altered. The Spitfire was extremely complicated to build, and it took 13,000 man-hours; its German equivalent, the Me-109, just 4,000 hours. Better management techniques could produce more equipment, but it was vital to decide how often to introduce improvements. If this was done too often output would fall because of continual disruption to production. If it was not done often enough, performance on the battlefield would suffer.

During the war the Spitfire went through twenty-four different marks and its speed rose from 355 mph to 450 mph. A naval variant was produced, and the Hurricane fighter was also adapted to a ground-attack role through the use of antitank cannon. The output of the Merlin engine, originally designed for the Spitfire, was doubled, and it was used to power the Lancaster bomber and the Mosquito. It also transformed the performance of the American P-51B fighter, the Mustang. This aircraft was ordered by the RAF in 1940, but when it was delivered in 1942 it was severely underpowered and was therefore ineffective. The introduction by the British of the Merlin engine and also disposable drop fuel tanks turned it into the aircraft that the USAAF (U.S. Army Air Forces) desperately needed but that two years earlier had been thought impossible: a long-range fighter capable of escorting bombers in daylight raids over Germany. When fully modified it had a speed of 455 mph at 30,000 feet and was capable of outperforming any German fighter, even over Germany, making it the essential weapon in securing Allied air supremacy.

The Soviet Union carried the policy of long production runs of a small range of types to its greatest extreme. They concentrated on only six basic aircraft: two fighters, one fighter-bomber, one medium bomber, and two trainers. The LA-5 fighter was given a new engine in 1943 and turned into the LA-7 with a speed of over 400 mph; armed with two cannons it was one of the best in the world. The Yak-1 was even more adaptable. It was modified to become the high-performance Yak-7, which when armed with a 37mm cannon became the Yak-9. Without the cannon it was a long-range escort fighter and with different armament again it became a highly effective tank-attack aircraft. One of the most successful tanks in the war, the Soviets' T-34, remained largely unchanged, apart from a higher-performance 85mm gun. The chassis of the T-34 was used as the base for the SU-122 self-propelled gun, which was delivered within a month of the first order being placed. In contrast with the Soviets, the Japanese had to cope with the complications caused by trying to maintain in service a multitude of different types. The Japanese navy had 53 basic aircraft with 112 variations, and the army air force had 37 basic models with 52 variants.

Another major focus of technological change during the war was greater mobility and increased firepower. The German army was heavily reliant on horsepower, but the Americans began with the objective, which in practice was not fully met, of a completely motorized army. The United States concentrated on the production of trucks (many of which went to equip the Soviet army) and also new types such as tank transporters to save wear and tear on the tanks themselves as well as new ideas such as amphibious vehicles and jeeps. Firepower was increased significantly in many fields through the use of more effective propellants and explosives and entirely new ideas such as the proximity fuse invented by the British and the German magnetic mine. On the Allied side, the infantry were increasingly equipped with recoilless rifles, bazookas, and other anti-tank weapons. Although tank armor was improved steadily, this was countered by the introduction of armor-piercing incendiary ammunition. In air warfare, bombs became much larger. During the Blitz on Britain the Luftwaffe were using bombs weighing only a few hundred pounds. The Allies produced not only highly effective incendiary bombs but also the 12,000-pound "blockbuster" bomb. By the end of the war the 22,000-pound "grand slam" was developed and the United States was working on a 44,000-pound bomb.

The substitution of materials was also an important focus of technological improvement. At first glance one of the most unlikely was the use of wooden aircraft. The British developed the Mosquito (against the strong opposition of the RAF), and it became one of the most effective aircraft of the war in a variety of roles: reconnaissance, light bomber, and target marking. Although unarmed, its speed was so high it could not be caught by any German fighter. Adoption of wooden construction by the Soviet Union saved over 30,000 tons of aluminum. Substitution of scarce materials was particularly important for Germany. By 1939 Germany was producing about 2.3 million tons of synthetic oil from coal; by 1943 it increased its output to nearly 6 million tons, which was about half its total requirements. Cut off from world rubber production it was already synthetically producing a quarter of its total requirements in 1939, and by 1942 it was producing more synthetic rubber per year than its entire prewar consumption of rubber. The United States had to go through a similar process after the loss of Malayan and Dutch East Indies rubber production to Japan in early 1942.

The one country that attempted to use qualitative superiority to compensate for quantitative inferiority was Germany. In 1943 the armaments minister, Albert Speer, convinced Hitler that the way to counter the greater productive capacity of the Allies was to develop advanced weapons that would prolong the war and wear out Germany's opponents. The problem with this approach was judging whether the scientific effort involved and the diversion of industrial resources was justified by the effectiveness of the new weapons. In some cases the effort was clearly worthwhile. Hitler's determination to develop the Panther tank and the later, even more heavily armored 75mm-gunned Tiger tank was clearly justified; the Tiger was perhaps the most effective tank of the whole war. It was a match for any Soviet tank, it outranged even the upgunned 76mm U.S. Sherman, and its frontal armor could not be penetrated by a Sherman except at very close range. As early as 1936 the German air force was working on the initial designs of what became the V-1, a jet-propelled, pilotless bomb guided by a gyromagnetic system. Full-scale production began in 1943 and the bomb was operational by the summer of 1944. It was relatively easy to make in large quantities (it took only 800 man-hours), and being made out of steel, it did not compete for scarce aluminum needed for aircraft production. The German army had a rival system, a long-range rocket that became known as the V-2 (A4 to the Germans). This project demonstrated the pitfalls of depending on high technology. The electronic system needed to control the rocket in its ascent stage was highly complex, and over three thousand test firings were required before it became operational—and even then it was far from reliable. It cost twenty times as much as a V-1, it could not be mass-produced, the electronic equipment could be made only at the expense of similar equipment for U-boats and radar systems, and although it could not be intercepted its military value was very limited.

The basic problem for Germany, though, was that these weapons could not be brought into service until too late in the war and superiority could be obtained only in a few limited areas. Germany did not have the resources to put some of its ideas, such as an air-to-ground missile, into development and production. The V-1 launch sites in northern France and the Low Countries were nearly all overrun within months of becoming operational. Advanced aircraft such as the Me-262 and the He-162 jet aircraft (the first in squadron service anywhere in the world) and the Me-263 rocket-propelled fighter with swept wings, although superior to any Allied design, could not compensate for the sheer mass of Allied aircraft. Fuel was short, and experienced pilots limited in number, and so by the time they were operational it was already too late.

The development of new weapons was not a risk-free process and all the combatants had some spectacular failures. The Germans produced two disastrous heavy bombers, the He-177 and Ju-88. The British developed aircraft that are now largely unknown, and de-servedly so: the Westland Welkin fighter, the Bristol Buckingham medium bomber, and the Vickers Windsor and Warwick bombers.

The intended replacement for the Spitfire and the Hurricane, the Typhoon, was inferior to the new German Focke-Wulf-190 fighter and had to be turned into a ground-attack aircraft. The second attempt, the Tempest, was little better. Attempts to cut down development time and rush designs into production were usually disastrous. The Churchill tank was developed in six months, but it took another two years gradually to eliminate serious defects in the design. Indeed, throughout the war the British had major problems in developing an adequate tank. The Crusader was so unreliable that normally a quarter of the fleet was nonoperational and in need of repairs. The Covenator was a total failure—it even had the engine radiator positioned in the crew compartment. The result of these failures was that the British had to rely on American tanks, at first Grants and Stuarts and then the excellent Sherman, and by the summer of 1944 two thirds of the tanks in the British army were U.S. models.

A major problem with the development of new weapons and equipment was the opposition's use of countermeasures. This was particularly the case with radar and electronic warfare and was a major feature of the bomber offensives by both Germany and Britain. Neither side could afford to neglect this aspect of the battle, which meant that considerable scientific effort produced only short-term operational gains rather than permanent superiority, because over time each side managed to cancel out the other. In 1940 the German bombers were using beams to navigate and determine when they were over their target, a system known as Knickebein. The British were able to develop countermeasures that could "bend" the beam but took until March 1942 to bring into service their own equivalent system, Gee. This was far more advanced than the German system and worked on the principle of very small time intervals in the transmission of the beam from three separate stations to enable the navigator in the bomber to plot his position on a special grid. Within seven months it was unusable, when the Germans deployed the Heinrich jamming system, and it was replaced by Oboe, a simpler beam system.

One of the major developments in the electronic war was airborne radar, which depended on the cavity magnetron, first developed in

Britain and shortly afterward by Germany. It was the basis of the H2S radar system that was capable of distinguishing some features on the ground, in particular, coastlines, lakes, and rivers. It was introduced in January 1943, but by September the Germans had deployed the ground-based Naxburg equipment capable of jamming H2S and by January 1944 they had an airborne jammer, Naxos, working. Both sides developed airborne radars capable of detecting other aircraft and both produced countermeasures. The Germans first deployed the Lichtenstein radar in February 1942 but by June 1943 the British had Serrate equipment, which detected Lichtenstein radar emissions and guided their fighters onto the German fighters. The British developed Monica to enable bombers to detect fighters approaching from the rear, but the Germans countered with the Flensburg system, which detected Monica emissions, and the British had to withdraw their equipment.

The use of I.F.F. (Identification, Friend and Foe) systems was equally problematic. Until the spring of 1944 British bombers kept their I.F.F. systems switched on over Germany in the belief that they jammed German radars, despite overwhelming scientific evidence that the Germans were using the transmissions to home in on the bombers. By October 1944 the British had developed Perfectos, an airborne transmitter-receiver that activated the German I.F.F. set and enabled fighters to locate their opponents. In July 1943 the British first used Window, strips of metal foil dropped by attacking aircraft that swamped German radar systems and made it very difficult to detect incoming bombers. Within three months the Germans deployed SN-2 airborne radar, which was not affected by Window, and a month later adapted their standard ground-based Würzburg radars to distinguish between Window and genuine aircraft. Not until September 1944 were the British able to adapt Window to jam SN-2 radars.

In chemical and biological warfare, weapons were developed but not used on a major scale, though the Allies were certainly prepared to use them if necessary. Chemical warfare had been used in the First World War, but its first use was banned by the 1925 Geneva Convention. In 1940 the British were prepared to use gas if a German invasion had been successful in getting troops onshore. However, by the autumn they decided against initiating its use because they believed that the Germans held larger stocks. In 1943 the British and the Americans agreed that if the Germans used gas against the Soviet Union, they would retaliate, and a public warning was issued. In the summer of 1944, after the first V-1 attacks on London, Churchill wanted "a cold-blooded calculation" made on whether it would be advantageous to use poison gas. In retaliation for the bombardment he wanted to "drench" the Ruhr and many other cities in Germany. The Chiefs of Staff opposed such a move, fearing that the British people would react badly in the face of German retaliation with their own gas attacks. By early 1945 the United States was drawing up plans for attacks on Japanese crops using defoliants.

The technology for chemical warfare was widely available, but biological warfare required considerable development aimed at deciding what type of germs to use and then how to transmit them. The Japanese had a special facility, Unit 731, operating in Manchuria, developing biological warfare and carrying out experiments on prisoners of war and captured civilians. Some successful attempts were made to spread plague in China, and the United States captured anthrax capsules from Japanese forces on New Guinea. The British also had an active program, again using anthrax, and they heavily contaminated one Scottish island during experimental work. In early 1942 Hitler decided that Germany would in no circumstances undertake offensive biological warfare operations, despite clear intelligence information about the British program. British efforts were dwarfed by Americans'. A major program, begun before Pearl Harbor, concentrated on anthrax, botulin, and cholera and, later, brucella (enough was produced to theoretically kill the entire population of the world), tularemia, and brucellosis. A 6,000-acre production facility was built in Indiana and three large testing areas were created. By 1943 production of four-pound anthrax bombs was started, and the production facility was geared to produce one million such bombs a month, together with 275,000 botulin bombs. The British ordered 500,000 anthrax bombs from the Americans and prepared millions of cakes of linseed feed impregnated with anthrax, which it intended to drop all over Germany. In the end, chemical and biological warfare were not used on any significant scale during the war, partly because of the fear of retaliation and the limited gains expected from its use.

One major new weapon that did mark a decisive change in the nature of warfare was developed and used: the atomic bomb. The state of the scientific knowledge necessary to develop a bomb was very similar on both sides, but decisions about its development illustrate very clearly their different strategic positions and economic strengths.

In late 1938 two German scientists first split the uranium atom and within a few months had confirmed that the splitting released high-speed neutrons and that a chain reaction and the creation of huge amounts of energy was theoretically possible. By mid-1939 scientists knew that the rare isotope U-235, which makes up less than 1 percent of natural uranium, was the fissile material. These results were published in scientific journals and were widely available just before the outbreak of the war. By September 1939 scientists were generally agreed that in theory a bomb was possible, but they were unclear as to whether it would work, what size it would be, or how to separate out U-235. Preliminary work on the feasibility of a bomb was under way in five countries: the United States, Britain, France, Germany, and the Soviet Union; the French work was abandoned in May 1940, and the Japanese started work at about the same time.

The next stages in the theoretical work were similar in all these countries and by the autumn of 1941 they had arrived at roughly the same point. By October 1939 the German army had established a team made up of senior physicists such as Werner Heisenberg working on uranium as an explosive. By the summer of 1940 they knew that energy production was possible, that U-235 would be explosive, and that a new element (later called plutonium), which could be produced in a reactor moderated by either heavy water or highly pure carbon, would be stable and highly explosive. In April 1940 I. G. Farben took over a Norwegian company and stepped up production of heavy water. For the remainder of 1940 and 1941 the German team worked on different methods of separating U-235.

In the United States, Albert Einstein told President Roosevelt just after the outbreak of the war that a bomb was theoretically possible. Teams of scientists were working on different aspects of the problem. Experimental separation of U-235 was achieved in late February 1940 at the University of Minnesota—enough to confirm that the material was indeed fissile. By late 1940 U.S. scientists had, like their German counterparts, carried out theoretical work on "element 94" (plutonium) and they knew it was possible to produce it in a reactor fueled with uranium, thereby avoiding the extremely difficult uranium-separation process. By the summer of 1941 the United States was still lacking an integrated program or a clear understanding on whether a bomb could be made.

That understanding was provided by the British. In Britain, two émigré scientists, Otto Frisch and Rudolf Peirels, had by early 1940 shown that uranium separation was theoretically possible, calculated that a bomb containing no more than a few pounds of explosive should work, that when the bomb was detonated it would be the equivalent of some tens of thousands of tons of conventional explosive, and that about a fifth of the energy would be released as radioactive debris causing contamination over a wide area. The British set up the MAUD committee in the summer of 1940 to take this work further. Within a year it had confirmed the main findings of Frisch and Peirels's work.

In 1941, each country apart from Japan, where research work was at a low level, made crucial decisions about whether to take its research efforts further and attempt to build a bomb. Soviet work had begun in 1939, too, and when prominent American scientists stopped publishing their research findings, Soviet scientists realized that the United States was working on a bomb. There is little reason to doubt that Soviet scientists had made the same theoretical breakthroughs as others. However, the German attack in 1941 meant that every effort had to be concentrated on survival and on producing equipment of immediate value. Scientific work on the atomic bomb was severely cut back. Work did not restart as a top priority until early 1943. The Germans undertook a major review of their project at the end of 1941. Their research work was as advanced as elsewhere, the emigration of Jewish scientists did not handicap them, and the scientific team worked as willingly on the project as those in other countries. They understood that building a bomb would need a major investment and guessed correctly that a bomb would not be operational for about three years and that it would therefore not be of use in a war they still expected to last no more than another two years. They believed that the effort involved would detract from the more important and immediate war effort. In early 1942 the project was cut back and nine small scientific teams were created to do research on specific aspects of the problem but with no intention of building a bomb. During the rest of the war, the separation and enrichment of uranium was obtained on an experimental basis and small reactors were built that were capable of a self-sustaining chain reaction to create plutonium. The Allies believed the Germans had decided to build a bomb and their attacks on Norwegian heavy water production were intended to stop the German program. In fact, these attacks had little effect.

The British were in the same position as the Germans. They knew that a bomb could be made but in 1941 decided that it was beyond their means during the war. The investment required would involve a substantial diversion of resources from the war effort and in addition there were concerns that German bombing might destroy any plants that were built. The British felt they had no alternative but to pass their information on to the Americans. When the Americans formally received the report of the MAUD committee in the autumn of 1941 it played a vital part in their decision to go ahead with a bomb project. When Roosevelt was briefed in early October 1941 the information he was given on explosive power, cost, and time scale for development was wrong. Nevertheless, the belief that the atomic bomb could be made, that the Germans were probably working on one, and that it would play a crucial part in the postwar world ensured that the Americans would go ahead. The British were offered a joint program but rejected the deal, fearing they would be dependent on the United States after the war. Within a few months they realized they had made a serious mistake but by then the United States would offer no more than limited cooperation in the U.S.-directed program.

After Pearl Harbor the United States gave the project top priority. A report to Roosevelt in March 1942 advised that there were five possible routes to the production of enough explosive: three ways of separating enough U-235 (a centrifuge plant, gaseous diffusion, and electromagnetic) and two ways of producing plutonium (a reactor moderated by either heavy water or graphite). Scientists had no idea which would work and none had been tried on more than a laboratory scale, some not even at that level. Roosevelt ordered that time, not money, was the most important element (the Americans thought the Germans might be ahead by as much as a year) and that all five routes should be developed simultaneously. In June 1942 the army took over the project, which gave them control of a vast construction effort and huge scientific program. The scale of the effort can be judged from the fact that when the Japanese abandoned their program in early 1943 they estimated that even one uranium-separation process would take up 10 percent of the nation's electrical capacity and half its copper production and still take ten years to complete.

In early December 1942 the first atomic "reactor" in the world, at the University of Chicago, produced a self-sustaining chain reaction. The route to the creation of plutonium was open. Production facilities were built even before it was clear that the processes would work on more than a laboratory scale. Electromagnetic and gaseous-diffusion plants were built in Tennessee at Oak Ridge (the latter required the production of over 5 million complex and chemically highly pure barrier tubes), and three reactors to produce plutonium were built at Hanford, Washington. Electromagnetic separation was achieved on an industrial scale in September 1943, but the process did not work properly until the spring of 1944. The gaseous-diffusion plant was not operational until January 1945. The two processes were in fact used in parallel to attain maximum enrichment. The Hanford plutonium facility began production in late December 1944. Apart from manufacturing the material required for an atomic bomb, a vast scientific effort was also required on bomb design, and extremely difficult theoretical problems had to be solved. By early 1943 initial work was well under way (the principle of the enormously more powerful H-bomb was understood and accepted as the postwar objective), and a special laboratory built at Los Alamos, in New Mexico. By the autumn of 1944 it was clear that Germany was not working on an atomic bomb, but the pace of the American work did not slow down. In early 1945 bomb-grade U-235 was available at the Los Alamos production facility, although some of the theoretical problems in bomb design were not solved until June. The first experimental bomb was tested on July 16, 1945, at the Alamogordo bombing range, and had the explosive power of about 18,000 tons of TNT, four times what the scientists had expected. Enough material was available to build a small number of operational bombs.

Scientific and technical effort was also vitally important in some areas of intelligence gathering and code breaking, though the use of agents required less scientific effort. Countries on both sides had a number of agents and spy rings operational. The Soviets were one of the most successful. They had a major group in Switzerland, the "Red Orchestra" and its subsection, the "Lucy" ring. Through an agent in the German High Command who is still known only by his code name, "Werther," they received high-grade information on German plans for a limited period, until the Swiss broke up the ring in the autumn of 1943. The Soviets also had an agent, Richard Sorge, inside the German embassy in Tokyo and penetrated British intelligence with agents such as Blunt in MI5, Philby in MI6, and Uren in S.O.E. (Special Operations Executive). In addition they had an informant, Fuchs, working on the American A-bomb program. The British obtained some information from discontented members of the German Abwehr. The Germans were also able to place some agents inside the Soviet bureaucracy such as Mishinskii, a senior commissar in the Moscow party organization.

Overall, however, the difficulty of recruiting and operating individual agents in wartime meant that intelligence from these sources was limited. There was also the danger that agents would be turned. The British managed to capture every German agent in Britain and through the "double-cross" operation were able to send false messages back to Germany for the duration of the war, which was particularly important in the period before D-Day. The Germans had their successes, too. In 1942 they penetrated most of the S.O.E. networks in Belgium and the next year had major triumphs in France—large numbers of agents were captured and most supplies dropped for them fell into German hands. The most spectacular of all the German efforts was "Operation North Pole" in the Netherlands. Using captured agents, the Germans sent over two thousand false messages back to London and gained control of all the S.O.E. networks in the country. Between June 1942 and the autumn of 1943, forty-three out of fifty-six agents dropped in the Netherlands were captured, and thirty-six of them were executed. All supplies dropped were captured by the Germans.

The most important area for scientific and technological effort was in the breaking of enemy codes; for example, by the end of the war the British and the Americans had produced the first primitive computers for this task. The Germans had some success at this level. The most important was probably their ability to read large parts of the Royal Navy's signals during the first four years of the war. This was crucial in operations such as the Norwegian campaign and was useful during the Battle of the Atlantic. Elsewhere their record was patchy. They were able to break some Soviet codes, especially of the army, at a tactical level where radio procedures were particularly poor. They read the U.S. military attaché codes in 1941 and early 1942, which provided valuable information about operations in North Africa. They also intercepted and unscrambled the radio-telephone circuit between Britain and the United States and occasionally listened in on conversations between Roosevelt and Churchill but learned little of any importance. Japan and Italy had little success at code breaking.

The most spectacular code-breaking successes were obtained by Britain and the United States. Using Polish and French work on the German Enigma coding machine used for nearly all German military radio communications, the British were able by the summer of 1940 to begin reading German signals with increasing frequency and speed. At first only Luftwaffe codes could be read, but in mid-1941 the capture of the U-boat *U-110* enabled naval codes to be read until February 1942. At that time changes to the naval Enigma machine again made signals difficult to read until early 1943. Army codes were broken in 1942 and also the system used to transmit messages from Hitler's headquarters to Army Groups. The British shared this information with the Americans from 1940, even though they were still neutral. After U.S. entry into the war the two countries developed a joint system for intercepting and decoding German messages and sending the results quickly to both political leaders and, more important, to military commanders so that they could make operational decisions on the basis of the material.

The Americans broke Japanese codes and in general shared most of the results with the British. They were able to read the Japanese diplomatic code ("Purple"), which gave important information about Japanese policy in the pre–Pearl Harbor period. It was of some use after 1941 in reading messages from the Japanese ambassador in Berlin, which often contained Hitler's assessments of the progress of the war and even some military information, such as the state of the beach defenses in France. From late 1940 the Americans were also reading the Japanese naval code. The code was changed just before Pearl Harbor and for a while the United States was able to read only just over 10 percent of a message. By April 1942 a major breakthrough was made and the code could be read fairly easily until August, when the Japanese made more changes. The ability to read the naval code was particularly important at this time. It enabled the United States to deploy its limited fleet most effectively. In the Battle of the Coral Sea in May, knowledge of the code made it possible to stop the Japanese invasion of Port Moresby in New Guinea. In June 1942 the Americans were able to position their fleet so as to defeat the Japanese attack on Midway. The Japanese army code was not broken until the spring of 1943 and then only on an intermittent basis until February 1944.

Access to good intelligence information did not guarantee that it would be acted upon, and the Allies in particular had some spectacular intelligence failures. The Americans were reading Japanese diplomatic messages in the period of the long negotiations between the two countries in the summer and autumn of 1941. They therefore knew that the Japanese were setting a deadline of the end of November for negotiations to succeed. When the talks broke down they failed to take adequate precautionary measures; they even expected a Japanese attack, but did not put their forces on alert. In the period before the German attack in June 1941 the Soviet leadership had extensive information that the Germans were preparing to attack. At a political level they were given warnings on six different occasions by the British, twice by their own ambassador in Berlin, once by the German ambassador in Moscow, and once by the Americans. At a military level their attaché in Berlin was sending a stream of warnings beginning as early as December 1940. From February their spy ring in Switzerland reported German troop movements to the east and gave an accurate date for the expected attack. Richard Sorge in Tokyo also gave a series of reports about the plan to invade the Soviet Union. The Soviet leadership discounted all this information. Those from Britain and the United States were thought to be designed merely to provoke the Soviets into a conflict with Germany. The information from the various spies was not always clear and was often contradictory about the date of the attack. The result was that, like the Americans later in 1941, the Soviet Union was largely unprepared to meet what seemed to be a "surprise" attack.

It is often claimed that the ability of the British and the Americans to read German messages sent via Enigma machines, "Ultra" intelligence, significantly shortened the war. There are, however, a number of reasons to seriously doubt that claim. The mere possession of intelligence information was not in itself a way of winning the war. During 1940 and 1941 the British had increasing success in breaking German codes and they were able to draw better conclusions about German strategy and intended operations than without this information, but their military weakness meant that they were unable to take advantage of this information. Thus, although they knew of the German intention to invade Greece, they were unable to send sufficient forces to take advantage of the situation and were subjected to a humiliating defeat. Near complete knowledge about German plans to invade Crete still did not enable the British to avoid another rapid defeat.

Detailed tactical information about German plans and the state of German forces was of little use if Allied commanders were unwilling to take advantage of the situation. This was particularly noticeable in Montgomery's handling of British forces after the initial success at El Alamein in November 1942 (where despite Ultra information he had embarked on an unimaginative frontal assault). As the Germans began to retreat the British knew that the two German Panzer divisions had eleven serviceable tanks between them, a quarter of their normal ammunition stocks, and enough fuel for four days. Montgomery's reaction was to sack commanders who showed any initiative in attacking the Germans. By November 17 Ultra showed that the Germans were virtually immobilized in Benghazi for lack of fuel. Montgomery then took twelve days to devise a plan for another crude frontal assault which was not to take place until December 17. By December 8 he knew that the Germans intended to withdraw if attacked. He only brought forward his planned attack by twenty-four hours. His failure to attack enabled the Germans to destroy the port at Benghazi. Montgomery repeated this performance at the end of December in front of Tripoli, when he waited three weeks before attacking despite the fact that he knew he had 532 front-line tanks and the Germans 37.

The campaign in Italy also showed little ability by Allied commanders to take advantage of Ultra intelligence. Similarly, in northwest Europe in 1944–45 Ultra intelligence did not lead to brilliantly conducted campaigns and there were often major failures, such as the German escape from the Falaise pocket in Normandy. Even in the Battle of the Atlantic, Ultra had only a limited impact. It was important in 1941 in enabling the British to reroute convoys away from the U-boats. Once U-boat numbers increased, however, this was no longer possible. Even knowing where the U-boats were operating was of limited use unless they could be attacked. Tactical improvements in the way naval battles were fought were crucial, as was the closing of the "air gap" by the provision of escort carriers and long-range patrol aircraft. In the last resort it was the American ability to build merchant ships far faster than the Germans could ever sink them that determined the ultimate outcome of the battle.

Even if the western Allies had been able to make good use of Ultra intelligence on the tactical level, its effect on the war would have been limited, because Ultra information could not compensate for failures in Allied strategy. The Anglo-American decision not to invade the Continent in 1943 and instead to invade French North

Africa followed by a Mediterranean campaign in 1943 prolonged the war. Most important of all, as far as is known the Soviets did not have the equivalent of Ultra intelligence and the British and Americans were not prepared to share the secret with them. Yet it was on the eastern front that the crucial battles of the Second World War took place and the German army was defeated. Intelligence successes were therefore similar in their impact to technological improvement. Both Germany and the Allies found that there was no shortcut to victory and no way in which the overwhelming importance of material superiority could be denied.

VII

COMBAT

THE SECOND WORLD WAR IS USUALLY SEEN AS A "MOD-
ern" war, in contrast to the First World War. The terrible experience
of four years of trench warfare, seared into the European conscious-
ness, is regarded as uniquely horrible. The 1939–45 conflict is viewed,
particularly in Britain and the United States, as a highly mobile war
in which tanks and planes were the dominant weapons and in which,
thanks to this firepower, casualties were relatively light. Although
British and American casualties were indeed low—for Britain, about
a quarter of First World War losses—there is a profound misappre-
hension of the nature of combat in the Second World War. Casualty
rates were in fact as bad as those of the First World War, and the
conditions of warfare in many cases, especially in the Far East, far
worse. In the primary conflict on the eastern front, loss rates on both
sides were very high and conditions were of a barbaric intensity un-
matched by almost any other conflict. The Second World War was
probably the most brutal war fought in modern times.

Overall the war was characterized by two features. First, the overwhelming majority of men conscripted never saw combat. In 1945
there were 11 million men in the U.S. Army, but only 2 million (less
than 20 percent) were in the ninety combat divisions, and of these,
just 700,000 (6 percent) were in the infantry. Similarly, the Germans
called up 10.5 million men for the army and the Waffen S.S. but only
210 combat divisions with 2.5 million men were maintained. And,

even within a combat division, only a small minority actually fought. A British infantry division normally consisted of 17,000 men, but only 4,000 of them carried weapons. The number actually involved in combat was even smaller. Postwar analysis in the U.S. Army showed that even in combat units, only 15 percent of men took any part in the fighting, and even under intense local pressure, only a quarter of the men who had weapons actually fired them. For the overwhelming majority of servicemen the war meant a routine job away from the fighting. In 1940, at the height of the Battle of Britain and despite claims of a pilot shortage, the RAF had more pilots sitting behind desks than in the whole of its Fighter and Bomber commands put together. In June 1944 the number of men in the U.S. Army qualified for overseas service but filling jobs in the interior of the United States exceeded the number of infantrymen in Europe and the Mediterranean combined, and they were often designated as healthier too.

Second, warfare was surprisingly "unmodern." The German army depended on horses for its mobility and the British continued to use pigeons for delivering messages in the Far East and North Africa, and aircrew also carried pigeons for release in case they were shot down over the sea. The Italians even carried out a cavalry charge at Keren in Eritrea in January 1941; not surprisingly, the casualty rate was nearly 70 percent. Some of the fighting was also extremely small scale. In Norway, total losses on both sides were less than 10,000 and in the Balkans in 1941 the Germans lost less than 5,000 killed. During the first eleven days of the fighting in France and Belgium in 1940 the British suffered less than 500 casualties. Although in retrospect the tank is seen as the dominant element in land warfare, in practice its contribution was very limited. Less than 8 percent of the German army consisted of Panzer divisions. Overall only 12 percent of the German army was motorized; the British were at about the same level and the Americans much higher, at 27 percent in northwest Europe. Although the Germans scored a remarkable success in the armored breakthrough at Sedan in May 1940, this was not typical of warfare as a whole. In North Africa the use of tanks was restricted by logistical problems. In general, tanks were heavily constrained by unsuitable terrain, as in Italy and the Pacific, and unreliability. In 1940, mechanical breakdowns made up three quarters of all British tank casualties. The situation was no better later in the war. During the battle for the Reichswald forest in February 1945 the Ninth Royal Tank regiment had 85 tank casualties, but only 20 percent were due to enemy action; 42 percent were caused by mechanical failure, and the other 38 percent became bogged down in the terrain. Neither the British nor the Americans showed much tactical flair in the handling of tanks, tending to avoid mass tank battles and preferring to use them as close support of the infantry. In practice, the main weapon for the British and the Americans was artillery. In 1944–45 in northwest Europe they fired over 48 million rounds at about the same rate as they had in the static trench warfare between 1914 and 1918.

Combat in the Second World War was not characterized by rapid movement. Campaigns such as France in 1940, the Soviet Union in the summer of 1941, and France and Belgium in the summer of 1944 were exceptions rather than the rule. Many campaigns, such as that in Italy in 1943–45 were slow or static, and First World War–style trench systems were common in northern France in the winter of 1939–40 and even in the North African desert (the "Knightsbridge box"). Combat was more likely to be close infantry fighting in concentrated areas as at Monte Cassino, Imphal, Guadalcanal, Iwo Jima, Salerno, and Anzio. For most soldiers engaged in combat, war meant a struggle over very small objectives—individual buildings and even piles of rubble—and often very heavy losses were incurred for minor gains. Even in relatively open country, actions usually came down to an infantry advance under fire with hand-to-hand fighting, as in the bocage of Normandy, the forests of western Germany, and especially during the Japanese defense of Pacific islands.

This sort of warfare was particularly common during fighting in the centers of cities such as Stalingrad in the autumn and winter of 1942–43. On the morning of September 14, 1942, the Germans opened their attack on Stalingrad Central Railway Station and captured it at eight o'clock. Forty minutes later the Soviets recaptured it. An hour after that the Germans were in control again, and in the early afternoon a second Soviet assault regained the station. Fighting in the area went on for days, with both artillery and air bombardment and units fighting over individual drainpipes in order to secure a supply of water. For months, fighting in the city was over individual factories, and at one point Sergeant Pavlov of the Thirteenth Guards Division held one house with sixty men for fifty-eight days under constant attack. Combat was at very small unit level, so-called "storm groups" (in the Soviet army) of six or eight men armed with machine pistols, grenades, knives, and sharpened spades used as axes, with more heavily armed groups using crowbars and picks. Most of the fighting was carried out at night in trenches, basements, tunnels, and craters.

The conditions in which combat took place were often terrible. Muddy conditions seem to characterize the trench warfare of the First World War, but mud was just as prevalent in the Second World War. Such conditions typified warfare in northern France in 1939–40, Tunisia in the winter of 1942–43, Italy in the winter, the eastern front every autumn, and northwest Europe in the winter of 1944–45. One British army lieutenant described conditions in the latter theater in terms that could easily apply to Passchendaele in 1917:

> After the first couple of days we had to stretch groundsheets and gas capes to catch rainwater for drinking. No chance of shaving, as any cut would have become infected; but I had a good wash in a shell hole. Men's hands and feet were rather swollen after the rain and exposure. Had only one blanket each . . . and had to sleep two or three together to keep warm.

Conditions on the eastern front were far worse, especially in the winter. One anonymous German soldier in Stalingrad in January 1943 wrote:

> My hands are done for, and have been ever since the beginning of December. The little finger of my left hand is missing, and—what's even worse—the three middle fingers of my right one are frozen. I can only hold my mug with my thumb and little finger. I'm pretty hopeless. . . . My hands are finished.

It is not known whether the soldier survived, but he very probably did not. At this time over seven thousand Hungarian soldiers simply froze to death around Stalingrad. In the winter of 1944–45 British troops in Italy died of exposure owing to their lack of winter clothing. When the Italians "attacked" the French in the Alps in June 1940 they lost more troops to frostbite than to battle wounds.

Conditions did therefore take a very high toll. In late 1944 in the Hürtgen forest the U.S. First and Ninth armies lost 57,000 casualties to the enemy, but 70,000 to exposure, fatigue, and disease. In the horrific winter of 1941–42 in the Soviet Union the German army had nearly 500,000 men affected by illness (including skin infections, typhus, and spotted fever) and frostbite. In other theaters the situation was even worse. In the Middle East sickness caused twenty times as many casualties as combat, and even accidental injuries were as common as combat wounds. In Italy in 1943 the main diseases in order of their impact were malaria, skin diseases, venereal disease, and respiratory infections, each of which alone caused more casualties than enemy action. Because of the climate and terrain in the Pacific, conditions were even worse there. During clearance operations in eastern New Guinea in 1944–45 the Australians lost 442 men killed and 1,141 wounded but had 16,203 hospitalized, mainly for malaria. In Burma during 1942 sickness accounted for 129 times more casualties than enemy action, and although this rate was significantly reduced later in the war, nearly two thirds of the troops were affected by malaria despite intensive precautions. Medical facilities in the British and American armies were effective, and only about half as many soldiers died of their wounds as in the First World War. Elsewhere the situation was worse. Statistically, the chances of a German soldier dying of his wounds on the eastern front were twice as high as for his predecessor in the 1914–18 war.

Combat casualties in the Second World War were as high as in the First World War and in some cases far higher. This was particularly so for the infantry, which suffered the highest proportion of casualties. In the German army in the Soviet Union in 1941, over 80 percent of all casualties were in infantry units, although they constituted only about a third of the army. In the eleven U.S. divisions that fought for nine months or more in northwest Europe in 1944–45 none suffered a death rate below 15 percent; in addition, about 45 percent were wounded. In the worst cases, over 80 percent of a division were either killed or wounded. The U.S. Ninetieth Division in Normandy lost (including replacements) 100 percent of its officers and 150 percent of its men in six weeks. By the end of the war the King's Own Scottish Borderers had on average just 5 men out of 200 in each rifle company who had survived since D-Day. On other occasions combat was fierce for a short period. On Omaha Beach on D-Day three U.S. regiments suffered 2,500 casualties in a few hours. During the Dieppe raid in 1942 the Royal Regiment of Canada landed in a gully leading to the cliffs, and within three hours out of a total strength of 554 men, 95 percent were casualties, including over 40 percent dead. The first wave of troops landing on the Normandy beaches suffered very high casualties as they tried to clear beach defenses under heavy fire. For those who landed later casualty rates were much lower.

Although the infantry bore the brunt of the casualties, other sections of the army could suffer difficult conditions and very high casualty rates. The five-man crew of a Sherman tank had to fit into a vehicle twenty feet long, nine feet wide, and eleven feet high that also had to contain the engine, gas tank, ammunition, stores, and a large gun. One direct hit was usually enough to kill the crew through high-velocity shells and twisted metal flying around inside the vehicle. Getting out of the vehicle was very difficult, and ninety gallons of fuel could turn it into an inferno very quickly. Losses in armored units could be very high, especially if poor tactics were used. At the height of the Battle of El Alamein, the Ninth Armoured Brigade assaulted the German defensive positions on Kidney Ridge, driving slowly uphill toward the German guns in what was almost a repeat of the charge of the Light Brigade at Balaclava in the Crimean War. Seventy out of a total of ninety-four tanks were lost without breaching the German defenses. Five months later the Seventeenth and Twenty-first Lancers made a frontal assault, one squadron at a time, across minefields into the German gun positions in the Foudouk Pass, in Tunisia. The consequence was a casualty rate of 80 percent. In total, allowing for the men actually engaged in fighting, British and American casualties in Europe were about 13 percent killed and 32 percent wounded, almost identical with rates in the First World War.

Casualty rates in the army were high but they were sometimes even higher in the other services. The highest rate during the war was among German U-boat crews. Of the 40,900 men who served, 25,870 were killed and about 5,000 were captured—a death rate of 63 percent and an overall loss of just over three quarters. Air operations were almost as devastating. Perhaps the longest campaign of the war was that of RAF Bomber Command. Overall 59,000 aircrew were killed, 47 percent of the total. This was far worse than for units that spent the whole of the First World War in the trenches, which had a death rate of about 25 percent. Until 1944, when German fighter defenses collapsed, Bomber Command death rates were well over 60 percent. (It was a sad epitaph for those in the RAF who claimed that a bomber offensive was a way of avoiding the carnage of the First World War.) In Bomber Command an operational tour consisted of thirty missions, but an average casualty rate of 5 percent on each mission (some were twice that) meant that on average a crew did not survive an operational tour, and normally individuals were expected to complete two tours before being posted to other duties. Squadrons normally flew about seven or eight missions a month, so that on average a crew could expect to live for just over two months.

Individual operations had even worse loss rates. In May 1940 seventy-one Defiants were sent to attack the bridges across the Meuse at Sedan, but only forty returned, a loss rate of 56 percent. Three days later out of twelve Blenheims sent on a raid on Gembloux, only one returned. In mid-August 1940, eleven Blenheims of the Eighty-second Squadron attacked Aalborg airfield in Denmark, and none returned. When the USAAF joined the campaign in Europe they learned all over again the lesson the RAF had learned in the first weeks of the war: daylight bomber raids were not sustainable without continuous fighter escort. During two attacks on the ball-bearing factories at Schweinfurt the Americans lost 120 planes out of the 667 dispatched. Daylight raids had to be abandoned until the Mustang long-range fighter was available.

Combat deaths were not restricted to military personnel. During the war the British merchant navy lost about 40,000 men killed, or about a quarter of its strength, which was a far higher proportion than the Royal Navy. Nor were deaths always the result of enemy action; training could be very dangerous. In 1943–44, 5,603 USAAF pilots and 6,376 aircrew were killed in training accidents. Overall, RAF Bomber Command lost 8,440 men killed in accidents, or one in seven of all deaths. One of the worst single incidents was at Slapton Sands in Devon in April 1944 during a live-ammunition practice for D-Day. Nine German E-boats attacked the exercise. Nearly 750 U.S. soldiers were killed and their bodies bulldozed by the Allied authorities into a mass grave, the wounded were quarantined on security grounds, and the number of dead and wounded were added to the figures for the Normandy invasion. Deaths in attacks from friendly units could also be high. During the invasion of Sicily the Americans shot down twenty-three of their own transport aircraft and badly damaged another seventy. At the same time the British dropped sixty-nine gliders into the sea by mistake (about half the total force), killing over 600 men. Many units were also bombed by their own side. Before the breakout from the Normandy bridgehead, the U.S. bombed its own positions, killing over 550 men. In the same week the British bombed the Fifty-first Highland Division, killing 60 men, and then, around Caen, attacked Polish and Canadian positions, killing and wounding over 400 soldiers. Obviously, there were similar incidents in German and Soviet operations but records are more fragmentary.

Combat in the Pacific for American and British forces was a very different experience from that in Europe. The war in the Pacific was, in many respects, a racial war—a survey among U.S. soldiers showed that only 18 percent of them felt more like killing the Germans after seeing them, but nearly half felt that way about the Japanese. Indeed, at the end of 1944 an opinion poll showed that more than one in eight Americans thought that all the Japanese alive at the end of the war (soldiers and civilians) should be exterminated. Admiral William Halsey described the Japanese as "low monkeys" and asked his men to kill as many as possible to make more "monkey meat." A 1942 U.S. film on the Pacific war was entitled *The Beast of the East* and in September of that year the commander of the Pacific fleet had to issue instructions that no part of an enemy body could be used as a souvenir. In fact, Japanese skulls were polished and sent home as trophies, and it was common practice to knock out the gold teeth of both the dead and the wounded. Neither side took many prisoners.

Both Japanese and American casualties were high. Until mid-1943, Japanese aircrews were not equipped with parachutes, and even afterward those who ditched at sea were not rescued. By 1944 Japanese naval pilots were not trained in deck landing and were supposed to fly to land if they survived combat. Not surprisingly they were losing 2,000 pilots a month. On land Japanese casualties were far higher than American: during eighty-two days of fighting on Okinawa the Americans lost 12,500 dead, the Japanese over 100,000. On Saipan the number of Japanese dead was ten times higher than the American number, and on Guadalcanal, out of the garrison of 250 (subsequently massively reinforced) just 3 survived to be taken prisoner. Sometimes, however, American casualties were very high. On Iwo Jima during a six-week battle fought over seven square miles of volcanic ash and rock, the Americans lost 6,821 killed and 21,685 wounded from the 60,000 men involved, a casualty rate of just under 50 percent. The island of Tarawa saw the worst fighting of all: on the first day 1,500 were either dead or wounded out of 5,000 taking part in the invasion, and the death rate was twenty-seven times that of the Italian campaign.

The reality of combat was far worse than the people at home imagined and bore no relation to its subsequent portrayal in films. As one U.S. marine wrote after spending eighty-two days fighting on Okinawa, during which he lost twenty-one pounds, was covered in body sores, and survived a casualty rate, including reserves, of 153 percent in his company: "We lived in an environment totally incomprehensible not just to civilians but to men behind the lines." He spent a week living in a foxhole with no latrine in an area covered with decomposing bodies of different colors and dominated by the stench of death, and thought it "an environment so degrading I believed we had been flung into hell's own cesspool." A British officer described a similar scene during the long battle for Imphal on the India-Burma border:

> The most lasting impression of all was caused by the stench of decaying bodies, half-buried or lying in the open between the lines. In some of the slit trenches, rotting bodies of Japanese were used to form the protective parapet. Space was so limited that dugouts, latrines, cookhouses and graves were all close together. It was almost impossible to dig anywhere without uncovering a grave or a latrine.

During the battle of Monte Cassino in Italy the dead were left in the open to decompose and had their throats torn out by packs of wild dogs.

Men did not die tidily, bloodlessly, and painlessly. They suffocated in submarines, froze to death in the Arctic Sea on the highly dangerous convoys to the Soviet Union, drowned in the convoy battles in the Atlantic, or died slowly and agonizingly in the skies over Germany; the crew of a bomber hit either by flak or in a fighter attack had a one-in-five chance of getting out alive before the plane crashed. Ground combat was just as bad. For the individual soldier, most battles were just noise, confusion, and odd incidents that had no rational pattern and in which they rarely saw the enemy. An American survey showed that before an attack virtually all soldiers suffered from signs of fear—increased heartbeat, trembling, and sweating—and nearly a third vomited, a fifth lost control of their bowels, and one tenth urinated involuntarily. The results of such attacks showed these to be understandable reactions. One German soldier described the scene at Dieppe after the Canadian raid in 1942: "The dead on the beach— I've never seen such obscenities before. There were pieces of human beings littering the beach. There were headless bodies, there were legs, there were arms, there were even shoes with feet in them." At Tarawa one U.S. marine commanding a landing craft went mad from steering through all the severed heads and limbs near the shore, and another did so when he stepped on to a pile of bodies near the shore. One American described the scene on one of the landing beaches at Iwo Jima on the first day of the invasion:

> It resembled Doré's illustrations of the *Inferno*. Essential cargo—ammo, rations, water—was piled up in sprawling chaos. And gore, flesh and bones were lying all about. . . . There seemed to be no clean wounds; just fragments of corpses. . . . You tripped over strings of viscera fifteen feet long, over bodies which had been cut in half at the waist. Legs and arms, and heads bearing only necks, lay fifty feet from the closest torsos. As night fell the beach reeked with the stench of burning flesh.

The rapid changes to the structure of the armed forces and the creation of fighting units using civilians trained in a few months caused major problems of morale and discipline for all the belligerents. On the whole the Germans coped with this problem best. Detailed American mathematical models worked out after the war showed that the Germans consistently outfought the British and the Americans; on a man-for-man basis they inflicted casualties at about a 50 percent higher rate than opposing American and British forces. On the eastern front the difference was far greater, mainly because of the inept and self-defeating Soviet tactics. From 1943 the Germans fought a series of well-conducted defensive battles against overwhelmingly superior forces on both fronts. In early July 1944, for example, Canadian troops attacked Carpiquet airfield near Caen. They used ten infantry battalions (nearly 7,000 men), a tank regiment, and 428 guns and also had naval gunfire support. They were defeated by 150 German infantrymen with the support of three tanks and a single artillery piece. Very ad hoc formations also had to be pressed into service. In May 1944 at Velletri in Italy, 377 German prisoners were taken and they came from fifty different parent units. Nevertheless German morale did not crack until the spring of 1945, when the country was on the verge of defeat, at which point units simply disintegrated and left the front line.

Both the British and the Americans faced considerable problems when units faced combat for the first time. At Dunkirk, discipline among the troops had to be maintained by armed naval personnel, men rushed the boats in their panic, and officers deserted their men. Later, other defeats caused similar problems, for example in Crete in 1941. In Malaya the British thought that Australian units were "yellow." Some American units also broke on their first experience of fighting—Tunisia in 1942–43 and the Seventh Division in the Aleutians in May 1943. In general, however, discipline and fighting qualities improved with experience. Mutiny as such did not occur in the British and American armies. There were only a few isolated incidents of refusal to obey orders. Desertion, however, was a problem. The British army had over 100,000 cases in the course of the war and the Americans about the same proportion once units were in combat. Considering that desertion was very difficult in some theaters, such as Burma and the Pacific islands, this was a high rate. The problem was so bad in North Africa in 1942 that the British general Claude Auchinleck asked for authority to impose the death penalty. Before D-Day, deserters were twelve to a cell in Glasgow police stations. Overwhelmingly, deserters were young and less well educated and came from the infantry, the units subject to the highest casualties. Here, the desertion rate was about one in twenty. The First World War term "shell shock" was replaced by "combat fatigue," which on average accounted for about 15 percent of all battle casualties in the British and American armies.

Some of the same problems were found in the RAF and USAAF. The worst times were late 1943 and early 1944 when the RAF was engaged in the Battle of Berlin: the "early return" rate (aircrew turning back from a mission for dubious aircraft defects) reached 25 percent in some squadrons. The number of men removed from Bomber Command for what was called "lack of moral fiber" is not clear but was possibly as high as one in eight. Outright refusal to serve was treated harshly with courts-martial and prison sentences. Less obvious cases were sent to what were euphemistically called "aircrew refresher centers," which were in reality open-arrest detention centers.

Inmates were subjected to physical training and lectures and then sent back to their squadrons. Those found medically unfit were offered a transfer to the army or the coal mines. Another problem among British and American bomber crews was deliberate landings in Sweden and Switzerland, where crews were interned for the rest of the war. Altogether, 370 aircraft were affected. In July 1944, USAAF authorities concluded that "the landings were intentional evasions of further combat service." Clearly, this was not the case on every occasion: some aircraft *were* badly damaged. Many, however, were undamaged and had enough fuel to return to base. There is also some evidence that USAAF fighter crews were briefed to escort bombers home and if necessary shoot them down if they were trying to reach a neutral country. About 80 percent of the aircraft affected were American, which suggests, because of the higher number of RAF aircraft involved in the bomber offensive, that the problem primarily affected the USAAF.

Discipline was also a problem in other areas. Overall, the United States brought 1.7 million men before military courts in the course of the war and 142 of them were executed. The British were more circumspect, preferring summary justice to formal courts-martial, though there were over 200,000 courts-martial during the war. (The Germans brought fewer men before military courts—630,000—but executed far more, 10,000.) The main offenses were absence without leave, using military vehicles without authority (in late 1944 Twenty-first Army Group was losing seventy jeeps a day in Brussels alone), and looting from both civilians and military stores for the black market. In 1939 a special squad of 500 policemen had to be sent from Britain to France to stop mass thefts from the army.

Another major problem was the incidence of venereal disease, which at times put more men in the hospital than combat. In Italy in 1945, among British troops nearly 7 percent were treated for VD and about 1 percent for combat wounds. In Burma in 1943 the comparable rates were 16 percent and about 1 percent. In the Canadian army the average monthly rate of VD infection was over 5 percent. On average each soldier had to spend twenty days in the hospital being cured. The British made a small deduction from pay, and the Americans put those affected in barbed-wire stockades with "VD" emblazoned on the backs of their uniforms.

British forces suffered a much higher rate of prisoners taken (9 percent) than the Americans (2 percent), but this partly reflected the long period of defeats between 1940 and 1942; after that date rates were roughly equal. At times the Americans also had very high numbers captured, particularly when units were first in combat. In the Philippines over 32,000 were taken prisoner, as against 4,800 killed and wounded. In Tunisia in 1943 there were as many prisoners as the total killed and wounded. British and American troops had no great hatred of German or Italian troops, but even so a German soldier surrendering still only had a fifty-fifty chance of surviving as a prisoner rather than being shot. In the Far East very few prisoners were taken. For the Japanese, surrender was the ultimate humiliation. They were expected to die and if captured to commit suicide. After nearly two years of war the Allies held about 300 Japanese prisoners, and even by the end of 1944 the total amounted to only 6,400. On Saipan, when some 12,000 Japanese civilians were about to be captured, two thirds of them committed suicide by throwing themselves off a cliff.

One feature of all the Allies' armed forces was racial discrimination and segregation. The French used a considerable number of African troops, more than in the First World War, and they bore a disproportionate share of the casualties in 1940. Vichy relied on local troops for the defense of West Africa and they formed a major part of the Free French forces. However, the Africans were removed from the French units in Britain before D-Day, so that only white troops would participate in the liberation of France. In September and October 1944, black troops were removed from all Free French forces as part of a policy of *blanchissement* ordered by de Gaulle. Black troops were left neglected in the south of France in the winter of 1944–45, and about seventy-five were shot when their discontent boiled over into riots. Black prisoners of war recaptured from the Germans were sent to labor battalions, and eventually all were repatriated, some after waiting for more than a year. The British maintained segregated units, those they raised in Africa and the West Indies and units in the Indian army and Gurkha regiments. All officers were white, and black infantry soldiers received one seventh the pay of a white soldier. There were also other forms of discrimination. In Burma, black troops were not given mosquito nets and were used to dig air-raid trenches for Europeans, which they were not allowed to use themselves. They were not allowed in cinemas, NAAFI (the services' welfare organization) did not serve them either in or out of uniform, and when they were in transit through South Africa they were not allowed out unless accompanied by a white. South Africa itself, a highly segregated society, had all-white armed forces, and in Australia the cabinet decided in March 1940 that "the admission of aliens or of British subjects of a non-European origin or descent to the Australian Defence Forces is undesirable in principle." New Zealand, too, maintained segregated units.

The situation in the American armed forces reflected the deep-seated discrimination and segregation found in the society. This discrimination was encapsulated by an incident during the war when a black soldier was refused service at a lunch counter in Salina, Kansas, even though German prisoners of war were being served. Before the war black participation in the American armed forces had been deliberately restricted. None were permitted in the Marine Corps, in the navy they were allowed only in the all-black messmen and servants branch, and in the army there were only small segregated black units. A so-called "war for democracy" did not change this policy. Although President Roosevelt was prepared to insist on a no-discrimination clause in government defense contracts, the armed forces were determined not to be subjected to what they saw as social experiments.

The marines admitted the first blacks in 1942, but they were kept in segregated units and not used in combat. In the navy about 26,000 blacks were recruited, but three quarters of them worked as messmen, servants, cooks, and waiters. Two small ships were given all-black crews. The army set a quota of no more than 10 percent of blacks and insisted that they be kept in segregated units. Three quarters of those who joined were sent to labor units and most of the rest to low-quality infantry units posted to remote outposts in the United States. Not until March 1944 did the army accept that black units could be used in combat. The first were used in the Pacific and briefly in Italy in the summer of 1944, but were quickly broken up. In the crisis of the Battle of the Bulge in the Ardennes in the winter of 1944, 2,500 black troops were rushed to the front. General George Patton commanding the Third Army refused to accept any black as a replacement, but some fought for a few days in integrated units—such was the scale of the crisis. Once the situation was stablized the black troops were rapidly withdrawn. Blacks were not allowed to join the U.S. Army Air Corps until 1940, and even then were allowed only in completely segregated units. A separate training school for black pilots was established and in April 1943 the first black squadron was operational in North Africa. However, white pilots refused to give it full operational status against German units. By 1945 there were nearly 140,000 blacks in the Army Air Forces but nearly all of them were in menial support roles, and there were just four all-black squadrons.

Overall, policy in the U.S. armed forces was that no black could be superior in rank to a white in the same unit. Nearly all officers were therefore white and usually only the worst were sent to black units. All recreational, eating, and health facilities were rigidly segregated. The severity of the discrimination led to riots in nine training units in the summer of 1943. With the approval of the Red Cross, the U.S. services also insisted that blood donors and the use of plasma be rigidly segregated so that whites were not "contaminated" by being given black products. The arrival of U.S. forces abroad also caused problems. Australia with its "white Australia" policy objected strongly to the introduction of black servicemen into the country as laborers. The British asked the Americans not to send black troops to Britain. When this request was rejected, the secretary of state for war, Edward Grigg, started a policy of educating the British army "to adopt towards the U.S.A. colored troops the attitude of U.S.A. Army authorities"—i.e., the recognition of segregation and discrimination. Attempts to foster this attitude met with little success and, despite another "education" program, the civilian population were generally tolerant and friendly toward black American troops. This caused resentment both in the U.S. Army and in the administration in Washington.

The British and American experience was not typical of combat in the Second World War. Of the roughly 20 million combat deaths in the war the British and the Americans accounted for less than 600,000, and even if deaths among troops of the dominion countries and other western Allies are included, the total is still well below 1 million. At least two thirds of the military deaths in the war occurred on the eastern front. Here it was a war of unimaginable brutality and atrocities, deliberately perpetrated by both sides—in the case of the Soviet Union, often against its own troops. By March 1945 the German army in the east had suffered total casualties of nearly 6.2 million (including about 2.3 million killed), twice its total strength at the beginning of the campaign in June 1941. Soviet figures are not clear, partly because of the very high death rate among prisoners of war, but the most accurate estimate suggests at least 13 million killed and probably about the same number wounded.

The Germans suffered very heavy casualties on the eastern front from the start: by late March 1942 there were over 1 million casualties (about a third of the army). In the first ten days of August 1941, one regiment lost 37 officers and 1,200 others. In the winter of 1941–42, around Moscow, the Twenty-third Infantry Division was reduced from nine battalions to three and had 1,000 men left out of an original 8,000. Fighting later in the war was even more brutal. At Kursk in the summer of 1943, the 106th Infantry Division lost 3,224 men (roughly 40 percent of its strength) in two weeks; even the worst hit British divisions fighting in northwest Europe in 1944–45 took six months to reach such casualty levels. Even during the successes of the summer of 1941 conditions were tough. In the first month of the 1941 campaign the Twelfth Infantry Division marched 560 miles at 15 miles a day and had to fight a number of battles on top of this physical effort. By August the men were spending forty-eight hours in the front line without any rest, followed by twenty hours in the rear trenches where they could "rest" in the mud, covered with tent sheets and with no opportunity to change or dry their clothes and boots. As the campaign went on into the winter the Wehrmacht regressed into a primitive army—military equipment was no longer of much importance. Troops were left to live in the open with temperatures down to −43° Fahrenheit without proper winter clothing; the army ordered them to loot felt boots from civilians and prisoners. Food was in short supply, and health was bad because troops were unable to change their clothes. They were covered with lice and skin diseases and by early 1942 there were outbreaks of typhus and spotted fever, just as in pre-twentieth-century armies.

Although German casualty levels were high, those of the Soviet forces were far worse because of the profligate way in which they used men and equipment. In the first five months of the German attack, between June and November 1941, the Soviets lost combat aircraft at the rate of 45 percent of their front-line strength every month, tanks at a rate of 41 percent, and artillery, 51 percent. These extraordinary loss rates were not simply the result of the severe defeats and massive encirclements of this phase of the campaign; when the Soviets went onto the offensive their loss rates were generally the same, and some even rose. Even after the summer of 1944, when the outcome of the campaign was no longer in doubt and the Soviets had a huge material superiority, they were still losing 2,000 tanks, 3,000 aircraft, and 10,000 artillery pieces every month. The Soviet loss of tanks was stupendous, even when the Red Army was battle-hardened. In the retreat to Stalingrad in the summer of 1942 the Soviets lost eight tanks for every German tank; in the drive back to the Dnieper it was still six to one; and in the battles of 1944 it was four to one. In two months, January and February 1944, the German Army Group South alone destroyed nearly 4,000 Soviet tanks, far more than the Germans deployed on the whole front in June 1941. Human losses were on a similar scale, almost six times higher than the German figure. Even allowing for the huge losses in 1941, Soviet losses were still three and a half times German losses. What this meant for Soviet society can be illustrated by what happened to the twenty-six pupils of the ninth form of School Number 25 in the village of Ilyinskoye near Moscow, who all enlisted on the day of the German attack. At the end of the war only four were left alive.

This destruction was primarily caused by Soviet tactics, which were characterized by repeated attacks (often five or six times) employing no initiative or variation until breakthrough was finally achieved. Infantry units were not normally expected to survive longer than about ten days, and so were provided only with supplies that they could carry. Units did not normally receive reinforcements. Whole divisions or corps would almost be destroyed before being withdrawn and then rebuilt from scratch. Special penal and punishment battalions were set up in the autumn of 1942 and carried out the most dangerous tasks, such as walking across minefields in order to clear pathways. In snowy conditions they wore black uniforms rather than white arctic clothing in order to draw enemy fire. Discipline was kept by special N.K.V.D. (secret police) and SMERSH security squads of about fifteen to twenty men per division and a network of informers that may have amounted to about one in eight members of the army. Behind the front line were "rear-area" security units, about six regiments per front, which were used as "blocking detachments" to stop retreats and if necessary shoot their own troops. Discipline was harsh. Many members of the armed forces, such as Alexander Solzhenitsyn, were sent to the Gulag camps and others were shot on the spot. Despite this level of internal control the Red Army often disintegrated. During 1941, N.K.V.D. reports disclosed widespread drunkenness, panic, incompetence, and self-inflicted wounds, all of which was partly countered by the security units' rounding up people almost at random and shooting them in front of their regiments. Nevertheless, in the last six months of 1942 German forces reported over 60,000 Soviet troops crossing to German lines and as late as the summer of 1943 deserters still accounted for nearly two thirds of Soviet prisoners of war.

The dominant feature of the war on the eastern front was its extreme barbarity. In western Europe atrocities were the rare exception, not the rule that they became in the east. In May 1940 British troops were using "dum-dum" bullets, and the S.S. murdered ninety men of the Second Battalion of the Royal Norfolk Regiment at Le Paradis after they had surrendered. In general, however, the Geneva conventions were accepted and applied by both sides. In the east the situation was different. For the Nazis the war against the Soviet Union was an ideological war in which all measures could be justified. Such views were widely accepted by the army and orders to implement this policy were issued. The defeat of the Soviet Union was expected to be a short operation and the army wanted to secure its place in the new order that was expected to emerge as the Nazi state was consolidated. The Wehrmacht wanted to show that it was reliable and large parts of the army fully accepted the Nazi ideology. In the early stages of the 1941 campaign General Walter von Reichenau told his troops that it was an attack on "the Jewish-Bolshevik system" and that its aim was "the complete destruction of the sources of power and the eradication of the Asiatic influence on the European cultural sphere." The German soldier was "the carrier of an inexorable racial concept" and "the avenger of all bestialities inflicted upon the Germans" and he therefore had to understand "the necessity of harsh, but just measures against Jewish sub-humanity." As a consequence, Soviet citizens and Jews were not to be treated according to the normal rules of war. As the war continued this determination to barbarize warfare grew. In October 1942 the German High Command issued an order to all officers on the eastern front that they "must have an unambiguous, completely uncompromising position regarding the Jewish question. There is no difference between the so-called decent Jews and others."

As part of this policy the German army on the eastern front enthusiastically cooperated with four specific instructions, each of which was criminal. The first was the so-called "commissar" order: all Red Army commissars and Communist officials were to be shot on the spot without question. In March, General Alfred Jodl told the army that "the necessity of liquidating all Bolshevik chiefs and commissars speaks for itself." The army therefore either shot the commissars it captured or turned them over to the security units run by Himmler for whatever measures they wanted to take. In total, about 600,000 people were killed as a result of this policy. The second order instructed the army to cooperate with the Einsatzgruppen, or mobile strike squads, organized by Himmler. Without this cooperation these small squads, in total no more than 3,000 strong, would not have been able to kill over 500,000 Jews, Gypsies, mentally ill, and "Asiatics" in less than six months. Although the army did not take part in the massacres (army commanders were worried only about the effect such participation might have on discipline) they often cordoned off the massacre areas and after October 1941 allowed these squads into prisoner-of-war camps in order to identify Jews and other people they wanted to kill.

The third and fourth orders concerned anti-partisan operations. In 1941 instructions were issued that authorized the shooting of partisans and civilians helping them on a ruthless scale; if no specific offenders could be found then collective measures were authorized. The army was to cooperate with the S.S. in these operations. The result was a widespread campaign of terror against the Soviet population. In August 1941 II Corps ordered that all partisans were to be publicly hanged and their bodies left to rot. In September 1941 a daytime curfew was applied, and anybody breaking it was automatically defined as a partisan and killed. Any Red Army soldier found behind the German front line was classed as a partisan and shot. Although there were Soviet partisan units operating on a relatively small scale, German army and S.S. sweeps against such groups really amounted not to military operations but to nothing less than the murder of the civilian population. Between July 1941 and May 1942 Army Group Center lost 1,100 German troops killed in "anti-partisan" operations but killed over 80,000 "partisans." In the next six months they killed another 20,000 "partisans" for the loss of less than 2,000 troops. S.S. operations in Belorussia between mid-November 1942 and February 1943 cost 135 German dead in return for the killing of over 30,000 Soviet civilians, or "partisans," as the Germans called them.

In addition to these specific instructions the army decided that its logistics resources were insufficient to sustain the campaign in the east and therefore most supplies would have to be looted from the population. Special units were formed to carry out these operations and then individual soldiers were left to loot whatever remained. No consideration was given to the long-term exploitation of the conquered territories. The result was that by the spring of 1942 much of the population was starving to death. Those who worked for the Germans in conditions of virtual slavery were given some food, but it was usually only half the rations of the German troops, assuming any food was available. The death toll from this policy is unknown. When the German army began to retreat in 1943 it carried out a scorched-earth policy: any remaining men aged between fifteen and sixty-five were arrested and shipped back to Germany, sometimes adult women were "evacuated" too, and then all houses were burned down. By the time areas were liberated by the Soviet army they were largely depopulated wasteland.

The conditions in which the German army kept Soviet prisoners of war were almost indescribable. During the course of the war they captured 5.7 million Soviet prisoners (equivalent to the size of the entire U.S. Army deployed overseas), and about 3.3 million died in captivity (equivalent to the entire British army). The overwhelming proportion of these deaths took place in 1941; in that year just over 3 million prisoners were taken, and by February 1942 60 percent of them, about 2 million men, were dead. The German army planners expected to take large numbers of prisoners but made almost no provision to look after them. Those who were not shot when they surrendered were kept in open stockades surrounded by barbed wire or marched to the rear with little food or water—official rations were less than those given to the guard dogs. The prisoners stripped trees in the camp and ate grass and nettles, and cannibalism was widespread. Beatings and shootings were commonplace. By the winter of 1941–42 some shelter was provided, but even then about 450 prisoners were expected to live on bare earth in a hut forty feet by eighty feet. There was no medical treatment and no soap and there were no delousing facilities; consequently typhus was soon at epidemic proportions. At the end of 1941 in a camp near Gomel, north of Kiev, of 12,800 prisoners over 400 were dying every day. Conditions were improved marginally in 1942, when the Germans decided that in a longer war they would exploit Soviet prisoners; they were then formed into work units or rear-area security units or were sent back to Germany as slave labor. However, they were still regarded as completely dispensable. The first humans Zyklon B poison gas was tried out on at Auschwitz were Soviet prisoners.

That these conditions were the result of deliberate German policy is shown by the fact that only 4 percent of British and American prisoners held by the Germans died in captivity, compared with 58 percent of Soviet prisoners. This was the worst treatment of any prisoners in the war; the death rate for German prisoners in Soviet hands was about 30 percent. Even the death toll of Allied prisoners in Japanese hands, normally regarded as particularly barbaric, was far lower than the rate for Soviet prisoners held by the Germans. On the Burma railway the death rate was 26 percent and on the Bataan "death march" the death toll among American prisoners was 14 percent.

The consequence of the German barbarity was that when Soviet troops began to enter German territory in late October 1944 similar crimes were committed with little or no attempt on the part of Soviet authorities to stop them. Indeed propagandists such as Ilya Ehrenburg constantly reiterated that all Germans were responsible for the crimes committed in the Soviet Union, that they were not human beings and should all be killed. The village of Nemersdorf, in East Prussia, provides an illustration of what happened across eastern Germany to those civilians who did not flee ahead of the Red Army. Almost the entire population was murdered; people were nailed to barn doors; women and children were shot in the back of the head; columns of refugees were deliberately run over by tanks; others had their heads cut open by spades and axes; as a matter of routine women were raped. The picture was confirmed by British and American prisoners of war in the areas "liberated" by the Red Army.

For many ordinary soldiers on every side the war was an insane event in which they were treated as disposable parts in a large, impersonal machine. They were given little or no choice about participation. Their aim was to try to survive and get the war over as quickly as possible. In December 1941 a young recruit in the Grossdeutschland Division wrote, "When will they at last pull us out of the line? What is all this for? When will we ever get back home?" Marine

E. B. Sledge, who started out as a believer in the idea of a crusade or at least of revenge on the Japanese for Pearl Harbor, wrote of his experiences on Okinawa, where in the slit trenches there were no latrines and excrement was slung out by a shovel to lie on top of the decomposing bodies:

> If a marine slipped and slid down the back slope of the muddy ridge, he was apt to reach the bottom vomiting. . . . [He] would stand up horror-stricken as he watched in disbelief while fat maggots tumbled out of his muddy dungaree pockets, cartridge belt, legging lacings, and the like. . . . We didn't talk about such things. They were too horrible and obscene even for hardened veterans. . . . It is too preposterous to think that men could actually live and fight for days and nights on end under such terrible conditions and not be driven insane. . . . To me the war was insanity.

VIII

CIVILIANS

I N THE 1914–18 WAR THE OVERWHELMING MAJORITY OF casualties were military. Civilians, apart from those in the immediate war zone, were not killed in large numbers. In the Second World War about 20 million service personnel were killed. This figure is put into perspective by the 65 million civilians killed, about 23 million forcibly deported or resettled, about 25 million refugees, and by 1945 about 60 million homeless. During the course of the war civilians were deliberately killed by both sides and the strains of war caused some societies to collapse into ethnic and religious conflict with widespread slaughter. However, the impact of the war on different societies varied enormously. Some, such as the United States, Canada, South Africa, and New Zealand, were not attacked, had no civilian casualties, and suffered very little apart from the introduction of conscription. Indeed, for the Americans the war was a time of full employment and rapidly rising living standards. Others, such as Britain, were subjected to bombing, rationing, and disruption to normal peacetime life. Germany and Japan suffered very heavy Allied bombing with high casualties. The worst-affected countries were the states of central and eastern Europe, some of which collapsed into virtual anarchy and internal conflict, in addition to which all of them had to withstand the impact of German occupation. In the Far East, China disintegrated under the pressure of war, and in India millions starved to death.

Civilian populations often knew little of what was happening in the war. In all the major combatants they were subjected to rigid censorship, together with major state-directed propaganda campaigns that emphasized national unity and mobilization to help those fighting at the front. All the governments and leaders tended to look back to the past to find conservative, nationalistic symbols that could unite the nation. By the autumn of 1941 the Soviet leadership was referring to the conflict as "the great patriotic war," not a war to defend communism. They emphasized figures and events such as Alexander Nevsky, Suvorov, Kutuzov, and the war against Napoleon in 1812. In Germany Hitler became obsessed with Frederick the Great, and Goebbels spent huge sums making epic films about the Prussian king as a way of boosting morale. In 1940, Churchill drew instances from the past—the defeat of the Spanish Armada in 1588, Trafalgar in 1805—as examples of Britain's resistance to the threat of invasion. Japan turned to the image of the *Kamikaze,* or "divine wind," that had saved the country from Mongol invasion in the thirteenth century.

The reality was that there was a significant gulf between government and people. Leaders might try to claim an identity of interests, as Stalin did in his first speech to the Soviet people after the German attack: "Comrades, citizens, brothers and sisters, fighters of our army and navy! I am speaking to you, my friends." However, they ran the war with the minimum of consultation. General Tojo said, "The masses are foolish. If we tell them the facts, morale will collapse." Churchill said privately in 1940, "In time of war the machinery of government is so strong it can afford largely to ignore popular feeling." The consequence of this attitude was that the population often had little idea of what the war was about, apart from their own survival. In September 1942 a Gallup poll was carried out in the United States, but its findings were so disturbing that they were kept secret. The survey revealed that 40 percent of the American people admitted they did not know "what this war is all about." Less than a quarter of the population had even heard of the Atlantic Charter, the supposed foundation stone of Allied objectives for a better postwar world, and only 7 percent could identify even one of the Charter's points. The picture was the same in Britain. In March 1942 a secret

Ministry of Information survey concluded: "The public has no clearly worked-out conception of the purpose of the war.... We have only vague conceptions, fluctuating between ideas of holding what we have got and ideas of right and wrong."

Governments also turned against their own citizens. In Germany, although low-level dissent was tolerated until well into the war, the attempted assassination of Hitler in July 1944 was the pretext for the imprisonment and murder of a large number of those who were opposed to the government. The Soviet Union practiced internal repression on a far greater scale than the Nazis. About 20 million people had died during the collectivization campaign of the early 1930s and the terror of the late 1930s. In June 1941 there were probably about 5 million people in the Gulag camps, compared to a concentration camp population of about 6,000 in Germany in the 1930s, which had risen to about 60,000 in 1942. During 1941 a large number of Gulag prisoners were either released—about one million fought in "penal battalions" clearing minefields and assaulting well-defended positions—or the prisons where they were held were overrun by German forces. About 750,000 were evacuated to the east as the Germans advanced. Many were also shifted into labor camps, which accounted for about 10 percent of the Soviet industrial labor force by 1945. As the amount of food and clothing available for the general population fell drastically in 1941–42, so did that for the prisoners in the Gulag. The result was a sevenfold increase in the already high death rate. During the war about a fifth of the population of the Gulag died every year, in total about 2 million people.

In Britain the government took the power to imprison people without trial and a few hundred fascist sympathizers were jailed. In June 1940 it was made a criminal offense "to make or report any statement likely to cause alarm and despondency." A month later a man was sent to jail for a month for saying Britain had no chance of winning the war and another for saying that "the rotten government holds three hundred ninety million Indians in slavery." During the summer of 1940 the British were also affected by a "fifth column" panic over the aliens in the country. Although just over 400 alien Nazi sympathizers had been imprisoned in 1939, there were in the country nearly 60,000 refugees who had fled persecution in Germany during the 1930s. In June 1940 the latter also were all suddenly interned, and no attempt was made to categorize people according to their background, with the result that Nazis and Jews were mixed together in squalid makeshift camps. At the Wharf Mills camp, in Liverpool, 2,000 internees were held in a disused, rat-infested factory with eighteen taps for washing, sixty buckets in the yard for toilets, and straw mattresses available only for the chronically sick. At the Huyton camp in Lancashire, an official investigation of two suicides reported a tragic outcome: "The two men who succeeded in committing suicide had already been in Hitler's concentration camps. Against these they held out, but this camp has broken their spirit."

The United States had a far greater German and Italian alien population, a total of nearly 900,000, but less than 1 percent, usually hard-line Nazi and fascist sympathizers, were interned. American policy toward Japanese aliens (about 47,000) and U.S. citizens of Japanese ancestry (about 80,000) was very different than toward those of German and Italian origin. The latter were allowed to work in defense industries, but in the early months of 1942 the panic brought about by the Japanese attack on Pearl Harbor was used as an excuse for a determined campaign against Japanese-Americans. In February 1942 General de Witt, the military commander in California, argued for the exclusion of American citizens of Japanese descent from important strategic areas. Under pressure from well-entrenched anti-Japanese groups, this demand was transformed into a policy of relocation. With no opposition from either the Department of Justice or Congress and with the enthusiastic support of Roosevelt, Executive Order 9066 was promulgated on February 19, 1942. As a result, a War Relocation Authority was set up, and over 100,000 people, 80,000 of them American citizens who had committed no offense other than to be of Japanese descent, were moved into special camps guarded by the army. They were allowed to take only clothing, bedding, and cooking utensils and therefore had to sell their possessions at whatever price they could get in the very short period given to them to settle their affairs. Overall they lost property worth about $350 million. They were forced to live in communal barracks and were not allowed to practice their religion. When there was a riot over the conditions at Camp Manzanar in California, two people were shot by the army. In the autumn of 1943 those who wanted to return to Japan after the war or who were regarded as "suspicious" (about 18,000 in all) were sent to a special camp at Tule Lake, California.

In the spring of 1944 Roosevelt concluded that there was no longer any military case for detention, but the detention order was not lifted until January 1945, after the presidential election. Most people had to be forced to leave the camps because they had no resources and no homes to go to. The Supreme Court upheld the government's decision until 1945, and it took the Japanese-Americans nearly forty years to obtain compensation. The American Civil Liberties Union refused to support an attack on Executive Order 9066 as unconstitutional because of the organization's overall support for Roosevelt.

Other governments followed the American example. In Canada the openly racist prime minister, Mackenzie King, was instrumental in removing 20,000 Canadian citizens of Japanese descent from the west coast, despite the advice of the military and the internal security organizations that there was no threat to Canadian security. All of the assets of these Japanese-Canadians were confiscated, and after the war they were offered the choice of being either "repatriated" to Japan—despite the fact that they were Canadian citizens—or forced to settle east of the Rockies; over half decided to go to Japan. In Mexico all Japanese, but not Germans or Italians, were interned, and in Peru the government expropriated all property owned by people of Japanese descent, while leaving that of German aliens sacrosanct, and distributed it either among themselves or to their friends.

The churches in every country were generally conservative and supported the war. In Britain, the Church of England gave wholehearted endorsement to the war with only a few dissidents, such as Bishop George Bell of Chichester, opposing the deliberate bombing of civilians. In France, the Catholic church was one of the major pillars of the Vichy regime and supported anti-Semitic measures; in Austria it supported the Anschluss; and in Italy it was nationalistic, with figures such as Cardinal Schuster of Milan backing Mussolini until the latter's death in 1945. In Germany, Hitler ordered that no measures were to be taken against the churches for the duration of the war, and in return both major denominations supported him. The Lutheran church officially stated on September 2, 1939, that "since yesterday our German people have been called to the fight for the land of our fathers in order that German blood may be reunited with German blood." Members of the Catholic hierarchy asked soldiers "in obedience to the Führer to do their duty and to be ready to sacrifice their whole existence." They went on: "We appeal to the faithful to join in ardent prayer that God's providence may lead this war to blessed success for fatherland and people." After the attack on the Soviet Union, the bishop of Münster said: "Day and night our thoughts dwell with our brave soldiers, that God assist them in their struggle against the Bolshevik menace to our people." Opposition to Nazi policy came from only a small minority of the clergy in any denomination. In the Soviet Union the League of Militant Atheists was suppressed in August 1941 and at the same time *Pravda* condemned Nazi attacks on religion. The Orthodox religion was given greater status as part of the appeal to a nationalistic past, and in return the church supported the state and the Red Army. In 1943 facilities for the church were greatly improved and a kind of "concordat" was agreed upon with Stalin.

In the unoccupied Western democracies the war brought about social disruption and short-term changes in the pattern of life. In Britain, although about 40,000 civilians were killed and some 800,000 houses damaged beyond repair during the air attacks in 1940–41, the threat of death was very small after 1941. In countries such as the United States this threat was nonexistent. Families were split up by conscription and evacuation, rationing was imposed (far more severely in Britain than elsewhere), more women went to work, there were blackouts, and travel was restricted—gasoline rationing in Britain meant that car travel was stopped for all but essential users and trains were less frequent. In all countries the effects of war were felt most strongly in cities; in the countryside controls were less strongly enforced and food was more easily available—much of it finding its way onto the widespread black markets. The black market was one manifestation of the growing amount of crime; in Britain the crime rate rose by 60 percent during the war, twice as fast as in the 1930s. Juvenile crime increased even more rapidly, by over 40 percent in the first year of the war alone. Looting was widespread. The police had to set up a special anti-looting squad in London during the Blitz; of those caught, nearly half were civil-defense workers. There was also a vast increase in prostitution, particularly in London as Allied troops arrived in Britain before D-Day, and during the war the VD rate rose by 50 percent. The number of illegitimate births rose by just over 40 percent and the divorce rate by 75 percent. In the United States during the war both the divorce rate and the number of illegitimate births more than doubled.

In a large number of areas, though, life in Britain continued as normal, including the inequalities that characterized British society. Cinemas, nightclubs, and restaurants remained open. At the time of Dunkirk 645,000 people were still unemployed. Of the children evacuated from Newcastle, one in eight did not have proper shoes, one in five was deficient in clothing, and half were infested with nits. In 1943, 10 percent of the population was described in an official government survey as "ill-nourished" or worse, and in 1941 an official survey of the nation's health revealed "a state of affairs that is a disgrace to a civilised country." Yet in September 1940 the wealthy Conservative M.P. "Chips" Channon had to make do with what he described as a "depleted" staff of six servants at his town house (he normally employed fifteen), although he was able to maintain the usual number at his country home. Channon also described the scene at the Dorchester Hotel, where many ministers and senior officials stayed during the Blitz, as the East End of London was battered by German bombers; the population huddled in tube stations; and the homeless lived in squalid rest centers and relied on assistance given under the Poor Law:

> Half London seemed to be there.... I gave Bob Boothby a champagne cocktail in the private bar.... Our bill must have been im-

mense for we had four magnums of champagne. London lives well: I've never seen more lavishness, more money spent, or more food consumed than tonight, and the dance floor was packed.

Conditions for the civilian population on the continent of Europe were far worse. People had to decide whether to abandon their homes and jobs and flee as refugees; otherwise they might be subject to resettlement, forcible deportation, or slave labor. They had to live with the uncertainty of occupation, the threat of starvation, and the disintegration of their societies into ethnic and religious conflict. If they were Jews in areas controlled by Germany they faced the terror of mass extermination. Others had to face large-scale bombing aimed at killing as many civilians as possible. Even if they survived the bombing they were threatened with homelessness.

Refugees were a constant element in the war, from the German attack on Poland until the last days of the Allied invasion of Germany. In May 1940 about 3 million Belgians and 7 million French people left their homes. In four days in mid-June, 2 million Parisians fled. The mass panic affected different communities differently. At Evreux, northwest of Paris, on the evening of June 11 only 200 inhabitants were left out of a population of nearly 20,000, yet in other towns nearby the overwhelming majority of the population stayed. In the small French village of Marlemont in the Ardennes, of 195 people 171 left. Twenty-six traveled only a few miles, but over 40 percent of the village reached the Vendée in western France. For most people this was a temporary phenomenon. Between July and October 1940 over 1.5 million Belgians returned home, many on special repatriation trains, and by the end of the summer over three quarters of French refugees had returned.

In the summer and autumn of 1941 about 16 million Soviet citizens (about a fifth of the population in the affected areas) fled from the advancing Germans. About 1.4 million people left Moscow, including 150,000 on the night of October 16–17, when the city was expected to fall. As they fled east the situation became chaotic. In some towns such as Kazan and Sverdlovsk the population rose by a third in a few months, and in Stalingrad the population of 400,000 doubled in nine months. Most of the refugees had to live in terrible conditions, and facilities collapsed under the sheer weight of numbers. Later, during the Soviet invasion of Germany, millions of Germans fled ahead of the advancing Red Army; by 1950 a third of the population of West Germany had been born outside its borders.

In Asia there was a strong racial element in the treatment of refugees. During the evacuation of Burma in early 1942, for example, Europeans were given places on ships and planes, whereas the Indians were left behind or expected to make their own way back to India. Over 400,000 tried to do so overland in terrible conditions, and about 50,000 died en route.

During the war there were a number of major population transfers that were agreed upon between states but not usually by the people involved. In part, this was a way of trying to clarify the confused ethnic map of central and eastern Europe, but it was also an attempt to secure ethnic predominance in newly acquired areas. It was also German policy to bring the German minorities into a Greater Germany. The process began in early 1939, when, as a precondition for signing the Pact of Steel, Mussolini demanded the removal of the German-speaking minority in the South Tyrol, acquired by Italy from Austria in 1919. The Italians bribed the German speakers with a very favorable exchange rate for their compensation payments and about 70 percent voted in favor. Over the next three years about 100,000 people moved out of Italian territory, mainly to the Austrian Tyrol. The German-Soviet Pact of August 1939 also contained provisions for the German minority living in the Soviet sphere of influence to be resettled. The German government decided to move most of them to the parts of Poland incorporated into Germany in September 1939. Sixty-three thousand people were moved from Estonia and Latvia and about 330,000 from the Soviet-controlled areas of Poland to the German-controlled area of Poland. In return, about 57,000 Ukrainians and Russians were moved from German-controlled Poland to the Soviet area. In 1941–42 the Germans also began a resettlement program of people of German origin from the territories they controlled in the Soviet Union, involving about 350,000 people, and also in Bulgaria and Yugoslavia, where about 60,000 people were affected. Alto-

gether, therefore, about 900,000 people of German origin were resettled during the war as part of programs agreed on and run by the
German government.

Other ethnic minorities were also transferred by agreement. The
largest group affected were the Finns living in the areas of Karelia
annexed by the Soviet Union in the spring of 1940. Overall, about
420,000 people, equivalent to over 10 percent of the prewar population of Finland, were evacuated from these areas. In 1943, when Finland controlled much of Karelia again, about 265,000 moved back to
their old homes, only to be evacuated again a year later as Soviet
troops advanced. The last population exchange came at the end of
1944, when 46,000 Ingermanlanders moved from Finland to the Soviet Union. There were also major resettlements in the Balkans. One
hundred eighty-three thousand Bulgarians moved to Bulgaria or Bul-
garian-controlled areas, 319,000 Rumanians moved to Rumania, and
a minimum of 210,000 Hungarians moved from Rumania to Hungary
or the Hungarian-controlled areas of Yugoslavia. In addition, 76,000
Croats moved from Styria and Serbia into Croatia, and 120,000 Serbs
moved in the opposite direction. Even neutral states were affected.
Between 1940 and 1943, about 6,000 ethnic Swedes were resettled
from Estonia back to Sweden. Overall, and not counting the multiple
movement of Finns in Karelia, about 1,400,000 non-Germans were
resettled in eastern Europe and the Baltic area during the war.

These agreed-upon population transfers were on a small scale
compared with the forced deportation of peoples. This process began
in Poland in the winter of 1939–40. About 2 million Poles were removed from the areas of Poland annexed by Germany and sent to central Poland. There were also other smaller German deportations in
the west—about 100,000 French people were expelled from Alsace-
Lorraine, which had been annexed by Germany, and sent to Vichy
territory, and 7,000 were deported from Luxembourg. The largest
forced deportations, however, were carried out by the Soviet Union
and also affected substantial minorities from within its own population. At the same time as the Germans were forcibly removing 2 million Poles from German-annexed territory, the Soviets were deporting
1.25 million Poles from the territory they occupied in September

1939. When the Soviets occupied the Baltic states most of those active in political and public life were deported, usually to the Gulag camps. In total, about 170,000 people were affected in the year before the German invasion, 35,000 from Latvia, 60,000 from Estonia, and 75,000 from Lithuania. In September 1941 the German minority in the Volga area, about 380,000 people, together with about 800,000 other Soviet citizens of German descent were forcibly removed to the east on the suspicion that they sympathized with the invader. About half, or around 600,000 people, were sent to the Gulag.

The most extensive Soviet deportations, however, were carried out as Soviet troops liberated territory in 1943–44. The people affected were the minorities living on the north slope of the Caucasus and the west bank of the Volga, who maintained their own languages and religions, primarily Islam but also Buddhism, and who had been largely unaffected by the strongly Slav and Orthodox elements of Russian culture. Some groups, such as the Chechen and the Karachai, had risen in revolt against the Soviets in the summer of 1942, before German troops arrived in the area. For others, such as the Kalmyks, Ingush, Balkars, and Crimean Tatars, deportation was collective punishment for suspected collaboration. For the 200,000 Meskhetians who lived near the Turkish border it was preemptive punishment: German troops had never been anywhere near their region, but they were nevertheless regarded as a potential future enemy. In total, about 1,200,000 were affected. During 1943–44 the Soviets deployed hundreds of thousands of troops to forcibly remove these people, and they were moved with few possessions in cattle trucks with little or no food and water. Probably about 500,000 died in transit or subsequently in the Gulag. The Soviet authorities removed all references to these people, and all materials in their written languages were destroyed. In total, the Soviets forcibly deported about 2,500,000 of their own citizens.

Defeat and occupation produced a new, uncertain world for the civilians affected. The first reaction was to try to return to normality as quickly as possible. This was particularly apparent in western Europe in 1940. In Belgium the coal miners of the Limburg resumed work under German occupation on May 25, before Dunkirk and the

Belgian surrender and while over a million refugees were still outside the country. In Paris the theaters were running at nearly full capacity throughout May, during the rout at Sedan and the collapse of the Anglo-French armies. There was a hiatus from June 10 until early July, during the mass departure from the city and the early days of the occupation. The Palace Music Hall reopened on July 6, the Concert Mayol a week later, and the Folies Bergères at the end of the month. The Opéra-Comique and the Opéra followed in August. Racing at Auteuil restarted in early October, and at the end of the year there was a gala performance at the Opéra, complete with the Garde Républicain, that was equal in grandeur to any prewar occasion. In occupied western Europe about 90 percent of railway lines were back in operation by the end of 1940. The Amsterdam stock exchange reopened in mid-July and the index quickly rose to prewar levels and even higher by 1942. By this date the Paris Bourse index had risen to five times its prewar level.

Perhaps the factor that had the greatest impact on the civilian population was the sheer randomness of life under occupation, together with a justifiable fear of what the future might hold. In general, civilians had to adapt to the conditions of a police state, with identity cards, curfews, strict rationing, lack of food, and prohibitions on various activities such as listening to Allied radio stations. There were street searches and roundups, and individual actions often had little to do with whether people survived or not. As the war continued, German demands for labor grew and the slow growth of the resistance meant that life became even more hazardous. In September 1941 Hitler issued a decree that 100 hostages were to be killed for every German killed and 50 for every German wounded. In practice it was not possible to carry out reprisals on this scale, but they could still be substantial. In the Netherlands during the war about 3,000 civilians were executed and 600 died in concentration camps in Holland and about 20,000 in camps in Germany. In June 1944 there was a partisan raid near Tulle in central France, and in return 99 French civilians were hanged from the balconies, window grilles, and lampposts of the town. In June 1944, the Second S.S. Division was moving from Toulouse to Normandy and faced a series of low-level partisan attacks. When the division halted near the village of Oradour-sur-Glane near Limoges, 700 people were herded into the church and killed and the village was burned. Although Oradour has remained a symbol of the barbarity of German occupation in France, in western Europe it was the exception rather than the rule. German occupation was much less brutal in the west, whereas in the east Oradour was repeated thousands of times. The "antipartisan" operations in the western Soviet Union killed millions of civilians. In August 1943 a highly trained elite regiment of the German army, the Ninety-eighth Infantry, killed 317 people in the village of Komeno in western Greece, including twenty entire families and 74 children under the age of ten. Two months later in the northern Peloponnese about 80 German soldiers were killed by guerrillas. In retaliation, twenty-five villages were burned to the ground and 700 civilians shot, including the entire male population of the town of Kalavryta. These actions were repeated week after week, month after month in Greece during 1943–44.

Occupation also meant forced labor. Until the spring of 1942 the German authorities were content to rely on large-scale volunteering by foreign nationals to work in Germany. Then, as the economy was fully mobilized for war, they turned to forced labor. By the end of 1942 there were nearly 4 million foreign workers in Germany, and by 1943–44, between 1 million and 2 million were being sent each year. In all, forced labor probably affected about 12 million people in Europe; 1.5 million came from the Ukraine alone in the first half of 1944. At first, targets were imposed on local administrations, but this was soon replaced by mass roundups in the streets. In early November 1944 in Rotterdam, 54,000 out of a total eligible male population of about 70,000 were caught in mass raids and sent to forced labor, the majority in eastern Holland. The Japanese carried out a similar policy. By 1945 about 2 million Koreans were forced to work in Japan in conditions of near slavery in the coal mines and factories. In the East Indies the Japanese took over 300,000 people to work in Siam and Burma, of whom about 230,000 died.

The country that probably suffered the most under occupation was Poland. After it was partitioned in September 1939, there is no doubt that conditions in the Soviet area were far worse than in the west under German rule. By 1941 the Soviets had killed about four times as many Poles as the Germans (about 480,000, compared with 120,000) and this from a population about half the size of that controlled by Germany. Three separate Soviet mass deportations removed over 1 million Poles, mainly from the intellectual and political elite, and overall about 10 percent of all adult males in the Soviet-controlled area were imprisoned and tortured. At Boryslaw people were killed by having their mouths sewn together with barbed wire, or their eyes gouged out, or by being pushed into boiling water. About 5,000 Polish officers were shot at Katyn on the Politburo's orders. People living in the border areas were forcibly resettled and an internal passport system was introduced to control movement. These eastern provinces were forced into the Soviet Union as nominally independent republics, a new school system was introduced, property was expropriated, and a campaign was directed against the Catholic church and Polish culture. When the Germans invaded in June 1941 all prisoners were either killed or deported by the Soviets; at Lvov prison 12,400 were killed out of a total of 13,000 inmates.

The German occupation system in Poland was geared to the unlimited exploitation of a subjugated population. Compulsory labor was imposed on all those over fourteen. About 1.5 million civilians together with 500,000 prisoners of war were sent to Germany—about one eighth of the population. There was mass impoverishment of the Polish people. By 1941 average income had already fallen to 40 percent of its 1938 level, and this was to become much worse later in the war. By 1942–43 about half the food in the country was being sent to Germany and was taken from the countryside by means of force and terror. About a quarter of the population of Warsaw became dependent on welfare agencies for food, the TB rate among the non-Jewish population tripled between 1940 and 1943, and although rationing was imposed, most rationed goods were never supplied. Overall, Poland suffered from a gradual disintegration of society and a breakdown of social bonds. There was a huge growth in the black market, which came to supply about 80 percent of all needs, and people could survive only by finding some time to deal in it. The Poles suffered from labor roundups, street shootings (about 300 people a week were shot in the streets of Warsaw by the Germans between October 1943 and July 1944), hostage taking, reprisals, denunciations (many to settle old feuds), and blackmail. In October 1943 the German administration was discussing a decree under which civilians keeping their hands in their pockets would be shot. Altogether, about a fifth of the Polish population died in the war, over 90 percent of whom, about 5.5 million people, were civilians.

The situation in Poland was characteristic of German policies. In August 1942 Göring told the German administrators of occupied countries: "I see the people living there stuffed full of food. . . . You haven't been sent there to work for the well-being of the peoples entrusted to you, but to get hold of as much as you can so that the German people can live." Starvation became widespread in occupied countries. One of the worst situations was that of Greece, following the widespread looting of supplies by the Germans, economic collapse, and rampant inflation. About 40,000 people died of starvation in the first nine months of German occupation. The situation became worse in Athens and catastrophic on some of the isolated islands, and by 1945 about 300,000 had died. The food crisis in Greece was so bad that it was the only country for which the British were prepared to allow supplies to pass through the blockade. Starvation also occurred in the occupied parts of the Netherlands in the winter of 1944−45. By the summer of 1944 the ration, measured in calories, was already at half the prewar levels and produced a steady weakening in the population. In the winter, with the Netherlands only partly liberated, the transport system broke down and the Germans had little food they could issue to the population. In the northeast of the country, rations were maintained at about 1,500 calories, but even here about 15,000 people died. The situation was far worse in the west of the country, where public food services were feeding an average of 300,000 people a day; by April 1945 rations were down to about 500 calories a day. The population was kept alive only by Swedish and Swiss Red Cross supplies. The Allies refused to help. Tens of thousands died and in Amsterdam it was impossible to bury the dead properly.

The death toll from starvation in German-occupied Europe was small compared with that elsewhere. The greatest single tragedy was in Bengal. Rising war expenditure caused inflation after 1942, which resulted in the hoarding of food supplies, withdrawal of stocks from the market, and general administrative chaos. Agricultural wages failed to keep pace with inflation, impoverishing large parts of the rural population and also fishermen, who suffered from the impounding of their boats under wartime regulations. In 1943, despite the largest rice harvest ever, millions of people found they could no longer afford to buy rice as the price rose eightfold. The British government refused to allow more food imports by reallocating available shipping space. They also rejected an Indian government request for the import of 600,000 tons of wheat. Partly as a result of this inaction by the British, about 3 million people starved to death in 1943–44.

The food situation in the Soviet Union was also acute. The average calorie intake fell by a quarter between 1940 and 1942 and did not regain prewar levels for the rest of the war. Averages mean little, though, because the largest amounts of food were given to the military and munitions workers. Peasants, children, and the old had little, and their official rations were often insufficient to sustain life. Malnutrition was pervasive, and the incidence of infectious diseases rose rapidly in 1942 and was kept under control only through the introduction of "disinfection points" and "sanitation control" points at major railway stations. Death rates were at their peak in 1942, and even in Siberia, well away from the fighting, they rose by a quarter.

The situation was bad in most of the Soviet Union but it was catastrophic in the besieged city of Leningrad. During the winter of 1941–42 nearly 100,000 people were dying every month, far more per month than the British civilian casualties for the whole of the war. Overall, about 1.3 million people died in Leningrad during the 900-day siege, more than the military and civilian casualties in Britain and the United States for the whole of the war. Most of the blame for this situation can be placed on the Soviet authorities and their failure to organize an adequate evacuation of the city, or plan its food supplies, in the weeks before the siege began.

As German troops advanced toward Leningrad in August 1941 no action was taken; although rationing had been formally imposed at the beginning of July, it had little effect because ration levels were actually above prewar consumption. No attempt was made to arrange the evacuation of the population of about 2.8 million, which included 500,000 children. Panic set in after German forces cut off rail links at the end of August and fighting spread into the suburbs in mid-September. The Germans decided against a protracted fight through the streets and settled down to a blockade, expecting the city to be starved into surrender. With the cutting of rail links the only supply route was across Lake Ladoga, but the lack of ships and adequate piers and warehouses meant that no more than a third of Leningrad's food requirements could be supplied in this way. Stricter rationing was imposed at the beginning of September, when stocks were already down to one month's supply and restaurants were closed. In October the first deaths from hunger occurred, and nonworkers and children were now expected to survive on a third of a loaf of poor-quality bread a day plus, per month, one pound of meat, one and a half pounds of pasta, three pounds of pastry, and some cooking oil. In practice little but bread was available, and that was usually adulterated with moldy flour.

By the beginning of November the situation became acute, after the Germans cut the rail link to the Lake Ladoga supply point. All ration cards were re-registered and loss of a card meant certain death from starvation. Rations were allocated inequitably. Nonworkers received 125 grams of bread a day, workers 250 grams, soldiers in the front line 500 grams; the bread was altered to include 25 percent "edible" cellulose (pine and fir bark). The result was that the young, especially those between fourteen and eighteen, died first, for their nutritional needs were the greatest and their ration the lowest. In early December the rail route to the now frozen Lake Ladoga was recaptured, but even the new ice road across the lake could not deliver more than 800 tons of supplies a day—not enough to keep the population alive. The city of Leningrad was slowly collapsing in the coldest winter in living memory. At the beginning of December the streetcar system stopped working and there was no electricity and little water, so fires started by bombs and artillery bombardment could not be put out. By January the limited stocks of fuel were running out, and with no coal and wood it was impossible to heat the frozen water from the river Neva to make bread. By December all the dogs had been eaten and by the new year all the rats, too. People were dying in the streets, and others were murdered for their ration cards by gangs of professional criminals and deserters from the army. People, especially children and lone soldiers (the latter were better fed), were also killed to be ground up and sold in "meat patties." Nearly 300 people were executed for cannibalism, but this number represented only the tip of the iceberg. People could not wash, food utensils could not be cleaned, and a major outbreak of disease was avoided only because of the cold weather. The army was too weak to counter the siege; most of its divisions were at a third of their nominal strength, and even though they were better fed they reported over 20,000 cases of scurvy. The exact death toll in the winter of 1941–42 in Leningrad is unknown but was probably about 650,000. Over 20,000 yards of communal graves had to be created by dynamiting the frozen ground.

Only in the last week of January did the Soviet authorities decide to move some of the population. About 550,000 were evacuated across Lake Ladoga by April, but many died en route or shortly after. As the population of the city fell through starvation and evacuation, rations could be increased slowly. By March 1942 the city was slowly struggling back to life: power was restored, the streets could be cleaned, and the streetcars started running again. By April, when the ice road had to close with the spring thaw, about two months' supply of food had been stockpiled, but about 100,000 people still died that month. In July 1942 Leningrad was reduced to a military city with the evacuation of a further 300,000 people, which cut the population to about 800,000, only a quarter of its prewar level. Soviet forces were unable to break the siege throughout 1942–43. Rations were better than in the winter of 1941–42 because the population was so much lower. The siege was finally lifted at the end of January 1944, when the key railway junction of Mga was recaptured, reopening direct links with the rest of the country. By then the population had fallen to less than 600,000. Leningrad remained a devastated city: over 700,000 houses and 500 schools had been destroyed. Even by September 1945 the population had grown to only just over 1 million, about a third of its prewar level.

Across eastern Europe, as states and societies collapsed under the pressures of war, ethnic and religious conflict surfaced out of deep historical conflicts. At the start of the war in September 1939 the last actions of Polish forces in the east of the country were not against Soviet troops but against the Belorussian and Ukrainian minority, and the slaughter was stopped only by the arrival of Soviet troops. The minority then took advantage of the chaos of the first days of the occupation to turn on the Poles and kill them. Later, between 1941 and 1944, Ukrainian nationalist forces operating in what had been eastern Poland killed about 80,000 Poles. In return, the Polish Home Army, loyal to the government in London, took reprisals and exterminated whole villages of non-Poles. There were similar conflicts in parts of the Balkans. During the Bulgarian occupation of northeastern Greece in April 1941 about 100,000 Greeks were driven out of their villages to make room for Bulgarian immigrants.

The greatest ethnic slaughter took place as Yugoslavia was carved up after the German invasion in April 1941. The creation of a separate Croatia under nominal Italian supervision but controlled by the fascist, Catholic, extremist Ustasha movement was the catalyst for the tragedy. The Croats had been a minority largely excluded from power in Serb-controlled Yugoslavia. Now, historic Croatia was expanded to include Bosnia-Herzegovina and other territories, and the Ustasha were left by the Italians to govern a population of nearly 7 million people, of whom about half were Croats, just over 2 million were Serbs, about 750,000 were Muslims, and a small number were Protestants and Jews. The Protestants and Muslims were tolerated and the Jews treated as in Germany. The minister for education, Mile Budak, made clear the Ustasha aims: "Our new Croatia will get rid of all Serbs in our midst in order to become one hundred percent Catholic within ten years." He spoke of killing a third of the Serbs, converting a third, and expelling the remainder. The leader of the Ustasha, Ante Pavelic, said, "A good Ustasha is one who can use his knife to cut a child from the womb of its mother."

Persecution of the Orthodox Serbs began with the banning of the use of the Cyrillic script and the closure of Orthodox schools and was followed by forcible conversion to Catholicism and indiscriminate slaughter. About 300,000 Serbs were "converted," but by the end of the summer of 1941 about 350,000 Serbs had been killed and by May 1943 this total had risen to over 500,000. Thousands were kept in prison camps where the conditions were so appalling they horrified even the German officials in the area. At Zemun camp about 50,000 out of a total population of about 70,000 died within a few weeks of the camp's being established. Orthodox priests were tortured and killed, normally by having their throats cut, and their bodies were then exhibited in local butcher shops. The actions of the Ustasha were strongly supported by the local Catholic hierarchy. Cardinal Stepinac, the head of the Catholic church in Croatia, rejoiced over this "progress of Christianity." Franciscan priests led the killing of the Serbs and even ran two of the worst prison camps, Jasenovac and Alipasin Most. Pope Pius XII received Ante Pavelic at the Vatican with the honors due a head of state and called him "a much maligned man." The Vatican retained a close relationship with the Ustasha until the end of the war, and after.

Even persecution and death on this scale is dwarfed by the German treatment of the Jews and other minorities. In September 1933 the German government had begun the compulsory sterilization of those with congenital mental defects and sufferers from schizophrenia, manic-depressive psychosis, epilepsy, and severe alcoholism. There was substantial "scientific" support for such a program, and a eugenics movement had been widespread in other countries in the early twentieth century. By the outbreak of war the program had spread to include all German colored children, and on September 1, 1939, Hitler gave retrospective approval for a program for killing incurable patients. A few months later about 6,500 mental patients from Polish hospitals were shot. In early 1940 the first experiments in killing mental patients with carbon monoxide began; by September 1941 over 70,000 had been killed, and by 1945 nearly 90 percent of patients in German mental hospitals had been killed. Gypsies, those of mixed Gypsy blood, homosexuals, and "psychopaths" were either killed or sent to concentration camps. The exact number who died is unknown, although at least 17,000 Gypsies were killed at Auschwitz. Throughout the operation of these programs there was widespread scientific collaboration in the selection of victims, the writing of reports, and the carrying out of so-called "medical experiments."

Anti-Semitism was nothing new in European history: there had been ghettos, expulsions, and widespread discrimination for centuries, supported by the churches and most states. When the Nazis came to power in January 1933 they had no overall anti-Jewish policy and no idea about where their policy might lead, apart from immediate discrimination and an attempt to solve what they saw as the "Jewish question"—probably in the long term by expelling the Jews from Germany and possibly from Europe as a whole. By 1939, however, the action taken against German and Austrian Jews was still limited to widespread and severe discrimination. They were removed from official offices and the professions; a "voluntary" sale ("Aryanization") of Jewish enterprises was encouraged and then enforced after November 1938; Jews were subject to wide-ranging restrictions; and Jewish culture was attacked. Thousands were encouraged to emigrate and had to leave nearly all their property behind.

The situation became more critical in September 1939 when Germany took over a large part of Poland and found itself ruling over 2 million Jews. The German authorities were far more brutal in their treatment of Polish Jews than German Jews—their treatment of all Poles was vicious—and the minimal legal restraints that still applied in Germany itself were abandoned. After an initial upsurge of violence against Jews, as had occurred in 1938 during the Anschluss with Austria, the German government drew up a longer-term policy. In the autumn of 1939 they decided that Jews were to be expelled from the areas of Poland incorporated into Germany and sent to the General Government, the part of central Poland subject to German occupation but not incorporated into the Reich. The movement began in December 1939 with the aim of forcibly resettling about 600,000 people, but it stopped in March 1940 when still short of the target. Jews in Poland were subject to forced labor and in early 1940 many were moved into labor camps under appalling conditions.

By mid-1940 German officials in the General Government reacted to the influx of Jews and their inability to expel them any farther east by creating ghettos on an ad hoc and local basis. They came into force at Lodz in April 1940, at Warsaw in October, and at Lublin in April 1941, but the process was not complete until the end of 1941. The ghettos were designed to strictly isolate all Jews, but the German authorities had little idea what to do next. The ghettos were run by Jewish councils under German control and the inmates were forced to work. In some ghettos municipal workshops were set up, but in others, such as Warsaw, private enterprise was allowed, and inevitably this resulted in some inmates exploiting others. During 1941 a new crisis emerged: only minimal rations were allowed into the ghettos, and this, combined with overcrowding and poor sanitation, resulted in a very high death rate. This did not worry the German authorities as long as enough Jews survived to work. By early 1942 about 5,000 people a month were dying in the Warsaw ghetto, while in Lodz about 30,000 died in the two years after the ghetto was established. Overall it is likely that about 600,000 Jews died in the ghettos and labor camps in Poland—about one in five of all Polish Jews.

The first step in the deliberate mass killing of Jews was taken during the preparations for the invasion of the Soviet Union. As part of the process of exterminating the Bolshevik intelligentsia (the "commissar order"), Hitler ordered the creation of Einsatzgruppen, one to be attached to each of the four army groups, amounting in total to about 3,000 men at first. They operated just behind the front-line troops and in conjunction with the army. Their task was to kill as many Jews and suspected Communists as possible, and in practice distinctions between the categories were largely ignored. After June 1941 the Einsatzgruppen carried out fairly standardized killing operations. They would move into newly captured towns in eastern Poland or the western Soviet Union and, usually with the help of the local community, identify and separate the Jewish population. There was no attempt, as in Germany, to define a Jew legally—anybody who was thought to be Jewish was included. These people were taken in batches, forced to hand over their valuables and clothes, and then shot in an open grave, usually an old anti-tank ditch or shell crater.

The slaughter was usually conducted on a semipublic basis, sometimes with members of the army or the local population watching. By the late autumn of 1941 the Einsatzgruppen reported that about 300,000 Jews had been killed. Security Police units (Sicherheitspolizei—Sipo) moved in behind the Einsatzgruppen and killed about another 100,000. The local population often took part, enthusiastically, in the slaughter.

A second anti-Jewish sweep began in the autumn of 1941 in the Baltic states. As conditions behind the front line became more stable a much more extensive and systematic operation involving the S.S., the Security Police, local units, and the army as well as the now greatly expanded Einsatzgruppen was mounted. The killings followed the same general pattern as earlier in the year. A mass grave was dug by Jewish forced labor, the ghetto was surrounded, the residents were assembled, the houses burned down in order to prevent anybody from attempting to escape, and people then taken in batches to be shot. Their killers were usually drunk, many of the victims were buried alive, and some crawled out of the mass graves only to be shot later. Only a few survived. In June 1942, when these operations were over, a special unit was formed to dig up the mass graves, burn the bodies, and eliminate as many traces as possible of what had taken place. In total this second sweep operation probably killed about 900,000 people. Altogether, therefore, the mobile killing operations in the period 1941–42 resulted in the deaths of about 1,400,000 people.

German policy on what the Nazi leadership saw as the "Jewish question" was still undecided in the summer and autumn of 1941. The Jews living in western Europe and Germany were subject to massive discrimination, their property was confiscated, and often they were forced to live in particular areas. In Poland, Jews had been driven from the territory annexed by Germany and sent to squalid ghettos farther east, where tens of thousands were dying. Large numbers living farther east were killed by the special mobile commandos. However, there was no overall plan about what would happen next. In January 1939 Hitler had told the Reichstag: "If international-finance Jewry inside and outside of Europe should succeed once more in plunging nations into another world war, the consequence will not be the Bolshevization of the earth and thereby the victory of Jewry, but the annihilation of the Jewish race in Europe." German policy from 1938 until the end of 1941 was directed toward finding a "solution" to the "Jewish question" in mass emigration—possibly to Madagascar or, as was envisaged when Polish Jews were moved eastward, settlement in the Soviet Union, probably in Siberia. In July 1941 Göring ordered Reinhard Heydrich, the head of the Security Police, to make all the preparations for a mass deportation program. Until the autumn of 1941 Hitler, too, was talking in terms of speeding up the pace of deportation to either Madagascar or Siberia once the defeat of the Soviet Union was achieved.

German policy changed in the autumn of 1941 when it became clear that the war would be prolonged and mass deportation from western and central Europe to the east would not be possible while the war with the Soviet Union continued. The Nazi leadership believed they faced a "Jewish question" now made worse by the conditions their policy had created in Poland. Mass killing was already under way on the eastern front. At the end of November 1941 invitations were issued for a conference on the "remaining work" in connection with the "final solution" of the "Jewish question." This took place on January 20, 1942, at Wannsee in Berlin and included representatives from all the government departments that would be involved in planning the operation. The German government was careful not to set out clearly and unambiguously that it intended to exterminate as many Jews as possible. However, the conclusions of the meeting were that there would be mass transportation to the east, forced labor for those capable of it, and "appropriate treatment" or "special measures" for the rest. By early 1942 the construction of special killing centers in Poland was under way, and arrangements were being made to transport the victims to the centers. This decision to create establishments that had no purpose other than the industrialized mass killing of a particular group of people is what distinguishes this barbarity from all others committed in the Second World War. No document has been found giving Hitler's authorization for this program. However, this policy could not have been adopted without his approval and knowledge and a formal order was neither required nor in conformity with his normal method of working.

The German government could act on its own in Germany, Poland, and the occupied Soviet Union. Elsewhere they needed the cooperation of their allies and the governments and administrations of the occupied countries. In western Europe, the first phase of the policy from late 1941 was the prohibition of any Jewish emigration, the beginning of internment in special camps, and even greater harassment and discrimination; the wearing of a distinctive yellow star was generally introduced in early 1942. The largest deportations were from the Netherlands and France; in the latter country the Vichy government was particularly cooperative. Some of the allies—Italy, Hungary, and Finland—refused to cooperate with German policy. The Germans were able to organize deportations from the first two countries only after they occupied them, in 1943 and 1944, respectively. Altogether, about 250,000 Jews were deported to the killing centers from western Europe. Ultimately only military defeat stopped the deportations: the last regular transit from the French internment center at Drancy took place on July 31, 1944, and that from the Netherlands just over a month later. The last transport from Italy to Auschwitz left on October 24, 1944.

The deportations from western Europe were relatively small compared with the numbers killed from eastern Europe and the Balkans; the Jewish inhabitants of these areas provided the overwhelming proportion of those massacred at the new German killing centers. The first killings by gas (carbon monoxide) used mobile vans and began in the Soviet Union and Serbia in 1941; by the last months of 1941 stationary vans were used at Chelmno, northern Poland, to kill about 100,000 people. This process was adopted at the first killing centers and also at the last to be opened, at Treblinka. At the Auschwitz center it was decided to use the more "efficient" Zyklon B (prussic acid), which had to be produced on a massive scale in the German chemical plants of a subsidiary of I. G. Farben. By July 1942 six killing centers at Chelmno, Auschwitz, Treblinka, Sobibor, Belzec, and Majdanek were operational.

Jews were transported to the killing centers under terrible conditions, spending days, often weeks, in grossly overcrowded cattle trucks with little or no food and water and no sanitation. Tens of thousands died before they reached the killing centers. On arrival at the camps they were forced to give up all their property; there was a complex operation to reuse every possible item, down to the hair of the dead, which was made into felt footwear for U-boat crews. Victims were then stripped before being sent directly to the gas chambers unless overcrowding meant they had to wait, without clothes and food, before being killed. Apart from Majdanek and Auschwitz the centers required only a few Jews to carry out the most revolting tasks. In these two camps, "selections" were made of those to work as slaves in the industrial plants run by the S.S. and major German companies. The numbers of workers required varied greatly. Auschwitz had 140,000 workers in December 1943 but only 67,000 four months later. The conditions for these workers were indescribable, and once they were either too weak to work, ill, or no longer required, they too were killed, as were the few Jewish workers at the other killing centers.

Those sent to die were crushed into gas chambers that were disguised as "sanitation" or "shower" rooms. At Auschwitz about 2,000 people were killed in each chamber once the pellets of Zyklon B sublimated on the floor and produced hydrogen cyanide gas. There was a terrible struggle to breathe the gas-free air at the top of the chamber, but within about four minutes everybody was dead. Many of the dead would have bled through the nose or foamed at the mouth and nearly all turned pink and their bodies were covered in green spots. Carbon monoxide, used in some centers, took much longer to kill its victims; it was usually about two or three hours before everybody was dead, and the conditions in the gas chambers afterward were horrific. The removal of the bodies was the task of the Jewish Sonderkommando, or special squads, who first had to pull out the gold teeth from the dead. Disposal of the bodies was a major problem for the German authorities. At Chelmno a bone-crushing machine was tried out and at Auschwitz there was a crematorium capable of burning about 12,000 bodies a day, but the gas chambers were often operating faster than that. Most of the killing centers burned the bodies in huge open pits. Auschwitz had eight pits, each sixty yards long, where the 2,000 or so Jews in the Sonderkommando collected in buckets the human fat that accumulated at the bottom of the pits and poured it back over the fire to hasten the burning process. By August 1944 Auschwitz was killing 20,000 people a day.

The killing centers carried out the industrialized mass killing over a very short period. Chelmno was effectively closed after March 1943 and Treblinka, Sobibor, and Belzec were evacuated in the autumn of 1943. Majdanek was overrun by the Red Army in July 1944, so that by the summer and autumn of 1944 only Auschwitz was still in use, during which period it was killing a huge number of Hungarian Jews. Himmler ordered its closure at the end of November 1944 and it was evacuated in January 1945; 58,000 of its inmates were sent on a forced march westward, during which most died. Some 6,000 ill and dying were left behind to be liberated by Soviet troops. The exact number who died at the killing centers will never be known. The most accurate estimate is about 4 million people. To this figure has to be added the approximately 600,000 who died in the ghettos and the 1.4 million who died in the mobile killing operations. In total, therefore, the number of Jews killed during the Second World War, simply for being Jews, was about 6 million. A large number of people in Germany, both in the government and private industry, were involved in arranging the deportations, operating the transport, and building and supplying the killing centers as well as running the slave labor camps.

The Second World War was the first conflict in which the bombing of civilians was adopted as a deliberate policy on a large scale, and the Allies killed by far the greater number. Before the war, military theorists suggested that the bombing of cities would be a way of attacking enemy morale and forcing an opponent to surrender short of defeat on the battlefield. In practice the combatants found that large-scale air attacks did not bring the results expected: no society collapsed under the pressure of bombing. At the outbreak of the war both sides accepted Roosevelt's call to avoid the deliberate bombing of civilians. The British pledged themselves "solemnly and publicly" to conduct hostilities with due regard to the civilian population. In

April 1940 the British and French agreed to refrain from air attacks if civilians were likely to be involved. Germany agreed on September 3, 1939, to confine air attacks to the zone of operations. The Allies ignored the German bombing of Warsaw in September 1939 but chose to regard the German attack in May 1940 on Rotterdam, which, like Warsaw, was certainly within the zone of operations, as breaking that commitment. The British opened the first bomber offensive deliberately aimed at civilian targets with attacks on the Ruhr in May 1940. On May 24, after these operations, Hitler authorized the bombing of Britain, but until September 1940 he insisted that the Luftwaffe should avoid attacking London and only changed this policy after the British began bombing Berlin. The German Blitz on Britain in the winter of 1940–41 was followed by the far more extensive Allied bombing of German cities and huge casualties in places such as Hamburg and Dresden. By 1942 the Americans had forgotten Roosevelt's 1939 initiative and joined the British bomber offensive. The final irony came in August 1945, when the Americans, who almost six years earlier had asked the combatants to avoid attacks on civilians, dropped the atomic bombs on Hiroshima and Nagasaki.

German bombing of civilians was almost entirely restricted to Britain. The period of greatest bombing was in 1940, when just under 37,000 tons were dropped; the total for the whole war was just over 74,000 tons. This figure is small compared with the Allied bomb load. They dropped just short of 2 million tons of bombs on Europe, including nearly 1.2 million tons in 1944 alone. The casualty rate reflected these figures. The bombing of Britain killed 51,000 people. The Allies, however, killed about 600,000 German civilians, 62,000 Italians, and over 900,000 Japanese. They also killed about 60,000 French people, even though bombing of occupied territory was not allowed before spring 1942. In Germany about 800,000 people were seriously injured and 7.5 million were made homeless. Overall the Allies killed at least 1,600,000 civilians through bombing.

People's response to bombing was remarkably similar in each country. The main effort was to flee the likely targets. At the outbreak of war the British government put into action an elaborate evacuation plan prepared before 1939, but many of the evacuees had returned by the time large-scale bombing began in September 1940. Within a few days half the population of the Borough of Stepney in the East End had left, and by October a quarter of London's citizens had fled the capital. The population of provincial cities reacted in the same way, a phenomenon rapidly christened "trekking." In parts of Southampton only one in five of the population were left. In Portsmouth, about 90,000 people a night were leaving the city. In Germany, nearly 5 million people fled the cities, mainly a voluntary movement since German evacuation plans were far less developed than those in Britain. In Italy the government organized huge convoys of trucks to evacuate the cities each night. In Japan, which suffered from the most highly concentrated bombing, 10 million people fled the cities, half of them from Tokyo, and 450,000 children were compulsorily evacuated. Most major Japanese cities lost about 60 percent of their population.

In general, governments were slow to organize effective civil defense and relief efforts for the bombed cities. In Britain, for example, there was no national fire service with interoperable equipment and no fire-watching service until the Blitz was over, in May 1941. Few effective shelters had been provided and the government tried to stop people using the Underground stations, fearing they would not come out again to work. Eventually the authorities had to give in and belatedly supply canteen facilities, chemical lavatories, and a proper system of tickets for entry. Provision for the homeless was also inadequate. By October 1940 only 7,000 out of the 250,000 who had lost their homes had been rehoused. The overwhelming majority therefore had to survive in government "rest centers," where they were subject to the indignities of the Poor Law designed for the destitute. In one center in Stepney nearly 300 people had to use ten pails or old coal scuttles as lavatories and make do with seven basins (but no soap or towels) to wash in. No facilities or assistance were provided for "trekkers," whom the government wished to discourage. People everywhere tried to carry on their lives as best they could because they had little alternative. There were few, if any, ways in which they could show their discontent and every belligerent government was powerful enough to control its population.

At first the techniques of destruction were relatively primitive. The German raid on Coventry in November 1940 took about 500 bombers to kill about 550 people. Even so, the Blitz in the winter of 1940–41 killed over 40,000 people, and the centers of some cities, especially London, were badly damaged. On May 30, 1942, the British launched, partly as a propaganda measure, a 1,000-bomber raid on Cologne. This effort killed 469 people. The development of more sophisticated techniques using a carefully calculated mixture of explosive bombs to blow open buildings and then incendiaries to set them on fire resulted in casualties on a scale not experienced before. The effect of these techniques was demonstrated in Operation Gomorrah, the Allied bombing of Hamburg in late July 1943. On the two nights of raids the aiming point for Bomber Command was not the U-boat and naval yards on the south bank of the Elbe but the residential districts to the north, but the effect of "creep-back," the tendency of crews to drop their bombs short of the aiming point, ensured that the full weight of the bombing was felt in the densely populated areas of the city.

The first raid killed about 1,500 people, but the second, when the incendiary load was increased by about a third, was devastating. The bombing was unusually concentrated and the fires coalesced into a single firestorm that expanded to cover an area of over four square miles. Temperatures at the center reached about 1,472° Fahrenheit, with hurricane-force winds as oxygen was sucked in by the firestorm. About 16,000 blocks of apartments caught fire, and although most of the residents were in basement shelters, they died because the oxygen was sucked out. Only a few survived in the open air by jumping into canals or water-filled craters. The firestorm lasted for five hours and about 40,000 people were killed (almost as many as died in Britain in the whole of the war). One resident of the Hammerbrook district described the scene in the immediate aftermath of the raid:

> Four-story-high blocks of flats were like glowing mounds of stone. . . . Women and children were so charred as to be unrecognizable. . . . Their brains tumbled from their burst temples and their

insides from the soft parts under the ribs. . . . The smallest children lay like fried eels on the pavement.

A mass exodus from the city followed—over 1 million people left. However, although about a quarter of a million homes were destroyed and 900,000 people needed rehousing, the war production lost was small (less than two months in total) and within five months the city was back to 80 percent of its normal output. In February 1945 a similar attack on Dresden, which was crowded with refugees from the east, probably killed about 70,000 to 80,000 people in a single night.

The American raid on Tokyo on the night of March 9–10, 1945, was even more catastrophic. The United States launched 334 B-29s loaded with 2,000 tons of incendiaries and targeted twelve square miles in which wooden housing made up, according to USAAF estimates, about 90 percent of the area. There was no military or economic target of any importance in the bombing area. The resulting firestorm covered an area of sixteen square miles; the flames could be seen 150 miles out to sea, and the air above the fire was so violent that bombers at 6,000 feet were turned over and crews had to wear oxygen masks. The official U.S. Strategic Bombing Survey concluded: "Probably more persons lost their lives by fire at Tokyo in a 6-hour period than at any time in the history of man." About 100,000 people died, 1 million were injured, and 1 million lost their homes. The fires were so intense that people who jumped into the canals of Shitamachi to save themselves were boiled alive. The head of the USAAF sent the overall commander of the mission, General Curtis LeMay, the following message: "Congratulations. This mission shows your crews have got the guts for anything." Over the next few nights the USAAF bombed Nagoya, Osaka, and Kobe in the same manner, killing about another 100,000 people. The raids stopped only because the U.S. units in the Pacific ran out of incendiary bombs.

The U.S. bombing of Japan was so intense in the period after November 1944 that the committee directing the A-bomb effort had to insist on the "reservation" of three cities so that there would still be targets left on which to drop the new weapon. The primary target was always Hiroshima. Nagasaki was added to the list at the last moment. Hiroshima had a population of just under 300,000, including about 43,000 soldiers. It was not a military center and there were no important war industries in the town. Anyway, the target committee agreed that the aiming point should be the center of the city, not the industrial areas on the outskirts. It was therefore a delusion for President Truman to write in his diary that "the target will be a purely military one." The first atomic bomb was dropped on August 6, 1945, and exploded at 8:16 A.M. at 2,000 feet above the Shima Hospital in central Hiroshima. In effect the whole city was destroyed in an instant. About 150,000 people were killed more or less immediately, and of the city's 76,000 buildings over 70,000 were destroyed or severely damaged. Another 50,000 people died by 1950 from the effects of radiation. Three days later the more powerful bomb dropped on Nagasaki killed about 70,000 people immediately, a toll that rose to about 140,000. In both cities just over half the population were killed.

The impact of the bomb was similar in both cities. Within an area of about half a mile from the explosion, 90 percent of the people were killed instantly—the majority who died were killed in this way. The only trace of some people was the shadows they left behind on walls and pavements. About a mile from the explosion skin was carbonized and viscerae were evaporated. Thousands of small black bundles were stuck to pavements and bridges, the remains of cremated humans. Even two and a half miles from the explosion skin temperatures reached 120° Fahrenheit, resulting in instant blistering. The blast wave traveling at two miles a second then ripped off this blistered skin. This wave also blew broken glass and bits of buildings into people. Others who jumped into civil-defense water tanks were boiled alive. Thousands of people were left walking around with the skin hanging off their bodies, eyes sticking two inches out of their sockets or attempting to walk on their ankles because their feet had been blown off. There was little or no medical attention for the wounded.

The descriptions given by the survivors are terrifying. One woman reported, "I heard a girl's voice clearly from behind a tree. 'Help me, please.' Her back was completely burned and the skin peeled off and was hanging down from her hips." A seventeen-year-old girl said, "I walked past Hiroshima station . . . and saw people with their bowels and brains coming out." One man described how he was horrified "at the sight of a stark naked man standing in the rain with his eyeball in his palm. He looked to be in great pain but there was nothing I could do for him." A sixteen-year-old boy said he saw "human bodies in such a state that you couldn't tell whether they were humans or what. . . . There is a pile of bodies in the road and people are writhing in their death agonies." A thirteen-year-old boy recalled: "men whose whole bodies were covered with blood, and women whose skin hung from them like a kimono, plunged shrieking into the river." An eleven-year-old girl remembered that "no matter where you looked there was nothing but burned people all around." One hospital patient spoke about the condition of the troops who had been exercising in the open with no tops on when the bomb exploded. They were "burned from the hips up; and where the skin had peeled, their flesh was wet and mushy. . . . And they had no faces! Their eyes, noses and mouths had been burned away and it looked as if their ears had melted off. It was hard to tell front from back." The suffering continued for years as tens of thousands of people succumbed to various radiation-induced illnesses.

Even after the two A-bomb attacks, while Japan was in the throes of surrendering and further atom bomb attacks were suspended, the USAAF launched over 1,000 aircraft, every one available, for one last raid on Tokyo. Twelve million pounds of high explosives and incendiaries were dropped, destroying half of the Kumagaya district, leaving tens of thousands dead. The USAAF was determined to show that it could win the war. Even before the A-bombs were dropped, Henry Stimson, the secretary of state for war and key adviser on the use to be made of the new weapon, emphasized to the committee directing the atomic program: "The appalling lack of conscience and compassion that the war had brought about . . . the complacency, the indifference, and the silence with which we greeted the mass bombings in Europe and, above all, Japan . . . as far as degradation went, we had had it."

IX

OCCUPATION

MILITARY CONQUESTS BY GERMANY, JAPAN, AND ITALY meant that they acquired vast new territories to rule. At its maximum extent the new German "empire" included over 260 million people, and Japan controlled much of China and nearly all of southeast Asia. Both countries proclaimed a "new order" in their spheres but although there was much that was new there was little order. The Japanese Greater East Asian Co-Prosperity Scheme was, in reality, no more than a Japanese empire; similarly, German policies were directed toward exploitation, not the building of a new Europe. Hitler remarked in February 1942, during one of his interminable after-dinner monologues: "Once I conquered a country should I ever restore its freedom? What for? Whoever spent his blood has the right to rule." While Japan ruled its new territories as a military empire, Germany produced an administrative shambles. Some parts of Europe were annexed (western Poland, Eupen-Malmedy from Belgium, part of Slovenia, Alsace-Lorraine, and Luxembourg de facto after 1942), some were protectorates (Bohemia and Moravia), some were Reich commissariats (central Poland, Norway, the Netherlands, and Ukraine), some were under military administration (Denmark after 1943, Serbia, Greece, and parts of France), and some had German supervision imposed (Denmark before September 1943 and Hungary after 1944). Some areas (Croatia, the Dalmatian coast, and parts of Greece) were left for the Italians.

Analysis of reactions by states and societies to foreign occupation has generally, both during the war and since, tended to categorize all activity as either collaboration or resistance. However, to do so dangerously oversimplifies a complex situation. Are the nationalist risings in the Baltic states, Ukraine, and Belorussia and their cooperation with German forces a form of collaboration, or should they be seen as resistance to Soviet rule? Should the nationalists in Burma, India, the Philippines, and elsewhere in southeast Asia be seen as collaborators with Japan or as leading the resistance to European rule? Into what category does the Jewish terrorist group, the Stern gang, fall? It approached the German Legation in Beirut and asked for German help in expelling the British from Palestine, and organized the assassination of leading British figures such as Lord Moyne. In his memoirs, written forty years later, Yitzhak Shamir argued that "in 1940 and 1941, it was reasonable to feel that there was little for Jews to choose from between the Germans and the British."

The use of two simple categories seriously distorts behavior that was neither collaboration nor resistance. For most people, whose livelihoods and welfare depended on the existing social and economic system, there was little choice but to adjust to the new circumstances of occupation and to try to carry on life as normally as possible. The overwhelming majority of people therefore chose neither of the extremes of collaboration or resistance. To some extent, though, merely carrying on their "normal" lives by going to work when a large part of industrial and agricultural output went to the Germans was a form of collaboration. In France, armaments manufacturers were accepting orders from Germany within three months of the armistice, and by 1942 over 3,000 aircraft and nearly 12,000 airplane engines were on order. In the Netherlands the railway workers union authorized its members to collaborate with the Germans. The railways organized ninety-eight trains to transport 112,000 Dutch Jews to the extermination camps. Were the workers who produced the munitions and ran the trains collaborators, or simply trying to keep their jobs? Individuals often had little choice but to make a number of adaptations to life under occupation, but this was not the case for politicians. They had a very clear choice about whether to try to continue to exercise power in very different circumstances from those of the prewar world.

Reactions to occupation, especially at the political level, cannot be understood within a purely wartime framework. They reflected divisions, often severe, in prewar political structures. For example, Greek wartime politics was largely determined by reactions to the king's involvement in the prewar Metaxas dictatorship, and the Vichy government in France was a conservative reaction to the politics and policies of the Third Republic. In India, Burma, and the Philippines, the nationalist groups that had demanded independence before the war split, with some members deciding to cooperate with Japan (and in one case Germany, too) in an attempt to obtain independence. In some states—especially Denmark before September 1943, Vichy before November 1942, and Slovakia—governments were able to adjust to the new circumstances. They retained considerable independence, particularly in the domestic field, and were willing, often enthusiastically so, to cooperate with Germany in foreign relations. In other countries, such as Poland, Belgium, the Netherlands, and Norway, governments did not survive the invasion. (In Belgium, King Leopold III stayed behind to negotiate an armistice but had no power.) However, prewar instructions to the civil services were that they were to cooperate with any occupier to ensure that the basic functions of the states continued and the welfare of the people could be protected as far as possible. After invasion, this situation posed major problems for the bureaucracies. To what extent should they cooperate with the German occupying authorities in carrying out their instructions, what room to maneuver did they have, bearing in mind that if they refused to cooperate, the Germans might find more pliant administrators? Where was the borderline between necessary cooperation and active collaboration? Even in Poland, a country that suffered one of the most draconian occupation regimes, about 280,000 people continued working in the civil service and other state functions.

Many political responses and movements were attempts to avoid the extremes of collaboration and resistance and to explore whether it was possible to devise a new politics that would be compatible with a German-occupied Europe. The prewar political structures in the Far East, European colonial rule, ruled out this option. Under both German and Japanese rule there were cases of weak, puppet regimes such as the Russian collaborators and the regimes in China and Manchuria. Only in a minority of cases was there active, ideological collaborationism with Germany. These groups had their origins in a variety of prewar movements—Catholic authoritarianism, small prewar fascist and semi-Nazi groups, and marginalized political figures—who saw occupation as a way of gaining power in alliance with the Germans. In general, the German government mistrusted these groups, recognizing that they had little support domestically, and refused to give them more than the trappings of power. Because Japan did not articulate an alternative political philosophy this form of collaboration was absent in the Far East. The problem for all these groups, particularly in German-occupied Europe, was that the occupying power was not interested in constructing a new framework that would be based on genuine cooperation between independent states, even though that cooperation would inevitably reflect the new balance of power—both Germany and Japan were primarily interested in exploitation and in entrenching their new dominance.

The progress of the war was vitally important in determining reactions to occupation, particularly in Europe. From the summer of 1940 until at least the American entry into the war, the overwhelming response was one of acceptance and adjustment. German domination of the Continent seemed to be an established fact, and therefore it was necessary to decide how to come to terms with the new reality, unpleasant though it might be. In this period resistance to German occupation was extremely limited. During 1942 and particularly in 1943–44, resistance grew as it became more clear that the Allies would eventually win. The much more open, even ambiguous, situation apparent in Europe between 1939 and 1942, which had given political groups and states such as Vichy France considerable room to maneuver, was rapidly disappearing, and the political situation was being polarized into pro- and anti-German positions. However, even in this later period the level of resistance should not be exaggerated. Much resistance activity developed very late and only as the Allied armies approached. Nevertheless, new political movements were emerging and attempting to ensure some influence in the political world that would emerge after liberation. In this period the collaborators, especially those who did so on an ideological basis, were so committed to Germany and the Nazis that they found it either impossible to disengage or were unwilling to do so.

Occupation, in its earliest stages, produced a number of reactions at the political level ranging across a spectrum from different forms of opportunism through puppet regimes to ideological enthusiasm for the occupier. In many countries adjustment to and acceptance of foreign control seemed the wisest policy, for example in the Czech lands between 1939 and the end of 1941, and in Denmark from April 1940 to August 1943. After Munich, President Benes was forced into exile and he was replaced by the conservative and nationalist Emil Hacha. When the Germans occupied Prague in March 1939 and established the Protectorate of Bohemia-Moravia, Hacha stayed in office and the Czech state continued to function. An extraordinary consensus emerged between the government in Prague and the group in exile. Benes kept in contact with the Hacha government and there was considerable cooperation between them, and they agreed that resistance would be self-defeating. In fact there was little, if any, resistance—by early 1940 the circulation of illegal newspapers went into steep decline, there was little sabotage, and by the end of 1941 General Homola, the leader of the Nation's Defense group nominally pledged to resistance, admitted that it had no arms and he was its only leader. Some members of the government in Prague escaped to join Benes in London with the approval of the prime minister, Elias. (Elias was eventually shot by the Germans as a "traitor" for maintaining links with Benes.) The rival presidents did not attack each other and accepted that they were both working in the national interest. Only slowly did the situation change. The day after the German attack on the Soviet Union Hacha praised the Germans, whereas Benes objected to any anti-Soviet action. Increasing German control of the Czech economy and supervision of the government led Hacha to call for full collaboration in November. It was only at this point that Benes finally broke with the Prague government and declared

Czech belligerency a month later. Resistance then had to be imported from outside.

The position of Denmark remained anomalous after the German invasion in April 1940, until full occupation took place at the end of August 1943. Denmark was technically still neutral, but subject to a light German occupation (there were only about two hundred German officials in the country). The Danish political establishment was determined to maintain the existing political system, and a four-party coalition was formed that shifted strongly to the right after the fall of France. Danish policy was aimed at accommodation and cooperation. The foreign minister, Scavenius, spoke of his "astonishment and admiration" at the quick German victories and argued that Denmark could find a new role in active cooperation with Germany. Denmark broke diplomatic relations with those states at war with Germany and in June 1941 imprisoned, without trial, the leaders of the Communist party, speaking of the German struggle against a power that "constituted a threat to the welfare and prosperity of the Nordic states." In August the Communist party was banned and in November 1941 Denmark signed the Anti-Comintern Pact. Danish workers were recruited to work in Germany, and industrial and agricultural exports to its neighbor increased significantly. In the end, the cooperation of the Danish establishment with Germany was halted by growing popular pressure and demonstrations, which resulted in a full German takeover.

On a more general level, acceptance of occupation can be found in the large number of voluntary workers supporting the German war effort. To some extent this reflected the relatively high levels of unemployment in occupied Europe and the lack of alternative employment, but until mid-1942 voluntary labor, in which about 2 million people were involved at any one time, was sufficient to meet all German requirements. As early as May 1940 there were about 800,000 voluntary workers in Germany, mainly from Poland. The conquest of western Europe increased this number significantly. By October 1941 there were 295,000 volunteers from this area—mainly from Belgium and the Netherlands, although eventually France was to supply over 650,000 volunteers—together with about 1 million from Poland; 400,000 from German allies such as Italy, Slovakia, and Hungary; and some from neutral countries, mainly Switzerland.

In many countries the main reaction to German occupation was not simply to adjust to the new circumstances but to use them to accomplish goals that seemed impossible in prewar politics—a response found in Slovakia, Vichy France, and the Netherlands. After Munich, Slovak politicians, who were assured of German support in seeking a separate republic, became less willing to tolerate what they had always seen as Czech domination of the Czechoslovak Republic. It was President Hacha's attempt to dismiss the Slovak government on March 10, 1939, that caused Hitler to invite its prime minister to Berlin, where he was told to declare independence. The Slovaks did so four days later and German troops then entered Prague. Slovakia became an independent republic run by the Catholic, authoritarian, and nationalist Slovak People's Party under its leader, Father Josef Tiso. The new government reflected a long tradition in Slovak opinion and politics with its emphasis on a corporate, Catholic social system. The government cooperated with Germany but resisted any attempt at nazification, and the German government supported Tiso rather than the more pro-German radicals because the Germans wanted stability and economic development to support their operations on the eastern front. The Tiso government remained extremely popular and there was no resistance organization in Slovakia until the end of 1943.

The French defeat in June 1940 brought about the dissolution of the existing French state. The two main French conditions for an armistice were quickly accepted by Hitler: no handing over of their fleet and the continuation of a sovereign, unoccupied French state. In theory, French sovereignty was maintained over the whole country, but German troops withdrew to a northern occupation zone running from Switzerland to the Spanish border along a line going almost as far north as Tours and giving Germany control of the whole Atlantic seaboard. The French government, originally at Bordeaux but later at Vichy, retained control of the rest of France and the empire. In the aftermath of defeat the politicians of the Third Republic, reflecting the animosities and divisions of the previous decade, voted in the

National Assembly by 569 to 80 to give full powers to Pétain, the new president, to draw up a new constitution and state. The consequence was the creation of a right-wing, authoritarian (but not fascist) government composed of many of the outcasts from the politics of the Third Republic and strongly influenced by the military and the technocrats of the civil service. Pétain dominated the government and fully exercised the powers he had been given. By the end of 1940 a relatively stable system had been established and the most fanatical advocates of collaboration with Germany had been dispatched to Paris to cooperate with the occupation regime.

The Vichy government had widespread popular support: the war was expected to end shortly and most French people wanted a new departure and an attempt to reestablish France's place in Europe. As late as April 1944 there were vast crowds in Paris to cheer Pétain— no doubt some of the same people who cheered de Gaulle on his entry into the capital just four months later. The new regime was fiercely anti-Bolshevik and developed an extremely conservative ideology that looked back to the late nineteenth century and took much from the Catholic tradition that advocated corporate authoritarianism as an alternative to both totalitarianism and liberal democracy. The old trio of verities, "Liberty, Equality, Fraternity," was replaced by "Labor, Family, Fatherland." In August 1940, the French Freemasons organization was dissolved and three months later so were all trade unions. All strikes and lockouts were prohibited. Strict censorship was enforced. A conservative family policy was introduced: divorce was made more difficult, abortion was outlawed, and a highly nationalist new education syllabus included lessons in morality. The main emphasis in Vichy policy was a shift away from individualism toward a more corporatist approach, with the introduction of state youth movements and the organization of the professions.

Without any prompting from the German authorities, Vichy introduced its own anti-Jewish policies. In August 1940 the law against slandering or libeling any racial or religious group was repealed. Two months later, French Jews (defined as those with half Jewish blood or more or those who practiced Judaism) were excluded from all elected and public functions and could not serve in the army, the media, or as magistrates. A quota was set for admission to universities and the professions. Businesses were to be taken over by non-Jews. In the spring of 1941, 40,000 foreign Jews were interned in special camps in the south of France. In December 1941 a special tax was imposed on the Jewish community, and in May 1942 Jews were required to wear the yellow star, were excluded from public places, and were allowed to shop only in the afternoon, when most food had already been sold.

The Vichy government had to decide how to adjust to the new balance of power in Europe. At the beginning of October 1940 Pétain called for "collaboration in every domain," provided that Germany showed "restraint in victory." The Vichy minister of state, Pierre Laval, was the most open in his determination to collaborate with Germany, but Pétain and other senior figures followed broadly the same policy. Laval was sacked from the government in late 1940, and Pétain refused to come to a deal with Hitler at their meeting at Montoire in late October and kept open his lines of communication to the British. However, this did not alter Vichy's general determination to try to exploit the new situation. In early 1941, under Admiral Darlan, the Vichy government embarked on a policy of state collaboration with Germany. The German determination to help Iraq against Britain in May 1941 led to a request by the Germans to use French bases and facilities in Syria. Vichy granted the facilities: over one hundred German planes used the bases, and four trainloads of supplies were sent to Iraq via Syria. In return Darlan was able to secure the first concessions from Germany since the armistice in June 1940. The administration of the demarcation line was softened, about 100,000 prisoners of war were released, some French warships were allowed to rearm, and—in return for a guarantee of French sovereignty over the empire—Darlan agreed "in principle" to the use by German forces of the Dakar naval base in West Africa, although this part of the agreement was never implemented. These agreements did not lead to a new status for France vis-à-vis Germany, and by December 1941, when Pétain met Göring, it was clear that Germany would not treat France as an equal.

In April 1942 Laval became premier of the Vichy government,

convinced that he was the one man who could negotiate with Germany and establish France's place in the new Europe. There was still no question of Vichy support for Nazi doctrines; Vichy had its own domestic political agenda and sought to exploit the new situation for the advantage of France. Almost immediately the German authorities asked for "voluntary" workers. Laval was able to bargain for the return of prisoners in the ratio of one for every three workers who went to Germany. In September Vichy mobilized all males aged between eighteen and fifty and all women between twenty-one and thirty-five for labor duties. Internal security was increased and prominent prewar politicians such as Blum, Daladier, Reynaud, and Mandel were handed over to the Germans. During the summer of 1942 Vichy freely cooperated with German anti-Jewish policies. All the non-French Jews who had been interned in the south since 1940 were handed over in return for a promise not to deport French Jews (in fact, over 23,000 were deported). Laval specifically asked the Germans to include children under the age of sixteen in the deportations. Despite these efforts Laval had not improved France's position by the time the Allies invaded Morocco and Algeria in November 1942. Vichy agreed to the deployment of German troops in Tunisia but cooperation with the Allies in Algiers resulted in German occupation of the whole of France, the disarming of the remaining French army, and the scuttling of the navy. The Vichy government continued but its situation and policies after November 1942 need to be viewed in terms of a different type of response to occupation than the relative degree of freedom it enjoyed in the two and a half years after the armistice.

In the Netherlands, unlike in France, no government remained in the country after May 1940, although a Dutch administration continued under German supervision. On July 24 a number of politicians led by Dr. Hendrikus Colijn, head of the Calvinist Anti-Revolutionary party and prime minister five times before the war, published an appeal to the nation for a movement called Nederlandsche Unie, or "Netherlands Union." It was meant to be a mass movement, filling the void left by the flight of the queen and the government, and called for unity and cohesion in the new circumstances. It looked backward to past values, including toleration, but there was nothing in the appeal about democracy. It was close to the Vichy appeal to a social Catholic rejection of both Marxism and capitalism and placed an emphasis on traditionalist, corporatist values but from a mainly Calvinist perspective. The movement accepted the new balance of power in Europe and tried to find a way in which the Netherlands could reassert itself. Colijn said, "Since a defeat of the Germans is no longer possible, [Europe] will in future be led by Germany [and therefore] it would be necessary to modify certain national establishments and institutions in accordance with the German model."

Nederlandsche Unie was intended to be the forum where the debate about how the country could adjust to the new situation in Europe could take place. It was immensely popular on a scale never seen before in the country; by late 1940 it had 800,000 members. Unlike Vichy, however, it was not able to implement its policies. Colijn tried to form a provisional government, but the German authorities did not give permission. Without access to power the movement continued to be little more than a debating society and a focus for hopes about Dutch national revival in the new Europe. The Germans remained suspicious of the movement, especially after it refused to back all-out mobilization after the invasion of the Soviet Union. Its popularity continued, however, and after the occupation authorities banned the public sale of its newspaper, over 250,000 people took out a direct subscription. During the second half of 1941 the German government became convinced that Nederlandsche Unie was basically anti-German, and the movement was banned at the end of the year.

The policies of the governments in Vichy and Slovakia and movements like Nederlandsche Unie had their roots in the prewar world and doubts about the effectiveness of liberal democracy. German success and national defeat were spurs toward attempts to find a more conservative, organized, and corporatist approach to national life. These policies were highly popular, and in Europe between 1940 and 1942, some governments had enough maneuvering room to enable them to be implemented. It was only as the war intensified and German defeat loomed that German policy increasingly closed off these options and forced governments to choose between Germany and the Allies.

In some areas, occupation seemed to provide the opportunity to achieve long-desired goals that had been effectively blocked in pre-war conditions. The German invasion of the Soviet Union and the Japanese destruction of the European empires in southeast Asia created a situation that nationalist groups seeking independence hoped to exploit. Although none were successful in the short term, their longer-term impact, particularly in the Far East, was substantial. During the chaos of the Russian revolution and civil war, various nationalities had achieved a short-lived independence between 1918 and 1922, which had been suppressed by the reestablishment of the Russian empire under Soviet control; the Baltic states retained their independence until 1940. The problem for all these nationalist groups in eastern Europe and the Soviet Union was that the German government, with its strong racial views about the inferiority of the Slav peoples, had no intention of allowing them any formal independence. The conquered areas were to be exploited by Germany and nationalist groups were allocated a role of only low-level collaboration with German occupying forces.

Ukrainian nationalism was a relatively recent development, and although a series of governments existed in the period 1917–20, the nationalists had split into numerous semifascist factions while in exile. For a few months after the Munich agreement, Ukrainian nationalists controlled Carpatho-Ukraine in eastern Czechoslovakia, and in September 1939 over six thousand guerrillas rose against Polish forces before the Soviet invasion of eastern Poland. Eighteen months later, nationalists followed German troops into Ukraine and on June 30, 1941, declared an independent state at Lvov. In the short period before the Germans arrested the nationalist leaders, in July, a series of atrocities against Russians, Poles, and Jews took place. On July 5, 70 Jews were blown up with dynamite at Tarnopol, and 130 were beaten to death with clubs at Kremenets. The German government had no intention of allowing an independent Ukrainian state, but they were prepared to accept Ukrainian help at a local level in administration. The Ukrainian Orthodox church was allowed to set up its own autonomous organization in August 1941 and provided major support for the nationalists. Local militias were vital in helping the Einsatzgruppen carry out their massacres; the militias were normally left to undertake the most revolting tasks, such as killing the children, which even the S.S. men disliked. Ukraine also provided one of the largest groups of S.S. volunteers in the conquered territory. The formation of the Galician S.S. was suggested by the main collaborator in Cracow, Professor Volodymyr Kubiovych, and over 100,000 men came forward. It was the German authorities who decided to limit recruitment to a level of 30,000. Militarily they were ineffective. Some of the nationalists remained uncommitted to the Germans, and in 1943 the Bandera wing of the main nationalist organization, the O.U.N., set up its own partisan army. Its task was to fight the Soviets, Poles, and Jews and it hoped to reestablish the independent Ukraine that had existed in 1918–20. It was about 50,000 strong and it remained in existence for several years after the war. Not until the last days of the war was the German government prepared to support an independent Ukraine. On March 17, 1945, an independent Ukraine was declared by a handful of exiles in Weimar—an irrelevant gesture.

In Belorussia the German authorities made it clear that they did not propose to create an independent state. However, the nationalists, led by Radaslav Astronski, who had arrived in the wake of the German invading forces, called for national mobilization and created about sixty battalions to assist the occupying troops. In December 1943 the existing "advisory council" of Belorussians helping the Germans was transformed into the "Belorussian Central Council" to act as representatives of the Belorussian people collaborating with Germany. In June 1944, as Soviet forces neared Minsk, a Belorussian Congress, composed of various self-appointed groups, met to declare that it was the legal successor to the independent Belorussian Rada (parliament) of 1918, but within a week its members had withdrawn into exile, in Germany.

In the Baltic states the German authorities viewed the local population as non-Slavs and thus superior to the other nationalities of the

Soviet Union. They were therefore allowed a greater degree of self-government, although the area was still reserved for German colonization. The Baltic states were the first to recruit units for the S.S.; the Latvian S.S. was 30,000 strong by 1943 and was headed by Rudolf Bangerskis, who had fought with Admiral Kolchak (the White Russian leader during the civil war) and who had been minister for war in Latvia in 1927. Local forces were also central to the anti-Jewish pogroms, drawing on a deep current of anti-Semitism in the Baltic states. In Lithuania, Bishop Brizgyz forbade the clergy to aid the Jews in any way, and the forces that rose in revolt as Soviet troops departed in 1941 rapidly turned their weapons on the Jewish population. In the Latvian capital of Riga 500 were killed in a single day, and in Lithuania 47,000 were killed in a three-month program of daily slaughter.

Farther east in the Soviet Union nationalist groups had far fewer opportunities to exploit the circumstances created by the war, partly because they were occupied by German forces for shorter periods. The group that contributed most to the German war effort was the Cossacks, who had generally been on the White side in the Russian civil war. Soon after June 1941 the leader of the Kuban Cossacks, Naumenko, and of the Don Cossacks, Krasnov, offered help to the German authorities as a way of reestablishing Cossack independence. They were ignored until November 1943 when, with German forces in retreat, they were promised their old lands back. In March 1944 Naumenko and Krasnov were put in charge of Cossack forces within the German army. The troops, together with many women and children, retreated with the Germans, fought the Yugoslav partisans, and in the spring of 1945 were granted by the Germans the area of "Cossackia" in Italy, near the Austrian border. In April 1945 the Cossack forces retreated into Austria to avoid fighting British units.

In the summer of 1942 German troops appeared to be heading toward conquest of the Caucasus region, an area regarded by German racial experts as Aryan though not intended for German settlement. Exile groups from this area had considerable influence over German policy, but little was achieved. The Chechen and Karachai rose in revolt against the Soviets as German troops approached, and a Karachai National Committee was formed and given some local power: collective farms were dissolved and local volunteer cavalry units were formed to fight with the Germans. Persecution of the Jews was instituted. German occupation lasted only a couple of months and there was therefore no time for the resentment of German occupation policies, typical of other areas of the Soviet Union, to emerge. Some local units retreated with the Germans in the autumn of 1942, and a year later a Turkic S.S. unit was formed, which took part, with singular lack of success, in antipartisan operations in Belorussia in 1944.

In Asia, the Japanese had an even greater level of nationalist discontent available to exploit, but like the German government they were primarily interested in the control of conquered territories rather than their development as independent states. There was also, as with Germany, an element of racial superiority in their attitudes toward the conquered peoples. Only as the progress of the war turned against them did the Japanese begin to make cautious moves toward allowing genuine independence—moves that were to have a major impact on the postwar world. From the start of the war, however, the Japanese adopted the *rhetoric* of liberation against European domination. A few days after Pearl Harbor, Tokyo announced that the war would be known as the Great East Asian War because it was "a war for the construction of a new order in East Asia," an order that entailed "the liberation of East Asian peoples from the aggression of America and Britain" and the eventual "creation of a new world culture." The Japanese prime minister, Tojo, announced in January 1942 that Asian development was to follow the Western model of industrialization but in a new order of "coexistence and coprosperity." This concept was superficial, and no real plans, other than for Japanese exploitation of the new territories, were developed before early 1943. Long-term Japanese plans envisaged Burma and the Philippines becoming puppet states like Manchuria, Siam and, Indochina, which were then developing into Japanese protectorates, while Malaya, Java, Sumatra, and the other islands remained colonies, like

Korea and Taiwan. The Japanese government believed that it could save Asia from the Europeans only by asserting Japanese dominance over the region.

By early 1943, as the tide of the war turned against Japan, the first attempts were made to construct a policy that would provide an incentive for nationalists to support the Japanese. In general, the Japanese had been widely welcomed in 1942, and the rapid collapse of the European empires—the British surrender at Singapore and the Dutch collapse in the East Indies—had destroyed the prestige of the colonial empires that had been carefully built up over the preceding centuries. Many of the nationalist politicians such as Aung San in Burma, Sukarno in Indonesia, and Subhas Chandra Bose in India had long been sympathetic toward Japan in its struggles with the West. A large number of societies and youth organizations were set up to support the Japanese, although the actions of Japanese troops often alienated the local populations. For the Japanese, the most important moment in their campaign to enlist nationalist support came in November 1943, with the Great East Asia Conference. The conference agreed on a policy of coexistence, coprosperity, mutual autonomy, and independence, cooperation, economic development, and no racial discrimination. For the Japanese this declaration was their Atlantic Charter enshrining opposition to British and American domination of the world. They did not live up to its ideals, however.

The first country to be granted independence was the Philippines. Before the outbreak of the Pacific war, the United States had already promised the country full independence in 1946. During the Japanese invasion President Manuel Quezon was so disillusioned by the American failure to defend the country that he asked Roosevelt for an immediate grant of independence so that he could negotiate with the Japanese. Roosevelt refused and Quezon was removed to America. His replacement, President José Laurel, was elected by the National Assembly, and in mid-October 1943 the formal grant of independence, promised by Japan five months earlier, came into effect. The Philippine government did not immediately declare war on the United States but allowed the Japanese to use military facilities on the islands. It was only after the U.S. bombing of Manila in September 1944 that the Philippines declared war on its former colonial power.

In Burma the local population had given little help to the British in defending the country in early 1942. The Japanese had before the war given limited training to the army led by Aung San, and after the conquest the Burma Independence Army rapidly grew to a strength of 200,000. In August 1942 it was replaced by the seven-battalion-strong Burma Defence Army. In early 1943 the Japanese began consultations with the nationalist leader, Ba Maw, who had been imprisoned by the British in 1940. In August 1943 Burma was declared independent. Ba Maw became head of government and Aung San took over as defense minister. In other countries the nationalists were less successful. The Chinese minority in Malaya was strongly opposed to the Japanese, and although the Malays welcomed the invader, no progress was made toward any form of independence. On Java a 34,000-strong volunteer army called Defenders of the Homeland was formed, which initially cooperated with the Japanese but eventually attacked them in February 1945 to try to establish independence before the Dutch returned. In Indonesia the nationalist movement under Sukarno ran a Pioneer Corps to support the Japanese, and very little help was given to the Allies during the war. However, the nationalists, who were Muslims, remained antipathetic to Japanese aims. Eventually, in September 1944, the Tokyo government promised independence, although nothing was achieved before the war ended. Later, in the chaos of the surrender and before the Dutch returned, the nationalists under Sukarno declared independence. In Indochina the Japanese were content to retain nominal French colonial rule until March 1945. During the war the British and the Americans cooperated with the nationalists under Ho Chi Minh, and as in Indonesia independence was declared in Hanoi in September 1945 before French control was reasserted.

One of the most difficult problems the Japanese (and the British) faced was how to deal with Indian nationalism. In the spring of 1942 the Congress party in India supported noncooperation with either side. In April 1942 Jawaharlal Nehru, a leader of the Congress party, declared, "Japan's quarrel is not with India. She is warring against the

British Empire. If India were freed, her first step would probably be to negotiate with Japan." Even before Congress officially switched to a "Quit India" policy, other elements in the Indian nationalist movement supported cooperation with Japan. In December 1941 Pritam Singh, who had been living in exile in Bangkok, had raised the Indian national flag in the Siamese village of Ha'adyai close to the Malayan border as Japanese troops moved south to invade British territory. After the fall of Singapore a much more serious movement began, when almost half of the 45,000 Indian troops captured joined the Indian National Army, the military arm of the Indian Independence League, led by Captain Mohan Singh. Unlike the British Indian Army, the I.N.A. was not organized along ethnic lines.

The main problem for the I.N.A. was that it lacked a leader of sufficient status. That role was eventually filled by Subhas Chandra Bose, who with Nehru had been general secretary of the Congress party in the late 1920s. At the outbreak of war he had been interned by the British but he escaped in early 1941 and traveled with Italian help (he was a great admirer of Mussolini) via Kabul and the Soviet Union to Berlin. In Germany he tried to recruit from among Indian prisoners captured in North Africa. However, the German government had little use for him, and the Japanese needed a convincing Indian leader after removing Mohan Singh at the end of 1942. Bose left Kiel in a U-boat in February 1943 and was transshipped to a Japanese submarine 400 miles off Madagascar in April; he eventually arrived in Tokyo after his round-the-world underwater voyage. In Malaya in July 1943 he became president of the Indian Independence League and in October head of "Asad Hind," the provisional government of free India. It had been given no more than a promise of independence from Japan and nominal control over the Andaman and Nicobar islands, although it declared war on both Britain and the United States. About six thousand I.N.A. troops were used during the Imphal battles of 1944, a situation where Indian troops were fighting for both sides, but they proved of only limited military effectiveness.

Both the Japanese and Germans were reluctant to encourage nationalist movements that might interfere with their exploitation of conquered territories—until the tide of the war turned in the Allies' favor. Nevertheless there were genuine nationalist movements in Ukraine, Belorussia, the Baltic states, India, the Philippines, Burma, and Indonesia that saw the war as an opportunity to achieve their aims. Although this meant cooperation with the invader, they did have a significant base of popular support. These movements were very different from the puppet regimes and groups that cooperated with the Germans and Japanese in situations where they had no effective freedom to operate and where they lacked a popular base. Such groups were found in the Soviet Union and across eastern and central Europe and as governments in China, Vichy France after 1942, and Mussolini's republic of Salo in northern Italy after the autumn of 1943.

Although western Europe contained numerous White Russian émigrés from the 1917 revolution, the German government refused to use them for more than menial tasks such as screening prisoners. They had no intention of allowing any alternative Russian government to emerge. They were prepared to exploit the Soviet population as workers and as auxiliary forces, and about half a million were used in this way. A few ex-Soviet local commanders, such as Kromiadi near Smolensk, Gil-Rodionov in Belorussia, and General Kaminsky near Bryansk, were allowed considerable discretion in their local areas. These men ran petty fiefdoms that flourished in the near anarchy of the eastern front. Kaminsky was a thug who publicly garroted his commanders and together with the local population of about 30,000 escaped the advancing Red Army in September 1943. His units then joined the S.S. and helped to put down the Warsaw uprising in August 1944. Once this task was completed Kaminsky was shot by the Germans.

The most significant defection to the Germans was that of General Andrei Vlasov, a Communist party member for over a decade and a brilliant commander who in 1941 had been promoted to lead the Second Assault Army. He was captured by the Germans near Volkhov in 1942 and rapidly became leader of a group of captured officers comprising Colonel Vladimir Boiarski of the Forty-first Guards Division, Major-General Malyshkin (who had been purged in 1938 but reinstated), Major-General Trukhin (chief of staff for the Baltic area), and Georgi Zhilenkov, a Moscow district party boss. In September 1942 Vlasov called for a separate peace and the creation of an anti-Stalinist government. Three months later he became head of the Russian National Committee. The German government allowed the formation of the Russian Army of Liberation from among Soviet prisoners. It was easy to recruit, given the prisoners' terrible conditions, and by mid-1943 the force consisted of about 160 battalions. For propaganda purposes Vlasov was appointed commander, but in practice the Germans were not prepared either to allow the army to operate as a separate formation or for Vlasov actually to command it. In early June 1943 Hitler ruled that Vlasov was to be kept out of all Soviet territory and the activities of his group restricted to propaganda from Berlin.

The situation changed only when Germany was on the point of defeat. In mid-September 1944 Himmler met Vlasov and agreed to the formation of K.O.N.R., the Committee for the Liberation of the Peoples of Russia, which was to be the forerunner of a government-in-exile, and a genuine Russian army. Two months later K.O.N.R. was founded in Prague at a meeting attended by no more than eighty people and largely shunned by the existing émigré organizations and the nationalities within the Soviet empire. At the end of January 1945 Vlasov took command of about 50,000 troops, who formed a ramshackle two-division army. It fought the Soviets around Frankfurt-on-the-Oder, but then, ignoring German orders, it moved across country to Prague, where on May 7 it helped resistance units fighting the S.S. before withdrawing toward Austria to avoid surrendering to the Red Army. Other groups in German-occupied areas were even more pathetic than the Vlasov organization. In Serbia, General Milan Nedic was allowed to command an "army" of 20,000 but he was never any more than a figurehead of a sham entity, unlike the extremist Ustasha in Croatia. In Greece, an ineffective government was allowed to hold nominal power. At first General Tsolakoglu tried to form a nonroyalist, non-Metaxas government, but no political figures would join, although in the summer of 1941 the socialist Giorgios Papandreou was prepared to discuss possibilities. The main advocate of cooperation with Germany was the finance minister Sotirios Gotzamanis, who, like many others, believed the German rhetoric about a new Europe and dreamed about a new order of freely cooperating states. In April 1943 Ioannis Rallis took over as prime minister; he and his government were mainly anti-Communist rather than pro-German and they wielded little political power.

The position of the Vichy government was transformed by the German occupation of all of France in November 1942. It no longer had any independent sphere within which it could operate, and although Pétain and Laval tried to convince themselves that little had changed, Vichy was in reality little more than a puppet regime maintained because the Germans found it useful. German "concessions," such as the abolition of the demarcation line in March 1943, were meaningless. Increasingly Vichy became a police state. In February 1943 the S.T.O. organization implemented a program of compulsory labor in Germany. At least 650,000 French citizens were affected. In the autumn of 1943 Pétain tried to sack Laval, create an elected assembly, and shift toward a policy of neutrality. He was under the illusion that he had as much freedom to maneuver as he had had in 1940–42; the German reaction showed that he did not. They banned his broadcast and although he refused to carry out any official functions for a month, he eventually gave in, reshuffled his government as the Germans instructed, and accepted a German "diplomatic delegate" in Vichy who supervised the government.

By early 1944 the Vichy government had become even more radical and right-wing. Hardliners such as Darnand and Henriot were brought in, "courts-martial" were introduced to try "terrorists," Pétain condemned all resistance groups, and the vicious militia was increasingly in control. Nevertheless the state continued to function, the administration and the police remained loyal, and the Catholic hierarchy remained supportive. When Pétain visited Nancy and Paris he was greeted with huge, enthusiastic crowds. Before the invasion of Normandy Vichy tried to open contacts with the Allies to see if a compromise settlement was possible, and after June they tried to negotiate with the Gaullists, but all their initiatives were rejected. In mid-August, Pétain, Laval, and a few other senior figures were forced by German troops to leave Vichy and travel east. On September 7 they were installed at Sigmaringen castle in Swabia and treated by the Germans as a provisional government of France, complete with a German ambassador. Pétain refused to carry out any functions or deal with the motley crew of collaborators the Germans had evacuated from Paris.

After his fall from power in July 1943 Mussolini was an even more pathetic figure than the Vichy regime. On September 12 he was released from Italian captivity at the Gran Sasso fortress in the Apennines by German commandos under Otto Skorzeny acting on Hitler's direct orders. Mussolini was taken to Germany to meet Hitler and plans were drawn up to reconstitute a Fascist government in Italy. When Italy had tried to withdraw from the war German forces interned over 600,000 Italian troops and established control over the country as far south as Rome. Mussolini's puppet government was put together in Rome on September 23, but it had to leave the capital because it was in the German military zone. Mussolini eventually settled on Lake Garda and instituted the Republic of Salo amid the chaos of the German occupation of northern Italy.

Mussolini, under German guidance, attempted to re-create the Fascist regime that had fallen apart in July. Within a month an organization of 250,000 members had been created and by November at the Congress of Verona a new, strongly fascist domestic policy was instituted. The monarchy, which had helped dismiss Mussolini, was dissolved, a strongly corporatist social and economic policy was instituted (though more in theory than in practice), and a special tribunal was established to try those members of the Fascist Grand Council who had voted against Mussolini in July. In January 1944 five people, including Mussolini's son-in-law, Count Ciano, were shot as traitors. A militia was established as well as an Italian S.S. unit. The Germans allowed the formation of an Italian army under General Graziani, which recruited from the internees held in Germany. However, it was restricted to four divisions and kept under strict control because the Germans feared another attempted defection.

Mussolini's power was minimal and the German occupation authorities were in real control of northern Italy. After the fall of Rome in June 1944 and the advance of the Allied armies toward the north, the formal German occupation zone encroached even farther into Mussolini's nominal zone of responsibility. The main task of the puppet government was to create the Black Brigades of party members that fought an increasingly vicious war against the partisans of the resistance as northern Italy slid into civil war. At the end of 1944 Mussolini tried to reconstitute his government and move it to Milan so as to detach it from German control and possibly open negotiations with the Allies. At least one attempt at negotiation was made in March 1945, but it failed and as the Allied armies finally advanced into Piedmont Mussolini fled north. He was captured by the partisans and shot.

Like all other occupied countries, China was not devoted to all-out national resistance, and this enabled the Japanese to establish puppet regimes. The earliest was in Manchuria, renamed Manchukuo, under the last deposed emperor, K'ang-te, in 1932, but it was no more than a facade for Japanese annexation. Similarly the Japanese authorities were keen to find as many people as possible to cooperate with them in the areas occupied after the 1937 invasion. In December 1937 they set up the Hsin-min Hui (People's Renovation Society), which promoted the idea of Asian rejuvenation, and by August 1942 there were 13,500 branches with 3.5 million members. The problem of finding an alternative government for China was more difficult. The Chinese figurehead chosen by the Japanese was Wang Ching-wei, who in the late 1920s and early 1930s had shared with Chiang Kai-shek a conciliatory approach to the Japanese. Wang continued this policy after the 1937 attack, strongly influenced by his fear of the Communists and of Chiang's cooperation with them and resentment of the Western powers' privileged position in China, particularly Britain's and the United States', and their failure to give effective help to the nationalists. In many ways he was an old-fashioned nationalist and, as a follower of Sun Yat-sen, looked to a revival of China on Asian, not Western, models. In December 1938 he left the Nationalist capital, Chungking, hoping to bring about military defections and make peace. His mission failed. A year later he returned to China from Indochina with Japanese support. In March 1940 the Re-organized National Government was established in Nanking and a few months later a Sino-Japanese basic treaty was agreed on that enshrined Japanese predominance. Wang Ching-wei operated only in Japanese-controlled territory, accepted Japanese advisers in his government, and recognized the Japanese conquest of Manchuria and autonomy for northern China, together with extensive Japanese military, political, and economic privileges in the rest of China.

The main problem for Wang Ching-wei's regime in Nanking was that the Japanese allowed it no armed forces, reinforcing its all too obvious position as a puppet regime. They also refused to allow it to declare war on Britain and the United States after Pearl Harbor, preferring it to retain its neutral status under the 1940 agreements. Although in early 1942 the Nanking government was used to try to influence the Nationalists in favor of peace, in China as elsewhere, the Japanese were very reluctant to undertake more than the rhetoric of pan-Asian collaboration against the Western nations. There were no fundamental changes until 1943. Then, in January, the Nanking government was allowed to declare war on the Allies, and later in the year the Japanese, like the British and the Americans with the Chiang Kai-shek government, agreed to give up their privileges under the nineteenth-century treaties. Although this was an attempt to increase the status of the Wang government, in practice very little altered. The Nanking government remained a pathetic puppet regime, although there was a considerable amount of Chinese collaboration with the Japanese. Somewhere between 500,000 and 1 million Chinese soldiers served with the Japanese, many of them defectors from the Nationalist armies (600,000 troops had defected by August 1943). Many of the local warlords opened up permanent trade routes with the Japanese using their troops to escort supplies and even granting extensive credit facilities. Even the Nationalist government in Chungking sold the Japanese tungsten, as well as many of their medical supplies provided by the Red Cross.

Although the Japanese adopted the rhetoric of a pan-Asian revival against the Western powers, Japan did not have a specific ideology that could be adopted by groups in other countries. In Europe, however, imitators of the Nazi philosophy and form of political action could be found in nearly every country. With one exception, the

German government had no time for these small, ineffective groups and did not trust them to take over the government of their countries, preferring to work either with local civil-service administrations, as for example in Belgium and the Netherlands, or through pliant governments, for example Vichy. The main value of the Nazi imitators as far as Germany was concerned was their willingness to play a role in internal security through the creation of militias and to provide recruiting organizations for volunteer units serving with the German army on the eastern front or becoming S.S. formations, all as part of a common war against bolshevism.

The only exception to this situation was in Norway, where Vidkun Quisling gave his name to a whole group of collaborators. Quisling had been minister for war in the early 1930s and later had founded his own movement for Nordic and national revival based on Nazi ideology. After 1938 he was supported by German money and in December 1939 he met Hitler and offered to mount a coup in Oslo. Hitler turned him down. When the Germans invaded on April 9, 1940, Quisling, in a comic-opera episode, appointed himself prime minister, and also minister of defense, minister of justice, and minister of foreign affairs. However, the civil service refused to cooperate, and a week later the Germans unceremoniously removed him from office and installed their own provisional government. Quisling and his party were only allowed to have ten of the thirteen seats on the powerless Provisional Council of State established in September 1940 and were given the privilege of being the only legal political party in Norway. Their membership rose from 4,000 in the summer of 1940 to 43,000 eighteen months later. The German occupation authorities considered Quisling too interested in asserting Norwegian independence within a German-dominated Europe. He was finally made prime minister in February 1942 but his government was given no effective power, apart from internal security under the thuggish Jonas Lie, who founded the Norwegian S.S. and was not a member of Quisling's party. About 5,000 Norwegians volunteered to serve with the German forces, including 2,000 in a special Nordic S.S. unit.

The other ideological collaborators in Europe did not achieve even this limited degree of recognition. In Denmark the main Nazi imitator was Fritz Clausen, but he had little support; in the March 1943 elections his party gained just 2 percent of the vote and the Germans preferred to work with the Danish government. A Frikorps Danmark fought on the eastern front as part of the Waffen S.S., and although Clausen himself joined the S.S. he remained of no political importance even after the full German occupation of Denmark. In the Netherlands a Fascist party, which was closer to Mussolini than Hitler, led by Adriaan Mussert had become the fifth-strongest in the country by the mid-1930s. Mussert was a not a Nazi, he refused to allow his supporters to join the S.S., and he hoped to preserve Dutch independence. Only a few fanatical Nazi sympathizers under Rost van Tonningen wanted the Netherlands to be absorbed into Germany. Mussert's party, the N.S.B., was ignored at a national level but was allowed to take power at local and provincial levels. Nevertheless there was a strong base of support in the Netherlands for collaboration with Germany. About 12,000 people joined the police and auxiliary units that supported the occupation authorities and 17,000 joined the S.S. in various units. Mussert and about 40,000 of his followers fled into Germany when Allied forces entered the Netherlands in late 1944.

Neighboring Luxembourg produced its own collaborationist movement. The V.D.B. ("Ethnic German Movement"), headed by Professor Damian Kratzenburg, was the only official party and had over 70,000 members by September 1941. Its main policy was to enforce German as the only official language of the country. In Belgium there were two collaborationist groups. The V.N.V. (Flemish Nationalist Party), under Staff de Clercq, favored a Greater Germanic Netherlands including Flanders. Again, the German authorities would not put the V.N.V. into power but were prepared to make it the only legal party and allow its members to take over local administration. In the Walloon areas of Belgium, members of the Rexist party, which had its roots in the Catholic tradition of authoritarian alternatives to liberalism, headed by Leon Degrelle were the main collaborators. Degrelle was a great favorite of Hitler, but like the V.N.V. the Rexists remained local administrators and a militia force to support the occupation authorities. As in the Netherlands there was a strong base of popular support for collaboration. Overall, about 50,000 people joined either the V.N.V. or the Rexists and about 20,000 were members of the militia. Degrelle was one of the 40,000 volunteers who fought on the eastern front and stayed with the Germans until the final battle for Berlin.

The greatest variety of collaborators were found in France, all of them acting independently of the Vichy government. Paris, in the German-controlled zone, was the center not just of a glittering social world but also of those politicians dedicated to full-scale collaboration with Germany. To a large extent they had failed in the prewar political system and now thought they saw the opportunity for revenge. Many came not from the existing far right but from the left, and some just wanted power. They tended to see themselves as the real revolutionaries compared with the old regime at Vichy and the leaders of a new France in a new Europe. They nearly all advocated internal repression, anti-Jewish measures, and concentration on the fight against bolshevism. Any lingering doubts about Germany were resolved by the attack on the Soviet Union. Their main problem was that, as elsewhere, the German authorities were not interested in giving them any effective power, and, of less importance, they were distrusted by the Vichy government. The result was impotence, intense rivalries, numerous splits, and an increasing radicalism as the progress of the war moved against Germany.

The first major movement, R.N.P. (Rassemblement National Populaire), was founded in early 1941 by Marcel Déat, an ex-Socialist and briefly a minister before the war and a close associate of Laval. He became a Fascist and was backed by the German ambassador in Paris, Abetz. In the autumn of 1940 Déat dismissed the German reannexation of Alsace-Lorraine: "As French people it is in our interest that there be no more frontiers and that we accept being a part of Hitler's Europe." He hoped to build a mass totalitarian party linking the trade unions and the radical right. Within months the R.N.P. split into left and right, the latter under Deloncle, who founded the Mouvement Social Révolutionnaire (M.S.R.), which had about 15,000 militants and paramilitaries. By early 1942 the M.S.R. had itself split and part of it was absorbed by the Parti Populaire

Français (P.P.F.) led by Jacques Doriot, the ex-Communist mayor of the Paris suburb of Saint-Denis, who had drifted to the far right. The P.P.F. had been founded in 1937, but it was not until after the occupation that it gained any real strength. By 1942 it had about 250,000 supporters and was strongly represented in the Parisian media; as late as 1944 its main newspaper was still selling 300,000 copies an issue. In November 1942, when German forces occupied the southern zone, Doriot offered to seize power from Laval, but the Germans were not interested.

Equally popular in France was the Anti-Bolshevik Legion, which was launched in the summer of 1941. Over 30,000 men volunteered to fight on the eastern front, but Hitler, who was reluctant to involve the French, limited the numbers to 15,000. The Legion was supported by the Catholic church and members of the Académie Française, who became honorary members. The Legion fought near Moscow but, like so many of the volunteer units, it was soon pulled back to concentrate on antipartisan warfare. The collaborationist groups in Paris struggled to control the Legion, but it was Laval at Vichy who recognized it in July 1942 as the Légion Tricolore, which was later expanded into the Légion des Volontaires Français. In July 1943 the Vichy government agreed to the formation of a French Waffen S.S. unit—the Sturmbrigade Frankreich, or "Charlemagne Division"—as long as it was not used against the French. It was 7,500 strong and recruited with propaganda that was an incompatible mixture of Christian crusade ideals and pagan Nazi ideas. It fought with the Horst Wessel Division of the S.S. in southern Poland in August 1944 and sustained heavy casualties. Some of its members fought in the final Battle of Berlin even after Hitler's death.

As the war turned in favor of the Allies the collaborationists in France became even more extreme. Déat remained convinced that Germany would still win the war and in September 1943 broke with Laval and called for a full-scale revolution: "France will if necessary be covered with concentration camps and the execution squads will operate without pause." After D-Day the increasingly desperate hard-line collaborators carried out their threats in what amounted to a civil war, including the torture and shooting of resistance figures and some prewar political figures such as Georges Mandel. As the secretary to Joseph Darnand, the leader of the paramilitary Milice, put it: "Not to have taken action . . . would have resulted in our entirely losing the confidence of the S.S." After September 1944 Doriot headed an impotent Committee for French Liberation based in Germany, but the internecine squabbles continued. In February 1945 Doriot was killed, probably as the result of a German plot hatched with other French collaborators and the Belgian Rexist leader Degrelle.

Until well into 1943, adaptation, adjustment, and opportunism were the overwhelming reactions to German occupation. These attitudes were not incompatible with a limited degree of low-level resistance. Many of the earliest manifestations of this nonacceptance of foreign occupation were symbolic, such as wearing royal symbols or national colors: as early as June 26, 1940, Prince Bernhard's birthday, thousands of Dutch people signed a book of greetings at the royal palace or wore either carnations (Bernhard's favorite flower) or orange-colored flowers. Two months later, about two thirds of the Danish population took part in various communal song festivals. In November 1940 thousands of French people took part in armistice day parades. The German authorities rarely worried about such activities because they remained compatible with cooperation, especially the production of goods and munitions for the German war effort. Another banned but widely practiced act was listening to Allied radio broadcasts; by 1943 the BBC was broadcasting five and a half hours of programs every day to France and even fifteen minutes a day, four days a week to smaller countries such as Albania and Luxembourg.

A step further along the road to resistance was active noncooperation. In the Netherlands and Norway the trade unions effectively dissolved themselves rather than be subjected to Nazi control. In Norway in February 1942 there was a mass refusal to attend a church service to mark the installation of Quisling as the head of the government, although thousands attended a nonpolitical service later in the day. As a result the dean of Trondheim Cathedral was removed, whereupon over 90 percent of the ministers in the established church resigned, and between 1942 and 1945 there was effectively no established church in Norway. In Luxembourg during the 1941 referendum on the incorporation of the country into Germany the occupation authorities decreed that it was inadmissable for voters to describe their nationality as "Luxemburgisch" or their language as "Letzeburgisch." In the referendum over 97 percent of the population used these terms. At this level it was also possible for workers and managers in factories or on the railways to engage in low-level resistance. There was plenty of scope for working slowly, not repairing machines, not adopting the most efficient methods, and generally creating as many difficulties as possible.

A more open form of resistance was the publication of underground leaflets, newspapers, books, and posters. Many were started by small groups of like-minded people and then snowballed, although often they had a very short life span. The Germans reckoned that there were over 3,500 illegal newspapers being produced in western Europe by 1944 and some, such as *Défense de la France,* had a circulation of about 450,000. Such publications were an important source of nonofficial information, and it required huge efforts to find the paper, premises, and money to sustain publication in a strictly rationed and controlled society and economy. It could also be a very dangerous occupation. One Dutch paper, *Trouw,* which had a circulation of about 60,000 copies, had over 120 of its helpers executed. Another form of resistance activity was to help in the escape of Allied aircrew and prisoners or Jews and other refugees. Well-organized escape routes were developed, which were able to help 3,000 aircrew to escape capture; in total, nearly 30,000 fugitives crossed the border from France into Spain, the main escape route. In addition, by late 1943 almost 25,000 Jews were being hidden by the Dutch underground organizations. This, too, could be highly dangerous work, usually leading to death if discovered. The twenty-three-year-old Andrée Dejongh ran the Comet escape line from Brussels which in three years was responsible for the escape of about eight hundred British servicemen. She was captured in 1943 but survived two years in Mauthausen concentration camp in Austria. Her father took over the Comet line but was executed in March 1944. Equally important and dangerous was the gathering of intelligence about German activities, deployments, and defenses. A network of informants, especially if they were within local administrations, could be a valuable source of knowledge for the Allies, as long as means could be found to ensure that the information reached them.

For most of the people who took part in such activities their participation was motivated by the maintenance of self-respect. It was also a calling that required great courage. Life as a full-time resistance agent depended on maintaining several false identities, living on false papers, living in constant fear, traveling regularly, staying in hotels, meeting other agents in public places, memorizing vast amounts of information about their false identities and security procedures for clandestine meetings. These agents depended on a network of helpers prepared to provide various forms of assistance, such as safe houses. Above all, there was the constant threat of discovery, torture, and death. The head of the French resistance, Jean Moulin, was tortured to death in Lyons by the Gestapo. Pierre Brossolette, a socialist journalist, escaped to London, was sent back to France as an agent, and was eventually captured in Brittany on his way back to Britain. He was tortured by the Gestapo and committed suicide by throwing himself out of a window to avoid revealing his knowledge of the resistance organization.

It is, however, vital not to overemphasize the importance of the resistance. Actions such as publishing newspapers and collecting information would not end German occupation. Also, resistance was not highly popular before the last two years of the war. Of the 43,000 French troops captured in Syria in the summer of 1941 only 6,000 volunteered to join the Free French; the remainder opted to be repatriated. More Norwegians died on the eastern front fighting in volunteer S.S. units than in the resistance. In the Netherlands before June 1944 the best estimate is that less than 1,200 people were fully engaged in the resistance, and before 1943 there were no major armed resistance groups in western Europe. The scale of British assistance should also not be exaggerated. Although the Special Operations Executive (S.O.E.) was set up in July 1940 with the aim of fomenting continual subversion and open rebellion, this aim rapidly gave way to supporting underground armies that would operate in conjunction with Allied strategy and only rise in revolt when the Allies were ready to invade. S.O.E. also had to deal with bitter conflicts with other groups within the British bureaucracy, such as MI5 and MI6. It was also restricted by the War Cabinet decision that no agents should be dropped into the Vichy-controlled zone, a policy that was not reversed until after November 1942. In a review of its first eighteen months of operations carried out in September 1941, S.O.E. was forced to admit that although thirty agents had been sent into France, only thirteen more had been recruited locally, in France. Among them they had two operational radios. Two agents had been dropped into the Netherlands but no reports had been received and just one person had been recruited to work in Italy.

Resistance activity in many areas was therefore inevitably very circumscribed. In France the first emissary from the Free French was not parachuted into the country until October 1941; de Gaulle was viewed with suspicion by many figures in the resistance. In some countries, such as the Netherlands and Belgium, which were heavily urbanized and lacked remote mountainous areas, guerrilla activity was not possible. The Dutch resistance was also extremely isolated: it was two years before courier links with Sweden were established and even longer before a route to Switzerland was open. The first underground newspaper was not smuggled out to Britain until 1942, and no useful intelligence was provided for the Allies until well into 1943. In Norway, which did have a terrain ideally suited to guerrilla warfare, the government-in-exile, supported by the British, stopped any open warfare from the underground army organization MILORG. In other countries resistance activity was organized only very late in the war. In Slovakia the National Council, dedicated to resistance, was not created until November 1943; in Hungary a Liberation Committee was finally formed in November 1944.

Although partisan warfare in Yugoslavia began almost immediately after the German conquest, by the autumn of 1941 the country was badly split and resistance activity was very limited. The Communist partisans under Tito had no outside support for over twenty months and in the autumn of 1941 were driven out of Serbia into a

remote area of Bosnia-Herzegovina, where they maintained themselves by a reign of terror over the local population. At the same time
the Chetniks, under Mihailovic, followed the advice of the government-in-exile and the British that they should not commit themselves to major activity because of the German policy of reprisals and
should instead wait for an Allied invasion. Mihailovic carried this
policy further than intended. He saw the partisans as the main threat
to a postwar restoration of the monarchy and concentrated upon containing them through cooperation with both the Germans and Italians in antipartisan operations. The overall result was a lack of
effective resistance and a growing civil war within Yugoslavia made
worse by the ethnic divisions.

Until well into 1942 resistance caused the Germans few problems.
During 1941 Germany was able to control the Balkans by using just
seven divisions as occupying forces. In Yugoslavia there were just
four divisions, half of whose troops were First World War veterans.
German counterintelligence activities were also extremely efficient.
In the Netherlands they penetrated the S.O.E. organization and in a
spectacular success created a phantom resistance organization and
captured nearly every S.O.E. agent dropped for nearly two years. In
the east they set up a fake Communist party of Bohemia-Moravia,
which succeeded in gaining Soviet recognition and which was able to
neutralize much of the resistance activity. The Germans also scored
considerable successes in France. In 1942 a quarter of air drops of
supplies to the resistance fell into German hands, and by 1943 the
proportion had risen to a half. They were also able to turn a number
of radio operators, so that at one point the Germans were running
eleven "resistance" transmitters and were even setting up dummy resistance groups that fooled the British.

In these difficult circumstances there were limits to how much resistance movements could achieve, even when they were formed and
operational. To some extent they had to be defensive, helping people
cope with the rigors of occupation. In the Netherlands, for example,
much of the activity was concentrated on two organizations. The National Relief Fund (recognized by the government-in-exile) had
15,000 people involved in distributing relief for those who had left

jobs rather than cooperate with the occupation authorities. Another organization helped those in hiding and by the summer of 1944 was supplying the underground with over 200,000 false ration cards and other forgeries. Help was also given to strikers. When Allied airborne troops landed at Nijmegen and Arnhem in September 1944 a railway strike was called. It was highly effective, but the strikers demanded full pay for the duration of the strike, plus overtime and a Christmas bonus. This was conceded but it meant that nearly half of all the financial aid sent by the government-in-exile to the resistance went to this one group of workers.

One of the most remarkable examples of defensive resistance was the rescue of the Danish Jews. Until the formal German takeover of the country in September 1943 no action had been taken against the Jews, and when the Germans did move, the resistance movements had been warned by the head of the S.S. in Denmark. There was time to organize an operation involving thousands of people in which 7,300 Jews were secretly moved across the country to a fleet of trawlers, which took them to Sweden. Other action ensured the safety of those who could not move: for example, Jewish hospital patients were "discharged" and reregistered under different names without moving from their beds. Only 2 percent of the Jewish population in Denmark (mainly the old) was caught in the German sweep. They were sent to Theresienstadt concentration camp, but the Danish king insisted that they be treated well, and under considerable pressure the German authorities allowed Danish and Red Cross representatives to visit the camp and provide supplies. The overwhelming majority survived until the end of the war.

However, the largest and most extraordinary example of defensive resistance occurred in Poland. In the Soviet-occupied zone, resistance was limited, partly because the head of the resistance army was an N.K.V.D. informer, and Soviet forces ruthlessly suppressed any activity. In the German zone the central organs of the Polish state effectively ceased to exist and the occupation authorities had no interest in encouraging collaboration—Poland was the only occupied country in Europe not to produce a collaborationist organization—and were instead interested only in exploitation. In June 1940 the government-in-exile under General Sikorski called off all resistance and sabotage operations as too dangerous and pointless, given the overwhelming German superiority on the Continent. Instead, activities were concentrated on trying to maintain the institutions of the Polish state and society so that they could reemerge at the end of the war.

The first steps toward creating such a structure were taken in Warsaw after the government fled the country. By early 1940 nearly all the prewar parties had set up underground organizations, but unity proved difficult to sustain in the isolated cell structure necessary under occupation. Parties split and split again because there was no incentive to stay united, and it was not until January 1944 that a Council of National Unity was established and a unified Home Army created, from which only the radical right and Communists stood aside. Gradually a highly bureaucratic underground emerged that was able to raise money from voluntary donations, some forms of taxation, and grants from the government in London. About half the money was spent on social welfare programs and education, officials were paid salaries, and even the political parties received "state" support. Over 1 million pupils were educated by 19,000 teachers, and by 1944 Warsaw University was effectively operating again with over 200 professors and lecturers in organized faculties and 1,700 properly enrolled students. The underground also operated its own criminal-justice system with courts, lawyers, and judges—it executed over 200 people during the war. An underground press was vital in countering German propaganda and breaking down the isolation of individuals and groups. More than 400 clandestine printing houses produced over 1,500 newspapers, more than anywhere else in Europe. Although the Home Army declined drastically after the summer of 1940, when the government called off open resistance, it had been rebuilt to a strength of about 350,000 by 1943.

Fear of extensive reprisals meant that some types of resistance, especially assassinations of prominent Germans or the killing of German soldiers, were only reluctantly authorized, if at all, by the governments-in-exile. They saw it as their responsibility to protect the civilian population as far as possible. This was particularly the case after Hitler's order in September 1941 that 100 hostages should be shot for every German killed and 50 for every German wounded. Although this order was not always carried out in these exact proportions, reprisals were brutal. As a consequence, governments and most local resistance groups except the Communists were reluctant to undertake such operations until liberation was at hand. Other forms of resistance—slowdowns, sabotage, noncooperation, producing newspapers, and providing intelligence—involved less risk for the civilian population.

The consequences of random assassinations were vividly and terribly demonstrated by the British-directed killing of Reinhard Heydrich, the head of the German Secret Police (Sipo) and Security Service (SD), the chief planner of the Final Solution, and the administrator of the Protectorate of Bohemia-Moravia. Given the lack of resistance inside the protectorate, the British had to use agents specially dropped for the purpose of shooting Heydrich on May 27, 1942. On hearing the news Hitler ordered martial law to be declared and 10,000 Czechs to be arrested; all prisoners were to be taken to concentration camps and shot, 100 of them immediately. The deputy administrator of the protectorate persuaded Hitler to rescind the order. Heydrich died of his wounds on June 4. There were over 1,000 denunciations of suspected figures in the resistance by Czech citizens, and after being given information from a local factory owner that the assassins had sheltered in the village of Lidice, Hitler ordered its destruction. The village was surrounded by German troops, assisted by the Czech gendarmerie. All 173 males were shot, 198 women were sent to Ravensbrück concentration camp, 17 children were deemed to be Aryan enough to be adopted in Germany, and the remaining 81 children were almost certainly gassed at Chelmno. The village was burned down and the 26 inhabitants who were absent during the operation were tracked down and shot. In addition to the deaths at Lidice, 24 people were shot at Lezaky and 11 children were sent to death camps. Then, a total of 1,331 people were killed after "trials." In total, over 1,600 people were deliberately killed as revenge for the death of Heydrich. The Czech government banned all further assassinations.

The acute problems caused by resistance were shown in their most brutal form during the Warsaw uprising of 1944. In mid-July the commander of the Home Army, Bor-Komorowski, told the government in London that an uprising in the city would be too dangerous and would only lead to heavy losses. Within a week there was a rapid change of mind as Soviet forces neared Warsaw. The uprising began at five P.M. on August 1, and no warning was given to the civilian population, so tens of thousands of people were caught in the wrong part of the city and were unable to return to their homes and families for the rest of the battle. The revolt was planned to last for a week and was designed to seize control of the city before the Red Army arrived. Instead it lasted for over two months and demonstrated total war at its grimmest. Warsaw was cut off from the rest of the world and was turned into a battleground. At first the Home Army was able to take the initiative and gained control of most of the old city, but they did not capture the bridgeheads across the river to enable Soviet troops to fight their way into Warsaw. Morale at first was high among the civilian population as liberation seemed at hand, but it soon began to disintegrate, although the population had little choice but to support the Home Army because of the brutal German reaction.

The Germans had few forces available to put down the uprising—only a small number of army units were used—and the bulk of the forces came from the S.S. and collaborator units such as the Kaminsky Brigade. During the first ten days German forces indulged in an orgy of destruction, looting, rape, and murder. In total about 50,000 people were killed in the Wola district, including 2,000 inmates of the Wolski hospital. After this initial phase the shooting of civilians became slightly rarer and most were deported to the transit camp at Pruszkow, where thousands died in foul conditions. Tens of thousands of refugees fled from the German forces and had to be accommodated in the areas of Warsaw controlled by the Home Army, causing huge problems of feeding and sanitation. At the end of August the Old Town was evacuated and the fighting continued in the Powisle district, where about 30,000 people were living in cellars without electricity or water and under constant German artillery bombardment. Discipline began to break down and capitulation was openly discussed.

At the end of the first week of September about 30,000 civilians were evacuated under Red Cross auspices, but for the rest of the month resistance continued in the Srodmiescie district to the south of the Old Town. The shortage of food was severe and supplies of water depended on wells dug during the uprising; by the end of September water was being sold. A cease-fire was agreed to at the beginning of October for the evacuation of civilians, and the Home Army then surrendered to the Germans. The number who died during the two months of fighting is very difficult to establish. The most accurate estimates suggest that about 15,000 members of the Home Army were killed, and over 200,000 civilians. In addition, about 400,000 civilians became refugees in German camps and the city of Warsaw was almost totally destroyed. Not only was the uprising a failure in military terms, it also failed politically: it did not alter the Soviet position on the future of Poland, neither did it establish the London Poles as a government, nor did it change the views of the British and American governments about the future of Poland. Its main consequence was the deaths of hundreds of thousands of civilians.

The most open form of resistance was the adoption of guerrilla warfare, but these groups did not achieve major success anywhere. The most highly organized partisan warfare occurred in the Soviet Union, where units were under the command of a central headquarters in Moscow and were supplied, at least intermittently, by the Soviet air force. In early 1942 there were probably about 30,000 in the partisan forces, but this rose to 120,000 a year later and to 175,000 in early 1944. They were organized into over 1,100 separate units, but during 1944, as regular Soviet forces swept westward, they were broken up and absorbed into the regular army. Overall they killed about 40,000 German and allied troops and were able to impose a form of counterterror on the civilian population in the occupied areas to reduce the amount of collaboration. The partisans probably killed at least as many of their own citizens as they did the occupying forces and lost about 55,000 people themselves.

In Yugoslavia, the Communist partisan forces under Tito were much smaller, about 19,000 in mid-1943, and they were engaged in a civil war as well as in fighting German and Italian troops. The partisans were able to tie down over 120,000 Axis troops and in September 1943, when Italy changed sides, they disarmed six Italian divisions, complete with their stores, and were then able to control a wider area and build up their forces to a strength of about 80,000. At this stage the British switched their support from Mihailovic to Tito as the only partisan actually fighting German forces. By early 1944 the partisans were able to move toward more open warfare against the low-grade German troops in the country, but it was not until the entry of Soviet troops into Yugoslavia that German forces were driven out. That most of the fighting within Yugoslavia between 1941 and 1945 was really a civil war rather than a war of resistance and liberation is illustrated by the operations in which the partisans suffered their losses. About 65,000 to 80,000 were killed in operations against German and Italian forces, and over 225,000 in combat with the Chetniks loyal to Mihailovic and the government-in-exile.

In Italy, partisan groups emerged in the north in the autumn of 1943 after the German occupation. The groups were strongest in Piedmont and Liguria, and were mainly linked to political parties: Garibaldi brigades (Communist), Matteoti (Socialist), and the Justice and Liberty groups of the Action party. They were controlled by a National Liberation Committee composed of the main parties. The Communists did not try to push a revolutionary war, arguing that the top priority was liberation. The partisans received little help from the Allied forces, who wanted to keep the resistance operating as small units tying down as many German troops as possible to help conventional operations. However, they did establish about thirty short-lived "partisan republics" in liberated areas. In the late autumn of 1944, with the advance of Allied armies into the north halted for the winter, the Allied commander, General Alexander, asked for the partisans to demobilize and wait for liberation. By the spring of 1945 the membership of partisan groups was about 200,000, and after the German front broke, general strikes spread and some towns were liberated by the resistance groups before the arrival of Allied troops. Overall, in the eighteen months of fighting during some of the most bitter partisan warfare of the war, 63,000 partisans and about 20,000 civilians were killed.

In northwest Europe partisan warfare was more limited. In Norway, Denmark, the Netherlands, and Belgium resistance armies played almost no role in helping the Allies, and even in France where the partisans, members of the "Maquis" (named for the south's tough vegetation), were much stronger, their role was essentially minor. Resistance in France did not begin to emerge on a major scale until the full German occupation of November 1942 finally ended Vichy as an independent government. The setting up of the S.T.O. to organize large-scale conscription of labor for work in Germany increased the incentive for people to join the resistance. From the spring of 1943, the creation of the C.N.R. (Conseil National de la Résistance) under Jean Moulin and his decision as well as that of other important politicians such as Léon Blum and Christian Pineau to back de Gaulle brought about a gradual convergence of internal and external resistance in France. Although the Maquis grew during the summer and autumn of 1943 as the S.T.O. began to bite, numbers remained small: no more than 40,000 as late as March 1944. The Free French organization in London and Algiers wanted to coordinate resistance activity with any Allied landing and overall the resistance had few resources. The British told the resistance in March 1943 that few arms drops and supplies would be available that year. Only in 1944, as invasion neared, were supplies increased. On D-Day de Gaulle called, in effect, for a national uprising, but within four days General Koenig, the Free French commander, ordered the maximum possible curb on activity, once it was clear that the Normandy landings were not going to produce a rapid German defeat. Although the resistance was able to carry out low-level sabotage that certainly impeded the Germans' activities and their ability to bring up reinforcements, there were strict limits on what they could achieve. In early July the resistance around Grenoble rose in revolt and took over the Vercors plateau to the west of the city. Despite large air drops from the Allies, the Germans were able to bring up two infantry divisions, part of a Panzer division, and Soviet defector units and within two days eliminate the resistance groups. Over one thousand died and the rest of the resistance was scattered.

Outside Europe, resistance to support the Allies was the exception rather than the rule. Installing agents was very difficult, and most of the population gave little support to the colonial powers as they attempted to reestablish their control. In Burma the British were able to gain support among the Karen and Kachin hill tribes who had always been a persecuted minority within Burma and had little incentive to see an independent Burma established. Their military impact was very limited. Toward the end of the war the British were able to open contact with the independent government established by Japan and by March 1945 the bulk of Aung San's Burma National Army was in open revolt against the Japanese. However, it would be difficult to interpret this as a pro-British move, and the Allied commander in southeast Asia, Mountbatten, had to negotiate with the head of the government, the ex–political prisoner Ba Maw, as an equal. These events presaged an end to British rule, not its reestablishment. In the Philippines the Hukbalahap, the People's Anti-Japanese Army, was formed in March 1942 under U.S. sponsorship, but in reality it was a strongly Communist-influenced, peasant, anti-landlord movement (the landlords collaborated strongly with the Japanese). Its military impact was limited, and once U.S. troops returned to the Philippines the Hukbalahap were rapidly involved in fighting the new occupying power.

In general, resistance groups developed outside the framework of prewar political structures. Many of their members strongly believed in a new departure at the end of the war, that the struggle for liberation would bring about a new type of politics and national life. In fact, their influence on liberation was very limited. Only Albania was liberated without the entry of Allied armies. Even here, however, it was the progress of Soviet forces that forced the Germans to withdraw and allowed the Communist resistance under Enver Hoxha, which had started eliminating its opponents even before liberation, to seize control in the autumn of 1944. The resistance had little actual impact on the liberation of their countries, which was determined by the progress of Allied armies and the policies and deals agreed between the Allies. However, resistance groups and activity did provide some kind of national spirit and hope in grim situations as well as forums in which people could feel that they were making at least some contribution toward ridding their countries of their vicious occupiers.

X

LIBERATION

By EARLY 1943 THE TIDE OF THE WAR HAD TURNED IN favor of the Allies. During that year, however, only Sicily and parts of southern Italy were liberated. It was not until 1944—as the Soviets finally recaptured their own territory and swept into the Balkans and eastern Poland, Allied armies reached Rome, and the Normandy invasion drove the Germans out of France and Belgium—that significant areas were liberated. For the people of many of these territories it meant the end of several years of rule by a vicious occupying power—the end of German reprisals, street arrests, forced labor, and the terrible uncertainty and fear induced by German policy. In eastern Europe, however, the effect of liberation was ambiguous. One occupying power was removed but the establishment of Soviet control and rule by local Communist regimes meant the imposition of a different form of terror: the arrest of those thought hostile to the new government, the reuse of German concentration camps as forced-labor camps for political dissidents, the establishment of a one-party state, and the introduction of a new secret police. In the Far East, liberation was a very different experience—it meant the reimposition of European colonial rule on unwilling populations and often the outbreak of new conflicts as nationalist groups sought independence.

The conquest of the Axis countries and the liberation of occupied territory posed major problems for the Allies in establishing new governments. The postwar interests of the different Allies were reflected in the different solutions proposed for these problems. In general, the occupation of enemy territory proved less contentious than the liberation of Allied territory. The Axis countries had functioning governments—the problem for the Allies was how to deal with them and how to remake them into the kind of governments they wanted. In some of the occupied countries, such as Norway and the Netherlands, governments-in-exile could be restored, but others faced a range of difficult problems. In countries such as Yugoslavia the government-in-exile no longer controlled events within the country; in others such as France there was no government-in-exile to restore, and there were disputes between the Allies over how to proceed. The most difficult case of all was Poland, which had two rival governments sponsored by the U.S.S.R. and Britain as well as a major dispute between the Allies over the postwar boundaries of the state. In the last resort, however, political authority usually flowed from the occupying army: the Soviets were able to establish the regimes they wanted in the areas they controlled, and Britain and the United States did the same.

Until 1941 the British (and the French while they were still in the war) studiously avoided any detailed commitments about peace, apart from a refusal to make any deal with Hitler. During this period the military situation facing Britain was so bad that thinking about possible peace terms was unnecessary. In many areas the complexity of the problems involved meant that it was best to avoid decisions. In this period it was extremely difficult, for example, to set out the peace terms involving Poland when part of the country was occupied by the Soviet Union, which was neutral in the war between Britain and Germany.

During the early months of 1941 Britain was forced to change its position under American influence. Once the United States had decided to rescue Britain and sustain its war effort through Lend-Lease, it made clear that it intended to take the lead in defining the postwar settlement. The British were required to reveal any secret treaties they had made about peace terms and were then barred from making new agreements without U.S. approval. In his State of the Union address in January 1941 Roosevelt began to define his war aims. He set

out the principle of the Four Freedoms: freedom of speech and ex-
pression, freedom of worship, and freedom from want and from fear.
When Roosevelt and Churchill met for the first time during the war
at Newfoundland in August 1941, the primary U.S. aim at the conference was to obtain a joint statement about war aims. Eventually,
eight principles were agreed on, which originally constituted the
communiqué from the conference but later grew in importance.
They became the Atlantic Charter, which by 1942 had become the
cornerstone of the aims enshrined in the Declaration of the United
Nations, signed on January 1, 1942, by the United States, Britain, the
U.S.S.R., China, and twenty-two other countries, and subscribed to
by every member of the alliance fighting the Axis powers.

Some of the eight principles, in particular the last four, were no
more than general aspirations: on collaboration between nations in
the economic field, the construction of peace after the defeat of the
Nazis, free passage on the high seas, and the hope that all nations
"must come to the abandonment of the use of force." The first four
principles, the most important ones, were to be the source of major
problems and were in practice ignored. The first principle, which
committed the powers to no territorial or other form of aggrandizement after the war, was not applied at the end of the war. The second
principle, that there were to be no territorial changes unless they
were "in accord with the freely expressed wishes of the people concerned," was not applied to any of the territorial changes agreed on
during the war. The third principle affirmed the "right of all peoples
to choose the form of government under which they will live." The
British decided unilaterally that this principle could not possibly
apply to their imperial possessions. The fourth pledged adherence to
free trade and equal access to raw materials after the war. The British
were extremely concerned about this point because it threatened the
system of imperial preference developed in the 1930s and seemed
likely to do little more than entrench American economic hegemony.
Discussions on this subject were postponed until after the war.

The British dealt with the first liberation of territory just before
they signed the Atlantic Charter, and their actions demonstrated
some of the complexities and ambiguities of policy-making in this

area. In East Africa, British forces conquered Italian Somaliland and then advanced, in 1941, to expel Italian troops from their prewar conquest of Abyssinia. Here the prewar ruler, Emperor Haile Selassie, was restored to the throne. In the Middle East, British forces, assisted by the Free French, conquered Syria and Lebanon, also in 1941, and removed the Vichy administration, which had allowed Germany to use the territory to aid the nationalist coup in Iraq. The British did not, however, allow the Free French to take over this territory, which had been allocated to France under a League of Nations mandate after the First World War. The British looked back to the clash of interests with the French that had occurred during that war and in the immediate post-1918 period and were determined to eliminate French influence from a region they regarded as being entirely within their sphere of influence. They argued, without any legal basis, that the Vichy government had forfeited the mandate and, correctly, that their agreements with de Gaulle did not pledge Britain to a restoration of all prewar French territory (they had already considered offering French Morocco to Spain if they kept out of the war). In September 1941 the British announced that there was to be no question of France maintaining its position in the Levant and there was to be no substitution of Free French for Vichy administration. Thus, almost the first successful British military action in the war was the removal of its main ally from control of one of its own colonies.

The problems involved in the liberation of Syria and Lebanon were minor compared with those raised in 1942 by the Anglo-American decision to invade French North Africa, which was still controlled by Vichy, a government the United States continued to recognize as legitimate and with which the British still had indirect dealings. During the planning for the invasion the Americans took the lead on the political aspects and were keen to make some arrangement with the Vichy government that would minimize the risk of any large-scale resistance to Anglo-American forces. They opened secret contacts and together with the British agreed that the aim was to bring over the existing Vichy administration in North Africa to the Allied side, leaving de Gaulle as a marginalized figure among a number who opposed a Vichy-based government. Three weeks before the landings the British and the Americans agreed that Admiral Darlan, one of the main advocates of collaboration with Germany earlier in the year, should be brought into the planning. De Gaulle was totally excluded.

When the landings took place on November 8 there was some initial resistance, but Darlan, who had traveled to North Africa three days before, was able to organize the surrender of Algiers and issue orders for a general cease-fire. Within days Darlan was de facto head of the French administration in North Africa, which was almost unchanged from the Vichy period, while pro-Allied Frenchmen remained in jail. Within a fortnight of the invasion, General Eisenhower, the Allied commander, had signed a full-scale deal with Darlan that recognized him as high commissioner. Thus, the first Anglo-American military action of the war was not an attack on Germany or Italy, but an invasion of the territory of an ex-ally, with a government that the United States still recognized as legitimate. They had also made a deal to keep in power men whom most of the public regarded as collaborators. There was a storm of protest from the public, the governments-in-exile, and the Soviet Union. If this was Allied policy, what would happen when other countries were liberated? The protests brought about no change of policy, but some of the problems were resolved when Darlan was assassinated on Christmas Eve by people believed to be royalist supporters of the Comte de Paris.

The complaints about the handling of affairs in North Africa were one of the main reasons why Roosevelt announced a new policy at the end of the Casablanca Conference with the British in January 1943. Until then the British had been working on the assumption that the war would end, as it had in 1918, with a request for an armistice and then negotiations with a German government, though not one controlled by Hitler. At Casablanca it was made clear that Allied policy would now be "unconditional surrender." There would be no negotiations, only total capitulation. This certainly solved the political problem of dealing with enemy governments and also helped to hold the Allies together by reassuring the Soviet Union of the western Allies' refusal to seek a separate peace and by postponing arguments about peace terms.

The first nation to surrender, be occupied, and liberated was Italy. Events revealed the deep divisions between the Allies, and the decisions eventually set precedents that were followed later in the war. The British had never been keen to apply the doctrine of unconditional surrender to Italy, and their draft surrender terms, produced less than six months after Casablanca, abandoned the principle by calling on the Allied commander to recognize the existing Italian government. The United States moved a little toward the British position in allowing some continuing role for a non-Fascist Italian government, but it was determined to impose military government, partly to avoid a repetition of the Algiers fiasco and to allay criticisms from the Soviets. The replacement of Mussolini by Badoglio only increased pressure from the British for a deal with the ex-Fascists. When the Italian armistice was finally signed on September 3 it was no more than a simple military agreement placing the Italian government and forces under Allied control. The full armistice imposed at the end of the month involved a near total surrender of Italian sovereignty: the Allies could occupy Italy and utilize all its resources, the Fascist party was to be disbanded, and relations with the Axis broken. However, the government under the king and Badoglio that had overthrown Mussolini and then fled from Rome to Bari was retained to administer Italy under Allied supervision.

The Soviet Union made it clear to the western Allies that the arrangements made for Italy would be a test case and would determine the degree of British and American influence in areas liberated by the Soviets. The British and the Americans, who had their own disputes over who should have the predominant influence in Italy, agreed that the Soviets should effectively be excluded. The Soviet demand for a powerful tripartite military and political commission based initially in Sicily, which would extend its functions to all other liberated countries, was rejected. Instead, the western Allies offered no more than an advisory body resident in Algiers made up of representatives of France, Greece, and Yugoslavia as well as the three major allies, with effective power lying in the hands of an Allied Control Commission (A.C.C.) run by the Allied commander on the spot. At the Moscow Foreign Ministers' Conference in October, Molotov made it clear that such arrangements would be a precedent for what would happen in eastern Europe, but still no changes were made. It was the first step toward a de facto division of Europe into spheres of interest.

Within Italy it was not until December 1943 that the Allies insisted that Badoglio begin a purge of Fascist elements within the administration. He refused to set up an independent agency and was in fact rebuilding the administrative structure using those who had operated the old regime; individuals vetoed by the A.C.C. in one post were simply appointed to another one. The British, however, backed Badoglio as the only leader who could provide the necessary support for the Allies. By early 1944 the United States was convinced that both the king and Badoglio would have to go and were backing politicians such as Count Sforza, whom they had helped bring back from exile. Eventually Britain and the United States agreed to wait until Rome was liberated, although by the spring of 1944 it was becoming increasingly clear that Italian opinion would no longer tolerate King Victor Emmanuel. A coalition government, nominally under Badoglio, was formed in April. On June 5, the day after the Allies entered Rome, the king abdicated in favor of his son, Umberto, and a six-party government under Ivanoe Bonomi replaced Badoglio's. The British, who supported Badoglio, were furious but could do no more than veto the appointment of Sforza as foreign minister, though they could not keep him out of the government. Only now did a sweeping purge of the old Fascists begin under Sforza's direction: over three hundred generals were removed and three quarters of the senators were suspended. However, the Allies rapidly sought to contain the anti-Fascist drive and supported Bonomi, who wanted to contain it for internal political reasons. During 1944, U.S. military assistance (six Italian divisions were fighting alongside the Allies by the winter) and major reconstruction assistance resulted in a significant increase in U.S. influence, and by February 1945 the Americans were able to insist on giving much greater powers to the Italian government and weakening the powers of the

A.C.C. The western Allies had been able to ensure that a sympathetic government was installed, but they had faced little opposition from the Communists: their leader, Palmiro Togliatti, who returned from exile in March 1944, cooperated with this policy.

As the Soviets had made clear, it was their intention that the Allied Control Commissions for the Axis countries in eastern Europe—Rumania, Bulgaria, and Hungary—followed the Italian model and gave wide-ranging authority to the representative of the liberating army and very little to the representatives of the other allies. In Bulgaria, a Communist-dominated Fatherland Front was established in 1942, and in September 1944, as Soviet forces crossed the frontier, it seized power in Sofia. The Communists took the key posts of deputy prime minister and ministers for the interior and justice, and although the Front split later in the year the Soviets were able to ensure Communist preponderance in the government. In Rumania in August 1944, King Michael attempted a volte-face from the Axis to the Allies: General Antonescu was imprisoned and a largely right-wing coalition military government was installed, although it did include previous leaders of the opposition during the war with the Soviet Union. Under Soviet occupation the coalition government split twice in the autumn, each time resulting in an increase in Communist influence. However, the government was still independent and little action was taken against war criminals. At the end of February 1945 the Soviets demanded that the king sack the prime minister and a week later a new pro-Soviet government took power. The Communists were in control of the key ministries of interior and justice and the government embarked on a series of major social reforms.

In Hungary, a National Independence Front government was established on Soviet-controlled territory at the end of December 1944. It was made up of three generals who had followed Admiral Horthy's call for an armistice with the Allies before the full German takeover of the country, together with representatives of all the major parties. It agreed to an armistice with the Allies, accepted Hungary's boundaries as they were in 1937, and started a program of moderate social reform: large landed estates were broken up and nationalization of key industries was begun. From April the new government was installed in Budapest. Although the Soviet military commander had major powers, the all-party coalition was maintained, and in the November 1945 election the liberal Smallholders Party won over 60 percent of the vote, the Communists and their allies getting about half that figure.

In dealing with Allied states, only three cases involving governments-in-exile were uncomplicated. In Norway and the Netherlands the respective governments-in-exile in London and the monarchs were reestablished as soon as the country was liberated, without any serious problems. In Czechoslovakia, the Benes government-in-exile accepted that the Soviet Union would play a key role in liberation and in December 1943 signed a twenty-year treaty of alliance. Benes also accepted that the Communist party would play a major role in postwar government. In a unique situation among Allied states, all parties participated in a temporary government, which was promulgated at Kosice in early April 1945. It contained six Czech and six Slovak parties led by the left-wing Social Democrat Zdenek Fierlinger and had strong Communist influence. Soviet troops entered Prague on May 9, and Benes then returned to the capital. He was confirmed as president by the National Assembly in October, and at the beginning of December Soviet and American troops withdrew from the country.

The liberation of Belgium was relatively straightforward, except for the position of King Leopold III, who had remained behind when the government left in 1940. The government-in-exile was split over the future of the monarchy, although most accepted that Leopold would have to abdicate. During the war most British assistance had gone to the secret army linked to the government-in-exile and not to the resistance of the Front de l'Indépendence, which was more left-wing. The first priority of Allied forces when they entered Brussels in early September 1944 was to disarm the resistance and provide arms for the gendarmerie to keep order. The government-in-exile resigned almost immediately after its return and was replaced by one that included the Communists and representatives of the resistance. This government split, and by November there were riots in Brussels over the demands for the surrender of arms by the resistance, which were put down by British troops. The resistance was eventually disarmed and the Allies were able to ensure the emergence of a pro-Western government under a new monarch.

The situation in Yugoslavia was confused because of the fundamental ethnic divisions and the split in the resistance. By early 1944 the British were swinging toward Tito and the partisans as the only group likely to fight the German occupying forces. At the same time they were putting pressure on the exiled King Peter to sack his government-in-exile and in particular Mihailovic, who was technically minister of war, although he was leading the Chetniks in Yugoslavia and collaborating with the Germans. It was hoped that getting rid of Mihailovic might increase the chances of an agreement with Tito. The king was forced to recall the exiled politician Ivan Subasic, a leader of the Croatian Peasant party, from the United States and in May 1944 appoint him prime minister. On this basis a deal was struck with Tito: he became commander-in-chief and Subasic became leader of a "progressive and democratic" government, but the king would not be allowed to return until decisions had been made about his future after the war. This agreement was essentially window-dressing, but it was the best the British could obtain—Tito held the real power in Yugoslavia.

In September 1944 Tito flew to Moscow and secured an agreement for Yugoslav civilian authorities to function in areas liberated by the Soviets and for the Soviet army to leave the country once operations against Germany were complete. On October 20 Soviet forces liberated Belgrade, and three weeks later they left Yugoslav territory. The new government, technically a coalition but dominated by the Communists, was recognized by all the Allies at the beginning of March 1945. Tito and the Communists had already set about establishing control. All members of Mihailovic's Chetniks, the Croatian Ustasha, Slovenian Home Guard units, and Yugoslav members of the S.S. were killed as a matter of policy. In total, 40,000 to 50,000 were killed, plus an unknown number of civilian refugees.

A more difficult problem arose in Greece, particularly for the British, who regarded the country as part of their sphere of interest. The government under King George II had fled into exile in 1941, but the king was tarnished by his association with the prewar Metaxas dictatorship, and almost all Greek politicians and resistance groups were opposed to his return. Resistance emerged in two movements: E.A.M. (National Liberation Front), a popular front, and the right-wing E.D.E.S. (National Republican Greek League). In exile the government was badly split, a situation made worse when the Greek army in Egypt mutinied against the king in March 1944. The mutiny was put down by British troops. In May, all parties except the monarchists agreed to a coalition government and a plebiscite about the return of the monarchy after liberation. As Soviet forces swept through the Balkans in the late summer of 1944 it was clear that the Germans would soon have to withdraw from Greece. The British, keen to establish control, prepared to send troops to Athens as soon as the Germans left.

In early October Churchill went to Moscow for talks with Stalin. He was determined to secure a deal recognizing the spheres of interest of each country. At the first meeting with the Soviet leader he passed Stalin what he described as "a naughty document" that conceded to the Soviets a 90 percent influence in Rumania and Bulgaria in return for equal shares in Yugoslavia and Hungary and 90 percent British influence in Greece. He insisted that Britain had to remain the leading Mediterranean power. Stalin accepted the deal and stuck to its terms. The agreement cleared the way for the British to impose the government they wanted on Greece. For over a year they had been concerned about the growing importance of E.L.A.S., the E.A.M.'s military wing. As early as November 1943, the S.O.E. (Special Operations Executive) in Cairo had taken the extraordinary step of allowing one of its agents in Greece, Don Stott, to hold talks with the head of the German secret field police in Athens about joint action against the Soviets. If E.L.A.S. was to be excluded from power, the British, desperately short of troops, might need to rely on the security battalions set up by the puppet government in Greece, which had acted with the German army. Stott also saw representatives of all the Greek factions except E.L.A.S.

The Germans eventually left the Greek capital on October 14,

1944. The British, who had already secured from the resistance an agreement to zones of occupation, quickly moved forces into Athens. E.L.A.S. could quite easily have taken control of the capital as well as other major cities such as Patras and Salonika but made no attempt to do so and stuck with the deal made with the British. The British also brought the Greek army from Egypt, purged of all but its royalist elements after the mutiny earlier in the year. The army was amalgamated with the security battalions, which only a month earlier had been fighting the partisans. The British expected a conflict with E.L.A.S. They were therefore worried when Giorgios Papandreou, the head of the all-party coalition, reached an agreement with E.L.A.S. on November 20 on the disbanding of their forces. Meanwhile, the British were rounding up members of the resistance, and 15,000 were interned and another 8,000 deported to camps in the Middle East.

In the first week of December, in the wake of complex negotiations over the demobilization of the partisan groups, demonstrations in Athens against the government, and threats of a general strike, clashes between the government and E.L.A.S. units occurred. They were low-level and could easily have been resolved, but the British used them as an excuse for a conflict with E.L.A.S. When Papandreou threatened to resign and allow a government including E.L.A.S. representatives to take power, the British threatened to imprison him until he changed his mind. The British commander, General Dobie, was instructed, "Do not hesitate to act as if you were in a conquered city," and was told that he should incur bloodshed if necessary. E.L.A.S. offered a general settlement but the British government refused, telling their representatives in Athens that it was important to defeat E.L.A.S.

The British had to bring in 70,000 troops to establish control in Athens. The sight of British troops fighting the resistance groups who only three months earlier had been fighting the Germans caused outrage in Britain and also in the United States—Roosevelt publicly disowned the British action. Stalin stood aside and accepted that Greece fell within the British sphere. At the end of December, in an attempt to increase the popularity of the government they were backing, the British finally persuaded the king to appoint the archbishop of Athens as regent, pending a plebiscite on the future of the monarchy. The regent appointed a new government under General Nikolaos Plastiras, who had earlier offered to form a pro-German government-in-exile in Berlin. In early 1945 E.L.A.S. demobilized itself, but a 60,000-strong National Guard was recruited, primarily of ex-Security Guard members, and in a right-wing terror campaign continued the fight against E.L.A.S. that they had been waging during the occupation. The British were happy to work with the ex-collaborators. Any attempt to punish those responsible for war crimes was abandoned and during 1945 a right-wing authoritarian government was established that was able to rig a plebiscite on the return of the monarchy. The British had been able to establish the government they wanted in Greece. They recognized, however, that their actions, especially fighting the ex-resistance groups, made it very much more difficult to criticize the Soviets for the way they imposed the governments they wanted.

The problems facing the British and the Americans in France were very different from those in Greece and stemmed primarily from the reluctance of the United States and Churchill (but not other members of the British government) to see de Gaulle established in power. Although the British and the Americans had tried to break with de Gaulle before the invasion of French North Africa in November 1942 and again during 1943, he was in effective control of the F.C.N.L. (the French Committee of National Liberation). Neither country, however, accorded this group a status greater than leadership of the Free French movement; they did not recognize it as a government-in-exile. In the autumn of 1943 discussions started about the policy to be adopted when Allied armies began to liberate France. The Americans insisted on a period of Allied military government before elections. De Gaulle and the Free French movement, which had fought alongside the Allies since June 1940, would not be given a special position. The British reluctantly went along with this plan, and the instructions given to the Allied commander allowed him to cooperate with any group, apart from the Vichy government, although this did not rule out dealing with Vichy-appointed local administrations.

De Gaulle was determined to avoid being sidelined by the British and Americans. On May 26, 1944, suspecting invasion was imminent, the F.C.N.L. declared itself the provisional government of the French republic. Eight days after D-Day, de Gaulle visited France and without consulting the British and the Americans set up a skeleton provisional government in liberated territory at Bayeux. It was a very important symbolic step for de Gaulle. Against the advice of the British, the other governments-in-exile recognized the new provisional government. Allied military commanders on the spot, who were still without instructions on how to proceed, decided to work with the de Gaulle administrators, who therefore became the de facto local government of France. Soon they were appointing prefects, subprefects, and mayors and removing Vichy appointees in the liberated areas. On July 11, in a major change of policy, the United States wrong-footed the British by accepting de Gaulle as "the working authority for civilian administration in the liberated areas"—equivalent to de facto recognition. In the absence of a clear alternative the western Allies found themselves with no alternative but to work with de Gaulle and the new provisional government as it took control behind the advancing Allied troops.

The fall of Paris in late August demonstrated de Gaulle's popularity and saw the provisional government take over control in the capital. However, large parts of the country remained outside its influence. Its first task was to control the F.F.I. (French Forces of the Interior, the armed forces of the French resistance within France), disarm them, and in some cases incorporate them into the new French army that was being formed. In the provinces it took time to establish control and much power lay with the departmental liberation committees. The Allies were content for the provisional government to gradually extend its control and establish the framework of political authority. At the end of September the British announced they were going to recognize the Italian government, but this privilege was not extended to de Gaulle. The official American policy still held, that nothing would happen until after elections. The Soviets had long recognized that France fell within the British and American sphere of influence and the Communists made no attempt to disrupt the gradual accretion of power to de Gaulle. Under the circumstances, Britain and the United States had little choice but to change their policy, and on October 23 they and the Soviet Union finally recognized the provisional government headed by de Gaulle. By the spring of 1945 the government in Paris was in effective control of the country and a sovereign France had been re-created.

Part of the process of taking control of France was a purge of the existing Vichy regime and the exaction of revenge against the collaborators, a process repeated in the other liberated countries. In 1943 the F.C.N.L. in Algiers had already decided to put Pétain and other members of the Vichy regime on trial, as well as those who collaborated, sent workers to Germany, or ordered French people to fight the Allies. By mid-December, nearly six hundred people had been interned in North Africa and a few months later the trials began. Pucheu, the Vichy interior minister, was put on trial, sentenced to death, and shot. In June 1944 the resistance leaders called for the execution of major collaborators, in particular the leaders of the Vichy militia, and the provisional government was planning to set up military courts to undertake rapid trials. In practice, much of the action was local, ad hoc and unauthorized. Some of the actions took place before liberation: at least twenty-five hundred "summary executions" were carried out by the resistance in the six months before D-Day. Immediately after liberation the process speeded up. Local courts were set up by the resistance and the most flagrant collaborators put on trial and executed. In total, probably over five thousand were executed in the months after D-Day. Female collaborators often had their heads shaved and were then paraded through their local town. Thousands were affected, but again, the total is unknown. Some idea of the scale of this punishment can be gained from the fact that in the small town of Nogent-le-Rotrou, near Chartres, sixteen women were treated in this way. Over 120,000 people were interned, including famous people such as the actor and dramatist Sacha Guitry, although about a quarter were released very quickly. Some of those released were later shot by the resistance in unofficial killings. By the spring of 1945 the worst of the outburst of revenge that followed liberation was over and a more regular judicial process took over.

Some of the most difficult questions about liberation arose in eastern Europe. Did the advancing Soviet armies come as liberators from German occupation or as oppressors to restore the Soviet empire and communism? In Ukraine, the nationalist partisans of the O.U.N. fought Soviet forces as they moved west and continued to do so for some years after the war. The Baltic states had been taken over by the Soviet Union in 1940 and as early as December 1941 Stalin made it clear to the British that the fundamental Soviet war aim was to reestablish Soviet borders as they had been in June 1941—in other words, the Allies would have to recognize the gains the Soviet Union had made in collaboration with Germany. The British originally dismissed this demand as being contrary to the principles for which the war was being fought. In practice, however, by May 1942 they had accepted that Estonia, Latvia, and Lithuania would be part of the Soviet Union after the war, and in 1944, as Soviet forces reentered these states, the British gave de facto recognition to the conquest. The Americans also accepted the situation.

The Soviet demand to retain its 1941 borders posed the greatest political and moral problems to the Allies, particularly the British, as it applied to Poland, the country for whom the British had gone to war. The problem was twofold: the borders of the country and the nature of the postwar government. In August 1939 the Polish eastern border was that established in 1920 after the Polish-Soviet war and was some 200 miles to the east of that provisionally drawn up at Versailles in 1919 (the Curzon Line). When the Soviets invaded in September 1939 they conquered the eastern part of the country and established the Soviet border along a line near to, but in some respects significantly different from, the Curzon Line. When Germany invaded the Soviet Union in June 1941 the Polish government-in-exile in London came under pressure to reestablish diplomatic relations with Moscow. Before they took this action, they sought an assurance from the British about their borders. In July the British stated that "His Majesty's Government did not recognize territorial changes affecting Poland made since August 1939." This was a clear declaration that they stood by the 1920 boundary. Again in 1942, during discussions on the Anglo-Soviet treaty, the British reassured the Poles that they would not make any agreement affecting or compromising Polish territory.

On April 13, 1943, the German government announced that it had found a mass grave containing about five thousand bodies of Polish officers and civilians at Katyn. They claimed that the murders had been carried out in 1940, when the area was controlled by the Soviets. The claim was true—the killings were carried out on the direct orders of Stalin and the Politburo. The Polish government-in-exile called for an investigation by the Red Cross, as did the Germans. The Soviets, who claimed the Germans carried out the killings in 1941, accused the Poles in London of acting in collusion with Germany and used this as an excuse to break off relations. Within days the British government had information from the Poles that gave almost incontrovertible evidence of Soviet guilt. Privately the British accepted this evidence and sent copies to the Americans but decided to say nothing in public and continued to blame the Germans. After April the Soviets set up a new army recruited from among the Poles remaining in the Soviet Union (most had left for the Middle East under the direction of the London Poles), whose officers were mainly Soviet citizens of Polish origin. The Koscuiszko Division was in action by October and by the spring of 1944 was 43,000 strong. In June 1943 a Union of Polish Patriots was established in Moscow. Both organizations seemed to be potential forerunners of a Polish government that would be an alternative to the government-in-exile in London.

At the first meeting between the Allied leaders at Teheran in late November 1943, it was Churchill who raised the subject of Polish frontiers with Stalin, in contradiction to his earlier sentiments and the pledges given to the Polish government. He suggested that the Soviet border should be pushed westward at the expense of Poland and that the Poles should be compensated by acquiring German territory. Roosevelt supported this position but wanted a final decision postponed because so many Polish-American votes were at stake in the 1944 U.S. elections. As a result it was informally agreed that the British proposal on Poland should be accepted and that the British should take the lead in trying to persuade their ally to accept the dismemberment of its territory. Negotiations with the Poles began at the end of December, but they were not told that their three major allies had already decided their fate. The Polish government protested that they could not possibly accept, with four million Poles living in the areas to be acquired by the Soviet Union and with Lvov, which the Curzon Line allocated to Poland, also going to the Soviets. The Poles were told that the Soviets had "a moral right" to this territory.

Meanwhile, in December 1943 the Soviets formed the Polish National Council, dominated by the Communists under Boleslaw Bierut and Wladyslaw Gomulka, which accepted the Soviet frontier demands. In early 1944 Soviet troops crossed the pre–September 1939 frontier, causing major political problems for the London Poles. The attempt by the Home Army, which they controlled, to conduct guerrilla operations in this area led to the arrest of members of the units in the Wilno and Nowogrodek areas and later around Lvov. The Soviets would tolerate no Polish operations in the areas that had been part of Poland until the Soviet invasion in 1939. At the beginning of August 1944, as Soviet troops entered areas that they recognized as Polish, the Polish National Council in Moscow was transformed into the Polish Committee of National Liberation, was established at Lublin, and was given control of the liberated areas. The failure of the Warsaw uprising ended what little power the London Poles might have had to affect events within Poland.

At his meeting with Churchill and Stalin in Moscow in October 1944, Stanislaw Mikolajczyk, the prime minister of the government-in-exile, offered concessions—a few Communists would be included in the government, an alliance would be signed with the Soviets, but the post–September 1939 border could not be accepted. The next day the Polish prime minister was told of the fait accompli agreed to by the main Allies. When Mikolajczyk protested he was subjected to a tirade of abuse from Churchill, who threatened to recognize the Lublin Poles. Mikolajczyk refused to agree to the British and Allied demands and instead resigned as prime minister a month later. The British still technically recognized the London Poles but had little to do with them.

On January 1, 1945, the Lublin Committee became the Polish provisional government and was recognized as such by the Soviet Union. By then some 200,000 troops were fighting in units controlled by the Lublin Poles and in mid-January the Home Army was dissolved. Fifty thousand members were deported by the Soviets, the Germans allowed one brigade of about 850 men to pass through their lines and make contact with U.S. forces, and some others formed part of a skeleton underground to oppose Soviet occupation. Much of the Yalta Conference between the three Allied leaders in early February centered around Poland. Agreement was reached regarding the eastern border—the Soviet position was accepted. In the end Churchill and Roosevelt abandoned any attempt to create an entirely new Polish government and accepted the addition of a few of the London Poles to the existing Communist-dominated Lublin provisional government. On the western border it was agreed that Poland should incorporate large areas of what had been Germany, territory that had an overwhelmingly German population. All the Allies were agreed that the Oder River should be Poland's western border, but Britain and the United States did not accept until the Potsdam Conference in July 1945 that in the north the border should follow the western Neisse River, incorporating still more German territory.

A month before the Potsdam Conference, after some leaders of the Polish underground had been arrested and put on trial in Moscow, a Provisional Government of National Unity, incorporating a few members of the London Polish government, was established in Warsaw. The British and the Americans recognized it in early July and then withdrew recognition of the Polish government-in-exile. By the end of the war, therefore, the Poland that had existed on September 1, 1939, had been dismembered. A large part of its territory in the east was annexed by the Soviet Union and it had been forced to take over large parts of historic Prussia and Germany. The western Allies had also accepted Soviet policy on what sort of government should run Poland. The Soviet Union had also annexed the Baltic states and

Rumanian Bessarabia, together with parts of East Prussia around Königsberg, and had made major territorial gains at the expense of Finland and even some in eastern Czechoslovakia. All of this was with the consent of the British and American governments and in flat contradiction of the terms of the Atlantic Charter. These actions violated Point 1 of the Charter, which committed the Allies to no territorial aggrandizement. They also broke the second point of the Charter, which stated that no territorial changes would take place unless they were "in accord with the freely expressed wishes of the people concerned." There had been no attempt to find out what these wishes might be. They also broke the third point, "the right of all peoples to choose the form of government under which they will live."

Allied policy-making concerning the liberation of Germany was, at least until the Potsdam Conference, relatively straightforward. It ensured that contacts with either German politicians in exile or the few resistance figures within Germany were minimal, rightly distrusting the latter as being essentially conservative and trying to retain as much German power as possible in any peace that might occur if Hitler were overthrown. All the Allies were agreed on harsh terms. Even before the Casablanca declaration Roosevelt was speaking of unconditional surrender: "we must then dismember her and subject her to the harshest possible quarantine, if need be for thirty years." The British always advocated dismemberment and harsh disarmament for a long period. As early as 1940 Churchill was reported as saying that he was becoming less and less benevolent toward the Germans, that there would be no "just peace," and he also talked of castrating all German males. In 1943 he told the cabinet that about three or four million German males would have to be forcibly segregated after the war and stopped from breeding until there was a balance of population with France. In September 1944 the British, under American financial pressure, accepted the plan drawn up by Henry Morgenthau for postwar Germany. It proposed dismemberment and destruction of German industry on a large scale in order to create a mainly agricultural economy.

At the Yalta Conference the three main Allies agreed on the division of Germany into occupation zones (one was also created for the French). The Americans reneged on the Morgenthau plan and now wanted to keep Germany within its 1937 frontiers, except in the east, rather than dismember it. Little was agreed upon about postwar Germany except that no German government would survive, as had happened in 1918. At the end of April 1945, Hitler, confined to his beleaguered bunker in Berlin as Soviet troops fought their way through the city, appointed Admiral Karl Dönitz as president and Goebbels as chancellor and expelled Himmler and Göring from the Nazi party for their attempts to make a peace deal with the Allies. He then committed suicide, as did Goebbels. Dönitz created his new government at Flensburg, near the Danish border, although it controlled little, apart from the area in the north of Germany not yet reached by Allied forces. Dönitz's policy was to avoid a general surrender and through a series of local capitulations give as much time as possible for units to move from the east, thereby avoiding capture by the Soviets. The British and Americans tacitly accepted this policy. Even after May 7, when the Germans formally surrendered to General Eisenhower at Reims, the western Allies allowed German units to move west. A total of about one million men were affected and an unknown number of refugees. Although the Allies were committed to unconditional surrender, the British opposed the arrest of the Dönitz government, which continued to function and administer large parts of Germany for nearly a fortnight after the formal surrender. The British insisted that for this cooperation Dönitz would have to have any sentence he received for war crimes reduced. The Dönitz government was finally arrested on May 19, with the British still dissenting, and on June 5 the Allies formally declared their total control over Germany.

Although the war in Europe was over, the Far Eastern war continued, and questions of liberation were much more difficult in this conflict. Were the British, Dutch, Americans, and French returning to their colonial territories as liberators from Japanese control or as imperialists reasserting foreign rule? The Americans only promised the Philippines independence "as soon as feasible," and on the former

Japanese-mandated islands it intended to take over, it wanted to entrench its position by making them subject not to the General Assembly of the new United Nations but to the Security Council, where the United States would be able to use its veto to ensure continued control. European policies on the future of their empires had changed little during the war. Regarding India, the British did not formally commit themselves to go beyond the 1940 declaration of dominion status at some undefined point in the future. The White Paper on Burma, published in May 1945, envisaged three years of direct rule after the war followed by a reversion to the 1941 position with no promise of any further progress toward independence. The Dutch promised a vague commonwealth scheme of internal self-government for all colonies but no independence. The Free French in early 1944 and again as the provisional government in March 1945 promised only that Indochina would be part of a federation and its population, citizens of France.

When Japan surrendered on August 15, 1945, the immediate task for the colonial powers was to move troops into their possessions because few had been liberated: the Japanese still held Malaya, Singapore, Indochina, the Dutch East Indies, Hong Kong, and Borneo as well as large parts of China, Manchuria, and various islands in the Pacific. In these chaotic conditions independence movements had some room to maneuver. The Indian National Army left Rangoon in April 1945 for Siam and later Singapore, where it continued to broadcast propaganda into India until the end of the war. The leader of the movement, Subhas Chandra Bose, died after an air crash in Taiwan in August 1945. Continued Indian pressure, however, was to ensure that within two years of the end of the war India became independent. In Burma the British had already been negotiating with Aung San, the leader of the Burma Defence Army, and had persuaded him to change sides as British troops entered the country. The other nationalist leader, Ba Maw, continued to support the Japanese until the end, but within a year he had been pardoned by the British and brought back to Rangoon. The British could not sustain their opposition to independence as it had been set out in the May 1945 White Paper and were soon negotiating with Aung San. Independence was finally granted in January 1948. British troops also reoccupied Singapore and, after long arguments with Chiang Kai-shek, Hong Kong, too. The Chinese had wanted to liberate Hong Kong as a way of reasserting Chinese control, and Roosevelt had also wanted the British to give up the colony.

The Dutch were forced to rely on British troops to take over in Indonesia, where the nationalists under Sukarno declared independence just after the Japanese surrender. British forces recognized Sukarno as being in de facto control of Indonesia, but as the amount of arms available to the nationalists from the Japanese-controlled militia and from the Japanese themselves rose, the British turned to using Japanese troops to maintain order. After months of fighting the British established control of the East Java city of Surabaya, but by the time Dutch troops arrived in the colony in the spring of 1946 the Indonesian independence movement was strongly entrenched. The Dutch finally recognized the inevitability of Indonesian independence in 1949.

Until 1945 Indochina was a backwater in the war, still run by ex-Vichy administrators but under Japanese control. In March the Japanese finally removed the last vestiges of French control and persuaded the emperor of Annam (a kingdom on the east coast of Indochina), Bao Dai, to declare independence. Similar action followed two days later in Cambodia under King Sihanouk, and a month later in Laos. In the north of Indochina the nationalist and Communist Vietminh guerrillas under Ho Chi Minh were strongly supported by the United States, which hoped to end French rule over Indochina after the war, and by August 1945 they had liberated large parts of the north but still had little support in the south. A week after the Japanese surrender the Vietminh took control of Hanoi, and five days later Bao Dai abdicated. At the Potsdam Conference the country was divided along the 16th parallel between Chinese and British areas of operations. In the south the British arrived in Saigon in mid-September 1945 and struggled to reassert French control in conditions of near anarchy between Japanese and French troops, Vietminh guerrillas, and their own forces. The Chinese moved into Hanoi in September, humiliating the French at every opportunity. French troops did not reenter the city until March 1946, and fighting with the Vietminh broke out within months.

The situation in other countries was equally difficult to resolve. For the British, Siam was an enemy country and they had consistently refused to make any guarantee not to seek territorial gains in Siam at the end of the war because they wanted to acquire the Isthmus of Kra to provide better defenses for Malaya. The United States was not at war with Siam and regarded it as an occupied country and backed the Free Siam movement operating in the United States. The British arrived in Bangkok in early September and began a period of military rule, and Siam was forced to give up its wartime gains in Malaya and Indochina.

Korea had been occupied by Japan in 1910, but the Allies agreed on postwar independence at the Cairo Conference in 1943. The Americans and the Soviets subsequently agreed on a demarcation line along the 38th parallel for their respective occupation zones. U.S. forces arrived in Seoul in early September 1945 and immediately began working with the Japanese administration to control the country and also used Japanese troops to fire on Korean demonstrators. In the north the Soviets sent 270,000 Japanese troops to labor camps in Siberia and through the Communist Korean People's Committee were the effective rulers of the country. By late 1945 a de facto division of Korea was becoming apparent.

In China, Soviet troops swept into Manchuria and allowed Communist forces under Lin Piao to take control. Elsewhere there was considerable cooperation between Chiang Kai-shek and the Japanese. In large areas under Japanese control, Japanese troops kept order and kept out Communist forces until the Nationalists were able to take over. In many areas such as Shansi province Japanese troops were still fighting the Communists as late as April 1949.

The Second World War was over and Allied troops had conquered all enemy territory and "liberated" Allied territory. By the end of 1945 governments were functioning in most of the liberated areas, and in Germany and Japan Allied military governments were in control. However, many major problems still remained to be resolved.

XI

AFTERMATH

WHEN DID THE SECOND WORLD WAR END? GERMANY and Japan formally surrendered in May and September 1945, respectively, but fighting in various parts of the world continued for years afterward. Underground resistance to Soviet forces in Ukraine and Poland lasted until the late 1940s. The war between the Nationalists and Communists in China ended on the mainland in 1949. In the Pacific a few Japanese soldiers fought on for decades. Lieutenant Onoda Hiroo finally surrendered on the island of Lubang off the coast of Luzon on March 10, 1974. In 1945 he had been instructed to continue guerrilla warfare, and at first with a few companions and then alone he did so for twenty-nine years. He kept his weapons, made new boots out of rubber, and continued to kill the local inhabitants. He would not surrender until his former commander, Major Taniguchi Yoshimi, came from Japan and read out a formal cancellation of his orders. Peace treaties with the allies of Germany were signed by 1947 and with Japan in 1951. No formal peace treaty was ever signed with Germany, and it was not until reunification in 1990 that the Federal Republic formally recognized the Oder-Neisse Line as the country's eastern boundary; it was 1994 before Allied troops finally withdrew from their occupation role in Berlin. Other conflicts took years to resolve. The dispute between Italy and Yugoslavia over Trieste was settled in 1954, but it was another twenty years before the fighting stopped in Vietnam, following the reunification of the country after the defeat of the American attempt to create a separate state in the south. By 1995 the last major problems that remained were the possible reunification of Korea and a peace treaty between Japan and Russia.

One of the first Allied actions in the immediate aftermath of the war was a massive deportation of enemy civilians. Over 20 million people were affected, compared with the approximately 1 million Germans and the 3 million of other nationalities resettled during the war. Three million Japanese were moved from southeast Asia and the Pacific to Japan, but the main movements came in Europe. Between 1944 and 1952 the Soviet Union deported over 500,000 people from the Baltic states, many to the Gulag camps, and moved in a large number of Russian nationals as a form of colonization. The Balkan states also expelled their German minority populations, 200,000 each from both Hungary and Yugoslavia and 110,000 from Rumania. In 1944 the Polish and Soviet governments agreed that Polish citizens living in the eastern parts of the country annexed by the Soviet Union could opt to move westward into Poland. About 2 million chose to do so, and another 500,000 from the minority populations in Poland (Ukrainians, Russians, Belorussians, and Lithuanians) moved eastward into the Soviet Union, although they were not allowed to live in the frontier districts.

The largest and most controversial movement of populations took place in central Europe: the expulsion of the Germans from Czechoslovakia and the previously German territories in Poland that were to be handed over to Poland as compensation for the extension of the Soviet Union into Poland. In Czechoslovakia the German population of the Sudetenland had been at the root of the crisis that led to the Munich settlement and the dismemberment of Czechoslovakia in 1938. Until August 1941 the Czech government-in-exile led by Benes negotiated with the German Social Democrat exiles in London on a policy of self-contained autonomous German districts and the cession of some territory to Germany (the policy Britain and France had adopted before and at Munich). The Czechs then made a major departure in policy, to total expulsion of the German minority.

This was accepted by the British in July 1942, at the same time that they repudiated the Munich settlement, and by the United States and the Soviet Union a year later. In May 1945, once the Benes government was installed in Prague, the German minority population was forced to wear special armbands and undertake forced labor, and some were sent to internment camps. The U.S. authorities later tried Vaclav Hrnecek, the deputy commander of the Budweis internment camp in Bohemia, and sentenced him to eight years in jail for the way he ran the camp. Between May and August 1945, about 750,000 Germans were deported from Czechoslovakia in harsh, largely unplanned movements. After the Potsdam Conference, when the Allies agreed on a policy of massive repatriation, another 1.8 million Germans were moved to Germany by the end of 1946. By 1949, after further "voluntary" movements, less than 200,000 Germans remained, out of a total of 3 million of German descent living in prewar Czechoslovakia.

The decision to move Poland westward necessarily involved the movement of millions of Germans. The territories in the west now allocated to Poland were ethnically German and had been for centuries, including East Prussia, Pomerania, Silesia, and Brandenburg. At Versailles under the principles of self-determination it had never been contemplated that they could be anything other than German territory. The Allies recognized that, as part of a policy of collective guilt, about 5 million people would have to be expelled if the Polish border was moved to the Oder River and another 3 million if it was pushed to the western Neisse River, as agreed de facto at Potsdam. To some extent the German people had partly solved the Allies' problems: about 4 million refugees had left the area ahead of the Red Army. The remaining population was crammed into internment camps, and one Jewish ex-inmate of the Theresienstadt camp thought the conditions were worse for the Germans than when it had been occupied by the Jews. At Lamsdorf internment camp, 6,488 people died out of a total population of 8,064, a death rate of 80 percent. Eventually, the remaining 4 million Germans were expelled westward. Altogether, over 12 million Germans were affected during the war and its aftermath. Of this total about 2 million died, half of them as refugees during the war and the remainder during the Allied expulsions.

Another deportation question affected Soviet citizens fighting in German uniform who were captured by the western Allies. This problem emerged after the Normandy landings, when a number of Soviet defector forces surrendered to British and American troops. From the beginning the British government decided they would have to be returned, forcibly if necessary, to the Soviet Union, where they would either be shot or subject to what were euphemistically described as "harsh measures." The British and the Americans were keen to give no excuse to the Soviets to maltreat any of their own prisoners of war liberated by the Soviets in central Europe. At the Yalta Conference the three powers agreed to a secret protocol to return their citizens. By the end of June 1945 the British had returned about 32,000 Soviet citizens (not all of whom were prisoners of war) by boat to Odessa and Murmansk. The only concession the British made was to recognize the August 1939 Soviet frontier as defining a Soviet citizen.

A more extensive operation had to be carried out in the Drau River valley in southeast Austria, where in the chaos at the end of the war the British army controlled about 40,000 Cossacks (including a large number of women and children) and 5,000 Georgian troops who had fought with the Germans. The British army decided that all were subject to the Yalta agreement, although some had been in exile since the Russian civil war and others had not been within the August 1939 boundaries of the Soviet Union. In addition, all the Germans captured were handed over to the Soviets. This was not a requirement of the Yalta agreement. By a series of deceptions and the use of force (the British shot about twenty of the Cossacks and a number committed suicide) the Cossacks were handed over to the Soviets. About 4,000 escaped, but about half were recaptured. The senior officers were hanged and the rest deported to the Gulag. The forcible repatriations ended in August 1945 and a new policy, developed by the Americans, was adopted: only ex-members of the Red Army and those who had actively collaborated with the Germans would be deported in future, and civilian refugees would be allowed to stay in the West if they wanted.

Preparatory work on the peace terms for the minor Axis powers was undertaken in the Foreign Ministers' Conference set up at the Potsdam Conference, and a formal Peace Conference was established at Paris in July 1946. Unlike at Versailles, the defeated were given a chance to make representations, but the minor Allies were given little say over the terms. The treaties were finally agreed on by early 1947. Rumania gained little from its volte-face in 1944 and recovered very little of the territory lost in 1940. The Soviet Union kept Bessarabia and Bukovina, and Bulgaria kept southern Dobruja. About half of Transylvania was regained from Hungary. Elsewhere, Hungary was forced back to its early 1938 frontiers and also lost Ruthenia to Czechoslovakia, which had to cede it to the Soviet Union to give the latter a border with Czechoslovakia. Bulgaria lost all its gains, apart from southern Dobruja. All three defeated states had to accept limitations on their armed forces and pay reparations. Unlike its stance in the Balkans and central Europe, the Soviet Union was content to see an independent, friendly, and non-Communist Finland, despite the latter's decision to join Germany in 1941. Reparations were modest and there was no interference in Finnish internal politics. The June 1941 frontiers were restored but with the addition for the Soviets of the Petsamo area and its huge nickel reserves. In return the Soviets gave up the base on the Hanko Peninsula, west of Helsinki, but they took over the Poskkala Peninsula (this area was returned in 1956). Finland did not carry out a major purge of war criminals, although Ryti, the president at the time of the attack on the Soviet Union in 1941, was imprisoned for ten years.

The British and the Americans had no intention of imposing harsh terms on Italy—it was too important strategically in terms of excluding Communist influence. When Italy decided to declare war on Germany in the autumn of 1943 it had been promised that terms would be eased. Strict limits were placed on the Italian armed forces, but the state of the economy ruled out the payment of reparations to all except the Soviet Union. Four small frontier areas were given to France, Rhodes and the Dodecanese to Greece, and the Adriatic islands and most of Venezia Giulia to Yugoslavia. Italy was allowed to keep the South Tyrol (Alto Adige) gained from Austria in 1918. The complex situation at Trieste was not resolved until 1954, when roughly half each was given to Yugoslavia and Italy, although the Allies had promised the Italians all of it in March 1948 in an attempt to boost the chances of the ruling Christian Democrats against the Communists in the national elections. Of the Italian colonies Libya was made nominally independent in 1952, although it remained under strict British tutelage. Somalia was placed under Italian trustreeship and eventually was united with British Somaliland. Eritrea was forced into an unwanted federal union with Ethiopia, and its full integration into Ethiopia in 1962 led to a twenty-year-long civil war. Italy was not allowed to join the United Nations until 1955, although it had been a founding member of NATO in 1949.

A treaty with Germany was never signed. The two rival blocs increasingly ran their occupation zones as separate entities, leading eventually to the creation of the Federal Republic from the American, British, and French zones, and the German Democratic Republic from the Soviet zone. The remaining two treaties, with Austria and Japan, became increasingly caught up in the opening phases of the Cold War. The treaty with Austria was technically not a peace treaty because the Austrians argued they were the first victim of German aggression in 1938, a point conceded by the Allies at the Moscow Foreign Ministers' Conference in October 1943. The Allies finally agreed, over U.S. objections, to a tripartite occupation in October 1944, and after the capture of Vienna the veteran Socialist leader Karl Renner, the first president of the Austrian republic, declared independence and was recognized by the Allies in October 1945. Long negotiations followed, but not until a thaw in the first phase of the Cold War, after the death of Stalin and after the Austrians had suggested that they should become permanently neutral, was a state treaty finally agreed upon, and Allied forces withdrew in May 1955.

At the Cairo Conference in November 1943, the Americans, British, and Chinese agreed that Japan should be stripped of her overseas empire, "which she has taken by violence and greed." The same could have been said of the European empires in the Far East. Manchuria, Formosa, and the Pescadores islands would be returned to China, and Korea would eventually become independent. The United States had run the Pacific war unilaterally and was determined to do the same with the occupation regime after the Japanese surrender. The initial planning for the peace treaty with Japan was dominated by the Cold War. The United States wanted the treaty drawn up by the Far East Commission of eleven countries where a two-thirds majority could ensure the adoption of any policy, thereby isolating the Soviet Union. The latter wanted the treaty to be drawn up by the Foreign Ministers' Conference, as in Europe, where the Soviets had an effective veto. The Chinese wanted a four-power group where they had a veto. By 1947–48 the Americans were already losing interest in Japanese internal reform, preferring to incorporate Japan into the Western anti-Communist system. By 1950 they advocated a separate peace with Japan, despite the fact that the Declaration by the United Nations of January 1942, signed by all the Allies, specifically ruled out such a step. Over the next eighteen months the United States, following the outbreak of the Korean War, worked on the terms of a separate peace and on persuading their initially reluctant allies to go along with the idea. At the San Francisco Conference in September 1951 a joint American and British draft treaty was presented. The Americans took the Bonin and Ryukyu islands (including Okinawa) as trusteeship territories for their own strategic purposes, and Formosa and the Pescadores were ceded by Japan to the Chinese, but the Nationalist Chinese on Taiwan, not the Communists on the mainland. The Soviet Union and its allies were present, but the conference agenda allowed no discussion of the provisions of the treaty, which was railroaded through against the opposition of the Soviet bloc and some other countries who wanted stronger terms. The Soviet Union, Poland, and Czechoslovakia refused to sign the peace treaty.

Cooperation between the wartime Allies did last long enough to mount trials of the main war criminals. The charges and the proceedings raised major legal, moral, and political questions. At the Moscow Foreign Ministers' Conference in the autumn of 1943 the Allies agreed that war criminals, when captured, would be sent back to the countries where they had committed their crimes for trial. The major war criminals would be punished jointly by the Allies in a way that was still to be decided. It was undecided because there were major differences between the Allies over how to proceed. The Soviets wanted immediate punishment on capture, but the British and the Americans wanted to postpone action until after the war in order to avoid any retaliation against prisoners of war. The British believed that any action was essentially political rather than legal and therefore wanted summary executions by the military, but Stalin rejected this proposal in the autumn of 1944. The French agreed with the British that it would be difficult to define many of the appalling acts committed by Germany as being either war crimes or against international law. The Americans wanted a full trial in a military court with formal charges, the production of evidence, and cross-examination of witnesses so as to set out a historical record of what had happened and how the international community punished such action. The Americans finally persuaded their allies to accept their views at the San Francisco Conference in 1945, which established the new United Nations organization. Their aims were laudable but led, as the other Allies had realized they would, to innumerable difficulties and charges of double standards.

There was plenty of evidence to prosecute a huge range of war crimes under the Hague and Geneva conventions: the barbarization of warfare on the eastern front, the treatment of Soviet prisoners, the shooting of British and American prisoners, among others. However, the Allies wanted to go further, because these definitions would not include many crimes, in particular aggression against other states and the deaths of six million Jews. However, to include charges of "crimes against peace" and "crimes against humanity" seemed to be defining the offense after the event because they were not previously offenses against international law. It was also unclear how the tribunal could try offenses committed within a sovereign state, Germany, against its own citizens and those committed before war broke out. Charges of conspiracy were also introduced, although this concept was unknown outside of the common-law systems of the United States and Britain. The United States also insisted on putting certain organizations on trial—the Reich cabinet, the Nazi party, the S.S., the S.A., the Gestapo, and the German High Command—so as to condemn them as criminal organizations, so that in future trials it would merely be necessary to prove membership in such an organization before finding an individual guilty. In the end the charter setting up the International Military Tribunal tried to avoid these problems by simply declaring certain acts as crimes and gave the tribunal jurisdiction. Another difficulty was that the judges were drawn entirely from the ranks of the victors, some were not judges, and some had been involved in drawing up the charges and establishing the tribunal.

The most difficult area of all was the category "crimes against peace" and "aggressive war." The only basis on which these charges could be brought was the Paris (Kellogg-Briand) Pact of 1928, in which all signatories had renounced war but not self-defense. "Self-defense" was not limited to the territory of the country concerned and was judged by that country alone. In the end it proved impossible to define "aggression." Neither the French nor (less surprisingly) the Soviet Union regarded aggressive war as a crime in international law as it then existed. Although the tribunal decided to disallow all *tu quoque* responses from the German defendants, the tribunal charter specifically defined aggression as applying only to Germany. This was essential to avoid two problems. First, Italy was not on trial, despite its record of aggression under Mussolini: Abyssinia, 1935; Albania, 1939; the declaration of war on Britain and France in June 1940; and its attack on Greece in the autumn of that year. More important, however, the Allies, in particular the Soviet Union, could equally have been charged with "crimes against peace" following the Soviet attacks on Poland and Finland in 1939, the forcible takeover of the three Baltic states in 1940, the demands for territory from Rumania later that year, the declaration of war on neutral Bulgaria in 1944, and the declaration of war on Japan in 1945. The British could have been charged with violating the neutrality of Norway, Denmark, and Iran (the latter jointly with the Soviet Union), the United

States with violating Danish neutrality and of complicity in the Soviet attack on Japan by soliciting it. Australia and Britain could have
been charged with violating Portuguese neutrality.

War crimes also raised difficult questions. Soviet treatment of German prisoners was almost as bad as German treatment of prisoners
taken on the eastern front. The Soviet Union had the audacity to insist that Germany be specifically charged with the Katyn massacre,
which they themselves had carried out. There was also the question
of suspected Allied war crimes; the German High Command had set
up a special unit in September 1939 to keep a careful record of these
allegations. The most important cases were the killing of 5,000 ethnic
Germans in early September 1939 by the Poles in Bromberg, Thorn,
and Pomerellen, and the death marches of German civilians. The
British were accused of shooting shipwrecked German sailors at Nar-
vik and Crete and with sinking the hospital ship *Tübingen* in the Adriatic near Pola in November 1944. The French were accused of
shooting German aircrew and eighty prisoners at Annecy in early
September 1944. The Americans were accused of shooting prisoners
in Italy and the Ardennes and suffocating to death 140 prisoners
while they were being transported across France in sealed boxcars.

The final problem about the tribunal was the inclusion in the definition of "crimes against humanity" of "inhumane acts against any
civilian population" and in the definition of war crimes as including
"wanton destruction of cities . . . or devastation not justified by military necessity." On this basis it would have been equally possible to
indict the Allies for their large-scale bombing of German cities and
for dropping the atomic bomb on Japan.

The next problem was whom to put on trial. The Soviets held a
small number of major figures, and the western Allies over fifty at
Mandorf-les-Bains in Luxembourg. Some of the most important
figures—Hitler, Goebbels, and Himmler—had already committed
suicide, and in the end it was decided to put twenty-four defendants
on trial, including Martin Bormann, Hitler's deputy in the last stages
of the war, who had not been captured and was thought to have died
trying to escape from Berlin in April 1945. The Americans insisted
on including Franz von Papen, Baldur von Schirach, and Konstantin

von Neurath, who were associated with the early days of the Nazi government but were non-Nazis of marginal importance. Dönitz was included, against the advice of the British Admiralty, who thought he had fought a fair naval war. The Russians insisted on including Admiral Erich Raeder and Fritzsche (Goebbels's deputy), whom they held despite the fact that they were minor figures. Julius Streicher was included, but, although he was a revolting anti-Semitic propagandist, it was difficult to see how he was responsible for any specific decisions. The biggest mistake was caused by a clerical error. The Allies were determined to put on trial one representative of German industry and eventually chose the Krupp armaments firm. However, they indicted Gustav Krupp, who was seventy-five, doubly incontinent, in a poor mental state, and who had handed over control of the firm to his son Alfried in 1940. It was Alfried the Allies had meant to charge. The result was that the judges refused to try Gustav. They also had doubts about the mental condition of Rudolf Hess, Hitler's deputy who had flown to Britain in 1941 in an attempt to secure peace before the German invasion of the Soviet Union. The Reich cabinet was also indicted as an organization because it seemed important; only afterward did the Allies discover that it had not met after 1937. The S.A. was also included, although it soon became apparent that it was of little importance after 1934.

The trial opened in Nuremberg on November 20, 1945, and lasted until the end of August 1946, with judgments and sentences being given a month later. It was an opportunity for the first time to set out a full catalogue of the terrible crimes committed by the German government and the Nazis. Evidence was produced on forced labor, the barbarization of warfare in the east, and the Final Solution, among other crimes. The judges began considering the judgments and verdicts in mid-July 1946, six weeks before the end of the trial. There were major disagreements, and some of the judgments were the result of political horsetrading. Eventually, against strong Soviet opposition, Schacht, von Papen, and Fritzsche were acquitted, as were the S.A. and, by implication, the German High Command and General Staff. The main defendants, such as Göring, von Ribbentrop, Ernst Kaltenbrunner (the Gestapo chief), Hans Frank (occupation chief in

Poland), and Arthur Seyss-Inquart (Reich commissioner in the Netherlands), were sentenced to death. Göring committed suicide by swal-
lowing a cyanide capsule, but the rest were hanged two weeks after
the verdicts were delivered, in the prison gymnasium at Nuremberg.

Some of the other sentences seemed inconsistent. Von Neurath,
the occupation chief in Bohemia-Moravia, received only fifteen
years because his regime was judged to be less harsh than elsewhere.
Von Schirach received twenty years, despite his involvement in
anti-Jewish policies. Fritz Sauckel, the director of the forced-labor
program, was sentenced to death, but Speer, who used the labor as
armaments minister, received twenty years after a politically adroit
performance during the trial. Hess and Raeder were imprisoned for
life, and Dönitz for ten years, despite the fact that the judgment effectively exonerated him. Of those sent to Spandau Prison in Berlin to
serve their sentences, Dönitz served his full term, as did von Schirach
and Speer. Von Neurath, given fifteen years, was released on health
grounds in 1954, as was economics minister Walther Funk, in 1957,
despite his life sentence. Only Hess served out his full life sentence.

The Tokyo trial of the Japanese followed many of the precedents
of Nuremberg. The defendants were subject to fifty-five counts,
eighteen of them "crimes against peace." The first of these was an
eighteen-year conspiracy to "secure military, naval, political and
economic domination of East Asia and of the Pacific and Indian Oceans." They were also charged with war crimes and crimes
against humanity. A new count not used at Nuremberg was introduced: "negative criminality"—failure to take adequate steps to stop
breaches of the law. Two men, including Foreign Minister Hirota,
were executed on this charge alone. Hirota was found guilty because
although he inquired about the atrocities committed by the Japanese
army at Nanking in 1937–38 he accepted the assurances given by the
War Ministry and did not take any further action. There were
twenty-eight defendants, deliberately drawn from a wide cross section of the Japanese elite, including fourteen generals, three admirals,
five career diplomats, and three bureaucrats. The most important
missing defendant was the emperor, against whom there was plenty
of evidence of crimes against peace. The Americans had at first con-

sidered indicting him but then decided he was needed as a symbol to rebuild Japan and therefore had to be found blameless. The defendants were instructed by the U.S. prosecutors that at no point in their evidence were they to implicate the emperor. The trial lasted two and a half years, ending in November 1948. Eventually, seven death sentences were handed down, including General Tojo, the prime minister who had been in office when the final decision to go to war had been made. There were also sixteen sentences of life imprisonment, one of twenty years, and one of seven years. The verdicts were not unanimous. The only expert on international law, Justice Radhabinod Pal of India, found all the defendants not guilty, arguing in his dissenting judgment against the very concept of the trials: "A trial with law thus prescribed will only be a sham employment of legal process for the satisfaction of a thirst for revenge. It does not correspond to any idea of justice." Of the eighteen people sentenced to jail terms, six died in prison and the others were all released early in April 1958.

Other countries held their own trials and investigations of those thought to be guilty of war crimes or collaboration with Germany. Norway, Denmark, and the Netherlands reintroduced capital punishment for those involved. The main collaborators such as Quisling and Mussert were executed, Jonas Lie committed suicide, and Clausen died awaiting trial. In total, in western Europe nearly 11,000 people were sentenced to death, although fewer than 2,500 executions were actually carried out. About 170,000 were sent to jail for various periods. The highest rates of sentencing were in Belgium and Norway, which in per capita terms were six times higher than in France. In Norway 46,000 people were found guilty of collaboration. Of these 18,000 were sent to jail (600 for more than eight years), 28,000 were either fined or deprived of their civil rights, and the remaining 5,000 were not punished. (In the occupied Channel Islands the British refused to accept that there had been collaboration despite widespread evidence to the contrary, and so there were no trials.)

The situation in France, where collaboration was more widespread, reveals many of the difficulties in dealing with the aftermath of occupation in Europe. Despite some of the promises made by the governments-in-exile and the resistance, it proved very difficult to proceed against more than the most important figures. The problem was that collaboration had been so deep-rooted that any effective purge would have left the state without administrators, judges, police, army, teachers, and industrialists. A special court was set up to try Pétain, Laval, and other senior Vichy ministers. The judges were career judges, but the jurors were parliamentarians who had voted against giving Pétain full powers in June 1940, and members of the resistance. The trials began with Admiral Esteva and General Dentz, the commanders in Tunisia and Syria. Neither was executed, despite their having fought against the Free French and the Allies. De Gaulle wanted Pétain tried in absentia but he gave himself up in late April 1945, even though the Swiss government was prepared to grant asylum. His trial began in July and was largely political rather than legal, with most of the evidence coming from former ministers. He was sentenced to death with a recommendation of mercy, which was granted by de Gaulle. Pétain spent the rest of his life in prison on the Ile d'Yeu off the Brittany coast and died in 1951.

Laval was not put on trial until October 1945. It was anything but a fair trial, was almost entirely political, and was conducted in great haste because the jurors wanted to start their election campaigns. De Gaulle rejected an appeal for clemency. Laval tried to commit suicide but his stomach was pumped out and he was tied to a post and shot, shouting, "Long live France." Darnaud, the head of the Vichy militia, was executed, and Déat was sentenced to death in absentia. In 1946 the trials of lower-ranking Vichy ministers began. Flandin, who had briefly been foreign minister, was effectively pardoned, but de Brinon, the Vichy ambassador in Paris, was executed; Vallat, the commissioner for Jewish affairs, was sent to jail; and Peyrouton, the interior minister who had opposed Laval, was acquitted, although he had already spent five years in prison. The trials continued into the 1950s, often of people who finally gave themselves up, but they usually received very light sentences.

Since 1943 the Interior Ministry of de Gaulle's F.C.N.L. in Algiers had begun drawing up lists of officials to be arrested or dismissed.

The first priority in 1944—45 was the police and judiciary. All police chiefs were dismissed (five were sentenced to death), as were some magistrates. In the army and the foreign service all promotions made by Vichy were declared void and the new French government refused to recognize any foreign ambassador who had been accredited to Vichy. In general, however, the purges were light and only the most severe cases of collaboration were punished. In the army purge, just 2,500 officers were dismissed, and in the civil service, 4,000 were dismissed without pension, 500 with a pension, 800 were forced to retire, and another 29 were not allowed to wear their medals. In the schools, just 200 teachers were stopped from teaching. The purges in industry were similarly very limited as a deliberate policy. There were only a few symbolic actions. André Laurent-Athalin, the president of the Banque de Paris et de Pays-Bas, which had helped to set up numerous Franco-German companies, was banned from running a bank. Some firms that had collaborated, such as the airplane engine manufacturers and Air France, were nationalized, as was Renault, whose head, Louis Renault, had chosen to return to Paris and collaborate with the Germans.

The only major industrial purge took place in the newspaper industry and was of direct interest to the politicians. In September 1944 a decree banned all newspapers that had published under occupation and all prewar ones that had continued for more than a fortnight after the armistice or, in the south, after the occupation of the Vichy zone. Over 900 papers were affected, but there were only 64 cases of total and 51 of partial confiscation. A blacklist of authors was drawn up but no major figures were put on trial. The Académie Française, always a conservative body, took action only against the major collaborators such as Pétain and Charles Maurras of Action Française, and even then their Academy places were left unfilled until after their deaths.

There were investigations of various entertainment stars, although the maximum penalty was only a one-year ban. However, no action was taken, even against those such as Mistinguett and Maurice Chevalier, who had appeared on Paris Radio or undertaken tours to Germany. Criminal proceedings against the most notorious of the collaborators, Sacha Guitry, were dropped. Many of those most deeply involved in collaboration were sheltered by right-wing Catholic clergy.

Overall, 124,000 cases were investigated for possible civil trial. Over a third (45,000) never came to trial, and another 28,000 were acquitted. Of the remaining 51,000, over 7,000 were sentenced to no more than "indignity"—the loss of civic rights for a period. The overwhelming majority of the remainder were sentenced to jail, just 2,700 for life, and although nearly 7,000 death sentences were passed—the overwhelming majority in absentia—only 767 were carried out. No one of any rank was seriously punished for French cooperation in the roundup and deportation of Jews.

The British were confronted with different but equally difficult problems when they decided to try members of the Indian National Army for collaborating with the Japanese. They deliberately chose one Sikh, one Hindu, and one Muslim for the first trial, which, ineptly, they held in the Red Fort in Delhi, a symbol of former Moghul glory. The atmosphere in India had changed decisively since the 1930s and members of the I.N.A. were widely seen as nationalist heroes, not traitors. The Congress party mounted a major support campaign and provided an impressive array of the most talented defense lawyers. The trial was essentially political and there was little doubt that I.N.A. members would be found guilty. They were sentenced to transportation for life, although the sentences were suspended. The Indian army, however, insisted that those involved should be cashiered. After independence the new government promised pensions to all those who had served in the I.N.A., although it stopped short of reinstating them in the army.

The impact of the developing Cold War was felt throughout Europe and the Far East and had a major influence on the treatment of war criminals and those associated with the Nazi and Japanese governments. During the war there had been a perceptible drift to the left in politics, a factor that was particularly evident in Britain. In occupied Europe the resistance also developed high ideals about a spiritual reconstruction after the war. Within a few years of the end of the war this trend was reversed. Radical reconstruction did not occur and the old order and values were reestablished. There was a drift to the right in politics; apparent in the United States as early as 1942, by the late 1940s it was characterized by a virulent anticommunism. Perceptions of national interest changed sharply and priority was given to new postwar concerns rather than the aftermath of the war. As the confrontation between the United States and its allies and the Soviet Union intensified, the western Allies rapidly lost their enthusiasm for digging over the past. Instead they gave a greater priority to building up a new state in western Germany that would fill the power vacuum in that part of Europe and support the emerging western alliance. After the Nuremberg trial, the Allies agreed that in future there would be trials only within respective zones, together with denazification proceedings affecting a large proportion of the population. In practice after some further trials of war criminals, such as the heads of the concentration and death camps, enthusiasm began to wane. This development partly reflected the lack of resources devoted by the western Allies to war crimes and investigation work, but also the changes in the international situation. The inevitable consequence was that the western Allies ended up working with, and eventually bringing back to power, some of those who had been involved with the Nazi government.

Denazification rapidly proved far more difficult than had been expected during the war. In November 1944 the U.S. Joint Chiefs of Staff instructed the occupying forces that the entire Nazi leadership was to be removed and, without exception, no active Nazis or even sympathizers were to be employed in public positions. Little had been achieved by the end of 1945, and German opposition to the process was growing—the churches were speaking out very strongly, something they had not done officially under the Nazis. The western Allies found that they could not proceed on the basis of excluding all who had been members of the Nazi party—the membership was simply too great. The U.S. authorities dropped the outright ban on employing former members of the party as early as March 1946. In the U.S. zone, just over 40,000 denazification cases were completed by the end of that year, but of these, nearly 30,000 were found to be just "followers" and were therefore not punished. Only 116 people were classified as major offenders. Most cases were left to subordinate German tribunals, and they were even more lenient, regrading over 80 percent of cases into lower categories. In the spring of 1947 the British decided to end the denazification process. Denazification was, superficially, a much more drastic process in the Soviet zone, but it was linked to the removal from power of existing elites in order to strengthen the position of the new Communist rulers.

In the western zones, the employment of former party members and even war criminals was widespread from the earliest days of the occupation. The British appointed Dr. Fritz Busch head of the German transport system, despite the fact that he had been designated for compulsory removal in view of his membership in the S.S. and his role as wartime head of German transport in the movement of millions of Jews to the killing centers. The British also appointed as head of the Hanover police a former S.S. officer, who then promptly recruited his former colleagues, despite the fact that the British had a full record of his wartime activities. This pattern was repeated in other towns, nearly all of whom had ex-Gestapo or S.S. officers in their police forces. In Düsseldorf the head of the criminal-investigation department, Dr. Bernard Wehner, was one of those who had investigated the 1944 plot on Hitler's life. In Munich the equivalent department was headed by Fritz Riedel, who as a member of the S.S. had worked in Latvia, while in Cologne the head of the criminal-investigation department was Kurt Geissler, a member of the S.S. and an agent for the Gestapo in Berlin. In the legal profession the situation was even worse. It was almost impossible to find any judges or lawyers who had not been compromised during the Nazi period. The United States imposed an arbitrary quota according to which not more than half of the posts were to be filled by ex-Nazis and sympathizers, but this quota was not adhered to. By 1948 three quarters of the state prosecutors in Bavaria were former Nazis, some of them ex-members of the S.S.

The result of this situation was predictable. German courts executed only three people for murdering other Germans during the Nazi period. For example, Hitler's favorite general, Sepp Dietrich of the S.S., who had directed the Night of the Long Knives (the killing of the head of the S.A., Ernst Röhm, and others in 1934) as well as war crimes in the east, was sentenced to eighteen months in jail. In the trial of Erbprinz Ernst Zurlippe, who joined the Nazis in 1928, became a member of the S.S., and openly claimed he knew about the death camps, the prosecutor asked for a sentence of only nine months, but Zurlippe was acquitted on the grounds that he did not know the S.S. were committing any crimes. August Heissmeyer, a confidant of Himmler, was prosecuted only for giving a false name after the end of the war. Dr. Otto Bradfisch, the head of Einzatsgruppe 8 who admitted to the murder of 15,000 people, was jailed for only ten years. The judge argued that only Hitler, Himmler, and Heydrich (all conveniently dead) had been fully responsible for all these crimes. In 1948 a German court acquitted five directors of DEGESCH, an I. G. Farben subsidiary that manufactured the Zyklon B gas used at Auschwitz. The defendants argued that they did not know how the gas was being used, even though 70 percent of their output was going to Auschwitz. The judge argued that "millions of people had been saved by Zyklon B gas from typhus and other epidemics."

The western Allies were showing a similar reluctance to continue with war-crimes trials. From the start there was a major lack of resources for tracking down war criminals, and in June 1947 the British stopped extraditing suspected war criminals from their zone, a policy the Americans adopted five months later. There was in particular a marked reluctance to put senior members of the military on trial for their complicity—and worse—in war crimes. It was easier to believe their protestations that they had not taken part in the atrocities and had indeed tried to stop them, which German records show to be largely untrue. The Italians put Field Marshal Kesselring on trial for the killing of 335 Italian hostages as a reprisal in Rome in March 1944. He confessed and was found guilty at his trial in Venice. The British, in particular Churchill, were outraged and protested. Kesselring was released in 1952. Even more of a problem for the British were the senior officers they held as prisoners, particularly after an American investigation in the summer of 1947 revealed strong evidence linking four senior commanders to war crimes: von Brauchitsch, von Runstedt, von Manstein, and Strauss. The Soviet Union demanded they be handed over for trial, but the British wanted the United States to carry out any trials; the Americans, however, were reluctant to undertake this task. In April 1948 the British cabinet decided to end all war-crimes trials by the beginning of September. It was agreed, very unwillingly and against the advice of senior members of the British army, to prosecute all four generals. Von Brauchitsch died, and it was then decided that von Rundstedt and Strauss were too ill to stand trial (the attorney general thought that in a British court they would have been ruled fit to be tried), and they were released without charge. The British refused to hand them over to the Soviets. Von Manstein was eventually tried in the autumn of 1949 and sentenced to eighteen years, of which he served three.

In the spring of 1945, senior S.S. officers, with the connivance of Himmler, had held separate surrender negotiations with Allied authorities in Italy. All of them escaped serious punishment. Walter Schellenberg was tried by the U.S. occupation authorities and found guilty of helping the Jewish extermination program in France. He was immediately pardoned and became an adviser to British intelligence. Walter Rauff, who had personally developed the gas-truck program for mobile killing operations, was held in a prisoner of war camp at Rimini but "escaped" to South America. Eugen Dollman, the head of the S.S. anti-Jewish program in Italy, was held by the U.S. authorities in 1947 but he too "escaped," to Switzerland. Karl Wolff, who had led the surrender talks, was tried by a denazification court in 1949 and was simply sentenced to time already served. The proceedings of the court were clearly a farce because in 1964 he was tried for war crimes—personal involvement in the deaths of 300,000 people and running the slave-labor program at I. G. Farben. He was sentenced to life imprisonment but released after seven years.

There was no greater enthusiasm for the prosecution of German industrialists involved in war crimes than for the prosecution of high-ranking military figures. The Allies' original intention was to have a second international tribunal after Nuremberg for major industrialists. This time, Alfried Krupp and two senior figures in the giant chemical company I. G. Farben were indicted, as well as Hermann Roechling, the Saar coal and steel magnate who had been convicted in absentia by the French after the First World War for war crimes, and a banker, Kurt von Schroeder. Disagreements among the Allies meant that the Soviets did not nominate any businessmen to be prosecuted, and the trial collapsed. It was left to each of the occupying powers to decide what to do. In May 1947, twenty-four I. G. Farben executives were charged by the Americans with planning a war of aggression and carrying out plunder and spoliation, together with slavery and mass murder, particularly at the Buna plant at Auschwitz. During the war the company took over a vast range of factories in the occupied countries and half of its workers were prisoners of war, foreign labor, or camp inmates. The conditions at the Buna plant, where average life expectancy was a few months, were so bad that even the S.S. complained about the poor rations provided by the company. In July 1948 all twenty-four executives were acquitted of planning a war of aggression, fourteen were acquitted of plunder and spoliation (nine were convicted on the latter charge), and only the five people who had detailed knowledge about Auschwitz and other plants were convicted of slavery and mass murder. Half the defendants were acquitted on all charges and two people were sentenced to eight years in jail, while most received light sentences of two to three years. Little action was taken against other companies involved in war crimes. For example, Siemens had an agreement with the S.S. for the use of cheap labor from concentration camps, and BMW used slaves from nearby Dachau concentration camp.

By the late 1940s, as the Cold War deepened and the Federal Republic was established under a right-wing government supported by the western Allies, enthusiasm for continuing with the investigation and prosecution of war crimes rapidly vanished. The western Allies decided to hand over all responsibility to the Germans. By 1950–51, as the Korean War seemed to presage a new world war, the Bonn government put pressure on the Allies to take a much more accommodating line over war criminals, including the early release of many of those convicted of crimes, as a way of rebuilding a strong Germany as part of the Western alliance. Eventually the U.S. occupation authorities decided that five convicted war criminals must hang, including the Einsatzgruppe commander Otto Ohlendorf and the head of the S.S.'s concentration-camp operation, Oswald Pohl. However, seventy-nine others had substantially reduced sentences and were released within a few months. These people included concentration-camp doctors, the top judges who had run Hitler's "people's courts," thirty-one out of thirty-five convicted Einsatzgruppe leaders, and all those involved in the trials over the use of slave labor by the Krupp armaments firm.

The same change of direction can be seen in the I. G. Farben case. In February 1947 the U.S. occupation authorities issued a decree breaking up all monopolies, but in fact the only target was I. G. Farben. In June another decree broke up the vast chemicals conglomerate into forty-seven independent units and imposed strict anti-monopoly and anti-cartel controls. This decree was almost immediately suspended because of the intensifying Cold War: the Americans felt that a strong West German economy was now vital to rebuilding Germany as an ally. The then owners of I. G. Farben demanded the smaller independent units be consolidated into its three original constituents before the amalgamation into I. G. Farben in 1926: Bayer, BASF, and Hoechst. In 1951 the western Allies compromised by dividing the 159 I. G. Farben plants in West Germany into nine companies, the original big three plus six others, such as Agfa. In 1953 the Allies compromised again by giving the big three almost total control of the smaller companies (Bayer was allowed to own all of Agfa), and only two small independent companies were set up. When shares in the new companies were allocated, priority was given to existing I. G. Farben shareholders, so that no confiscation actually took place. By the late 1950s all the small companies had been reabsorbed into one of the big three.

The handing over of responsibility for prosecuting war crimes to the West German authorities resulted in a quick loss of interest in continuing the work. In 1950 the German authorities brought about 500 indictments; by 1955, when the Federal Republic became a sovereign state, the number had fallen to 21. After growing international protests about the lack of action the Bonn government set up the Central Office for the Investigation of War Crimes in the late 1950's. Its real sympathies can, however, be judged from the fact that it was set up by the minister of justice, Fritz Schäffer, who had been sacked by the U.S. occupation authorities for his Nazi sympathies; he appointed as the office's first head Erwin Schüle, a former member of the Nazi party and the S.A. Until 1964 it had a staff of only ten, who simply read files. It could only investigate crimes committed outside Germany, yet under federal government rules it was not allowed to approach any of the governments in central and eastern Europe for evidence. The result was that not a single crime committed in the Soviet Union was investigated. Federal government rules also prevented the extradition of German citizens to face war-crimes trials abroad. The government went even further and created a secret department within the Foreign Ministry to aid suspected war criminals who were put on trial abroad. Since 1958 about six hundred people have been convicted of war crimes in German courts, but the difficulties of obtaining convictions are increasing as witnesses become older, memories become less clear, and very strict standards of evidence are insisted upon. Also, trials began to take up more and more time: in 1962 they lasted three to six years, but by 1978 the average duration had risen to over twelve years.

The consequence of this lack of commitment among the western Allies and the Germans has been that the majority of war criminals have never been punished. It has been estimated that at least 250,000 Germans were directly involved in war crimes (far more were indirectly involved in the bureaucracy, industry, and the armed forces), and of these only about 36,000 have been convicted of crimes. The overwhelming majority, about 30,000, of these convictions have been by Soviet, Polish, Yugoslav, and East German courts. The former western Allies convicted just over 5,000, nearly half of them in France, and the West German authorities just under 800. The limited impact of this process can be judged from the fact that about 10,000 Germans worked at the Majdanek killing center but only 1,300 have been identified, 387 investigated, and just 16 charged with offenses. In general, the major figures were prosecuted at Nuremberg and a number of other key figures elsewhere, but efforts have concentrated on those at the bottom of the German command structure. The large mass of middle-ranking figures and especially many of those in positions of authority, particularly the bureaucracy and industry, who had a large measure of complicity in what was taking place have remained unpunished.

These members of the German political, financial, and administrative elite not only remained unpunished but reemerged in the Federal Republic in positions of responsibility. One of the first actions by the Federal Parliament (Bundestag) after it took over responsibility for such affairs from the occupation authorities in 1951 was to reinstate all civil servants removed by the Allies for their Nazi sympathies, return them to their old positions, and promote them if they were entitled under civil service regulations. Throughout the civil service key figures were closely associated with the Nazi government. Chancellor Adenauer employed as his state secretary (the highest civil service adviser) Hans Globke, who in 1935 drafted the Nuremberg anti-Semitic laws for Hitler. He was to be a key figure in rebuilding the Bonn civil service. At least five other state secretaries had been closely associated with the Nazis. At the federal government's Ministry of Finance, Alfred Hartmann had worked closely with Globke on confiscating Jewish property. Günther Bergmann, at Transport, had supervised the plundering of Serbia; Ludwig Westerick, at Economics, had managed the aluminum industry, where 80 percent of the labor force were slaves; Rudolf Sentack, at the Refugees Ministry, was a senior member of the S.S. who had worked in the Reich Resettlement Office; and Franz Thedieck, at German Affairs, had betrayed a group of left-wingers to the Gestapo in 1933. The diplomatic adviser to Chancellor Adenauer was Gustav Hilger, who during the war had been the Foreign Ministry liaison officer with the S.S. on the eastern front and was therefore fully aware of the atrocities being carried out; he also acted as the link to the Vlasov collaborators. By the 1960s, sixty West German ambassadors were ex-members of the Nazi party and four of them had been in the S.S. The Bonn government also paid pensions to former S.S. members and their widows, including the widow of Heydrich, the man who drew up the plan for the extermination of the Jews, because they had been state employees. In addition, compensation was given to members of the S.S. at concentration camps for goods that were confis-

cated by the Allies at the end of the war and given to the slave workers the S.S. had exploited.

The pattern was the same outside the government. Hermann Abs,
who though not a member of the Nazi party had been an important
member of the managing board of the Deutsche Bank—which had
expanded its assets fourfold under the Nazi government and also
funded the I. G. Farben investment at Auschwitz—after the war went
on to become chairman of the Deutsche Bank and a key figure in
postwar German financial and industrial affairs for several decades.
Before the war Abs had been the foreign director, responsible for the
forcible takeover of assets such as the Creditanstalt Bank in Austria
and other institutions throughout occupied Europe. He was on the
Allied list for arrest as a war criminal but was protected by old ac-
quaintances from the City of London who were running British financial policy in their occupation zone. He was eventually arrested
under American pressure but was released without charge. Hans
Martin Schleyer, the president of the Federation of German Em-
ployers, who was assassinated by remnants of the Baader-Meinhof
gang in 1977, had joined the S.S. in 1935, run the Nazi party training
school, and worked closely with Himmler in the Reich Security Office.

The pattern was the same in Japan. At first a limited purge was carried out and a new constitution was imposed that prohibited Japan
from maintaining armed forces. Almost immediately the American
government began to see Japan less as a defeated enemy and more as
a useful ally against communism, particularly after the Communist
takeover in China and the outbreak of the Korean War. Little or no
action was taken against leading Japanese industrialists or the major
corporations, which all survived into the postwar world. The political and bureaucratic elite also survived remarkably unscathed. By
1953 the U.S. vice president, Richard Nixon, was even calling for the
abolition of the restriction on armed forces and for Japanese participation in the Western security system. As in Germany, figures
tainted by their role in the war soon reemerged into Japanese government. Shigemitsu Mamoru, the foreign minister from 1943 to 1945,
who had been sentenced to seven years' imprisonment at the Tokyo

war-crimes trial for waging aggressive war and failing to stop breaches of the laws of war, was released early in 1950. By December 1954 he became foreign minister again and remained so until 1956. Kishi Nobusuke served throughout the General Tojo cabinet that had made the decision to attack the Western powers; he had been listed as a "grade A" war criminal and considered for prosecution at the Tokyo trial. In the 1950s he was both foreign minister and prime minister and in 1960 renegotiated the Mutual Security Pact with the United States.

The Allied involvement with war criminals went far beyond a reluctance to prosecute after an initial burst of enthusiasm. Even before the German surrender, plans had been laid by all the Allies to recruit key German personnel. Within months war criminals were knowingly being employed and sheltered by the Allies and in some cases were allowed to escape justice. The first efforts concentrated on finding and exploiting key German scientists—it was a race among all four major Allies. The Allies knew little about the German nuclear research program, and in 1944 the Americans set up the Alsos mission, which operated just behind the front line in order to locate key scientists and stocks of uranium and heavy water. There was some cooperation between British and American teams—key figures such as the chemist Otto Hahn and the physicist Werner Heisenberg were taken to Britain before being moved to the United States, but the Americans reached the French occupation zone first and removed the key scientists before their allies arrived. The Soviets had their own teams, which captured and immediately took to the Soviet Union a number of key figures at the Aver company, which had worked on uranium. Most of the key scientists, however, were captured by the Americans and were given no choice but to travel to the United States and cooperate with members of the U.S. nuclear program.

Other U.S. teams worked to secure key figures in other areas. Within days of the surrender Professor Herbert Wagner, the chief missile designer for Henschel, was taken to the United States to carry on his work for the Americans. Henschel had created the HS-293 guided missile, the first in the world, and a radio-controlled antiaircraft rocket at the underground complex at Nordhausen concentration camp, where 20,000 slave laborers died. Key figures in the areas of Saxony and Thuringia, which was initially occupied by U.S. forces but which lay within the Soviet occupation zone, were forcibly removed days before Soviet forces took over the area. The Zeiss optical and research institutes were removed en bloc. In July 1945 the United States started Project Overcast to take 350 German rocket scientists and engineers to the United States. Among those included in the program were Dr. Arthur Rudolph, who, evidence at the Nuremberg tribunal showed, had been involved in atrocities at Nordhausen; General Walter Dornberger, who had also worked at Nordhausen and eventually became vice president of Bell Aerosystems in the United States; and Wernher von Braun, an honorary S.S. officer for ten years who later worked on the program to launch the first U.S. satellite in 1958.

In the spring of 1946 an expanded recruitment program, Operation Paperclip, was approved by President Truman—on the condition that it remain strictly secret. It involved recruiting about a thousand German and Austrian scientists to work in the United States and granting them U.S. citizenship. The rules of the program excluded war criminals and "ardent Nazis." However, if it seemed likely that the U.S. Immigration Service would reject a candidate who was wanted by some other government agency, the candidate's personal files would be altered to provide an innocuous background. Overall, in the ten years after the end of the war 765 German and Austrian scientists and engineers were taken to the United States. About 80 percent of them had been members of either the S.S. or the Nazi party, but only three individuals were forced to leave the United States. One area in which the U.S. authorities had a particular interest was biological warfare. The head of the German wartime program, Dr. Kurt Blome, who had carried out experiments on concentration-camp prisoners, was recruited by the Americans to carry on his research for them. In Japan the Americans also captured the records of the notorious Unit 731 biological warfare unit and took unit members to the United States to assist their program. Despite clear evidence of barbaric experiments on prisoners and civilians, none of the Japanese involved were prosecuted for war crimes, in order to keep the extent of U.S. knowledge of the program secret. The Soviet Union had its own program to recruit German scientists, called Operation Osava-kim. Three eminent nuclear scientists, professors Fritz Vollmer, Gustav Hertz, and Peter Thiessen, plus Siegfried Günther from the Heinkel aircraft firm, Adolf Betz, an authority on swept-wing aircraft, and many others, were taken to the Soviet Union and forced to work on Soviet research projects. They were paid twice as much as their Soviet counterparts and most were released within about three years.

The recruitment of Germans with highly dubious pasts was even more extensive in the military and intelligence areas. Within weeks of the German surrender the United States was using S.S. generals such as Reinefarth ("the butcher of Warsaw") and Rode and the Wehrmacht generals von Luttwitz, von Vormann, and Guderian to advise them how to conduct a campaign against the Soviet Union. None were prosecuted for their involvement in war crimes. In March 1945 Reinhard Gehlen, Germany's top military intelligence officer on the eastern front, microfilmed all of his records, and on May 22 he surrendered to U.S. counterintelligence officers and handed over some of his files. Within days U.S. intelligence agencies were competing to recruit him. In August he was sent to the United States for debriefing and by early 1946 the Americans had reestablished Gehlen in a former Waffen S.S. site at Pullach, near Munich, where he began re-creating his intelligence organization—this time working for the Americans rather than the Nazi government. Much of Gehlen's information came from captured Soviet prisoners who had been kept in bestial conditions, and although he promised the Americans that he would not employ former members of the S.S. and Gestapo, he broke that promise from the start, with U.S. knowledge.

Among his first recruits was Emil Augsburg, who had led an Einsatzkommando in the Soviet Union and then become director of the Wannsee Institute, where the meeting that initiated the Final Solution was held in 1942. He was wanted for war crimes, but he simply continued his previous work, this time for Gehlen and the Americans. He was joined by Hans Sommer, who had burned down five synagogues in Paris in 1941, and Fritz Schmidt, the Gestapo chief in

Kiel. Franz Six, who was a close adviser to both Himmler and Eichmann on the Final Solution and was personally responsible for atrocities on the eastern front, was recruited in 1946. He was eventually prosecuted as a war criminal and sentenced to twenty years in jail. He served only four before he was pardoned by the American authorities and was immediately reemployed by Gehlen. He later gave evidence for Eichmann's defense during the latter's trial in Jerusalem. Gehlen's station chief in Damascus was Alois Brunner, the "expert" used by Eichmann to organize deportations of Jews throughout Europe. He was a war criminal wanted by France and sentenced to death in absentia. By the mid-1950s he was running a C.I.A. program training Egyptian security forces. This C.I.A. program also used other Gehlen employees such as his organization chief and a former member of the S.S., Otto Skorzeny, who had rescued Mussolini from captivity in 1943, and Fritz Bünsch, another veteran of Eichmann's "Jewish Affairs" group. In the ten years after the war the United States spent over $200 million and employed over four thousand people in rebuilding Gehlen's intelligence empire. This German intelligence officer and his organization, employing a large number of convinced Nazis, had a major influence in shaping U.S. perceptions of the Soviet Union in the critical postwar years. In 1954, while keeping his contacts with the C.I.A., Gehlen became head of the new West German Bundesnachrichtendienst (B.N.D.) intelligence agency.

By the end of 1947 the United States had at least six large-scale programs for recruiting and using former S.S. and German intelligence personnel, including Operation Apple Pie, which was a joint program with the British for the direct recruitment of former members of S.S. security units to provide briefings on Soviet economic and industrial targets. A major rival to the Gehlen organization was run by Baron Otto von Bolschwing for the C.I.A. Von Bolschwing joined the Nazis in 1932, became an agent in the Middle East, where he acted as an "educator" of Eichmann on Jewish policy, and after 1939 became German security chief in Bucharest. In this role he provided arms for the fascist Iron Guard units and then helped smuggle out of the country the perpetrators of an anti-Jewish pogrom in January 1941. In this action about 1,000 Jews were killed, 60 of whom had their throats cut, were skinned alive, and were hung on hooks in the municipal abattoir and branded as kosher. As early as 1945 von Bolschwing was selling information to the Americans; he then worked briefly for Gehlen before setting up his own operation. Between 1949 and 1953 he worked as a top C.I.A. contract employee in Europe with a string of agents in Hungary and Rumania, many recruited from the Iron Guard, which the United States authorities were now keen to use. In 1954 the C.I.A. ensured his immigration into the United States by supplying him with false papers and a false background. Within the government the C.I.A. admitted that it was fully aware of his background as a war criminal.

The Soviet Union followed similar policies, though on a much smaller scale. Fritz Grobba, the German spy controller in the Middle East, went over to the Soviets in early 1945. Carl Clodius, a Nazi finance expert involved in supplying slave labor from the Balkans, became head of the Cominform Balkan division. S.S. General Hans Rattenhuber, who had commanded Hitler's personal guard, became a senior East German police official in Berlin, and General Rudolph Bamler, who had worked in the Abwehr, became deputy head of the Stasi, the East German secret police. Ernst Grossmann and Karlheinz Bartsch were members of the S.S., and Grossmann had been a guard at Sachsenhausen concentration camp. Both became members of the Central Committee of the East German Communist party. Only when their pasts were exposed in West Germany did the East German authorities find it expedient to purge them.

In the late 1940s the U.S. authorities began Operation Bloodstone, aimed at the recruitment of former Nazi collaborators and émigré groups, as part of an anti-Soviet drive. Gehlen had already begun reactivating his contacts and funding ex-collaborative groups such as the Vlasov army and the O.U.N. Ukrainian nationalists. Now the United States went further and brought many war criminals to the United States, in violation of immigration laws, and used them as "experts" on the Soviet Union. Nikolai Poppe had defected to the Germans in 1942 and worked at the Wannsee Institute helping the S.S. locate Jews and other minorities within the Soviet Union. In 1945 he worked for British intelligence, but he was then transferred to the Americans because the Soviets, who wanted to try him for war crimes, had found out he was working for the British. He was sent to the United States as an expert on Soviet minorities (the same task on which he had worked for the S.S.) and became part of the McCarthy anti-Communist crusade.

As early as 1947 the United States recruited the Ukrainian Mykola Lebed, who had worked for the Gestapo in 1939 and become head of police and security in the Ukrainian O.U.N. "government-in-exile" created by the Germans in 1944. The U.S. counterintelligence authorities described him as a sadist and collaborator, but he was nevertheless taken to the United States under a false name, as was General Pavlo Shandruk, the chief of the Ukrainian "government-in-exile," who had first been recruited by the British. The United States also kept a list of former members of the Ukrainian S.S. who could be mobilized in the event of war with the Soviet Union. Other collaborators were recruited for various tasks. These included members of the Russian fascist collaborators, the N.T.S. Vladimir Porensky was originally imprisoned as a war criminal but was released in 1946, under pressure from Britain's MI6 intelligence agency, in order to set up the covertly funded N.T.S. Possev publishing house in Munich and produce anti-Soviet literature. Other groups, such as the Georgian "government-in-exile" (similarly, a creation of the Nazis) and members of the Belorussian Rada did the same, reusing the propaganda material they had produced under the Nazis. Roman Redlich, a former member of the sadistic Kaminsky Brigade, who had directed the German program to recruit Soviet defectors as Nazi agents, was immediately hired by the United States to train their agents at the Regensburg base and was later used by the C.I.A. at the Bad Homburg agent-training school. Stanislaw Stankievich, a Belorussian Nazi whom the S.S. had appointed as mayor of Borisov during the anti-Jewish pogrom, became a leading member of the C.I.A.-funded Institute for the Study of the U.S.S.R. in Munich. U.S. intelligence agencies also recruited Midhat Frasheri, who had headed the collaborationist Balli Kombetar organization in Albania, and other leaders of the Albanian S.S. unit as experts on Albania.

The C.I.A. funded other refugee groups in the United States.

These included the Belorussian "government-in-exile" run by Radislaw Ostrowsky, a self-confessed collaborator with the S.S. and Gestapo, both of which had funded this group during the war. The Latvian group funded by the C.I.A. was dominated by former members of the Latvian S.S., in particular the Daugavas Vanagi group, which was set up in 1945 specifically to help ex-members of the S.S. to escape justice and assume new identities. The Committee for a Free Latvia was run by Vilis Hazners, a senior security officer in Riga during the anti-Jewish atrocities.

The American involvement with collaborators went much further still. In 1946 men from the Vlasov collaborationist army (all wanted in the Soviet Union as traitors) were sent to Morocco under American, British, and French sponsorship, nominally as employees of construction companies but in practice to train for a liberation battle against the Soviets. In 1947 the Pentagon started studying the outlook for guerrilla operations against the Soviet Union after a potential nuclear exchange. Both the British and the Americans had already set up labor battalions in Germany using recruits from the Baltic states, many of them former members of the S.S. The first Latvian labor company, formed by the United States in June 1946, was run by Voldemars Skaistlauks, a former Latvian S.S. general, and six of his senior colleagues. The 8850th Labor Company was headed by Talivaldis Karklins, a senior officer at the Madonna concentration camp in Latvia, and other major war criminals such as Eduards Kalinovskis, a member of a Latvian death squad, and Janis Zegners, deputy head of the Riga security police, were also recruited. By 1950 these groups had been armed with chemical-warfare equipment and given a role as a post-nuclear-strike guerrilla force. The U.S. occupation authorities even went so far in 1950 as to set up and fund the B.D.J. (Bund Deutscher Jugend, or the League of Young Germans), recruited mainly from former members of the Waffen S.S., whose task in the event of a Soviet invasion was to assassinate leading members of the German Social Democratic party.

The Americans not only recruited and trained former war criminals, they also helped them escape justice. The United States gave major assistance to a so-called "ratline" that was run by a Croatian

Catholic, Krunoslav Draganovic, with close links to the Vatican and to the Ustasha, which had killed about 500,000 Serbs during the war. The ratline sheltered ex-members of the Ustasha in Rome and then organized their escape to South America—almost certainly the route used by Ante Pavelic, the head of the Ustasha. Draganovic had close links with the C.I.A. until the 1960s. The C.I.A. was also running the International Refugee Organization in Rome, which issued exit papers to enable people to emigrate. The Draganovic ratline was used by U.S. intelligence to enable one of the most wanted war criminals to escape: Klaus Barbie, the "butcher of Lyons."

Barbie worked in the security side of the S.S. after 1935 and at the outset of the war was in Holland before moving to head operations in Lyons. There he personally tortured to death the leader of the French underground, Jean Moulin. From the start he was on the French list of most wanted war criminals. In the early months of the Allied occupation of Germany he had been captured by the British but had been allowed to "escape" after betraying a Nazi underground group of which he was a member. He went to ground in the chaos of occupied Germany and in April 1947 persuaded a wartime friend who was working for U.S. intelligence to take him on as an agent. When he was recruited by U.S. intelligence he confessed his links with the British and also his wartime past. The Americans used him to work against his old wartime enemies—their wartime allies—and penetrate French intelligence networks operating in the U.S. occupation zone. In 1947 Barbie was condemned to death in absentia by a court in Lyons. Two years later the French, who had located Barbie in the U.S. zone, made a formal request to the U.S. authorities for his extradition. Barbie was kept in an American "safe house" while American intelligence people lied to both their own government and the French, denying they knew where he was. They then used the Draganovic ratline to help Barbie escape justice. In an appallingly tasteless touch, he was given a new identity as Adolf Altmann, the chief rabbi of Trier (Barbie's hometown), who had actually died in Auschwitz. Barbie was retrained as a mechanic and given $8,000 and with his family was sent down the ratline to start a new life in Bolivia. There he rapidly became involved in crime, the arms trade, espionage, and right-wing terror activities. Thirty-two years later he was finally extradited to France to stand trial.

The Americans knowingly recruited Barbie, a war criminal, and then deliberately hid him from the justice of one of their wartime allies, even though he was no more than a low-level agent for them. They then provided him with a new life via another organization dominated by war criminals to try to ensure that he escaped justice for the rest of his life. The whole operation was a sordid epitaph to the Second World War. The high ideals professed had not lasted long in the world of Realpolitik and new alliances. Wartime declarations about the priority to be given to the task of bringing the vast number of war criminals to justice were rapidly forgotten. After 1945 war criminals and their organizations even became groups to be courted for their usefulness in the new world. With almost indecent haste the wartime Allies forgot most of what they pledged to do after the war; other priorities and other conflicts became more important.

XII

ARMAGEDDON

THE LIMITED EUROPEAN CONFLICT THAT BEGAN OVER
Poland in September 1939 led to six years of war, a war that eventually embraced nearly every part of the globe. It was the most devastating war in human history. About 85 million people were killed, if estimates based on the recently declassified 1939 Soviet census are accurate. About three quarters (65 million) of the dead were civilians. During the war and its immediate aftermath, 25 million civilians were refugees and another 23 million were forcibly resettled or deported. By 1945 about 60 million people were homeless, about 40 million of them in China. In the defeated states conditions were harsh. In 1946 the German gross national product was a third of its 1938 level, in Italy it had fallen back to 1911 levels, and in Japan it was less than 60 percent of levels in the mid-1930s. Conditions in the victorious states were often little better and sometimes a great deal worse. In the Netherlands the Germans had removed 60 percent of the railway coaches and all but 4 percent of the freight cars. Huge floods had also been created as the Germans opened the sluice gates of the dikes. In France, the transport system was nearly unusable and G.N.P. was less than half its prewar level.

Conditions were far worse in eastern Europe, where German occupation policies had been harsher. In Poland about 6 million people had been killed and 1.5 million homes had been destroyed, along with 14,000 factories, 200,000 shops, 375 hospitals, 6,135 schools,

2,500 railway engines, 84,000 railway wagons, and 3,600 miles of railway track. In addition, 60 percent of the farm livestock had been lost and a quarter of the forests destroyed. Even this level of destruction seemed relatively light compared with the situation in the Soviet Union. The total population loss is difficult to estimate but a consensus is beginning to emerge that the losses may have approached 50 million, or a quarter of the prewar population, with most of the deaths concentrated in the western republics of Ukraine and Belorussia. Most of the people killed were males, thus producing a massive population imbalance. Of the women twenty years old in the period 1929–38 only two thirds eventually married because there was an excess of at least 13 million women in that age group. Economically, the Soviet Union lost about a third of its prewar capital assets, and in the occupied areas the figure rose to two thirds. Over 4.5 million homes, 84,000 schools, 40,000 hospitals, and 32,000 industrial enterprises were destroyed. On the railways 39,000 miles of track, 15,800 locomotives, 428,000 freight cars, and half of all railway bridges were destroyed. In agriculture the situation was even worse. The cultivated area had been reduced by a quarter and because of the shortage of inputs grain yields were only half of their prewar level. Altogether, 17 million cattle, 27 million sheep and goats, 7 million horses, and 20 million pigs had been killed, and it was not until 1955 that Soviet agricultural output recovered to the levels of the mid-1930s. The total cost of the war to the Soviet Union was equal to about ten years' gross national product, and if the huge population losses are taken into account the figure rises to over twenty-five years' GNP.

The world in 1945 was a very different place than it had been only six years earlier. Trends latent in the previous decades matured. The old European balance that had existed in various forms since 1648, the end of the Thirty Years' War, was destroyed. A new balance was imposed from outside by the United States and the Soviet Union. The German question, which had dominated European relations since 1871, was resolved for nearly half a century by the de facto division of the country, which was formalized by the late 1940s. The other two major European powers were both badly damaged by the war, even though they were on the winning side. France had suffered occupation and considerable destruction and its political position took time to rebuild. Britain was still the strongest European power, but it too had been damaged by the war. In 1940 it was technically bankrupt and by the last year of the war its economic state was parlous. It was the largest debtor in the world and was in debt even to parts of the Empire such as India and Egypt. A large proportion of its overseas investments had been sold to finance the war. Its export trade had collapsed, and estimates suggested a balance-of-payments deficit of at least £1 billion a year in the immediate postwar period. The government recognized that Britain's prospects after the end of the war depended upon either the continuation of Lend-Lease or a massive loan from the United States. When Lend-Lease was stopped a few days after the Japanese surrender the British had no alternative but to try to negotiate a loan. However, the terms were tough: convertibility of sterling and the effective end of imperial preference, leaving Britain heavily dependent upon the United States. Although the British, like the French, continued to act as though they were a world power, their economic and financial strength was increasingly out of line with their pretensions.

The anomalous international power structure of the interwar years—when the two strongest powers, the United States and the Soviet Union, had either stood aside or been excluded from the European balance, a situation that produced many of the problems giving rise to the war—was ended. The Soviet Union made major territorial conquests in alliance with Germany between 1939 and June 1941 and it kept these gains as part of the Allied alliance. Indeed, it improved its position still further at the expense of Finland in 1944 and Czechoslovakia in 1945 and by taking over parts of what had been East Prussia in 1945. In the Far East, the Soviet Union's last-minute declaration of war on Japan regained the territories lost by Czarist Russia in the 1904–5 war and enabled it to take control of others, such as the Kurile Islands. In eastern Europe, by 1945 it was in the process of building up a cordon of satellite states.

The greatest transformation, however, was in the role of the

United States. Apart from the deaths of 320,000 service personnel (1.5 percent of the Soviet level), it suffered almost none of the adverse effects of the war. Instead, the demands of the war economy produced a massive increase in national wealth. G.N.P. increased by 50 percent, whereas in western Europe it fell by a quarter. By 1945 the United States produced over half the world's manufacturing output, supplied a third of the world's exports, and owned half the world's merchant shipping and two thirds of the world's gold.

Militarily its position had also been transformed. In 1939, despite its economic predominance the United States had weak armed forces. A major rearmament program beginning well before its entry into the war and continuing through until 1945 made it the only global military power. By 1945 the United States had 1,200 major warships, 3,000 heavy bombers, 69 divisions in Europe, and 26 divisions in Asia and the Pacific. It was also the only country to possess the atomic bomb (a monopoly it lost in 1949).

The result of these trends was to end the long period (perhaps stretching back to the sixteenth century) during which Europe was the predominant region of the world. Although the decline of the European empires was not complete for another two decades, the old Europe already lay in ruins. Twice in the twentieth century the United States had intervened in European quarrels. After 1945 Europe was divided into a new order by the contest between the two extra-European powers, the United States and the Soviet Union. During the war it had become increasingly clear that the world's power structure was shifting from one of European predominance to a bipolar world dominated by the two massive continental powers. During 1942 the United States and the Soviet Union were edging toward this constellation, which became fully apparent by 1943 with the first conference of Allied leaders at Teheran. Twice before Teheran, Roosevelt had suggested to Stalin a bilateral meeting without Churchill, and at the conference the President held three bilateral meetings with the Soviet leader and none with Churchill. The British were becoming increasingly marginalized, a process that was even more apparent at the Yalta and Potsdam conferences, where the key decisions were made by the United States and the Soviet Union. By

1945, however, the full extent of the rivalry between the two powers was still unclear, although the huge gulf between their military and economic power and that of the other major powers was already apparent.

The end of most of the fighting in September 1945 did not herald a new era of peace. Although the United States and the Soviet Union did not fight each other directly, their power struggle shaped the next forty years of world history. Within a few years Europe was deeply divided as never before and the proxy battles between the two continental powers blighted the lives of millions of people outside Europe.

GUIDE TO FURTHER READING

The literature on the Second World War is vast, running into tens of thousands, if not hundreds of thousands, of volumes. Rather than providing an exhaustive bibliography of all the sources consulted in the research for this book, this section lists thirty of the more stimulating books about the Second World War. It is an eclectic and idiosyncratic list, mainly of works published in the last decade or so, but the reader might like to consult some of them in order to pursue further some of the themes developed here.

Barber, J., and M. Harrison. *The Soviet Home Front 1941–45*. London, 1991.
Bartov, O. *The Eastern Front 1941–45: German Troops and the Barbarization of Warfare*. London, 1985.
————. *Hitler's Army: Soldiers, Nazis and War in the Third Reich*. New York, 1991.
Bower, T. *Blind Eye to Murder*. London, 1981.
Calleo, D. *The German Problem Reconsidered: Germany and the World Order 1870 to the Present Day*. Cambridge, 1978.
Cesarini, D., ed. *The Final Solution: Origins and Implementation*. London, 1994.
Ch'i, H. *Nationalist China at War: Military Defeats and Political Collapse 1937–45*. Ann Arbor, Mich., 1982.
Van Creveld, M. *Fighting Power: German and US Army Performance 1939–45*. London, 1983.
Djilas, M. *Wartime*. London, 1977.
Ellis, J. *The Sharp End of War: The Fighting Man in World War Two*. Newton Abbot, 1980.
————. *Brute Force: Allied Strategy and Tactics in the Second World War*. London, 1990.
Foot, M. *Six Faces of Courage*. London, 1978.
Fussell, P. *Wartime: Understanding and Behaviour in the Second World War*. Oxford, 1989.

Havens, T. *Valley of Darkness: The Japanese People and World War Two.* London, 1982.

Hirschfeld, G., ed. *The Policies of Genocide: Jews and Soviet Prisoners of War in Nazi Germany.* London, 1986.

Iriye, A. *Power and Culture: The Japanese-American War 1941–45.* Cambridge, Mass., 1981.

Kedward, H. *In Search of the Maquis: Rural Resistance in Southern France 1942–44.* Oxford, 1993.

Keegan, J. *Six Armies in Normandy.* London, 1982.

Knox, M. *Mussolini Unleashed 1939–41: Politics and Strategy in Fascist Italy's Last War.* Cambridge, 1982.

Lukacs, J. *The Last European War: September 1939–December 1941.* London, 1976.

Mazower, M. *Inside Hitler's Greece: The Experience of Occupation 1941–44.* New Haven, Conn., 1993.

Milward, A. *War, Economy and Society.* London, 1977.

Polenberg, R. *War and Society: The United States 1941–45.* Westport, Conn., 1972.

Rings, W. *Living with the Enemy: Collaboration and Resistance in Hitler's Europe.* London, 1982.

Salisbury, H. *The Siege of Leningrad.* London, 1969.

Schulte, T. *The German Army and Nazi Policies in Occupied Russia.* Oxford, 1989.

Simpson, C. *Blowback: America's Recruitment of Nazis and Its Effects on the Cold War.* New York, 1988.

Stafford, D. *Britain and European Resistance 1940–45.* London, 1980.

Tusa, A., and J. Tusa. *The Nuremberg Trial.* London, 1983.

Thorne, C. *The Issue of War: States, Societies and the Far Eastern Conflict of 1941–45.* London, 1985.

INDEX

ABOUT THE AUTHOR

CLIVE PONTING, the author of eight other books including *A Green History of the World,* is a professor of politics at the University of Swansea, Wales. Formerly he was an assistant secretary at the Ministry of Defence in the Thatcher administration.

ABOUT THE TYPE

The text of this book was set in Janson, a misnamed typeface designed in about 1690 by Nicholas Kis, a Hungarian in Amsterdam. In 1919 the matrices became the property of the Stempel Foundry in Frankfurt. It is an old-style face of excellent clarity and sharpness. Janson serifs are concave and splayed; the contrast between thick and thin strokes is marked.